W9-DHI-704

EUROPEAN IMMIGRANTS AND AMERICAN SOCIETY

A Collection of Studies and Dissertations

•

Edited by
Timothy Walch and
Edward R. Kantowicz

•

A Garland Series

PORTUGUESE EMIGRATION TO THE UNITED STATES, 1820–1930

•

Maria Ioannis Benis Baganha

GARLAND PUBLISHING, INC. • NEW YORK & LONDON • 1990

Library of Congress Cataloging-in-Publication Data

Baganha, Maria Ioannis Benis.
Portuguese emigration to the United States, 1820–1930/
Maria Ioannis Benis Baganha.
p. cm.—(European immigrants and American society)
Revised version of thesis (Ph. D.)—University of
Pennsylvania, 1988, with title: International labor
movements: Portuguese emigration to the United States,
1820–1930.
Includes bibliographical references.
ISBN 0-8240-7421-1 (alk. paper)
1. Portuguese Americans—History. 2. United States—
Emigration and immigration—History. 3. Portugal—
Emigration and immigration—History. 4. Immigrants—
United States—History. I. Title. II. Series.
E184.P8B29   1990
304.8'730469—dc20   90-46975

●

Printed on acid-free, 250-year-life paper.
Manufactured in the United States of America

Design by
Julie Threlkeld

To the memory of my grandmother,
Maria, who taught me the fundamentals

INTRODUCTORY NOTE

This work is a revised version of my Ph.D. Dissertation "International Labor Movements: Portuguese Emigration to the United States 1820 - 1930", University of Pennsylvania, 1988.

Some small changes were done in all chapters but only chapter IV was substantially revised. Some new material and bibliographic references were included in order to further clarify some points.

ACKNOWLEDGMENTS

When I came to the United States, I did not know I was about to have five of the best years of my life. Some very special people and some wonderful friends were greatly responsible for the good things that came my way.

Loretta Blume found me a good school district for my children and a comfortable apartment, and she introduced me to the beauties of shopping in the States. Loretta and her family made Christmas merry even away from home.

The University of Pennsylvania along with the Mellon and the Gulbenkian Foundations supported my research. The History Department staff at Penn endured my English with a smile and guided me around. The Population Studies Center made me feel welcome, and whenever I needed help on my computer programs Steve Taber and Mark Keintz never failed to rescue me. Dr. Ira Glazier gave me superb working conditions at the National Immigration Archives (Temple University), and pertinent comments on my work.

Every one I worked with was pleasant and helpful, but some made a real difference. Dr. Thomas Childers, with whom I truly enjoy to argue, helped me develop my critical reasoning. Dr. Michael Katz, whom unfortunately I met only in my last year at Penn, gave pertinent and very helpful comments on several chapters of this work. Miriam King, whom I met because she liked quantitative methods as much as I do, became a great help in my battles with the English language. She edited almost all my works at Penn and along the way we discuss at great length their content. Many new insights came out during those discussions.

My advisers, Drs. Lynn Lees, Ann Miller, and Martin Wolfe, worked very closely with me, and whatever their schedules, they always made time to meet and advise me. I know I was extremely lucky to have worked with them. But I was also fortunate in having their support and friendship along the way. I have a special debt of gratitude toward Lynn Lees. Without her support of my application to Penn, I probably would never have had the chance to know and work with any of the others.

Like other European students who come to the States, I began my graduate work in my own country, under the supervision of Dr. Vitorino Magalhäes Godinho. He was one of the very few people who encouraged me to come to the States, and during those years never once did he fail to advise, to encourage, and to comment on my research when needed.

While I was back in the States finishing my thesis, my youngest son was run over by two drunk British marines. He was seriously injured and was hospitalized for a long time. My children called to tell me not to dare appear without the dissertation. My parents cancelled their departure to Greece, and my husband put his professional life on hold so that I could stay in Philadelphia. I always took their support for granted, but in those months they simply overdid it.

TABLE OF CONTENTS

Page

LIST OF ILLUSTRATIONS

INTRODUCTION

Emigration has deep roots in Portugal. In the second
half of the seventeenth century, Severim de Faria (1655)
advised the Portuguese not to abandon their motherland for
some foreign stepmother (1). Almost a century later (1748-
1756), the Azoreans were insistently asking the King to let
them go to Brazil. Demographic pressure and bad harvests,
they claimed, were making their lives intolerable (2). By
the end of the eighteenth century, the Azoreans were
leaving, usually without the King's permission, as
crewmembers on American whaling vessels touching their sea-
shores (Morison, 1961 and Trindade, 1976).

During the same century, the mainlanders were also
departing, some to Brazil, others to neighboring Spain.
Godinho (1978:9) estimates that the Brazilian's gold and
diamond rushes of the eighteenth century drove half a
million Portuguese out of the country between 1700 and 1760.
Departures to Spain generally went unrecorded, but
Brettell's latest work (1985) gives strong evidence that a
significant share of the Portuguese northern peasantry was
leaving for that country.

Historical evidence suggests that, by the end of the
eighteenth century, the Portuguese migratory flow was
already exhibiting some of the main traits that would

---

1 References to growing emigration during the same century
can also be found in Duarte Ribeiro de Macedo, _Discurso
sobre a Introdução das Artes no Reino,_ 1675. Macedo
attributed the loss of population in the mainland to growing
emigration.
2 Serpa, 1976:8-11;Piazza, 1982:465-492.

characterize it during the following centuries. At least
part of the flows, to Spain and the United States, was
already an international labor movement with a significant
clandestine component (3).

The nineteenth century began badly for Portugal. The
country was ravaged by the Napoleonic invasions (1807-1810).
The King fled to Brazil (1808), and power fell first to
Junot and then to Beresford. Foreign invasions were
followed by domestic instability: war between liberals and
absolutists (1832-1834), coups d'etat and dictatorship
(1835-1846), popular revolts (1846), and civil war (1846-
1847).

Political turmoil, especially the absolutist persecutions
(1828-1834), drove a great number of Portuguese abroad.
Godinho (1978:10) estimates that the yearly average number
of departures during this period was around four thousand.
Contrary to the migratory wave of the eighteenth century,
which was mainly economically motivated, the migratory flow
of the first half of the nineteenth century seems to have
been substantially politically determined.

By mid-century, the country was at peace. In the course
of events, however, Portugal's richest colony (Brazil), was

---

3 We can not classify the Portuguese migratory flow to
Brazil as a international migratory movement until 1822
because Brazil was until that date a Portuguese colony.
Transfers of population within an Empire are different from
international migratory movements. First, transfers of
population within an Empire involve, at both ends of the
trajectory, only one central government; second, the
migrants are usually colonists and are protected by the
sending country; finally, migrants usually have higher
status then natives.

lost; its rural/domestic industry was destroyed (4); and the crown became burdened by foreign debt (5).

The Portuguese intelligentsia of the 1850's and 1860's seem to have believed firmly in the country's potential for recovery, for modernization, for "progress" as they would have said. Rodrigues de Freitas, for example, in his book Notice Sur Le Portugal (1867), wrote on the evident economic development the country had undergone since the end of the civil war. He gave examples of growth in a variety of sectors and activities: import/export trade; communications; commercial banking; agricultural credit; basic and industrial schooling; agricultural and industrial expositions; spread of newspapers and books; laws favoring transfers of fixed property and concessions of credit; and taxation for investment. "In sum [he claimed], the ideas and the tendencies of the people are undergoing an admirable betterment" (Freitas, 1867:48-49) (6). Pereira (1971), who has studied this period concluded that:

> Until 1870, Portugal was generally considered a
> rich country, its soil and sub-soil hiding
> resources yet to explore ... the industrial
> progress was faced with similar optimism.
> (Pereira, 1971:18)

The Portuguese people seem to have subscribed to a different view of the country's potential for recovery and

---

4 According to Perry (1979:96, 1st ed. 1893) while the French destroyed the cotton factories at Alcobaca, Alcanena and Pernes, the British destroyed the silk factories at Chacim and Bragança. Pereira (1900:42) went much further and wrote on the total destruction of the industry by the invaders.
5 To maintain the efforts of the war, both D.Pedro (liberal) and D.Miguel (absolutist) contracted debts that later were transformed in public debts.
6 Others, such as Rebelo da Silva (1868) emphasized the agricultural improvements taking place.

economic development. From the 1850's until the late 1920's, they left the country in unprecedented and growing numbers. Legal departures alone went from an average of eight thousand per year between 1855-1875, to twenty one thousand between 1876-1900, and to thirty six thousand between 1901-1925 (7).

Not surprisingly, there is an extensive literature on the Portuguese migratory wave of this period. The flow to Brazil, country of destination for the overwhelming majority of the Portuguese migrants, received particular attention. But the smaller flow to the United States second to the Brazilian flow in volume until 1925 (Keith, 1971:8), never captured the same attention.

ORGANIZATION OF THIS WORK

There is widespread agreement that international labor migration is a socio-economic process rooted in geo-economic inequality. Its inner dynamics do not, however, evoke the same sort of consensus.

7 Computed from Godinho, 1978:11. In relative terms, Portugal became from the 1850's on one of the main suppliers to the international labor-market. As early as 1854 the Dictionnaire de L'Économie Politique ranked Portugal as a major European migratory country. Fifty years later only Scotland, Italy and Ireland had higher rates of emigration (Carqueja, 1916:395). Recent scholarship goes even further. Livi Bacci (1971:35) remarked that, excluding Ireland, Portugal is the European country with the highest rate of net migration from the end of the nineteenth century on. The Portuguese were, of course, not alone in their growing exodus to the New World. Between 1840 and 1914, over forty million Europeans emigrated to America (Tomaske, 1971). But instead of choosing North America, as approximately two-thirds of the European inter-continental migrants did (Maldwyn, 1960:1), the Portuguese overwhelmingly chose Brazil as their destination.

Neo-classical economists describe the migratory process as spontaneous and thoroughly self-regulated (A.Lewis, 1955). They postulate that comparative economic advantages in the receiving society are a necessary and sufficient condition for initiating and sustaining labor migratory streams (Tapinos, 1974). Marxists and dependency theorists see the process as forced and developing from the inner inequalities of the capitalist system (G.Myrdal, 1957). They maintain that labor surplus is forced to emigrate when population growth exceeds agricultural productivity and the industrial absorptive capacities of the region (Kamphoefner, 1986).

In the last two decades, a growing number of historians and sociologists studying migration in different regions-- including Latin America, Africa, and Southern Europe-- have found these two explicative models to be incapable of covering the complexities of the migratory processes they analyzed. Thus, for example, Portes (1978) and Piore (1979) found that direct recruitment by the receiving economy has been necessary historically to break the inertia of a sending society. Massey (1987) emphasized that once a migratory movement begins, it tends to be self-sustained by migrant networks. Finally, Zolberg (1983) and Straubhaar (1986) maintained that both the shape and the volume of a migratory flow can be, and usually is, dependent on political scrutiny at both ends of the trajectory.

One of the goals of this work is to test the explicative power of both the classic (neo-classic and dependency) models and the recent additions to theory just noted. As a case study, I focus on Portuguese emigration to the United States, from its beginning in the late eighteenth and early nineteenth centuries until its forced reduction during the late 1920's.

Another goal is to isolate the individual characteristics of the migrants and of their sending and receiving communities. Because migration is a highly selective process, those that left must be compared with those that stayed behind. It is also necessary to determine which specific sending regions participated in this movement, and how their socio-economic characteristics differed from those of the non-migratory areas. Finally, I consider the socio-economic structure of migrant communities in the receiving society, and the extent to which they followed a common pattern or were recast by the specific characteristics of regions within the receiving society.

Portuguese emigration to the United States is a particularly appropriate case study for several reasons. Surviving records in both countries enable me to test both the classic models and new contributions to migration theory. There is almost no bibliography on this migratory current, and the Portuguese immigrants have been one of the least studied ethnic groups in the United States. Portugal is, however, one of the European countries with the longest migratory traditions, which allows me to place the migratory flow to the United States in a broad historical context.

This work is, thus, divided into two major parts. First, I weigh the evidence on the creation of the Portuguese migratory flow, to establish whether a pull/push model adequately explains its inception or whether recruitment proved to be essential to break the initial inertia (chapter I). Second, I consider the development of the Portuguese migratory stream, and test the explicative power of both macrolevel economic models and networking dynamics.

Migration policies at both ends of the trajectory, and labor market evolution in Portugal constitute the core of the next two chapters (chapters II, and III). These two chapters complete the study of the macrolevel parameters within which the Portuguese migratory movement took place.

International migration differs from all other migratory movements because it takes place between nation-states which can regulate the flow at their borders. It is this unique characteristic that led Bhagwati, among others, to remark that:

> one cannot begin to analyze international migration unless one first understands the immigration control system pertinent to any given parametric situation. (Bhagwati, 1984:679)

Chapter II thus pays particular attention to the migratory policies of the United States and Portugal.

In chapter III, I consider the evolution of the Portuguese labor market, for the Portuguese migratory flow was essentially a labor movement. Recently, some scholars have argued that the extent of economic stagnation in Portugal during the late nineteenth and early twentieth centuries has been exaggerated (8). I thus address the

---

8 Examples of these revisions are the works of David Justino and Jaime Reis. Justino (1987) that found the values for the Portuguese GNP per capita were, at the end of the nineteenth century, much higher then the values indicated by

following question: were the Portuguese leaving because there were no job vacancies at home, or despite increasing job opportunities ?

Although macrolevel political and economic issues set the context for migration, the decision to emigrate or not was made by individuals. In the second part of this work, I look at microlevel data and establish the specific characteristics of the migratory areas and of the migrants themselves. I begin by making some educated guesses about the volume and regions of origin of the Portuguese migratory flow, and then move on to the socioeconomic and demographic characteristics of migrants (chapter IV). Here, I adopt a comparative perspective, considering not only the Portuguese flow to the United States but also the Portuguese flow to Brazil, and to other European flows to the United States.

The work concludes with an analysis of the characteristics of Portuguese communities in the United States. The question I was interested in addressing was: what are the main factors affecting the social mobility of immigrants drawn from the same socio-cultural backgraound? Based on a sample of three communities collected from the 1910 census manuscripts of the United States, I establish the household structure and socio-economic characteristics of first generation Portuguese immigrants in Massachusetts, California, and Hawaii. Further, I identify what these communities had in common, and what set them apart from each

---

Bairoch, and Reis (1987) contends that Portuguese industry was growing at the turn of the century at European speed. Industry, not agriculture, Reis claims, was the dynamic sector of the Portuguese economy during this period.

other. What makes the Portuguese migratory experiences particularly interesting is that, this migrant group was one of the most culturally homogeneous group entereing the United States at that point yet, they presented quite different patterns of social mobility after settlement.

Methodological issues are dealt with in a statistical appendix. This section is partly the result of my battles with discrepancies between published and manuscript sources on Portuguese emigration. I believe that it sheds some light on this conflicting testimony comparing and linking records surviving in both Portugal and the United States.

MAIN CONCLUSIONS

Although rooted in the imbalances of the Portuguese socio-economic structure, Portuguese emigration to the United States was only initiated after direct inducement from the American economy. The inner dynamics of the Portuguese migratory process, once begun, are best captured by considering the migrant networks active at both ends of the trajectory and the migratory policies implemented by both countries. Both the neoclassic and the dependency models of international migration determinants performed poorly when not adjusted for political change. Even when migration policy changes were taken into account, models of emigration decision-making based on Portuguese economic structure prove to have greater explanatory power than models based on the economic advantages offered by the United States.

The typical Portuguese emigrant to the United States was a single male aged 16 to 29, who became an unskilled industrial worker in Massachusetts, or an agricultural laborer in California, depending upon his place of birth in the Azores. Members of a third Portuguese migratory current to Hawaii were more likely to be older, married, and accompanied by family members; they largely entered sugar plantation work.

The household structure and the socio-economic characteristics of Portuguese immigrants in United States were different in Massachusetts, California, and Hawaii. Extended family households, for example, were far more common in California than in the other two destinations. Upward mobility was also far more common in California than in the other two destinations. The differences found in the socio-economic characteristics of the Portuguese immigrants in these three regions, suggest that the socio-economic conditions of specific regions in the receiving society shaped the characteristics of the Portuguese migratory flow and the structure of the Portuguese immigrant community. Furthermore, the analysis reveals that , for the Portuguese case, the main determinants of social mobility were: 1. the way they entered the United States, i.e. as free emigrants or as contract laborers; 2. the strength of the migrant group network; and 3. the job and land opportunities in the region of settlement.

CHAPTER I - THE CREATION AND DEVELOPMENT OF THE PORTUGUESE
MIGRATORY STREAM TO UNITED STATES

It is usually recognized that international labor
movements have three phases. In the first phase, involving
small numbers, sporadic contacts give away to permanent
flows. In the second phase, the volume of the migratory
flow increases. During this phase of development migratory
streams follow cycles within a general tendency toward
growth. In the third phase, the flow recedes and finally is
halted or remains at insignificant levels.

There is controversy over the dynamics behind each of
these three phases. This section considers the main
hypotheses in migration theory for on creation and
development of international labor migratory streams, and
tests them using evidence on the creation and development of
the Portuguese migratory flow to the United States.

NEOCLASSIC THEORISTS

Neoclassical economists define labor migration as a self-
regulated process spreading spontaneously from the existence
of economic advantages in the receiving society. They
regard the existence of higher wages in the country of
destination as the main determinant for the creation and
development of a labor migratory stream (Lewis, 1955).
Using this logic, George Tapinos (1974) proposed a formal
model of emigration decision-making that postulates:

> it is a necessary and sufficient condition for
> [permanent] emigration to occur that the economic
> motivation to emigrate [brought about by the
> inequality between the expected real income in the
> region of immigration and the effective real
> income in the region of origin], exceeds the non-
> economic costs of displacement. These costs are
> higher if the cultural difference between the two
> countries is great (Tapinos, 1974:61,62).

A plausible scenario, fitting Tapinos' reasoning, can be
constructed to explain the Portuguese migratory stream to
the United States. We need only to picture the Portuguese
emigrant as an economically-rational decision-maker who, in
order to maximize his personal chances of economic success,
trades his job opportunities in his native country (with its
sluggish economic rates, low agricultural productivity and
growing unemployment) for job opportunities in another
country (with a prosperous and growing economy). After
designing this plausible scenario, all we need is to see how
well it holds up empirically.

The explicative power of Tapinos' model for the creation
and development of the Portuguese migratory flow to the
United States can be tested for the period between 1891 and
1930. For this period, we have the necessary information,
save for a measure of what the author calls the "non-
economic costs of displacement". The importance of this
variable can, however, be disregarded after the 1890's. We
have evidence that regular migratory contacts had existed
between Portugal and the United States at least since 1820.
By the 1890's, such established contacts must have reduced
considerably the non-economic costs of displacement.
Moreover, the growth of the Portuguese migratory flow to the

United States after 1890 would have further reduced these non-economic costs.

To test the neoclassical model, I hypothesized that the variation in the annual probability of emigrating from Portugal to the United States between 1891 and 1930 is explained by the variation in the annual ratio of United States G.N.P. per capita to Portuguese G.N.P. per capita (here used as a proxy for Tapinos' variable, anticipated and effective income) (1). The regression equation used to test this hypothesis was

$$EMIGR_T = \alpha + \beta GNPRATE_T$$

where: $EMIGR_T$ is the annual probability of emigrating from Portugal to the United States in period T (1891 to 1930); α is a constant representing the non-economic costs of displacement; and $GNPRATE_T$ is the annual ratio between the gross national product per capita of the two countries during the same period.

The results of this test indicate that there is a slight positive relationship between of the two variables, but not strong enough to predict the probability of emigrating from Portugal between 1891 and 1930, based on the knowledge of the comparative economic advantages existing in the United States. The R^2 equals only .0691, and the null hypothesis is not rejected at the .05 level of significance (see Appendix Model I).

Model I is a myopic model, in which it was assumed that the decision to emigrate and information occur

---

1 The notation and the variables used in the models presented in this chapter are described in Tables A:2 and Table A:3 in Appendix 1.

simultaneously. To correct for this limitation, Model I was redone with broader time frames (2). In Model II, instead of the yearly differences of G.N.P. per capita I used a three-year moving average. The results of Model II are given in Appendix 1 and are as poor as the results obtained for Model I. Finally, Model I was rerun twice each time adding a new variable reflecting the impact of earlier emigration. The new variables were Portuguese emigration to the United States with a time lag of three and five years respectively. These changes did not significantly increased the predictive value of Model I.

In sum, our test indicates that economic advantages in United States are probably a necessary, but not a sufficient condition to explain changes in the Portuguese migratory flow to this country. The Portuguese case confirms what researchers have found for other ethnic flows. As Philip Taylor (1971:106) noted, "The relationship between economic conditions and changes in emigration ... must not be made to seem too close..."

MARXISTS AND DEPENDENCY THEORISTS

The second hypothesis for the creation of a labor migratory stream (subscribed to by marxists and dependency theorists) postulates that population growth and lower agricultural productivity during phases of unbalanced

---

2 The need to include in models of emigration determinants time for information to be disseminated and migrant networks to act upon the decision to emigrate has been noted by several scholars, e.g. Tomaske, 1971.

industrial development will force a portion of the surplus population out of the country. Kamphoefner (1986) argued that German emigration to the United States during the first half of the nineteenth century is best explained by this framework. He wrote:

> But taken together, all the evidence presented here strongly suggests that protoindustrialization and subsequent deindustrialization were much more important factors in European emigration during the first half of the nineteenth century than has been previously realized. (Kamphoefner, 1986:195)

This hypothesis seems tailored for the Portuguese case during the late nineteenth century. In 1881, half of the Portuguese industrial workforce was still working at home (3). Also, at that time industrial work was centered in northern rural areas of the country and was performed mainly by women. By 1930, the majority of these domestic industries and the female industrial jobs they had furnished no longer existed. The regional distribution of the industrial workforce had shifted to the south, particularly to Lisbon. The industrial area which persisted in the north had contracted around the urban area of Oporto. The country's industrial development was, moreover, too slow to absorb population growth between 1890 and 1930. Over this period, a growing share of the population of working age could not find jobs or found them in the tertiary sector -- in domestic or personal services for women, in transportation or commerce for men.

---

3 The remaining 50 percent were equally divided between craft workshops and factories. Abstracts of the Industrial Enquire of 1881, in <u>Annuario Estatistico De Portugal - 1884</u>. Lisboa, 1886:394-396.

If we assume that without the complement of domestic industry a growing segment of the Portuguese rural population found it hard to survive (particularly in regions of lower agricultural productivity), then the hypothesis that a growing share of the Portuguese rural population was forced out of the country between 1891 and 1930 is quite plausible. It is also reasonable to assume, as Kamphoefner did, that the number of agricultural dependents (4) in the agricultural population is a good measure of the capability to stay and survive or of being forced to emigrate. Using a linear regression model, I measured how much of the variation in the annual probability of emigrating to United States during this period was explained by the ratio of dependents of agricultural workers to the population gainfully employed in agricultural activities. The explicative power of this hypothesis for the Portuguese migratory stream to the United States, between 1891 and 1930, is even weaker than the explicative power of the first hypothesis tested (5). The R^2 was .0006, and the null hypothesis is not rejected at the .05 level of significance (see Appendix - Model III). In sum, the quantitative evidence suggests that, if the Portuguese rural population was being forced out of the country, the dependency ratios of the agricultural population do not by themselves capture such a dynamic.

---

4 As agricultural dependents I considered everyone indicated in the census as a dependent of a gainfully employed agricultural worker.
5 Reruns with time lags of one and three years in the dependent variable of Model III produced only slightly better results.

Recently neo-classic theorists have been controlling for political change in their models (e.g.,Straubhaar,1986). Given the size of the Portuguese migratory flow pre- and post- 1921, it is probably redundant to try to prove that political scrutiny conditioned the migratory process and the individual decision to move. But it is not irrelevant to test the explicative power of the political variable over time. The linear regression in Model IV measures how much of the variance of the temporal series of the probability of emigrating is explained by the changes in American immigration policy (USA: 0= American immigration policy between 1980 to 1921 and 1= that policy afterwards). The R^2 in Model IV explains 35 percent of the fluctuation of the dependent variable and the null hypothesis is rejected at the .01 level. Another way to state the main point made in Model IV is to note that the probability of emigrating from Portugal to the United States fell from 11 per 10 thousand (between 1891 and 1920) to 2 per 10 thousand (between 1920 and 1930). This precipitous decline can be attributed to changes in American immigration policy.

Once the effect of political scrutiny on the migratory process is established, we need to reconsider the hypotheses proposed by the neoclassic and the marxist/dependency theorists. We have seen that neither comparative economic advantages in the receiving society nor deteriorating economic conditions at home were sufficient to initiate and sustain the Portuguese migratory flow to this country. The results of the tests do not, however, reject the hypothesis that these were necessary conditions.

My main hypothesis is that variable reflecting conditions
both at home and in United States (6) have intrinsic value
for explaining the migratory process, when adjusted for
political scrutiny. Models V and VI test this hypothesis,
and their results strongly supported it. They indicated,
however, that the dependency rates of the agricultural
population (that is, deteriorating economic conditions in
the sending society) are more relevant for understanding the
migratory current than are the differences of gross national
product per capita between Portugal and the United States
(this is, economic advantages in the host society). Model
V, where only changes in American immigration policy (USA)
and dependents in agriculture (AGRDEP) are considered as
independent variables, has an R^2 of .6249, while Model VI,
where USA, AGRDEP, and GNPRATE (differences in G.N.P. per
capita) are considered, has an R^2 only slightly higher
.6512. In other words, the introduction in the model of the
variable GNPRATE only minimally changes the explicative
power of the model.

THE CREATION OF PORTUGUESE LABOR STREAMS TO UNITED STATES

The third and last hypothesis for the creation of a labor
migratory stream postulates that such streams are created
through the receiving economy's direct recruitment of labor
in the sending society. Only qualitatively can I test this

6 For a full list of the factors considered in what is
normally called a pull-push approach, see Qualey, 1980:36-
38.

hypothesis. I will thus briefly survey the existing
evidence on the creation of Portuguese migratory streams to
the United States over the period we are considering.

PORTUGUESE EMIGRATION TO NEW ENGLAND

It is undisputed that the establishment of a permanent
Portuguese migratory current to the United States was
initiated by direct recruitment of Azorean seafaring men for
crew members on American vessels on the whaling route. We
cannot be too precise about when this temporary recruitment
of seafaring men gave way to a regular migratory stream and
to a permanent Portuguese settlement in New England. The
secondary sources surveyed make a strong case for placing
this turning point somewhere in the late eighteenth century
(7).

According to L. Pap (1949), the creation of a regular
migratory flow from Portugal to the United States occurred
during the second half of the eighteenth century, when Aaron
Lopez (a Portuguese refugee Jew) moved to New England where
he became a leading merchant in Newport and a key force in
the American whaling industry (Cheyet, 1970). Lopez seems
to have supplied his whaling vessels largely with Azorean
crews (8). Newport harbor soon proved to be inadequate to

7 Taft (1967:411) dated the commercial ties and the
migratory flow between New England and the Azores from the
1830's and 1840's. Bannick (1917:4) placed these beginnings
in the 1820's. Pap (1949), Morison (1961), and Trindade
(1976) give evidence that regular commercial relations and
labor flows between Azores and New England were established
during the eighteenth century.
8 Aaron Lopez owned a whaling fleet of over 30 vessels at
the end of the eighteenth century (Pap, 1949:4).

the growing needs of the whaling industry. The bulk of the industry and of the fleet moved then to the more spacious harbor of New Bedford, Rhode Island (Pap, 1949:4,5).

Samuel E. Morison (1961) established the connection between the Azores and the New England region by tracing back the trade routes and the development of the American merchant fleet of this region. In his work, evidence is given of ties between Massachusetts and the Azores dating back to the late eighteenth century. These relations grew out of the increasing labor and supply needs of the Massachusetts fleet. Such needs led Bostonian merchants to open mercantile houses in strategic foreign ports along the Mediterranean trade route for logistical support. Shortly after 1780, Thomas Hickling of Boston founded one of these mercantile houses in the Azores (Morison, 1961: 180).

The opportunity for neutral trade created by the Napoleonic wars, until Jefferson's embargo of 1807, meant growth for the American fleet and prosperity for the merchants of Massachusetts. Correspondingly, these conditions stimulated demand for Azorean crew members on those American vessels plying the Azorean coast on the whaling, the Mediterranean, and the Baltic routes.

Passage of the Embargo Act temporarily halted Massachusetts merchants' overseas trade. The Act interdicted American vessels from clearing, and fishing vessels from landing their cargoes, in foreign ports (Morison, 1961:187). Consequently, this period must have seen little contact between the Azores and Massachusetts. But as soon as the Embargo was lifted,

> Fayal in the Azores, where John B. Dabney, of
> Boston, was the American consul and leading
> merchant, became a new St. Eustatius, a go-between
> for nations forbidden to trade with another
> (Morison,1961:193).

Once foreign trade was free from governmental
restrictions, the Azores reclaimed its place in American
trading routes. An increasing need for crewmen went hand in
hand with the growth of foreign trade. But new job
opportunities in Massachusetts and surrounding areas,
combined with the harsh working conditions and low status of
seafaring, discouraged New Englanders from entering marine
life. By 1850, crews of American vessels were increasingly
composed of all nationalities except Americans. In
Morison's words, "[American] clipper ships were ... manned
by an international proletariat of the sea" (Morison,
1961:353). A growing number of these proletarians came from
the Azores, more specifically from Fayal.

Well-versed in the maritime craft and located in a
strategic point of passage for an increasing number of
American vessels, Azoreans constituted a constant source of
fresh labor for the merchant fleet of Massachusetts and the
whaling fleet of Rhode Island throughout the nineteenth
century. Morison has summarized the role of the Azores, and
more precisely the position of Fayal, on the American trade
routes as follows:

> Fayal in the Azores, where in any year (save
> three) between 1807 and 1892 one would discover
> the principal merchant to be a Dabney of Boston,
> was an outpost of the Mediterranean trade. The
> outward-bound whalers stopped there to pick up
> cheap labor, and to unload their early
> acquisitions of oil, which the Dabneys then
> shipped to Boston in their own vessels,...

> Baltic-bound vessels would often stop at
> Fayal to top off their cargoes with oranges, whale
> -oil, and wine. For Massachusetts approached
> Russia... by a long detour in Southern waters.
> (Morison, 1961:293, 294)

The strategic geographic position of the Western Islands
in the Mediterranean and the Baltic trade routes led to
permanent commercial ties between the Azores and
Massachusetts. The increasing need of the American merchant
fleet for constant renewal of crews created the background
against which a permanent migratory current was established
from the Azores to United States. Along with oranges, wine,
and whale oil that the Dabneys shipped from the Azores to
Boston came the sailors to man the vessels carrying these
products, and in time their women followed (Morison, 1961:
322-323).

In sum, the evidence indicates that the first Portuguese
migratory stream to the United States was induced rather
than spontaneous. Such a movement was founded on the needs
of the American whaling industry and its merchant fleet
along the Mediterranean and Baltic routes, and was preceded
by the establishment of American mercantile houses in the
sending society.

PORTUGUESE EMIGRATION TO CALIFORNIA

The strongest Portuguese migratory stream created after
the migratory current to New England flowed in the direction
of California. The discovery of gold in that state in the
mid-nineteenth century promoted an unprecedented
multinational race to the Pacific coast. The Portuguese

were among the many nationalities suffering from gold fever
(9).   They quickly gave up gold prospecting, but from the
mid-nineteenth century on they established a steady
migratory flow and a permanent Portuguese settlement in
California.   The Portuguese immigrants tended to enter
farming, and particularly dairy production, in San Francisco
and the surrounding area.

According to Pap (1949:5,6), from 1848 on Portuguese
immigrants came to the West Coast via several routes:
sailing directly from the Azores or from New Bedford to Cape
Horn and from there on taking the railroad; or, most
frequently, deserting their clippers or whaling boats around
San Francisco.   This last method was eased by the
establishment of whaling stations in California.   According
to Morison (1961: 331-338), it was not uncommon during this
period for entire crews to desert their vessels upon arrival
at San Francisco (10).

The census of 1850 recorded only 109 Portuguese
residing in California.   Ten years later there were 1580
Portuguese in California.   A few Portuguese were still
engaged in mining (e.g. 88 Portuguese miners in Trinity
county), but the majority was either engaged in whaling and
fishing or in farming.

The Portuguese owned and directed several whaling
stations in California in the 1850's and 1860's, e.g. at
Portuguese Bend, at Monterey, and at Bay of Carmelo (Brown,

9 In 1849 a booklet was published in Oporto with information
about California gold mines (Brown, 1944:51).
10 Of the 512 vessels abandoned in front of S. Francisco in
July 1850, at least one was Portuguese (Brown, 1944:51).

1944:51-53, and Pap, 1949:5). Some of the most prosperous Portuguese residing in California in 1860 were, however, engaged in farming, "financially speaking a trend which has continued down to the present time" (Brown, 1944:58).

In 1870 the Portuguese in California numbered 3453 individuals. Ten years later they were 8061. In sum, from 1850 onwards the Portuguese migratory flow to California was permanent and grew until the Portuguese community in that area became as important as the one previously established in New England. As far as I was able to document, this stream was primarily established by Portuguese immigrants already residing in the United States. Thus, it seems that the creation of a Portuguese migratory stream to California had nothing to do with direct recruitment from the receiving economy and very little to do with the sending society.

PORTUGUESE EMIGRATION TO LOUISIANA

Another Portuguese migratory stream created in the mid-nineteenth century took the direction of Louisiana. Between 1890 and 1930 it was a small but regular flow (11). This migratory flow to Louisiana was initially based upon contract labor (12). The first available reference dated this settlement from 1840, when a group of Portuguese males was contracted for sugar plantations. We know that this

---

11 Report of the Commissioner-General of Immigration For The Fiscal Year ended June 30, 1897 ... 1908 and 1920... 1932.
12 Bannick (1917:10) mentions that:"Prior to 1847 a few Portuguese settled in New Orleans, Louisiana. These settlers had been engaged in the slave trade." Bannick does not offer any evidence in support of his statement, and I did not find any other reference to such settlers.

group founded a mutual-aid society in 1851, the "Lusitanian-Portuguese Benevolent Association", that the majority married creole women, and that after 1865, with the abolition of slavery, the group scattered from the area. Many of them moved to California (Pap, 1949:5).

Soon after the disintegration of the original group and the departure of the majority of its members from the region, a new inflow of contract laborers arrived from the Portuguese mainland. The fate of this group, which arrived during the late 1860's and early 1870's, was the subject of several official inquiries and correspondence between Portuguese representatives in United States and the Lisbon government. The bulk of this documentation, published in 1874 (13), directly concerns the fate of 229 Portuguese emigrants who arrived in Louisiana between January and July of 1872, on board the vessels Saint Louis and Memphis.

These emigrants, seventy-nine of whom were under 12 years of age, were miserably exploited by their contractor, Carlos Nathan (14), and in certain cases, physically abused by their employers. Some of them succeeded in running away and presented formal complaints to Portuguese authorities in other states, which led to an official inquiry into the whole affair. The story that unfolds from this investigation contains all the usual ingredients that made

---

13 Documentos, 1874:241-250F. The Documents presented to the Portuguese Cortes in 1874 indicate that the contract labor system was used much more by the Brazilians to attract Portuguese emigrants than it was by Americans.
14 In an anonymous publication (Um Negociante Logrado) of 1872, this labor contractor was described as directly responsible for luring the Portuguese emigrants to New Orleans.

the process of contract labor recruitment so widespread during this period: low economic risks and high returns for the contractor's investment, and promises of ready cash and future large savings for the emigrant.

The press of the time, particularly in migratory districts, often claimed that contract labor and contract labor advertisements were the worst evils of emigration (Benis, 1979:90). But, their pleas or criticisms were ignored. As an editorial concluded, "Either the people do not read, [or if they read] they do not trust the press" (A Persuasão, Ponta Delgada, 1554, October, 1981).

Contract labor was slow to disappear and ceased only when forbidden by law (15). Advertisements of the "travel now, pay later" type attracted applicants without ready cash. The added promise of a lump sum at the term of the contract captured the more hesitant candidates (16). For the Portuguese peasantry, with its chronic starvation for cash, the contract labor advertisements proved difficult to resist.

---

15 In United States contract labor was formally forbidden in 1885. But according to the Immigration Commissioners, it took American authorities more then a decade to bring the process under control (see, for example, the Immigration Investigation Report for 1895). It is interesting to note that as early as the 1870's a segment of the anti-slavery movement in Brazil opposed slavery on economic grounds. This group argued that the slave owner was reducing his profits by preferring slaves to colons for the plantations. The "Gazeta de Campinas" of October 6, 1870, offers a table of expenses and profits for the two types of labor and concludes: "For the above, we can see that the slave leaves the plantation owner with less 127$000 [reis of profit when compared to the profits brought by the colon], plus [slave labor is subject to higher risks, such as] runaways, long sicknesses, death, etc, etc." Quoted in Ademir Gebara, 1977:135, 136.
16 Documentos..., 1874; Benis,1979.

While it lasted, contract labor induced a considerable number of Portuguese to cross the Atlantic, and led to the establishment of new migratory streams to Brazil and to United States. The mechanics of the system were the same in both receiving countries, as were the motivations of contractors, employers, and emigrants (17). In Brazil, the phenomenon attained enormous dimensions, involving tens of thousands. In United States, contract labor was never as significant, encompassing only a few thousand Portuguese. It was, however, this type of direct recruitment that induced Portuguese to emigrate to Louisiana and created a new Portuguese migratory flow to the United States.

PORTUGUESE EMIGRATION TO HAWAII

The third and last migratory stream I was able to document took the direction of Hawaii, then not yet part of the United States. During the first half of the nineteenth century a tiny Portuguese community was formed in the Sandwich Islands by deserting whaling crew members. In the 1850's they numbered no more then 60 persons. In 1872 the Portuguese numbered 395 individuals, ranking their community as the third largest foreign community in the islands (18).

17 The figures for the Louisiana case indicate that the contractor made a net profit of 100 percent from his transaction, the employer saved 50 percent in wages, and the emigrants had a promise of 60 to 100 dollars at the term of their three year contracts. See also the discussion of this topic by the Portuguese Minister in the United States in 1872 in Documentos..., 1874:242:243.
18 Documento Parlamentar, of May 22, 1882, quoted in the Boletim da Sociedade de Geografia de Lisboa, 3@ Serie, n.4, Lisboa, 1882,p. 224. See also: Adams,1937: 34,35; Freitas, 1903:148,149, and 151.

The Hawaiian Census of 1878 registered 435 Portuguese residents, 420 of whom were Azoreans, according to the Portuguese Consul in Honolulu (19).

This first Portuguese settlement in Hawaii was created by deserting crew members and later enlarged by runaways from Louisiana, but until the late 1870's there was not a regular migratory stream to the islands. This situation changed drastically during 1878-1879, when two vessels brought 540 Portuguese from Madeira as contract laborers. In the following two years 1,152 more contract laborers came from the Azores (S.Miguel).

Even after a great number of departures, in two years (1878-1880) the number of Azoreans living in Hawaii had practically doubled, numbering 813 at the end of 1880. The Madeirense numbered 440 individuals. The fate of a great number of these contract laborers resembled that described above for contract laborers in Louisiana during the 1870's. Similar abuses also motivated official inquiries that were later published in the Diário do Governo of April 19, 1882.

The flow of Portuguese to the Hawaiian islands increased further after the Portuguese and the Hawaiian governments signed a treaty of commerce and emigration in 1882. This treaty overtly promoted the flow of contract emigrants from the Western Islands to the Sandwich Islands.

The Portuguese migratory flow to Hawaii differed in some ways from the Louisiana flow. In the Hawaiian case, there was direct government involvement, and Portuguese hands were

---

19 Registered under a different heading, the Cape Verdians numbered only 120 individuals in 1878, and the number had not changed by 1880.

contracted to substitute for Chinese rather then slave labor. But as in the Louisiana case, at least half of the arrivals departed quickly, with the majority travelling to California, and a few returning to their homeland (Freitas, 1930:151). Those who left were, however, soon replaced by new shipments.

CONCLUSION

In sum, I found that the first labor migratory stream from Portugal to the United States was initiated by direct recruitment of seafaring men for crew members of American whaling and merchant vessels of New England. For subsequent migratory flows, I found that two out of three were also created by direct inducement-- with Portuguese laborers contracted as plantation workers. Of the three hypotheses on the creation of labor migratory streams considered in this section, the one that stresses interference and recruitment from the receiving society best fits the evidence on the creation of the first Portuguese migratory current to the United States, and on the subsequent creation of new streams (20).

---

20 During the nineteenth century, one more Portuguese settlements was created. This settlements was, however, an event without continuity. It was created, in 1848/49, by a few hundred converted Protestants from Madeira, who entered the United States, via West Indies, under the protection of the American Protestant Society. These Portuguese refugees settled in Illinois (near Springfield and Jacksonville), in an area still called today "Portuguese Hill" (Norton, 1857). This comunity, without further inflow, soon lost their ethnic roots.

THE DEVELOPMENT OF THE PORTUGUESE MIGRATORY FLOW TO UNITED
STATES

NETWORK DYNAMICS

No one denies the importance of migrant networks (21) in
the decision to emigrate and in the development of migratory
streams. What varies is the degree of importance accorded
to their impact on the whole migratory process.

Researchers of international migration occurring prior to
the Second World War usually lack the information necessary
to measure quantitatively the importance and impact of
migrant networks (22).   They have tended, however, to
stress the "power of the American letter", the "importance
of the prepaid ticket", and other related aspects of the
functioning of migrant networks (23). As Bodnar (1985:57)
put it, "The immigrant would not enter America alone".

Researchers of today's migratory streams with access to
direct testimony have assessed the impact of migrant
networks on the migratory process more precisely. The most
recent approach is direct sociological inquiries in migrant
communities at both ends of the trajectory; its analysis has
been preferentially based on logit models of decision-making
(e.g. O'Grada, 1985; Massey,1987). These recent works have

---

21 I am using the concept of migrant networks in a broad
sense. The term here refers to both kin/community based and
impersonal structures of information and support. The term
would encompass what MacDonald and Macdonald (1964) called
chain-migration and impersonally organized migration, and
what Tilly and Brown (1967) called "auspices of kinship" and
"auspices of work". The evidence on the Portuguese
emigration of this period strongly suggests that
kin/community migrant networks were more relevant than
impersonal structures of information and support.
22 There are exception, e.g., Tomaske (1971) included
migrant networks' influence in his analytic model.
23 E.g.,Taylor, 1971; Graves, 1977; Morawska, 1985.

shed light on the inner mechanisms that convince people to move, and they have also alerted scholars to the important role played by family and community in individual decisions to emigrate (24).

Unfortunately, the Portuguese migrants who are the subject of this work are almost all dead, making direct surveys impossible. Moreover, these emigrants rarely left behind letters, diaries or autobiographies that would help us reconstitute the migrant networks of their period. One of the few exception is a series of interviews conducted by Mayone Dias (1982) among Portuguese immigrants in California (25). The author's goal was to collect representative life stories and migrant experiences of the Portuguese community. In the course of providing their life stories, these Portuguese immigrants also gave their reasons for emigrating and described in passing the functioning and strength of the Portuguese migrant network in California and the Azores. Eleven of these life stories are particularly relevant here since the respondents emigrated from the Azores to the United States between 1903 and 1930.

The personal reasons for emigrating given by these eleven respondents are quite diverse. Fernando Pimentel, for example, emigrated in 1913 to evade military service; Lawrence Oliver and his sister emigrated in 1903 to run away from an unpleasant stepmother; and Mary Teixeira crossed the

---

24 A theoretical framework to the approach essayed here has been recently published by Wellman and Berkowitz, 1988.
25 The remaining exceptions are a few scattered interviews (e.g.,Leeder, 1968; Graves, 1977) and a few biographical accounts (e.g, Vieira, 1963; Andrade, 1968; Oliver, 1972; Namias, 1978).

ocean in 1913 to see how it was like on this side (26). It
is striking, however, that, despite the different personal
rationales for emigrating, all these life stories describe a
similar migratory process and show some common traits
regardless of sex, age, or the economic activity the
immigrant came to exercise in United States. These common
traits shed some light on the impact and importance of the
Portuguese migrant network for California.

One of the common elements for the respondents was a lack
of financial means for emigrating. In all these cases, a
relative either paid or advanced money for the ticket and
related expenses. These migrants also left at a very early
age, with the majority being between 16 and 18, and made the
crossing in the company of a relative or a neighbor. Given
their age and their lack of means, their decision to
emigrate must have had a significant familial component.

Upon arrival at Boston, Providence, or Ellis Island those
migrants who were not met by relatives were met by
Portuguese agents who conducted them to the train station or
to a Portuguese boarding house according to what seems to
have been a pre-arranged plan between the agent and the
emigrant's relative in United States. Just as family
networking at both ends of the trajectory was necessary to
finance the initial displacement, so too were these
Portuguese agents needed to reduce the cultural costs of
moving to the United States. They were part of the
Portuguese migrant network that received and directed the

---

26 Mayone Dias, 1982:221-242 (interview with Fernando
Pimentel), 317-341 (interview with Lawrence Oliver), 245-269
(interview with Mary Teixeira).

new arrivals, ignorant of the English language and
unfamiliar with the new country, to their various
destinations.

In all eleven cases, the first destination was a place
where a relative, as close as a brother or as distant as an
aunt or a cousin, was already established. And all the
respondents except one went to work with and for a
Portuguese immediately after their arrival. Offering
readily available work in a setting where the spoken
language was mainly Portuguese was another of the important
roles performed by the Portuguese migrant network for the
new arrivals.

The strength of the Portuguese migrant network is also
well documented in these interviews. Several of the
respondents mentioned their lack of incentive to learn
English after years of living in the United States-- a clear
symptom of the self-sufficiency of the Portuguese immigrant
community that they joined in the United States. This self-
sufficiency and self-containment was reinforced by three
factors: inter-marriage, occupational segregation, and
illiteracy. Only one respondent married outside his ethnic
group. The majority of the respondents worked all their
lives either for Portuguese or with Portuguese, and few of
them (two cases) had formal schooling prior to or after
arrival. In other words, the need to interact outside their
own ethnic group was restricted as far as possible.

Finally, these interviews suggest how the migrant network
functioned to reinforce the migratory stream itself.

Several of the respondents specifically mentioned that they were brought by a relative visiting the Azores or that they were called over by a relative already established in the United States. Later on, some of them perpetuated the process by bringing in other family members who had remained behind. Frank M. Rosa is certainly an extreme example of this tendency to perpetuate the chain between the sending and receiving communities. Arriving in 1904, by 1917 Rosa had already sent for three brothers, a sister, and his parents (in, Dias, 1982:271-296).

Another element of the migrant network moved beyond familial ties. Several of the respondents mentioned that after establishing themselves in various occupations (fishing, dairy, transportation) they sent for or employed newly arrived laborers from their original communities. In other words, jobs abandoned by Portuguese immigrants during the process of economic and social climbing were preferentially filled by members of the sending community who were called over or had recently arrived to United States.

These interviews suggest the existence of a kind of tacit agreement between those who were already established and those who were arriving. Those who were already established patronized the new arrivals by finding them housing and jobs. Those who had just arrived worked for members of the Portuguese community for less than the prevailing wages. When the immigrant had saved enough to pay his initial debts and to buy a truck, a piece of land, or some cows (the eleven life stories have happy economic endings), he in turn would employ newly arrived immigrants or send for relatives or neighbors that would work for wages below the current levels (e.g.interview with Manuel Mancebo Jr., in Dias, 1982:89-111). This kind of initiation fee in return for network support reinforced the Portuguese migrant network while sustaining the Portuguese migratory stream to California. Network dynamics were, in sum, mutually advantageous (27). For those already established in United States, they were a source of cheaper labor; for those willing to leave the Azores they offered assurance of finding a job, and logistical and cultural support. Although informal, the Portuguese migrant network seems to have been an effective "formal" information system able to support efficiently a labor market based on both sides of the Atlantic (28).

The Portuguese migratory network in California shared some characteristics with other regional Portuguese networks to this country-- specifically the family component and the network of support upon arrival-- but it also had some unique elements. In no other state was the number of Portuguese employers so large and so centered on primary activities identical to these that the emigrant had left in his sending community. Thus, in no other state could the Portuguese network be as self-sufficient and as self-contained as in California.

---

27 Parallel mechanisms existed in almost all migrant groups (the auto-biographical accounts in Namias, 1978 are a good example). For the Italians, a migrant group with great similarities with the Portuguese, see for example, Ratti, 1931, and MacDonald and MacDonald,1964.
28 On the importance of informal information in labor markets, see Rees, 1966.

The qualitative evidence on the functioning and strength of the Portuguese migrant network for California supports the hypothesis to be tested in this section-- that is, once a migratory stream begins, it tends to be self-sustained by the creation of migrant networks. A quantitative way to test this hypothesis is to look at one point in time to see whether or not the decision to emigrate was conditioned by the functioning of the networks in place.

THE DYNAMICS OF THE MIGRANT NETWORK IN TERCEIRA IN 1901

The Azores are an obvious choice for this type of analysis because they were one of the main migratory areas of Portugal, as well as the area of origin of the vast majority of Portuguese emigrants to United States. Moreover, they presented a dichotomous flow-- a portion of the Azoreans went to Brazil, while another portion chose instead the United States. The flow to Brazil was much longer-established than the one to United States. Thus we can observe not only the dynamics of a young network vis-a-vis an old network, but also see how networking conditions the decision to emigrate and filters the choice of direction.

I chose to focus on the island of Terceira and the year 1901 for three reasons. First, 1901 is the first year for which I have complete information on who decided to emigrate either to Brazil or to the United States and on who elected to stay. Second, since the capital of the district of Angra is located in Terceira, I can observe whether rural or urban residence played any significant role in the decision to leave or stay. Finally, Terceira entered the migratory flow to the United States later than other Azorean islands (29), and the specificities of a young network were more likely to be captured by looking at this island.

My main hypothesis was that networking is in fact a fundamental determinant in the decision to emigrate. More specifically I expected to find that the decision to emigrate was more or less the same regardless of the area of residence, but the direction of the flow (United States versus Brazil) was highly dependent on the area of residence.

My first step was to compute for each of Terceira's 26 parishes the percentage of the population at risk (de facto population minus foreigners recorded by the census of December of 1900) of departing for United States and departing for Brazil. The mapping of these percentages (shown in Figure 1 in Appendix 1) indicate that there were three groups of parishes. Group 1 parishes predominantly furnished emigrants to Brazil, with more than 60 percent of the flow having that destination (hereafter also referred to as GR1. Group 2 consisted of parishes that furnished emigrants to both the United States and Brazil, with the migratory flow more or less evenly divided between these

---

29 Between 1864 and 1870, 5811 Portuguese arrived to the United States (Annual Report on Immigration presented to the House of Representatives of the United States. 1864 to 1871). My survey of the registers of passports for the district of Angra during the same period indicates that only seven passports were issued to the United States to residents of Terceira. These seven passport holders were male, single and born in the city of Angra do Heroismo.

destinations (hereafter also referred to as GR2). Group 3 was composed of parishes that mainly furnished emigrants to the United States, with more than 60 percent of the flow taking that destination (hereafter also referred to as GR3).

The first fact revealed by the mapping of these percentages is that the first group of parishes (GR1) is the only group with regional cohesion. Since emigrants from GR1 predominantly took the direction of Brazil, we may infer that over time migrant networks tend to gain regional cohesion and to interlink among themselves. Group 2 and 3 were dispersed over the island, suggesting that each one of the groups was in itself more than one network, and that network formation is initially a very localized process-- perhaps initially occurring at the parish level.

The second step was to see if the probability of emigrating was similar in these three groups of parishes. Since the probability of migrating was identical, I then computed the probability, conditional on emigrating, of going to Brazil or to United States. These probabilities and the results of the statistical test of dependency used are given on the next two tables.

TABLE I:I - PROBABILITY OF DECIDING TO EMIGRATE
BY GROUP OF PARISHES

Decision	Group 1	Group 2	Group 3	Chi-square Test	
Stay	.988	.985	.985	Value	4.986
Leave	.012	.015	.015	Prob	.083
N	9512	17954	21285		

TABLE I:II - PROBABILITY OF EMIGRATING TO THE UNITED STATES
VERSUS BRAZIL BY GROUP OF PARISHES

Direction	Group 1	Group 2	Group 3	Chi-square Test	
U.S.	.233	.489	.799	Value	130.615
Brazil	.767	.511	.201	Prob	.000
N	116	270	323		

Source for Tables I and II: Census of December 1900 and
Register of Passports for Angra for 1901.

Table I:I indicates that the probability of leaving was
quite similar for residents of the three groups of parishes.
The Chi-square test indicate that the hypothesis of
statistical independence between the decision to emigrate
and the residence of the emigrant is accepted at the .10
level.   Table I:II shows that, for those who did emigrate,
the probability of going to Brazil or to United States was
almost reversed in the parishes of Group 1 and 3, and
practically the same in the parishes of Group 2.   The Chi-
square test indicates that there is strong statistical
dependency between the choice of destination and the area of
residence of the emigrant.

Given that the probability of emigrating affects all the
residential areas of the island, and is quite similar across
areas of residency and that the chi-square test rejects the
null hypothesis only at the .10 level, it cannot be argued
that the decision to leave or to stay is determined by some
specific geo-economic feature (e.g., urban versus rural or
farmholding's size in an area).   What can be argued is that
given the differences in probabilities found between the
choice of direction (Brazil or United States) and the high

statistical dependency found between destination and area of residency, the decision to emigrate was highly conditioned by the local migratory network.

A further question is whether individual and collective characteristics of the migratory flow from Terceira differed according to the area of residence of the emigrant, and the corresponding migrant network(s). My objectives are threefold: first, to characterize the emigrant group vis-a-vis the population at risk of emigrating; second, to examine the filtration each network exercised on the migrant population; and third, to see whether migrant characteristics differed according to network and place of destination (30).

The analysis will focus on the 709 emigrants who left Terceira either for United States or for Brazil during 1901. The characteristics known for each emigrant were as follows: place of birth (31), age, sex, marital status (single versus

_____

30 Ideally such an analysis should consider three groups of the population-- 1) the population at risk of emigrating; 2) the group emigrating to United States; and 3) the group emigrating to Brazil-- broken down by such characteristics as sex, age, occupation, and place of birth. Unfortunately, the available information on the population at risk of emigrating is limited to place of residency and sex. My first objective thus cannot be carried much further than what I have done in Table I:I. The second and third objective can, however, be pursued.
31 Parish of birth was used as place of residency because according to the Census' figures 96 percent of the Portuguese population in Terceira resided in their parish of birth. The place of residency in collective passports was considered to be the place of birth of the passport holder except when there were clear indications that the family had changed residency. In this last case the residency chosen was either the modal place of birth of the group or the place of the residency of the youngest member of the group.

married and widowed), occupation (32), type of passport
(individual versus collective), and previous personal or
familial migrant experience (33).

I used a logit model (Model VII, in Appendix 1) to test
whether the decision to emigrate to United States or Brazil
was a function of the known personal characteristics of the
migrants (34). The results are given in Table I:III.

---

32 Only given for males over fourteen years of age. This
information was coded in the following way: 1 if laborer 0
otherwise.
33 This characteristic means that either the migrant (if
travelling alone), or the migrant or one of his/her family
members (if travelling in a group) was born either in United
States or Brazil.
34 On the formalization of probabilistic-choice models see
Madala, 1987: 59-147.

TABLE I:III - LOGIT MODEL PREDICTING THE 1901 MIGRATORY
DIRECTION PROBABILITY BY AREA OF RESIDENCY AND
SELECTED OTHER CHARACTERISTICS

Variables	Model For Males		Model For Females	
	β	P	β	P
Migrant Characteristics Area of Residency				
Parishes (GR1)	- .6019	.1308	-1.4221	.0005
Parishes (GR3)	1.7953	.0000	1.5594	.0000
Individual Passport	-1.0746	.0020	- .4861	.2190
No Migrant Experience	-1.6091	.0003	-1.6970	.0000
Personal Characteristics Age Groups				
Child (<14)	- .6019	.2497	.5196	.3580
Young (14-25)	1.3913	.0032	.9664	.0314
Middle (26-40)	.5633	.1527	.7981	.0724
Single	1.3778	.0005	.4313	.2616
Occupation	.9416	.0040	....	....
Intercept	-1.1756	.0031	- .6097	.1275
Model Chi-square	147.14		116.92	
Model R^2	.501		.476	
No. of Emigrants	380		329	

Note: the Passport Registers do not recorded occupation for
females.

Table I:III presents, by sex, the coefficients that
measure the partial effect of each independent variable on
the logit probability, conditioned on emigrating, of
choosing the United States versus choosing Brazil. The
values in column one confirm what has been said about the
strength of migrant networks. The coefficient for GR3
(Group 3 of parishes) has the strongest positive partial
determinant of the decision to go to United States, while
Previous Migrant Experience and GR1 (Group 1 of parishes)
have the strongest partial negative effect on making such a
choice. They also confirm that the Terceira's migratory
experience to United States was relatively recent and that

it had not yet had time to create a significant re-migratory
component.

The coefficients for the individual characteristics
behave as would be expected in a flow still in formation
vis-a-vis a well-established one. Male children (child)
have a negative coefficient, and the strongest positive
relationship exists for the age group 14 to 25 years of age
(young) diminishing significantly afterwards. The other two
individual characteristics positively related to the choice
of going to United States versus to Brazil are marital
status (single) and occupation (laborer). In sum, the
relative strength of the logit parameters on the choice of
migratory direction indicate that the broader socio-economic
context, such as the migrant network active in the area of
residency of the migrant and personal or familial previous
migratory experience, were more relevant in determining the
migrant's choice of direction than were individual
characteristics such as age or marital status.

The values presented in column two indicate the logit
coefficients for the characteristics considered for women.
These values confirm that for women as well place of
residence and previous personal or familial migratory
experience had the strongest partial effect on the choice of
migratory direction. It follows from Table I:III that the
migrant more likely to go to the United States, whether male
or female, lived in one of the parishes of Group 3 (GR3),
was single, was between 14 and 25 years of age, and had no
previous personal or familial migratory experience.

The significance of changes in the log-odds (β) resulting from a unit of change in the odds (X) is hard to convey directly. I thus rearranged the information in Table I:III by estimating the changes in the probabilities resulting from changes in the independent variables (35). The result of these estimates are given in Tables I:IV, and I:V.

TABLE I:IV - ESTIMATED DIRECTION PROBABILITIES FOR A FEMALE
AT DIFFERENT PHASES OF HER LIFE CYCLE AND OTHER SELECTED
CHARACTERISTICS BY AREA OF RESIDENCY

Female Between 14 and 25 Years of Age
And Residency by Groups of Parishes

Select Characteristics	No Previous Experience=0			Previous Experience=1		
	Group 1	Group 2	Group 3	Group 1	Group 2	Group 3
Individual Passport						
Female Single	0.246	0.575	0.865	0.056	0.199	0.541
Female Married	0.175	0.468	0.807	0.037	0.139	0.434
Collective Passport						
Female Single	0.347	0.687	0.913	0.089	0.287	0.657
Female Married	0.256	0.588	0.872	0.059	0.207	0.554

Female Between 26 and 40 Years of Age

Select Characteristics	No Previous Experience=0			Previous Experience=1		
	Group 1	Group 2	Group 3	Group 1	Group 2	Group 3
Individual Passport						
Female Single	0.216	0.533	0.845	0.048	0.173	0.499
Female Married	0.152	0.426	0.779	0.032	0.120	0.393
Collective Passport						
Female Single	0.310	0.650	0.898	0.076	0.254	0.618
Female Married	0.226	0.547	0.852	0.051	0.181	0.513

---

35 The formula used for computing these changing probabilities was: $P=1/(1+e^{-\beta x})$, where X is a vector of assumed characteristics, and β is a vector of parameters pertaining to X (Petersen, 1985:130 and Massey, 1987:12).

TABLE I: V - ESTIMATED DIRECTION PROBABILITIES FOR A MALE AT
DIFFERENT PHASES OF HIS LIFE CYCLE AND OTHER SELECTED
CHARACTERISTICS BY AREA OF RESIDENCY

Select Characteristics	Males Between 14 And 25 Years of Age And Residency by Groups of Parishes					
	No Previous Experience=0			Previous Experience=1		
Individual Passport	Group 1	Group 2	Group 3	Group 1	Group 2	Group 3
Male Single and Laborer	0.702	0.812	0.963	0.321	0.463	0.838
Male Married and Laborer	0.373	0.521	0.867	0.106	0.179	0.567
Male Single with a Skill or Property	0.479	0.627	0.910	0.156	0.252	0.669
Male Married with a Skill or Property	0.188	0.298	0.718	0.044	0.078	0.338
Collective Passport						
Male Single and Laborer	0.874	0.927	0.987	0.580	0.716	0.938
Male Married and Laborer	0.635	0.761	0.950	0.259	0.389	0.793
Male Single with a Skill or Property	0.729	0.831	0.967	0.350	0.496	0.856
Male Married with a Skill or Property	0.405	0.554	0.882	0.120	0.199	0.599

Select Characteristics	Males Between 26 And 40 Years of Age					
	No Previous Experience=0			Previous Experience=1		
Individual Passport	Group 1	Group 2	Group 3	Group 1	Group 2	Group 3
Male Single and Laborer	0.508	0.653	0.919	0.171	0.274	0.694
Male Married and Laborer	0.206	0.322	0.741	0.049	0.087	0.364
Male Single with a Skill or Property	0.287	0.423	0.815	0.074	0.128	0.469
Male Married with a Skill or Property	0.092	0.156	0.527	0.020	0.036	0.182
Collective Passport						
Male Single and Laborer	0.751	0.846	0.971	0.377	0.525	0.869
Male Married and Laborer	0.432	0.582	0.893	0.132	0.218	0.626
Male Single with a Skill or Property	0.541	0.683	0.929	0.191	0.301	0.724
Male Married with a Skill or Property	0.229	0.352	0.765	0.056	0.098	0.395

Source: Table I:III

The first generalization that follows from both Tables
I:IV and I:V is that, whatever the combination of
characteristics considered, the probability of going to the
United States relative to Brazil diminished significantly
when the migrant had previous personal or familial migratory
experience. Thus, for example, the chances of going to
United States for a returned migrant laborer, single,
between 26 and 40 years of age, travelling alone, and
resident in GR2 (where both migrant networks were equally
active) were 2.4 times less than the chances he had of doing
the same if he had no previous migratory experience. This
finding suggests once more that a well-established migratory
flow (in this case the flow to Brazil) has a significant
component of re-emigration. This fact is important for two
reasons: first, the periodic homecoming of successful
migrants reminded those at home that chances for success
existed outside their society; second, return migration
maintained open and active channels between the receiving
and the sending community.

The second notable pattern is that the probability of
going to the United States increases, in both tables, from
left to right, regardless of the combination of
characteristics being analyzed. This is, the probability of
going to the United States grows accordingly to the strength
of the network in place. Thus, for example, a married
laborer between 26 and 40 years of age was 3.6 times more
likely to go to the United States if departing from GR3 than
if leaving from GR1. Similarly, a married female in the

same age group has five times more chances of going to United States if she resided in GR3 than if she inhabited GR2. Moreover, the probabilities for GR2 and GR3 are closer for males than for females, suggesting that the Brazilian network in GR2 was losing ground to the American network.

Although losing ground relative to the United States, Brazil's attraction increased with the migrant's age and skills. The probability of migrating to Brazil was consistently higher for migrants between 26 and 40 years of age than for migrants between 14 and 25 years of age, and was equally consistently higher for males with some skill or property than for laborers. Given what we already know about the re-emigration component of the Brazilian flow, these additional findings suggest that network support was particularly determinant in early phases of the migrant's life cycle and more so if he was an unskilled laborer. This inference is also supported by the migrant life stories reported at the beginning of this chapter; all the respondents mentioned their personal lack of financial means to cover the initial costs of displacement.

Finally, we may remark that the male migrant with the highest probability (96 to 99 percent chance) of coming to the United States from Terceira in 1901 was an unmarried laborer, between 14 and 25 years of age, residing in GR3 and without previous migratory experience. Conversely, the migrant most likely to emigrate to Brazil (98 percent chance) was married, resident in GR1, had a skill or property, and had previous personal or familial migratory experience.

For a female migrant, the odds of coming to United States were greater (91 percent) if she resided in GR3, was single, was between 14 and 25 years of age, travelled in a group, and had no earlier personal or familial migratory experience. The odds of making that decision were lowest (3 percent chance) for a married female, between 26 and 40 years of age, resident in GR1, who had previous personal or familial migratory experience.

In sum, the longitudinal cut on the Portuguese migratory flow indicates that networking was a main determinant of the decision to emigrate as well as of the direction taken. Moreover, the relevance of the network was greater for earlier phases of the migrant life cycle, and more so if the migrant was an unskilled male. Network inner dynamics seem to prolong a migratory current, even when migration from a region is changing direction. This probably results from the strong family and neighborhood component we found in the Portuguese migratory network, and from the fact that family reunification could only be accomplished in stages, due to the financial limitations of the population involved in the migratory process.

CONCLUSION

The Portuguese migratory process to the United States was rooted in socio-economic disparities existing between Portugal and the United States. The imbalances of the

Portuguese socio-economic structure pressured a part of the population to leave while the growth of the American economy demanded the inflow of unskilled labor.

Despite these existing preconditions, I found that direct recruitment from the American economy was necessary to initiate the first migratory stream to this country and at least two of the subsequent currents. Migration models postulating that economic advantages in the receiving society are a sufficient condition to initiate and sustain migratory currents were shown to be of weak explicative power for the Portuguese case. Migration models postulating that deteriorating economic conditions in the sending society are a sufficient condition to create and develop a migratory current were also found to be poor analytical tools. When, however, deteriorating conditions at home are postulated to be only necessary conditions, they greatly enhance our understanding of the Portuguese migratory process to this country.

For the development of the Portuguese migratory flow to the United States, I found that networking was a main determinant of the Portuguese migratory process as well as a powerful filter of the direction of the migratory flow. The analysis of migrant networks proved to be a useful tool for capturing the Portuguese migrant experience. Perhaps because migrant networks channeled home dreams of opulence as much as they found job opportunities for new arrivals, they stand for the measurable and the immeasurable elements of the migratory experience (36). Moreover, embodying in its functioning both the economic conditions of the receiving society and the bitterness of those leaving and remaining behind, networking can have a pace of its own that does not need to agree entirely with either the fluctuations of the American economy or with the economic deterioration of the Portuguese economy.

In sum, I found that the Portuguese migratory process to this country, at least until 1930, was best understood by the combined dynamics of the Portuguese migrant networks and of the American immigration policy. The first process explains how the flow was sustained, the second how it was halted.

The social and economic pressures encouraging emigration, and the obstacles set up by the sending and receiving societies to discourage it, are the themes addressed in the coming chapters.

---

36 The excitement and the dreams return migrants created in their communities were autobiographically described to me by the Reverend Julio da Rosa. Reverend Rosa offered me <u>Gente das Ilhas</u> by M. Rosa (n.d), which in his opinion, contains the best description of an emigrant arrival. I entirely agree with him.

CHAPTER II - STATES AND SOCIETIES: THE SOCIO-POLITICAL
FRAMEWORK OF
PORTUGUESE EMIGRATION TO THE UNITED STATES (1)

International migratory flows are different from all
other migratory movements in that they occur between nation-
states with specific boundaries, which can and usually do
interfere with the migratory flow at each end of the
trajectory. By promoting, restricting, or being indifferent
to the outflow or inflow at their borders, states have been
much more than bystanders to international migratory flows.
They have been an integral part of the whole process
(Zolberg, 1983:3, Bohning, 1984:3).

Migration theorists have been slow to integrate this
distinctive political feature of international migration
into their conceptual frameworks. Scholars have instead
favored approaches based on two separate postulates: 1. that
international mobility results from voluntary individual
movements in response to imbalances in the regional
distribution of economic and social opportunities; or, 2.
that international migration is a transfer of population
from the economic periphery to core areas of the capitalist
system, regulated according to the needs of the center (2).

The first approach implicitly denies the importance of
the political dimension to the overall process of
international migration; the second only recognizes the

---

1 A small part of this chapter has been published in "Social
Marginalization, Government Policies and Emigrants'
Remittances Portugal 1870 - 1930". Estudos e Ensaios Em
Homenagem a Vitorino Magalhães Godinho. Lisboa, 1988.
2 Examples of these two approaches can be found in Lee,
1969: 282-297 and Petras, 1983: 44-63, respectively. For a
detailed appraisal of both approaches see Zolberg, 1983: 3-
27.

political dimension as enacted by the receiving society. The problem with this latter approach lies not in its fundamental premise, that capitalism is a structurally uneven world system, but rather in its secondary postulate that international migration is generated, shaped, and thus explained by that same unevenness. As generally elaborated, this postulate leaves little or no room for the roles played by individuals, sending states, and dominant cultural values in generating and shaping international migratory flows.

A. Zolberg has recently published a critical appraisal of both approaches (1983: 3-27); evidence of the critical impact on the migratory flow exerted by the state in the sending society can also be found in the work of B.Heisler (1985: 469-484). Both works convincingly argue that any analysis of international migratory flows must take into account the political framework, at both ends of the trajectory, in which international mobility takes place.

The interlinkage of several layers of socio-political decision-making which involves and affects the process of international migration was addressed by Zolberg (1983). Attempting to interrelate and categorize the various elements in the migratory process, he writes:

> On the societal side, the notion that exit and entry are controlled in accordance with certain collective interests must be understood in a very broad sense. Control includes not only the erection of more or less restrictive barriers to free movement across state boundaries but also a policy of permissive indifference or benign neglect ... To basic policy orientations must be added incentives or sanctions devised to induce or prevent certain movements. On the entry side, control also includes all aspects governing naturalization and legal provisions concerning nationality in general. ... What matters is that

the resulting regulations are binding on
individuals and affect their lives even if they
themselves are not involved in the migration
process. ...
international migration conceptualized in this
manner entails not only a tension between
individuals and societies at each end of the
trajectory, but also involves a tension in the
same sense between sending and receiving states or
societies, each of which regulates migration in
accordance with goals of its own. (Zolberg,
1983:8)

The notion that departures and entries must be controlled in

accordance with certain collective interests can result, in

receiving societies, in either open door policies which

maximize the labor supply or in a quota system which

preserves cultural and political integrity. In sending

societies, control of the emigratory flow may lead to

selection, promotion, or restriction of emigrants'

departures by the state. For the individual, departure can

either represent a solution to an economic conflict between

the person and his or her own society, an act of political

participation (since by staying or leaving individuals are

voting with their feet, even when such rights are denied by

law), or both.

Because I am looking at international migration over a

long period and because the predominant social groups

controlling the process of decision-making at the socio-

economic and political level changed over time, I will

survey the attitudes toward migration revealed by

legislation in both the United States and Portugal. Such a

survey suggests the parameters within which individual

decisions to leave or stay were made between 1860 and 1930.

More concretely, I will address the following

questions. For the receiving society-- when did American

elites perceive that the immigratory flow was a threat to social integrity? What mechanisms of expulsion or absorption were used to reduce this alleged threat? When and how did this perception affect the Portuguese migratory flow to the United States? For the sending society-- was emigration used by the Portuguese political elites to achieve goals of their own? If so, what were the mechanisms used to achieve these goals? In what ways did they shape the Portuguese migratory flow?

UNITED STATES IMMIGRATION POLICY

A survey of American immigration policy (here defined by the laws regulating the entry, the departure, and the naturalization of foreigners in United States between 1860 and 1930) clarifies the research questions discussed above for the receiving society. By analyzing the legislation of the period, we can see the socio-economic and political goals that immigration policies were designed to achieve. In addition, the socio-political discourse associated with the legal apparatus can suggest what social groups were struggling for the control of society's perception of the migratory flow.

W.Bernard has divided American immigration policy from the colonial period to the present into five phases:

> the colonial era (1609-1775); the Open Door era (1776-1881); the era of regulation (1882-1916); the era of restriction (1917-1964); and the era of liberalization (1965 to the present). (Bernard, 1982: 75).

According to this periodization, between 1860 and 1930
there were two major shifts in American immigration policy,
defined by tightening of the borders and increasing federal
regulation of the migratory inflow (Bernard, 1982: 80-103).

While I agree with Bernard that the turning points of
American immigration policy were marked by heightened state
centralization and selectivity in admissions, I think that
our conceptualization would be improved by a slightly
different periodization, which emphasizes the changing
intentions of the immigration and naturalization laws and
the power structure enacting them. I divide immigration
policy from 1860 to 1930 into three periods: the period of
permissive indifference, 1860-1874; the period of
intervention and regulation, 1875-1920; and the period of
preservation of the "original stock," 1921-1930.

THE PERIOD OF PERMISSIVE INDIFFERENCE, 1860-1874

The years between 1860 and 1874 are part of a larger
period initiated in 1776 (often described as the "Open Door"
phase), during which American immigration policy was guided
by one predominant goal, the recruitment of manpower.
Maximizing the country's labor supply and its demographic
weight took precedence over other concerns. Years later,
government spokesmen would look back at this period with a
certain uneasiness, as the following commentary by the
Immigration Investigating Commission of 1895 documents.
Wrote the commissioners,

> ... as late as 1864 public sentiment sanctioned
> and encouraged indiscriminate immigration. No
> safeguards were provided to protect our people
> from the worst classes of foreign population;
> idiots, criminals, assisted persons, paupers, and
> those suffering from loathsome diseases were
> admitted without inspection or examination ....
> (Report of the Immigration Investigating
> Commission, 1895: 11)

It is not, however, totally accurate to speak of this
period as one with no safeguards on immigrants' entry.
True, until the early 1860's there were no federal
immigration laws, which creates the impression of an "Open
Door" policy. But in practice, this gap was filled by
state and local governments' legislation.

State governments' right to legislate on immigration was
first affirmed in an 1837 ruling of the Supreme Court, in
the case "City of New York versus Miln." The ruling read:

> We think it as competent for a State to provide
> precautionary measures against the moral
> pestilence of paupers, vagabonds, and possibly
> convicts, as it is to guard against the physical
> pestilence which may arise from unsound or
> infectious articles imported, or from a ship, the
> crew of which may be laboring under an infectious
> disease. (City of New York versus Miln, 36 U.S.
> 102, extract in Abbott,1924: 121)

This extract reveals that mechanisms of defense against
unwelcome foreigners could be legally activated if a state
wished to do so, and that, at least in New York, they were
being activated. However, permissive indifference at the
federal level towards immigration allowed for great variety
of admission regulations for steerage passengers at the
local level. Some states allowed unrestricted immigration
to their territories; others, particularly those with many
immigrants arriving each year (such as New York and

Massachusetts), institutionalized "precautionary measures" from the 1820's on.

In New York legislation was passed to reduce the socio-economic costs of immigration to the state's taxpayers (Abbott, 1924:97). As early as 1824, a statement on the physical condition of each passenger was required of the vessel's captain, and a penalty of seventy five dollars was imposed for each unrecorded passenger. Sureties not exceeding 300 dollars for each passenger were to be given, and were to be used (within the next two years from the day of the ship's arrival) if any passenger or one of his descendents became pauperized or sick and had to be cared for by the city. If any of the recorded passengers was found likely to "become chargeable to the said city," entry was to be refused and the ship carrying the passenger was to be compelled to return him to the port of origin (3). The overall result of New York's regulations on immigration was believed by immigration authorities to be qualitative selection of those allowed to enter. In 1870, F.Kapp, one of the New York state immigration commissioners, wrote:

> New York [where more than five-sevenths of the immigrants land] protects and shields the immigrant in his health and property, and the rising communities of the West flourish upon the fruits of her vigilant care. Our State acts, so to speak, as a filter in which the stream of immigration is purified; what is good passes beyond ; what is evil, for the most part, remains behind. (F.Kapp, _Immigration_ (1870), extract on Abbott, 1924: 165)

---

3 "An Act concerning Passengers in Vessels Coming to the Port of New York, February 11, 1824", _New York Laws_, 1824, chap.37, extract in Abbott, 1924: 106-108.

In fact, the spirit and the letter of the 1824 Act of New York state was already quite close to the federal acts that would be passed some decades later. We must keep in mind that about two-thirds of the migratory flow to United States during this period entered the country via the port of New York and thus fell under that state's regulations.

The attitude of permissive indifference towards immigration at the federal level left to state and local authorities the power to restrict or accept the inflow of foreigners, as well as migration's promotion and recruitment. Since these were understood to be state and local affairs, they were dealt with in a variety of ways. Some states appointed agents to recruit immigrants at New York harbor; others collected mailing lists of suitable possible candidates still living in Europe; others advertised, in multiple languages, their state's advantages when compared to stagnant Europe. In its 1870 pamphlet, the state of Iowa compared the opportunities the Midwest offered for individual freedom and wealth to Europe, where "the majority ... must live out their days as dependent laborers on the land of others" (4).

States' promotional campaigns had great support from some elements in the private sector. Until the last decade of the nineteenth century, help came from railroad land companies interested in potential emigrants as prospective customers for their trains, as land purchasers, and as settlers along their rail lines (5).

---

4 Iowa, the Home for Immigrants (1870), in Taylor, 1971:73.
5 After the 1890's transatlantic shipping lines increasingly replaced the railroads in setting up networks for attracting

The federal government's attempt to directly interfere with immigration on economic grounds, through the 1864 "Act to encourage immigration," was partially justified by the temporary absence of a significant part of the American labor force in the army, but it nevertheless faced strong opposition and was repealed two years later (Immigration Investigating Commission, 1895: 11). Another proposed act to promote immigration did not even make it through Congress in 1872. In this period, each state claimed the right to regulate immigration and settlement within its borders, while federal attempts at homogenization resulted in either total failure or in short-lived victory.

The federal government did, however, exercise control of immigration in one specific area-- the entry of Asian immigrants. By the Act of 1862 (February 19), Congress debarred from entry coolies from China, Japan, or any other Asian country when imported to be disposed of, sold, or transferred as servants or apprentices, or to be held in service or labor. This law was reinforced and supplemented by other acts of similar character passed in 1869 and 1875, and was followed by the very restrictive Chinese immigration Act of 1882.

---

potential emigrants. The steamship companies, with their extensive European network of agents and subagents, are believed to have thrust "down recruitment roots more firmly and widely than either state governments or railroad land companies" (Erickson, 1957:77). Still, Taylor (1971) and Erickson (1957) suggest that the greatest support to the promotion and recruitment of new emigrants probably came from the "American letter", that is immigrants' letters to their relatives and friends in the old country. An overview of the promotional campaigns of the several states, railroads and transatlantic companies can be found in Taylor, 1971:66-90, Erickson, 1957: 67-78, and Bernard, 1982:84,85.

In the immigration laws to stem the "Yellow peril" we find one of the constant traits of American immigration policy, racism. Racism can be understood as a symptom of fears about losing economic predominance, cultural integrity, or political power. The evidence suggests that cultural concerns were, in this case, the main motivation, and that they furnished sufficient political justification for the lawmakers of the time. In one of the Reports of the U.S. Industrial Commission of 1901, the Act of 1882 is justified by the fact that:

> The Chinese were of a distinct race and religion, unacquainted with representative institutions, not bringing their families, expecting to return to their native land, and while temporarily here resorting to low practices and filthy abodes. ("Immigration", Reports of the U.S. Industrial Commission, XV (1901), extract in Abbott, 1924: 187)

It was also on racial grounds that naturalization laws selected a posteriori those among the foreign stock who were granted political participation. From a very early period (1790), federal law established that only free white persons living in United States for at least two years could acquire American citizenship. In sum, since a very early period, mechanisms of selection were in place to help preserve the country's cultural and political integrity by denying political rights to a segment of the alien element in the country. Naturalization laws during this period made political participation dependent upon the possession of three individual characteristics: a certain status (to be free); a certain race (to be white); and a certain length of permanence in the country (2, 14, and 5 years respectively) (6).

With the naturalization laws, an á posteriori mechanism for selection of the citizenry by the concession or denial of political rights was set in place. This mechanism had a dual advantage: it did not enter in conflict with the desire to maximize the country's labor supply, yet it protected the country's cultural and political hegemony as defined by the elites of the time.

By the early 1870's, the predominant social groups in United States began redefining what goals should guide immigration policy and what power structure should regulate immigration. The statement of the Immigration Investigating Commission of 1895 is quite suggestive on this point. The Commissioners remarked:

> Between 1872 and 1882 public sentiment regarding immigration underwent a change. Not only were laws promoting it no longer discussed, but restrictions were demanded. (Immigration Investigating Commission, 1895: 11)

This change in attitude towards immigration coincided with a change in the composition of the migratory flow to the United States, brought about by the growing inflow of eastern and southern Europeans. I am not implying that the changes in the ethnic composition of the migratory flow were immediately noticed and perceived by contemporaries as irreversible changes. I agree with Higham (1985: 12-34)

---

6 In 1798, in order to assure electoral victory against the Republicans, the Federalist party pushed through Congress a new law raising the residency requirement to fourteen years. This law was repealed in 1801, after the Republican victory, and the residency requirement was lowered to five years (Bernard, 1982:81,82).

that such consciousness came later. But the lack of consciousness is of no relevance to the argument being made.

What is relevant is that during this period a larger number of eastern and southern Europeans were coming to United States, and that their inflow led to an increasingly hostile interaction of larger segments of the American population with these "new immigrants". Think, for example, of the events taking place during the 1870's in the coal fields of Pennsylvania where Hungarians and Italians were brought in to break up labor conflicts, or of the negative reactions induced by Jewish peddlers from eastern Europe in New York. Larger segments of the American population were solidifying racist and economic arguments against a new stratum of the migratory flow during the 1870's. In the literature of the time, we find arguments that helped to consolidate the anti-immigration positions in the 1880's and 1890's, when it became clear that the changes in the ethnic composition of the migratory flow were not a temporary phenomenon.

Part of the change in the ethnic composition of the migrant population can be attributed to a combination of European legislation on steerage passengers and new shipping capabilities. Both resulted, between the late 1860's and the early 1870's, in remarkable improvements in the conditions of transatlantic crossing that extended America's attraction to larger segments of the European peasantry.

The Reports presented to the Secretary of the Treasury of the United States in 1873 on the conditions on board for steerage passengers furnish evidence on the extent of improvements. Some of them reflect such an elitist stand

that it can be argued they constitute poor evidence. For

example, investigator Helen M. Barnard indicated that

steerage conditions on respectable lines were good as

"judged by the popular standard of what is due the poor and

ignorant classes in return for value given by them" (7).

But others, like the one from the supervising surgeon of the

United States Marine Hospital Service, use more reliable

measures of the amelioration of steerage conditions during

this period. This investigator remarked that the best proof

of the extent of these improvements was the decrease in

deaths during the ocean voyage. The frightening high

proportion of deaths on route in 1867, 11.67 percent on

sailing-vessels and the 1.03 percent on steamships, were

reduced to 5.42 and .45 percent respectively by 1872.

Moreover, death rates were likely to continue to fall since

steamships were increasingly replacing sailing-vessels (8).

These improved conditions in comfort and safety went hand

in hand with increases in speed; sailing vessels in 1867

still took as much time as they did in 1843, an average of

44 days, but steamers were making the crossing from Europe

to United States in 14 days. Furthermore, regularity and

accessibility of passenger services now spread over Europe

to key points like Antwerp, Havre, Marseille, Naples, Fiume,

and La Coruna (Gould, 1979:612-615) (9). These factors

---

7 "Reports to the Secretary of the Treasury by Special
Investigators", Unite States 43d Congress, 1st session,
Senate Ex. Doc. N.23 (1873), extract in Abbott, 1924: 51.
8 Ibidem, p.48, 49.
9 This new availability and regularity of emigrant services
is well exemplified by the increasing number of regular
ships arriving the New York harbor from the major European

combined with the railroad boom in Europe and the marketing
campaigns of American railroads, ship companies, and other
private entrepreneurs helped to extend to new areas of
Europe and to temporary migrants the attraction of United
States (10).

The annual average influx of immigrants, which during the
1870's was around 281000, jumped to 525000 during the
following decade. Moreover, the once minute migratory flow
from eastern and southern Europe became increasingly visible
during this period. Between 1861 and 1870, immigrant
arrivals from eastern and southern Europe accounted for a

---

ports. In August 1891, for example, weekly emigrant ships
arrived regularly from Havre to New York. These ships of
close to 3 thousand tons carried their passengers with
increasing comfort and safety; they were: La Gascogne
(arrived August 3-- 617 passengers), La Touraine (arrived
August 10-- 538 passengers), La Bourgogne (arrived August
17-- 765 passengers), La Champagne (arrived August 24-- 707
passengers), La Normandie (arrived August 31-- 811
passengers) (Balch Institute, Manifests for New York,
numbers: 1154, 1236, 1249, 1286, 1332).
10 As remarked by Gould (1979:613): "speedier transport (by
rail on the European continent, of course, as well as by
steamer on the high seas) offered a financial inducement to
temporary migration, as well as, more obviously, making this
physically more feasible." Transatlantic costs must have
decreased considerably during this period, helping to extend
the attraction of America to poorer elements of the European
peasantry. Evidence on at least one of the components,
ships' fares, does not entirely support this hypothesis.
The cost of transatlantic crossing seems to have varied
widely until the 1860's. By the 1870's, when sailing
vessels ceased to dominate the emigrant trade, steamer
companies seem to have succeeded in restraining competition
and thus fares dropped substantially. The problem is that
ships' fares are just one of the variables in the cost of
transportating an emigrant across the ocean. Other
variables such as the region of origin, the accessibility to
a railroad system and its cost, length of the journey, and
lodging during the journey, are as important factors as
ships' fares, for an estimation of transatlantic costs.
Since consistent, comparable, and long-term statistics that
would enlighten this problem are more or less impossible to
construct, the cost of transatlantic emigration will remain
a debatable issue (Gould, 1979:611-613; Hyde, 1975:81-84;
and Taylor, 1971: 6-9, 55-56, and 93-96).

meager 1.4 percent of the total migratory flow to the United States, against 87.8 percent from northern and western Europe. In the next decade, however, eastern and southern European participation rose to 18.2 percent, while northern and western Europe's share dropped to 73.6 percent (Immigration Commission, 1911, V.I: 57,61-63). The new ethnic composition of the migratory flow and its increasing volume would soon invite revision of American immigration policy.

THE PERIOD OF INTERVENTION AND REGULATION, 1875-1920

Two events marked the year 1875 as a turning point in American immigration policy. First, the Supreme Court's ruling on "Henderston versus Mayor of New York"-- a case similar to that of 1837-- found state laws on immigration to be unconstitutional because they usurped the exclusive power of the Congress to regulate foreign commerce. The 1875 ruling read:

> The laws which govern the right to land passengers in the United States from other countries ought to be the same in New York, Boston, New Orleans, and San Francisco ....
> We are of the opinion that this whole subject has been confided to Congress by the Constitution; that Congress can more appropriately and with more acceptance exercise it than any other body known to our law, state or national (Abbott,1924: 170-171).

Also suggestive of an underlying policy change was an act passed by Congress debarring convicts and prostitutes. In sum, the tone of the period was set: federal direct

intervention on immigration was firmly recognized by the
Supreme Court, and legal á priori mechanisms of selection of
"suitable" immigrants, based upon individual
characteristics, begun to be systematically codified (11).

W. Bernard (1982: 87) is correct in stressing that the
new underlying goal of the American immigration policy
during this period was the restriction, under Congressional
control, of the migratory flow to those healthy and
employable. But the achievement of this goal went hand in
hand with other goals, which were also reflected in the
legislation of the period.

A good example of the mixed motivations guiding
immigration laws is given by section 1 of the Stump Law
(March 3, 1891), where those immigrants to be denied entry
were listed. The act reads:

> That the following classes of aliens shall be
> excluded from admission into the United States, in
> accordance with the existing acts regulating
> immigration, other than those concerning Chinese
> laborers: All idiots, insane persons, paupers, or
> persons likely to become a public charge, persons
> suffering from a loathsome or a dangerous
> contagious disease, persons who have been
> convicted of a felony or other infamous crime or

---

11 I am aware that American scholars postpone until 1882 the
beginning of this phase. The 1882 Act has received special
emphasis because of its comprehensiveness. I, however,
would argue that this act did not modify the main features
of American immigration policy set out in 1875; it merely
reinforced them. I am also aware that my position seems to
dispute Higham's genarally accepted position on this period.
A position usually accepted. According to Higham (1985) the
1870's were an age of confidence in which "It was an article
of faith that this land of opportunity had leveled all the
barriers to individual mobility; and the corollary that a
completely free society was an unshakable one appeared
hardly less certain" (ibidem, p.36). I do not dispute the
idea that the 1870's were an age of confidence but I
certainly dispute that its corollary was a completely free
society, as the above legislation indicates.

misdemeanor involving moral turpitude,
polygamists, and also any person whose ticket or
passage is paid for with the money of another or
who is assisted by others to come, unless it is
affirmatively and satisfactorily shown on special
inquiry that such person does not belong to one of
the foregoing excluded classes, or to the class of
contract laborers excluded by the act of February
26, 1885; but this section shall not be held to
exclude persons living in the United States from
sending for a relative or a friend who is not of
the excluded classes under such regulations as the
Secretary of the Treasury may prescribe: Provided,
That nothing in this act shall be construed to
apply to or exclude persons convicted of a
political offense, notwithstanding said political
offense may be designated as a "felony", crime,
infamous crime, or misdemeanor involving "moral
turpitude" by the laws of the land whence he came
or by the court convicting. (extract in
Immigration Investigating Commission of 1895:13)

It is quite clear here that economic motivations were not

the only ones guiding American lawmakers.

A brief synopsis of the immigrant categories successively

debarred from entry will help clarify the various underlying

goals. The denial of entry to prostitutes and convicts (act

of 1875) was primarily defended on moral and cultural

grounds; however, it can be argued it was also based on

economic concerns (12). The restrictions on entry of

children unaccompanied by parents (act of 1907) were passed

as much to protect the child from being abused as to protect

taxpayers from the expenses of their eventual

institutionalization. The debarment from entry to

polygamists (act of 1891) can hardly be explained by

economic reasons; it is more easily attributable to the

---

12 Prostitutes and convicts were thought to be more likely
than other immigrants to become institutionalized and thus
more costly to the taxpayers; greater stress was, however,
put on the moral damage their entry represented to the
American society.

desire to preserve the predominant cultural values of the country. The desire to preserve the "American original stock" underlay the restrictions on Asian immigration (acts of 1875, 1882 and 1885 against Chinese immigration, and the Gentlemen's agreement between U.S and Japan in 1907, and the virtual ban of 1917). Public health concerns led to the barring of carriers of contagious diseases, such as tuberculosis (act of 1907). The exclusion of political radicals, particularly anarchists (act of 1903 and 1918), was primarily motivated by political concerns (13).

The prohibition on importing contract laborers codified in the acts of 1885, 1887, 1888 (14), 1891, 1893, and 1907 was justified at the time on economic and political grounds (as unfair competition for native workers and a threat to the stability of political institutions), and has been attributed to successful lobbying by the Knights of Labor (15), at this point already "on a track of prejudice and fear with regard to immigration" (Erickson, 1957:VII). But together with the naturalization act of 1906 (that made knowledge of English a requirement for naturalization), and the Immigration Act of 1917 (that made admissibility dependent upon literacy), these provisions on contract labor were also a mechanism for deterring contamination of the "American original stock" by the huge influx of "inferior

13 The above synopsis of American immigration legislation is based primarily on Immigration Investigating Commission (1895), Abbott (1924), Bernard (1982), Levine (1985).
14 These last two acts allowed for deportation upon arrival. I will deal with contract-labor laws in more detail later.
15 See for example: Report of the Immigration Investigating Commission, 1895: 20,21 and particularly p.54 and ff. transcribing labor opinions on immigration.

races" entering after 1870. In sum, if, in reviewing any of these acts (1885, 1891, 1906, and 1917), we try to weigh the evidence to decide which of two concerns-- economic or nativist-- motivated the policy-makers of the time, I believe we must say both factors were important.

All these legislative barriers were not powerful enough to keep growing numbers of eastern and southern Europeans from emigrating to the United States. Transatlantic migration to the United States appeared to contemporaries to be limited only by ships' carrying capacities, "and immigration of unprecedented volume was believed to be impending" (Hutchinson, 1956:8).

By 1897-1914, the migratory flow had become predominantly composed of eastern and southern Europeans (16), described by nativists as

> hirsute, low-browed, big-faced persons of
> obviously low mentality....[who] look out of place
> in black clothes and stiff collar, since clearly
> they belong in skins, in wattled huts at the close
> of the Great Ice Age (Ross, 1914:285-286).

If the "American original stock" was to be saved, more radical measures were needed.

---

16 The "Old" immigration still dominated between 1890 and 1896, when 1,562,797 migrants from Northern and Western Europe arrived in the United States, against 1,194,189 of the "New" immigrants from Southern and Eastern Europe. But between 1897 and 1914, the "old" immigrant arrivals numbered just 2,983,548, against 10,057,576 immigrants of the "new" stream ("Report of Mr.Dillingham, from the Committee on Immigration, April 28,1921", U.S. 67th Congress, 1st session, Senate Report N.17, extract in Abbott, 1924:233). This new stream included east central and southern Europeans, but from the 1890's on the Italians constituted the largest segment of this flow (Easterlin, 1982: 16-17).

THE PERIOD OF PRESERVATION OF THE "AMERICAN ORIGINAL STOCK", 1921-1930

The Quota Act of June 19, 1921 marks a new turning point in American immigration policy. With this act, the defense of predominant socio-cultural motivations took political precedence over economic considerations. I am not implying that the predominant economic interests were hurt by the new legislation. The Act of 1921 was passed as a temporary experimental measure in the middle of an economic recession and growing unemployment, so it could hardly hurt economic interests. The important point is that contemporary rhetoric based its arguments for the new legislation on the need to protect the "old" American blood from contamination. Anti-immigration arguments focused on the defense of the country's political institutions much more than on its economic institutions, and industrial employers could "grudgingly" accept the 1921 act (Higham, 985:315) (17).

---

17 Stan Vittoz (1978) disputes this interpretation. He argues instead that the anti-immigration laws of the post-World War I were only passed after a change in the American economic structure-- from labor intensive to capital intensive-- made anti-immigration laws welcomed and desired by American industrial employers (Vittoz, 1978:77). Vittoz gives us convincing evidence that such a change in the country's economic structure occurred between 1919 and 1929 (ibidem, p. 64-65). The current interpretation does not dispute that, when the anti-immigration Act of 1924 was passed, changes in the American economic structure were sufficiently underway to win industrial employers to the side of the proponents of anti-immigration legislation (see for example, Higham, 1985:312-330). For Vittoz argument to be substantiated evidence that the changes in the American economic structure were practically concluded before 1921 is crucial. Unfortunately, the author does not gives such evidence.

In sum, what Vittoz give us is a very strong and insufficiently substantiated conceptual position. This conceptual position can be broadly expressed by the following question: do socio- cultural motivations need to converge with economic imperatives to be politically

It is also important to remark that by 1921 there was already enough "policy feedback" to enact more coherent legislative solutions to stop the inflow of unwelcome foreigners. I am using the term "policy feedback" in the sense proposed by Weir (1986: 3, 34), who contends that: "A nation's politics creates social policies, they in turn remake its politics, transforming possibilities for the future". In other words, the legislative constructions of the 1920's could build upon the anterior and tested body of anti-immigration legislation to avoid unwanted outcomes.

The slogan of the defeated Know-Nothings of the 1850's, "Americans must rule America", had found a new voice in Senator Albert Johnson. Claiming to speak for the American people, Johnson said:

> [They] have seen, patent and plain, the encroachments of the foreign-born flood upon their lives. They have come to realize that such a flood, affecting as it does every individual of whatever race or origin, cannot fail likewise to affect the institutions which have made and preserve American liberties. It is no wonder, therefore, that the myth of the melting pot has been discredited. It is no wonder that Americans everywhere are insisting that their land no longer shall offer free and unrestricted asylum to the rest of the world (...).
> The United States is our land. If it was not the land of our fathers, at least it may be, and it should be, the land of our children. We intend to maintain it so. The day of unalloyed welcome to all peoples, the day of indiscriminate acceptance of all races, has definitely ended. (Quoted in, Bernard, 1982: 97)

The days "of unalloyed welcome to all people" had disappeared long before Senator Johnson' speech. Indeed,

---

effective? His answer is yes. My conceptual position is that socio-cultural motivations do not need to converge; to be politically effective it is enough that they do not conflict with economic imperatives.

they had never really existed during the nineteenth century, as I have tried to show above. What was truly at issue was not "indiscriminate acceptance of all races," nor even that "Americans must rule America," but rather who should be American, and which Americans should rule America. To the politically-dominant white, predominantly Anglo-Saxon, and Protestant segment of the American population, the answer was obvious-- themselves. All that remained was determining the best means of meeting their goal.

The nativist position of the early twentieth century was not entirely new; its seeds were nourished in earlier periods (18). And dogmatic theories about race had provided a rationale supporting legislation passed prior to 1921 (Taylor, 1971:243). What was new was the political will to set up radical mechanisms that guaranteed the achievement of numerically and ethnically restricted immigration. As the Republican platform of the 1920 put it:

> The immigration policy of the United States should be such as to ensure that the number of foreigners in the country should not exceed that which can be assimilated with reasonable rapidity, and to favor immigrants whose standards are similar to ours. (Quoted in, Taylor,1971:250-251)

The question the policy makers faced was clear: from where, and how many, immigrants could the American social fabric absorb without being ruined? Specifically, what measures of immigration were needed to ensure that future demographic trends did not endanger the white, Anglo-Saxon,

---

18 At least since the 1850's when the Know-Nothings achieved political dominance in some states and fought vigorously for federal anti-immigration legislation on nativist grounds.

Protestant supremacy (19)? A trial answer was given in 1921, when entry quotas were set at 3 percent of the number of foreign-born individuals of each non-excluded nationality, as recorded in the 1910 Census. The total number admissible during fiscal year 1921-1922 was set at 356,995 (Report of the C.G.I., 1922:5).

As scholars have pointed out, this quota system limited almost exclusively European immigration (Levine, at al., 1985:18), since the Asiatic flow was already banned. The 1921 act was also a temporary measure; the National Origins Law (or Johnson Act) of 1924 reduced the annual quota for each admissible nationality to 2 percent of the number recorded in the 1890 Census. The National Origins Law also barred from entry aliens ineligible for citizenship and established the Border Patrol to enforce its directives.

Finally, in 1927, Congress approved the national origins system, laid out in 1924, on a permanent basis. The principal numerical limitations of the law were as follows:

> Sec.11.(a)The annual quota of any nationality
> shall be 2 per centum of the number of foreign-
> born individuals of such nationality resident in
> continental United States as determined by the

---

19 There are abundant literary examples of this xenophobia in the literature of the time, e.g. Fairchild, 1926. Perhaps Niles Carpenter's work (1927), because it was so mild compared to the racist hysteria of the period, is a good example of the depth the phenomenon attained in United States during the 1920' and 1930's. Particularly interesting on this topic are what we may call "neutral" documents, such as the catalogue of races for use of the Statistics Bureau since 1891. This catalogue constructed for efficiency purposes and claiming to apply strictly scientific racial divisions, turns out to be a ranking of the world population into superior and inferior races. In my view it is more representative than any individual position that I could quote since it represents the accepted view of the American bureaucracy (Abstracts of Reports of the Immigration Commission, 1911, V.I: 209 and ff).

> United States census of 1890, but the minimum
> quota of any nationality shall be 100.
> (b) The annual quota of any nationality for the
> fiscal year beginning July 1, 1927, and for each
> of the fiscal years thereafter, shall be a number
> which bears the same ratio to 150,000 as the
> number of inhabitants in continental United States
> in 1920 having that national origin ... bears to
> the number of inhabitants in continental United
> States in 1920, but the minimum quota of any
> nationality shall be 100. (Report of the C.G.I.,
> 1925:5)

W.Bernard synthesized the effect of the new quota system

this way:

> In the end, northern and western Europe (including
> the British Isles) received 82 percent of the
> total annual quota, southern and eastern Europe 16
> percent, with 2 percent left to remaining quota-
> receiving nations. (Bernard,1982:98)

By 1927, then, American policy-makers had responded fully

to pressure from the dominant social groups to reduce the

influx of "unsuitables" to what were perceived to be

assimilable proportions. In other words, the pool of

potential undesirables-- politically ignorant, carriers of

"monkish traditions" or "popish" influences, or unfit

procreaters of future Americans-- was reduced to a maximum

of eighteen percent of the future migratory flow to the

United States. The system was fully operational by 1929.

CONCLUSION

American immigration policy between 1860 and 1930 can be

divided into three distinct phases. In the first period

(1860-1874), economic interests and local governmental

control dominated over cultural integrity and centralized

policy. But while maximization of the country's supply of

manpower took precedence over cultural and political concerns, these latter issues were not totally absent from the patchwork of immigration and naturalization laws.

During the middle period, 1875 to 1920, the state claimed and obtained the sovereign right to regulate the flow into and the permanence of foreigners in United States. This period was also one of transition, during which economic interests, nativists, and political power groups struggled for control of immigration policy.

The last period, 1921 to 1930, was one of definition. The state exercised its regulatory power, and society's predominant groups agreed upon the catalogue of "virtues" which foreigners ought to have to enter and became part of American society. Devices to achieve these goals were carried to their logical end in the 1920's, as a concept of racial fitness was embodied in law to ensure the future survival of the "American original stock".

THE EFFECT OF THE AMERICAN IMMIGRATION POLICY ON THE PORTUGUESE MIGRATORY FLOW

American immigration policy had virtually no effect upon the Portuguese before the 1880's but became highly restrictive after the 1920's. This change in American immigration policy corresponded to an increasingly narrow definition of the "melting pot", first limited in the 1860's to the exclusion of the "yellow peril" and later broadened to control the "new immigrants," which included the Portuguese.

During the first phase of the American immigration policy, between 1860 and 1874, the Portuguese migratory flow to the United States went unnoticed. Regulations on immigration at the federal and state level barely touched upon the Portuguese entrants. This is understandable, given their numerical insignificance.

We have seen that, between 1860 and 1874, the underlying goal of American immigration policy was maximization of the country's supply of manpower. Portugal, like other European countries, was a potential reservoir of labor for the United States. But, unlike some other nations, Portugal only supplied labor for a few specific activities, like whaling, fishing, and staffing merchant vessels. American entrepreneurs did not need to use promotional campaigns to attract this type of labor. At Portuguese ports, it was easy enough to find seafaring men willing to sail on American vessels (Morison, 1961: 322).

The evidence suggests that Portugal also supplied contract labor for at least some Louisiana plantations. As was done for other nationalities, this labor was recruited in Portugal by agents of American entrepreneurs who specialized in supplying this share of the labor market (Documentos, 1874:250D-F). It is possible that other flows of this type headed for other destinations; given that only a few hundred Portuguese arrived in America between 1860 and 1874, they could not have been more than a partial solution to labor shortages in the United States. In sum, Portugal's insignificant demographic weight as a supplier of manpower, among the potential European candidates, did not justify

more than casual promotional measures by private
entrepreneurs. I have found no evidence that American
states ever directly promoted Portuguese emigration to the
United States.

It is also unlikely that federal or state regulations
could have affected significantly the volume or composition
of the Portuguese migratory flow between 1860 and 1874.
Moreover, American naturalization laws, the a posteriori
mechanism of selection of the foreign stock at national
level, were during this period favorable to the Portuguese
immigrants.

The bulk of the Portuguese immigrants to the United
States were western islanders from the Azores and Madeira,
and they were predominantly illiterate and poor. These
migrants had, for the most, been excluded from political
participation in their own country. The blacks or "Bravas"
coming from Cape Verde, who are usually dealt with by
migration studies as a part of the Portuguese migratory flow
to the United States, were indeed not so. The Portuguese
were the inhabitants of the mainland and of the Atlantic
archipelagos of Madeira and Azores on the European coast,
or their descendants. The native inhabitants of the
Portuguese possessions in Africa, Asia, and Oceania were
part of the empire, but not part of the kingdom of Portugal.
As colonized peoples, they had no political rights. Their
political fate could have been no worse in the United States
than in their colonized land.

American state legislation on immigration, particularly
the provisions relating to foreign paupers, could have had

some direct effect on Portuguese immigration to the United States. But these regulations were efficiently applied only to steerage passengers arriving in New York harbor, and between 1860 and 1874 only 2 percent of the Portuguese flow to the United States entered that port. The great majority of the Portuguese, 79 percent, arrived at the port of Boston, thus falling under Massachusetts' regulations, which were only casually enforced (20).

Massachusetts' regulations for the admission of foreigners were similar to those described for New York. In 1794, the state of Massachusetts had passed legislation to deport "to any place beyond the sea where he belongs" any pauper, and had established a penalty of one hundred pounds on shipmasters knowingly bringing any convict or "notoriously dissolute" person to the state (21). In 1820, more detailed legislation was passed to reinforce the Act of 1794. The new act was similar to the one passed four years later by the State of New York, imposing a head tax per immigrant, bonding on the ship for future liabilities the city might incur with poor relief, and guidelines for interdiction of any passenger on steerage based on

20 On the enforcement of the immigration legislation in New York, and on its casual nature in Massachusetts, see Bernard, 1982:82. Several Immigration Commissioner reports for the 1890's also refer, in retrospective on immigration legislation, to the superior efficiency of immigrants inspection at New York port, compared to any other American port of arrival.
21 From "An Act Providing for the Relief and Support, Employment and Removal of the Poor, February 26, 1794", quoted in Abbott, 1924:105-106.

inspection of the shipmaster's list of immigrants carried
(22).

There was, then, no major difference between New York
and Massachusetts legislation. There was, however, a great
difference between the two states in the allocation of
resources to enforce the law. At New York, there was a
permanent body of inspectors; at Boston, the supervision of
immigrant admissions was left in the hands of casual
volunteers.

Although we have no direct evidence for this early period
of denials of entry, later evidence suggests that its effect
could not have been of great significance. When, during the
1890's, Portuguese arrivals were massively entering New York
harbor and federal legislation on immigration was in place,
together with a body of inspectors to enforce it, only a
small share of the Portuguese were debarred from entry (1
percent of those admitted between 1897 and 1910). The
majority of those debarred (68 percent) were denied entry
because they were paupers or were likely to become a public
charges. But this group, together with those debarred from
entry under categories excluded until the 1870's,
represented only .75 percent of the Portuguese inspected and
admitted into the United States. It is thus unlikely that
state regulations could have significantly affected any

---

22 "An Act to Prevent the introduction of Paupers from
Foreign Ports or Places, February 25, 1820", quoted in
Abbott, 1924:108.

part of the Portuguese migratory flow between 1820 and 1874 (23).

The situation was quite different during the second period of American immigration policy, 1875 to 1920. The alien contract-labor laws and the literacy test requirement, enacted during this period, both directly affected the Portuguese migratory flow to the United States. This is not surprising since the legislation was enacted to select and to limit eastern and southern Europeans arrivals, including those from Portugal.

The first of these laws was passed in February 26, 1885. Section 1 prohibited prepayment of transportation of any alien or foreigner under contract to perform labor of any kind in the United States. Section 2 made such contracts void, while sections 3 and 4 imposed penalties on the contracting parties and on shipmasters who were knowing parties. Section 5 dealt with exemptions for professional actors, artists, lecturers, singers, and persons employed strictly as personal or domestic servants. This same section also stated that nothing in the act

> shall be construed as prohibiting any individual
> from assisting any member of his family or any
> relative or personal friend to migrate from any
> foreign country to the United States for the
> purpose of settlement here. (quoted in,
> Immigration Investigating Commission, 1895: 12).

The effect of the 1885 act on contract-labor and of its enforcement in 1887 and 1888 were considered to be of slight effect by the immigration authorities, due to the escape

---

23 Particularly since the vast majority of Portuguese arrivals entered Boston or minor ports (e.g. New Bedford) where immigration regulations were laxly enforced.

clause of section 5 in the 1885 act (24). As the
Immigration Investigating Commission of 1895 recognized,

> this clause had almost nullified its operation,
> for employers easily induced their workmen to send
> for relatives and friends in Europe, so that
> nearly every contract laborer detected had a
> relative or friend who had secured him work prior
> to his leaving his home. (Immigration
> Investigating Commission, 1895: 13)

If these acts were ineffective in regulating the general
migratory flow to the United States, they were particularly
ineffective in curbing the Portuguese flow. Portuguese
immigration functioned via personal networks making the
avoidance of the law in the way described by the Commission
of 1895 particularly easy. Moreover, domestic service, the
main occupational activity of Portuguese females arriving to
the United States during this period, was one of the
categories exempted by section 5 of the 1885 act.

The problem created by the final clause of the 1885 act
was solved by the "Stump Law" of March 3, 1891. In this new
act, the wording "or any relative or personal friend" were
stricken from the law (25).

The 1891 corrections to the wording of section 5 of the
1885 act left prepayment of passages and assistance to
immigration open only to family members, and in theory made
the enforcement of the law much more effective. In fact,
after 1892 the annual reports of the Immigration

---

24 The acts of February 23, 1887, and October 19, 1888 did
not change the wording of the 1885 act; they only allowed
deportation of aliens imported under contract to be
undertaken upon arrival.
25 The 1891 act also added new exemptions: religious
ministers, persons of recognized professions, and professors
of colleges and seminars. But these new exemptions had
little impact on the Portuguese flow, which was mainly
comprised of unskilled laborers.

Commissioner claimed that increasing numbers of immigrants were debarred from entering the United States or were deported within one year after landing because they had been found to contravene the alien contract-labor clause. Four years after the publication of the "Stump Law", the Immigration Investigating Commission also stated:

> A considerable number of contract laborers have been debarred each year since the passage of the Contract Labor Law, and it is now very rare for employers to attempt to import contract laborers in large gangs, as they did formerly. (Immigration Investigating Commission, 1895: 20)

The American labor movement seems to have also thought that immigration authorities were effective in limiting contract labor. The president of the American Federation of Labor, Samuel Gompers, praised the immigration officials in his address to the fourteenth annual convention of the Federation in the following terms:

> I desire to call attention to the satisfactory spirit in which the United States immigration officials have for the past year and half cooperated with the Federation of Labor, as well as with kindred organizations. (...) [immigration authorities] uniformly exhibited a desire to aid in excluding foreign laborers in all cases where the law would support such action. (quoted in, Immigration Investigating Commission, 1895: 20-21)

Not everyone, however, believed the anti-contract labor laws to be effective. As late as 1901, the Secretary of Industry distinguished between the efficiency of the law in deporting alien contract-laborers and its inefficiency in convicting contract-labor promoters. He wrote:

> Owing to the strict construction of the law there have been very few cases in which the importer was fined. But there have been over 8,000 deemed contract laborers sent back [from 1885 to 1901] by immigration inspectors. The reason for the difference are plain. The prosecution and

conviction of the importers depends upon district attorneys and judges, who must necessarily follow the strict rules of evidence and must hold themselves to exact definitions of a contract. But the deportation of an immigrant turns upon the circumstantial evidence presented to administrative authorities and the inferences which may be drawn therefrom. ("Immigration", Report of the U.S. Industrial Commission, XV (1901), extract in Abbott, 1924: 187-188)

Seven years later the Secretary of Labor produced a similar opinion on this subject, when he remarked:

The greatest violators of the contract labor laws are the American manufacturers, who as a rule, do not act directly, but indirectly through agents and sub-agents. It is very difficult to secure evidence in such a form as will be sufficient in detail to enable suit to be brought under the penal provisions of the act, though from an administrative point of view the circumstances are often sufficiently convincing that the law has been surreptitiously evaded. In practice it is less difficult to secure the evidence upon which deportation proceedings can be instituted against the laborers who have been imported. (Report of the Secretary of Commerce and Labor (1908), extract in Report of the Commissioner-General of Immigration, 1908: 215)

What is puzzling about contract-labor laws is not the difficulties faced by authorities in convicting the importers, but rather the fact that the number debarred or deported was so numerically insignificant, despite consensus that debarring or deporting alien contract-laborers was not difficult.

The documents from the period imply that alien contract-laborers posed a great danger to American workers, and they stress the fact that the alien contract-labor laws were a direct response to demands from American workingmen for protection against "the invasion of paupers laborers from the Old World" (26). Shall we believe that American workers

---

26 Immigration Investigating Commission, 1895: 12.

would have been seriously endangered if the two thousand alien contract-laborers found, out of nearly nine hundred thousand immigrants inspected between 1894 and 1896, would have entered the United States?

Given the results of the law, this emphasis on contract-labor is odd. We must remember that the legislative innovation the acts of 1885 and 1891 was the exclusion of alien contract-laborers. Legislative provisions for debaring potential or actual paupers had been in place for some time. Thus the contract-labor laws must be judged by their effect on contract-labor.

Since aliens entering the country under contract were not recorded separately before 1885 and their numbers were insignificant afterwards, we are faced with the following question. Was the volume of alien contract-labor before 1885 as high as it was claimed to be by the American trade unions and the proponents of the bill in Congress? Or was fear of competition from contract labor ill-founded, as the small number of those so identified after the law was passed suggests?

Even if we admit as valid the remarks of the Commissioner -General of Immigration for 1897 (p.4), who stated that contract-labor laws were effectively enforced only after the passage of the acts of 1891 and of 1893 and " the establishment of immigrant stations under Federal supervision at the several principal ports, each with a

---

In the same vein the Industrial Commission of 1901 stated that, "The alien contract-labor law was enacted almost solely at the demand of organized labor". ("Immigration", Reports of the U.S. Industrial Commission, XV (1901), extract in Abbott, 1924: 186).

corps of men charged solely with the execution of these laws," still the numerical results remain insignificant. In the two following years, the flow of immigrants was only reduced by .2 percent by the application of the clause on contract laborers (27).

There is another way to look at the statistics of the period. The report of 1897 remarked that the annual average number of immigrants entering the United States between 1884 and 1893 was 472,063, and that in the following four years, the annual average of admissions decreased markedly to 279,566. This decrease was attributed by the Immigration Commissioner to a combination of factors: the American economic recession of the period; the 1882 act; and the contract-labor laws. The Commissioner confidently forecast that:

> With the present laws energetically enforced, however, I do not apprehend that immigration will ever reach the volume of past years, notwithstanding the most prosperous conditions in our country. (Report of the Commissioner-General of Immigration, 1897: 4-5)

The Commissioner's forecast was probably reasonable in 1897, but it was also totally wrong. As soon as American economy recovered, the migratory flow returned to its previous volume and then attained unprecedented numbers, while the number of immigrants debarred from entry and deported for being contract-laborers continued to be insignificant. For six years, between 1902-1907, nearly six million immigrants were admitted to the United States, while only about

---

27 The respective numbers were for 1894-1896: inspected and admitted 887534; entry was denied to 2023 for falling under the contract-labor clause (Report of the General Commissioner of Immigration for the given Years).

fourteen thousand (a meager .2 percent of the number admitted) were denied entry for falling under the contract-labor clause (28).

One answer to this apparent paradox is to accept that the volume of alien contract-labor before 1885 was exaggerated by the supporters of the bill in order to gain wider support for their predominantly nativist stand towards the "new immigration" stream. Another possibility is to assume that after 1885 widespread information discouraged some potential contract-laborers to come and helped others pass inspection at Ellis Island without being detected. More readily available labor sources within the country at this time, further reduced the need for alien contract-laborers. The number of contract-laborers caught could thus be insignificant.

In sum, numerical evidence suggests that, when alien contract-labor laws were passed, they addressed a problem that internal labor-market mechanisms had already greatly changed. Private immigrant agencies and the "Padrone system", both working within the United States, were recruiting and employing immigrants upon arrival for wages considerably lower than those paid to American workers for the same kind of work. Moreover, immigrants furnished by these private immigrant bureaus in United States or directly employed by agents of American manufacturers at Ellis island were being used to break up labor conflicts in strike after strike. These threats to the American labor movement were

---

28 The respective number were: admitted 5731242; debarred under the contract-labor clause 13893 (Report of the Commissioner-General of Immigration, 1925: 126, 156, 157).

coming from inside the United States not from outside, contrary to what was being claimed by proponents and supporters of the alien contract-labor clause. This internal threat was the real problem facing the American workers and their labor movement during the 1880's, but the law did not address this reality.

Erickson (1957) has convincingly argued that, between the legislation supporting the importation of contract-labor (1864) and its prohibition (1885), the American labor movement under the leadership of the American Federation of Labor embarked "on a track of prejudice and fear with regard to immigration which has become tradition and policy" (p.VIII). She further argues that this lobbying had little to do with reality because contract-labor had ceased to be numerically significant after the Civil War and "never reached the proportions claimed by the advocates of the law against its importation" (p.VII). The contract-labor laws were battling a ghost of the past, competition from imported alien contract-laborer.

Although the effect of the contract-labor clause can be considered negligible, the law gains a new dimension if we see it as another legal device to get rid of "undesirables", designed to supplement the "pauper and likely to become a public charge" clause. Viewed in this light, alien contract-labor laws becomes an integral part of the legal mechanisms enacted between 1885 and 1917 to check the "new immigration". If alien contract-labor laws could not stop a nonexistent danger, the allegedly vast importation of contract-laborers, they could help curb the eastern and southern European emigration to the United States.

By requiring the immigrant to prove that he could support himself and simultaneously requiring him to prove that he did not know in advance of any job, the law created a contradiction that left room for maneuver to immigrant inspectors. In effect, if the immigrant did not prove the first condition, he was liable as a potential public charge, but if he proved the second, he was liable to charges of illegally displacing American workers ("Immigration", Reports of the U.S. Industrial Commission, XV (1901), extract in Abbott, 1924:186). This odd contradiction in the legislation increased immigration authorities' effectiveness in denying entry to those deemed undesirable.

The direct effect of the contract-labor laws on the Portuguese migratory flow is more straightforward. A brief overview of Portuguese emigration during this period clarifies the effect of this American legislation on the Portuguese migratory flow to the United States.

Portugal's sluggish economic development and the work of emigrants' agencies raised the number of candidates for emigration to dramatic proportions during the second half of the nineteenth century. Available evidence suggests the lack of state supervision and its acceptance of contract labor organizations allowed agents and agencies to supply themselves with emigrant workers quite freely. Brazilian agents workings in Portugal were never efficiently curbed, despite media and public protests. When official inquiries found evidence of misconduct and exploitation of the emigrants contracted to Hawaii in the late 1870's, the facts did not stop the Portuguese government from signing a treaty with the Hawaiian government, formally agreeing to maintain the flow (29).

If American entrepreneurs had wished to contract labor in Portugal, they would not have faced serious obstacles from the Portuguese side. Had American law not forbidden it, the 2,511 Portuguese contract-laborers that went to Hawaii between 1885 and 1899 probably would have chosen to come to the United States instead. In fact, at least half of these Portuguese emigrants to Hawaii ran away to California as soon as they found an opportunity to do so (Freitas, 1930: 151).

We cannot estimate numerically the effect of the American alien contract-labor laws on the Portuguese migratory flow to the United States. We can, however, be sure that these laws had a direct effect in at least reducing the volume of Portuguese emigration to United States.

If we try to assess the effect of the literacy test of 1917, we face the following problem: there was no significant reduction in the immigrant flow from those nationalities considered to have higher illiteracy rates, except during 1918 and 1919, when the war was also holding down emigration. Moreover, this decrease is in line with the general trend in the migratory flow to the United States since 1915.

It is thus difficult to discern whether the literacy test or the war was more important in reducing the migratory flow

---

29 See Chapter I.

in 1918 and 1919. Further, we can never know how many illiterate potential emigrants changed their intention of coming to the United States after the 1917 act was passed. This last point is of particular interest because contemporaries saw the literacy test functioning as a preventive deterrent as well as a direct check. As the Commissioner-General of Immigration remarked some years later:

> Like other preventive measures, its effect is to be measured not only by the number of those who attempt to enter in spite of it and are rejected but to a much greater degree by the number who are deterred, owing to their knowledge of this requirement, from starting to this country. (Report of the Commissioner-General of Immigration, 1920: 13)

Unless we assume that in a very short time the great majority of potential migrants to the United States could have learned how to read or write, which is unlikely, the law, if enforced, should either have curbed considerably the flow coming from eastern and southern Europe or the socio-economic composition of the flow should have changed significantly.

In the Portuguese case, neither outcome occurred. This is particularly odd, given the fact that, between 1899 and 1910, the Portuguese flow had the highest percentage of illiterates (68.2 percent) of all the ethnic groups arriving in the United States (Immigration Commission, 1911, V.I: 98-99). The characteristics of the Portuguese migratory flow, in terms of sex, and occupation, were, however, practically the same before and after 1917. Table I summarizes some of

these characteristics before and after the literacy test was
enacted.

TABLE II:I - **CHARACTERISTICS OF THE PORTUGUESE MIGRATORY
FLOW TO THE U.S., 1915 AND 1920** (30)

IMMIGRANTS OVER 14 YEARS OF AGE

YEAR	TOTAL ADMITTED	PERCENTAGE DISTRIBUTION FEMALES	UNSKILLED	ILLITERATE
1915	3738	32%	87%	54%

IMMIGRANTS OVER 16 YEARS OF AGE

YEAR	TOTAL ADMITTED	FEMALES	UNSKILLED	ILLITERATE
1920	13596	32%	84%	6%

SOURCE: Reports of the Commissioner-General of Immigration
for the given Years.

As Table II:I indicates, the Portuguese flow increased in
volume almost fourfold between 1915 and 1920, while its
composition, in terms of the percentage of females and
unskilled, did not change significantly.

During this five-year span, the new Portuguese immigrant
became, if we were to believe the American immigration
authorities' figures, overwhelmingly literate. There are
two possible solutions to this puzzle. Either there was
major educational change in Portugal, or the rate of
illiteracy for 1920 is wrong (31).

----

30 NOTES: 1. As unskilled I considered-- laborers, farmers,
servants, and people without occupation;
2. The rate of illiteracy for 1920 was computed by
considering as illiterate those that the law exempted from
the test (e.g. wives joining husbands with American
citizenship) and those debarred from entry by being unable
to read.
31 Another possibility is to consider that the information
for 1915 is wrong. It is hard to suppose that it could be
so since the information was given on voluntary basis by the
emigrants, and there is no reason why would they report
themselves as illiterates without being so.

Because the Portuguese censuses give information on illiteracy, we can detect any real changes in educational attainment in the sending society. The 1911 census recorded 70 percent of the population over seven years of age as illiterate, and the corresponding figure in the 1920 census was 65 percent (32). We can then hardly speak of a major change, but rather just a slight decrease in illiteracy. Moreover, the 1920 census (Vol.I, 1923:XII-XIII) remarks that illiteracy rates were particularly high for the islands from which the majority of the Portuguese flow to the United States came.

We must then conclude that, the figures recorded by the American immigration authorities on the literacy of the Portuguese immigrants are wrong. It follows that, at least for the Portuguese, the 1917 literacy test did not have the intended result of keeping the illiterate out of the country.

It may be that immigrants with unfamiliar languages, like Portuguese, who were given literacy tests in their own language, could easily contravene the law by seeming to read some prayer they knew by heart or by learning to write their names. This hypothesis is at least easier to accept than the alternative-- a huge real increase in the literacy rate for Portuguese immigrants in absence of a major shift in the composition of the migratory flow.

---

32 Among the drafted men inspected in 1920, 62 percent were illiterate. It cannot be argued that the slight decrease noticed is biased by the inclusion of the literacy rates of the older age groups.

In conclusion, we may say that the second phase of American immigration policy was a period of transition; during which, by trial and error, legal mechanisms of defense against those deemed threatening or unsuitable were strengthened. The Portuguese were part of the group of nationalities deemed undesirable, and American immigration policy was thus directed against them. But because contract labor laws were enacted late, because Portugal had a relatively small population to export, and because Portuguese was a language unfamiliar to the American immigration authorities, the anti-immigration laws of the period had little impact on Portuguese migrants.

The third and last phase of the American immigration policy, 1921 to 1930, was devastating for southern European migration to the United States, and the Portuguese flow was no exception. The quota Act of 1921 set the upper limit for the Portuguese immigration at 2,520 per year. The number was revised to 2,465 for the fiscal year 1921-1923, and by the National Origins System of 1924, which set the Portuguese quota at 503 persons per year (Report of the C.G.I., 1922:5, and 1925:6).

In sum, the size of the Portuguese flow after 1921 was reduced to the levels of the 1880's, and, after 1924, it was further reduced to the levels of the 1870's (a few hundred immigrants every year). American cultural values and legal mechanisms of defense against unwelcome intruders were finally in harmony.

PORTUGUESE EMIGRATION POLICY

The main legal characteristics of the Portuguese
emigration policy were established during the 1860's, but
their administrative enforcement and social sanctioning
varied over time. Such variations were a function of the
Portuguese elites' perception of their socio-demographic and
foreign exchange needs, and of the level of administrative
and social enforcement they were able or willing to impose
(33).

The first objective of this section is to describe the
makings of the Portuguese emigration policy between 1860 and
1930 and to show how its selective character shaped the
emigratory flow independently of the direct shaping imposed
by the receiving society. It is my contention that between
1860 and 1930 the Portuguese political elites increasingly
pursued an imperialistic/colonial orientation which,
associated with the labor intensive character of the
Portuguese economy, could have been expected to have
resulted in a policy of no-exit. Such did not happen
because during that same period demographic growth and
economic backwardness made a substantial part of the
population redundant; the chronic need for foreign currency
made it advisable to trade national labor for foreign
exchange. Entangled in a colonial vocation and
contradictory socio-economic needs, the Portuguese elites
opted for an emigratory policy aimed not to stem but rather
to select the emigrant element. This was enforced by legal-

33 For a more complete survey of the political determinants
of emigration policies see for example: Portes,1978,
Zolberg, 1983, and Bohning, 1984.

administrative restrictions and by the social
marginalization of the emigrant.

My rational for the Portuguese emigration policy of
this period is slightly different from the one presented in
the most recent approach to this topic (34). For Miriam
H.Pereira, the Portuguese emigration policy is one of
apparent paradox characterized by restrictive legislative
measures towards emigration in a country dependent upon
emigrants' remittances. Pereira concludes a policy, which
formally barred exit, and in practice tolerated emigration
(Pereira, 1981:53).

The underlying assumption of such a position is that
the Portuguese political elites were either inept or were
prone to follow circumstances, rather than to design
policies. The acceptance or rejection of this assumption
can only take place after answering the following question:
is there any rational behind these apparent contradictions
(35) ?

In summary, my findings are that the Portuguese
policy-makers of the late nineteenth and early twentieth
centuries were able actors. Their anti-emigration laws were
not a part of a failed policy of no-exit, but rather a part

---

34 Miriam Halpern Pereira, A Politica Portuguesa de
Emigração 1850 - 1930. Lisboa, 1981 (specially p.7-58).
35 The position being taking here stresses the endogenous
decision-making forces at play. It does not imply any
denial of the existence of strong constraints created by the
Portuguese peripheric position in the economic world system.
What is being done is to revise the alternatives that within
such peripheric position remained open to the endogenous
dominant groups. The works of Portes (1978 and 1984),
Zolberg (1981 and 1983), and Berend and Ranki (1980, and
1982) are examples of the type of revision being made.

of a real solution to their problems (36). The
restrictions on exit and the dependency on remittances are
heads and tails of the same coin. This is, restrictions
created mechanisms that promoted family dispersion, which in
turn insured the flow of remittances. I will argue that the
Portuguese emigration policy followed between 1860 and 1930
exemplifies the use by the Portuguese elites of an available
alternative, within the specific world economic system of
the period, capable of easing their several needs. It
protected the import-export and banking groups by increasing
the country's consumption power and increased foreign
exchange supply without putting in danger the country's
labor supply or promoting changes that could have endangered
the entrenched interests of the landowners' elite.

36 I know of only one approach to the Portuguese emigration
similar to the one taken here-- Elizabeth R. Leeds, Labor
Export, Development, and the State: the Political Economy of
Portuguese Emigration, PhD Dissertation, M.I.T., June 1984.
Like Leeds, I subscribe to the idea that a full
understanding of a migratory flow requires analysis of the
sending countries' emigration policies. As the author
remarks, emigration policies "were responses to external
conditions made in the context of internal political and
economic variables" (p.15).
    Leeds work and my own differ, however, on some important
points. First, our time-frames are different. Leeds focuses
on the Salazar-Caetano regime, that is, she begins where I
end. Second, she sees the Portuguese emigration policy of
the pre-Salazar and of the Salazar period as fundamentally
similar policies, both mainly characterized by a state
promotion of emigration. I disagree with Leeds'
interpretation of the Salazar emigration policy; and the
present work contests the idea that there were no changes in
emigration policy over time.

RULING ELITES AND SOCIO ECONOMIC NEEDS

Landowners' Interests

At the turn of the century, Portuguese social structure was still quite characteristic of the Old Regime systems. This anachronistic structure was described, for the nineteenth century, by Godinho (1980), and for the rest of our period by Marques (1973) in the following way:

> The changes [occurring during the] nineteenth century allowed for the growth of primary activities [related to] agricultural production, although [they came] late and with hesitations, but [they also] allowed for the maintenance of a dominant hypertrophic stratum which claimed for itself an excessive share of the national product, and that for this reason did not leave space for the formation of a strong secondary sector of modern outlook. Between the oligarchy and the masses an incipient bourgeoisie existed, active, well informed, but whose action did not result in choices of new routes for the country. (Godinho, 1980:155)

> A class of wealthy bourgeoisie, linked to the bank, the big trade and landholdings, allied with the old and more or less pure landowner nobility which went on existing, governed the country oligarchically in the beginning of the twentieth century. (O.Marques, 1973: 209)

There is some dispute on what specific oligarchical or bourgeois interests most influenced the design of Portuguese politics of the period (Reis, 1984:2-9). There is, however, no dispute about the key role played by landowner interests on Portuguese politics (37).

---

37 Overall, the political stand of the Portuguese landowners' elite was quite coherent. They supported anti-emigration legislation in association with economic protectionism, an aggressive colonial policy, and an intransigent defense of the status quo. Examples of this position, almost fifty years apart, are the writings of the Viscount of Coruche (1886) and of Jose Pequito Rebelo (1931).

Furthermore, landlords' interests have been directly linked to anti-emigration legislation through the assumption that emigration was indeed creating labor shortages and increasing wages (Pereira, 1981:52).

Evidence, however, indicates the reverse was the case. At least after 1890, the Portuguese population in working age was increasingly hurt by unemployment. A comparison of two simple indicators will support my contention (38) that landlords' claims were political constructed issues without any link to the labor supply of the period. The first measure is a ratio of the population 10 years of age or under plus the population 60 years of age and more, over the population between 10 and 59 years of age (39). This ratio measures, in a crude manner, the potential labor supply of the country vis-a-vis those too young or to old to belong to the labor force. The second measure is a ratio of the population gainfully employed over the non-active population, roughly a ratio of producers over consumers. A comparison of the results of these two indicators allow us to see if the labor market structure was the result of a demographic bias or of labor conditions.

The results are as follows. The ratio between those elements of the population both too young and too old to participate in the labor force and those in working age remained more or less stable over the period. It was respectively .49 in 1890 and .47 in 1930. During the same

---

38 A detailed analysis of the Portuguese labor market between 1890 and 1930 is given in the next chapter.
39 This ratio is usually labeled "demographic potential for poverty" (see for example, A. Armstrong, 1974: 48,49).

period, however, the ratio between producers and consumers
went from 1 in 1890 to .58 in 1930, indicating that the
relationship between gainfully employed and inactive
population worsened markedly. Since this unfavorable
relationship between active and inactive population can not
be attributed to a demographic bias in favor of the too
young and too old within the Portuguese population, we have
to attribute it to increasing unemployment.

In conclusion, we may say that in Portugal, between
1890 and 1930 (the period with the highest levels of
emigration) what was scarce was job opportunities not labor
supply. In such a setting, claims of wage increases due to
labor shortage deserve small credit. The complaints of the
landowners' elite must be seen as simple periodical
restatements of a dominant group's principles, which not
being threatened did not need to have its principles
enforced through legislation (40).

Export-Import, Banking and Government Needs

Landowners needed only a large enough labor supply to
carry on agricultural work and enough surplus reserve to
insure low wages and seasonal internal migration. We have
seen that none of these needs could have been seriously hurt
by the emigratory flow of this period.

40 The credibility of these claims is also undermined by the
fact that during this same period the Portuguese government
overtly support temporary emigration to Spain.

But the mercantile sector and the government had broader interests. Merchants needed to increase, artificially or not, the country's purchasing power and to ensure an abundance of foreign currency to back up transactions with the London market. The state needed outside funds to satisfy international payments on a growing foreign debt. The traditional hypertrophy of the mercantile sector and the inability of the government to control public finances became, after the 1830's, major characteristics of the Portuguese economy. The mercantile and the public sectors were thus the most directly interested in encouraging emigration in return for foreign currency.

These traits of the Portuguese economy are best seen after the 1880's when they induced an increasing debate among sociologists and economists of the period. At the turn of the century contemporaries like Marianno de Carvalho, Oliveira Martins, and Emygdio Navarro considered the Portuguese public sector as one of the great malaises of the country's economy. Others, like Anselmo de Andrade and Bento Carqueja estimated that public expenditures were roughly 20 to 30 percent of the country's national income. This was a very high share when compared with almost all other European countries. In another small country, Switzerland, they accounted for only 6 percent of the G.N.I. (41). But, even with one of the heaviest fiscal systems of

41   Marvaud, 1912: 77-85, 111.

Europe (42) the Portuguese public sector went on being
unable to balance its budget and cover the deficit with
internal and external loans, further drying the country's
capabilities for investment.

In sum, disproportionate public spending was
necessarily leading to disproportionate fiscal charges,
inducing what today's economists call the "crowding out"
effect (Gordon, 1978:123-131) that tries to explain why
money becomes extremely expensive (43), and how the public
sector can dry up the resources for investment of a country,
hampering in the long run its economic development. In the
short run the more direct result of drying up the country's
capabilities for investment was to increase the dependence
of the Portuguese economy upon foreign capital and on
emigrants' remittances to pay its interest.

The importance of emigrants' remittances for the
Portuguese economy (44) and particularly for the annual
payment of the Portuguese foreign debt, the second largest
per capita in Europe (Macedo, 1979:6), grew in step with the
country's financial chaos. And it was dramatically
highlighted during the 1891 financial crisis. What Oliveira
Salazar called, "The vicious cycle of contracting a deficit

---

42 According to the <u>Times</u> of Feb 18, 1911 the Portuguese
fiscal system was only comparable to the Likin system of
China
43 J. Relvas wrote specifically on the expensiveness of the
Portuguese money where interest rates were never below 10
percent and sometimes attained an amazing 75 percent (quoted
in Marvaud, 1912:77-78
44 The importance of emigrants' remittances was emphasized
by many contemporaries (e.g. O.Martins (1891): Sampaio
(1893); Marvaud, 1912; Poinsard, 1912; Salazar, 1916; Young,
1917). The annual volume of remittances is not accurately
known and contemporary estimates vary. A summary of these
estimates was published by E. Mata, 1984:13-14.

to pay the debt, making debts to pay the deficit" (Salazar
1916:77) increasingly weakened the Portuguese financial
structure, which finally collapsed in 1891.

Depreciation of the Brazilian currency in the London
market in the previous year was not the only factor that
brought about the country's financial collapse. But, the 80
percent reduction in the customary million pounds in
emigrants' remittances from Brazil were among the crucial
factors (Salazar 1916: 80-81, Macedo 1979:7).

Similarly, by the end of the 1920's, when the
American borders began to be closed and the effects of the
Depression were felt outside Portugal, the consequences of
an interruption of remittances were serious (45). As a
governmental publication of 1932 observed:

> Many thousands of Portuguese families that lived
> almost exclusively off the money that relatives
> send them from Brazil. . . are presently
> struggling with the greatest possible difficulty
> and the capacity for consumption among a part of
> our population is thus seriously diminished. The
> value of property is extremely sensitive to the
> lack of remittances from Brazil and North
> America, since our emigrants . . . would employ
> the largest part of their savings in the purchase
> of landholdings. They were the ones that in the
> villages would make the value of the property go
> up. Today, the emigrants do not buy, and some
> even sell what they once possessed. (Boletim da
> Providencia Social, 1932, #23, p.41, in Pereira
> 1981:43)

In summary, remittances had become not only extremely
important to back up Portuguese finances but also, as the
last passage suggests, to sustain a segment of the country's
population. But, as also indicated by the above passage,

---

45 In 1917, for example, remittances from Brazil and the
United States accounted for half of the national total
incomings, 30 million dollars (young, Oxford, 1917:313).

remittances were, until the end of the period,

preferentially spent on consumption or invested in land,

never reproductively channeled, nor used to foster economic

change (46).

The Defense of the Status-Quo

It was the incapability or unwillingness of the

Portuguese elites to foster economic change that, in first

place, drove a segment of the Portuguese population out of

the country (47). Moreover, the volume of emigration was

never large enough to change significantly the labor

conditions of those remaining in the country. And, because

emigrants' remittances were primarily used either to

maintain unproductively a segment of the population or to

purchase land, they never significantly influenced the

economic structure. What in fact both emigration and

remittances did was to help postpone economic change.

As we have seen, the Portuguese population grew at

annual rates that could not be absorbed by the job market.

We can reasonably presume that the 1.5 million legal

emigrants and the half million clandestine emigrants who

46 Pereira's (1981) summary of the use of emigrants'
remittances goes in this same direction. She wrote: " from
1870 to 1930, remittances from Brazil, not only constituted
an instrument in the spread of money circulation within
rural areas, and a stimulus to investment in land and
buildings, but it also had a determinant role in the
Portuguese balance of payments and the exchange rate
situation."(Pereira, 1981:43).
47 In Portugal, emigration was, as remarked by O. Martins,
"not the result of the spirit of adventure, or of ambition,
but, and fundamentally, of the lack of means of subsistence"
(O. Martins (1891), 1956 ed., p.220).

left Portugal between 1891 and 1960 (Evangelista, 1971 :91; Serrão, 1977:30,31) were a surplus population. According to the official statistics the legal migratory flow was mainly constituted by males with no or unknown occupation and by unskilled laborers (O.Martins,1871: 228-231; Serrão, 1977: 129; Emigração Portugueza - Doc.s ..., 1874: 226); the probability of their being other than marginal to the Portuguese labor market is thus at best slim. And we can also infer that, if the "safety valve" mechanism had not been at work during this period, the retention of more than two million additional people plus their offspring might well have disrupted the Portuguese social fabric and have created a serious threat to its elites.

The threat to authority posed by the surplus population was accurately depicted, in 1882, by a anonymous Portuguese emigrant. He wrote:

> Each citizen who emigrates, shows by this same fact, a defect in his homeland that must be corrected. This citizen, although ignorant of all elementary notions of a basic education, realizes that he is a surplus, and leaves (...)
> If he were to understand the causes of this phenomenon ... The day would come, that those who had decided not to emigrate, would ask for detailed accounting of the country's patrimony-- wasted, dishonored, without name, without value, with nothing that one could call a country (Uma Memorável Sessao do Parlamento Portuguez, 1882:2)

In this passage, two key ideas -- that emigrants are surplus population and that they pose a threat to constituted authority-- are clearly laid out (48). This potentially

---

48 It is also interesting to remark that the author makes the level of the threat dependent on the amount of information circulating. He clearly indicates that in the Portuguese case, the threat was reduced by lack of education among the surplus population, which prevented them from identifying the causes of their marginalization within their

dangerous situation was aggravated by the fact that urbanization was practically non-existent, apart from Lisbon and Oporto, and that the country's agrarian base, rudimentary technology, and limited productivity (49) gave almost no alternative to the growing demographic pressure other than emigration or change.

The demand for labor in the international market-- especially from the American continents-- partially solved this potential dangerous situation. The regulation of emigration by the dominant social groups in Portugal through legal and social controls produced a selective migratory flow that in the long run postponed changes in the socio-economic structure, and in the short run produced a selective migratory flow.

In sum, the removal of much of the male surplus population and the flow of remittances reduced the pressure on the Portuguese elites to favor policies which might have lead to economic development and perhaps to their own displacement from power, or more concisely "emigration maintained archaic structures, these archaic structures explain and sustain emigration through the centuries" (Godinho, 1974:267).

---

native society. In other words, mechanisms were in place (in this case illiteracy) which helped hold Portuguese society together and perpetuated its elites.
49 Bento Carqueja's (1916: 93) figures on the country's wheat production within the European context are a good example of the low agricultural productivity I am referring to. He indicates that the wheat production per capita in Portugal between 1911 and 1915, was .5 hectoliters, that is, below the production per capita of Spain (1.7), France (2.7), Germany (.7), or Italy (1.3) during the same time period. Marvaud (1912:111) also refers this comparatively low agricultural productivity as one of the worst problems of the Portuguese economy.

LEGAL APPARATUS AND ADMINISTRATIVE ENFORCEMENT

The Portuguese elites never openly favored the use of the "safety valve" mechanism to reduce the marginal population. The whole period was formally characterized by restrictive emigratory measures. Even economic deterioration did not change the elites' attitude towards emigration, except when the destinations were areas of the empire.

Although the whole period was marked by restrictive policies, there were nuances (50). Between 1860 and 1880, without an alternative project for the reallocation of the marginal population, the government maintained legislative restrictions on emigration set up during the 1850's and 1860's, but did not enforce them. These earlier laws were intended to select the emigrant element and to regulate the conditions of transport. The more important legal text on emigration passed during this period was the law of April 7, 1863. For the present discussion the relevant article of this law is article 10 where the conditions for obtaining a passport were stipulated. These conditions prohibited anyone under twenty five years of age not emancipated and any male that had not fulfilled his military duty from leaving; also public servants without permission of their hierarchically superiors; married women without prior authorization from their husbands; single women without parental authorization; and young males, between fourteen and twenty one years of

---

50 For further detail consult Afonso Costa, 1911: chapter V, pp.161-167.

age, without paying a fine as insurance of their return to fulfill military service, or if eighteen years or over without making financial compensation for their military duties. The candidate would also have to prove he paid his passage or to present his labor contract in the country of destination.

The legal restrictions that, if enforced, were to select the emigratory flow were thus in place since 1863; but we find very little reinforcement in the form of additional legislation, or official memoranda to the district governors or to the customs directors. Such lack of reinforcement is understandable. Emigration was relatively low, between 1866 and 1890, when compared to the next decades. The annual average number of legal departures (51), between these two dates, was 10.6 thousand emigrants against 21.6 thousand between 1891 and 1900, and 27.2 thousand between 1901 and 1911 (Evangelista, 1971:91).

This situation began to be drastically changed during the 1880's in response to the new conditions of the international labor market. The end of the Paraguayan war and new legislation to ban slave traffic sparked increasing demand for unskilled labor in the Brazilian market, a demand that the Portuguese emigrants were eager to satisfy. Such eagerness would oblige the Portuguese elites to revise the precautionary measures enacted during the 1850's and 1860's to regulate the migratory flow.

---

51 The following figures only concern emigrants' departures from the mainland.

This revision of the Portuguese emigration policy
between 1880 and 1910 appears, however, connected with the
promotion of the colonial option. Already initiated in the
1870's, policies favoring the reallocation of the surplus
population to the colonies were implemented. Passports for
Portuguese Africa were free beginning in 1896 and no longer
required by 1901. In parallel with legislation favoring
migration to the colonies, restrictions on emigration to
other destinations were tightened. Passport prices were
increased, and, in 1886, 1894, 1896, 1901, and 1904
legislative measures were passed to restrain both
clandestine emigration and agencies of emigration. And
concrete measures were adopted to backup these laws -- a
special police force was created to restrain clandestine
emigration, and in trials of clandestine emigrants the jury
was surpressed (52). An abundant number of circulars,
official memoranda, and recommendations to the "Procurador
Geral da Corôa", the district Governors, and superintendents
of the special police force reflect the existence of a
strong will within the political elites to control the
emigratory flow by an administrative reinforcement of
emigration regulations (53).

In 1905 and 1907 these measures were further
strengthened. This last law is particularly interesting
since it reduced the taxes for emigrant ships while raising
them for emigrants' passports (A.Costa, 1911: 166-167). A

---

52 Particularly: laws of April 23, 1896, and May 11,1904.
53 A synopsis of these legislation is given in 'Emigração
Clandestina', Biblioteca Popular de Legislação, Lisboa,
1904:77-79.

more detailed account of its content clarifies the elites'
position towards emigration (54). The law of April 25, 1907
abolished the need for passports for foreigners, for
nationals leaving or returning from the colonies, and for
nationals not considered emigrants. According to this law
emigrants are the nationals leaving on vessels or steamships
travelling in steerage for foreign overseas ports and the
nationals "trying" to leave either by sea or land to fix
residence in foreign overseas ports. The first group, that
I will call travellers, if they wished could obtain a
passport by a single payment of 2000 reis. The second
group, the emigrants, must previously to their departure
obtain a passport. The cost of this compulsory passport was
7000 reis-- 6000 for the state and 1000 for the local civil
government issuing the passport. Moreover, if male and over
fourteen years of age, but at risk of being called for the
army (18-21 years of age), prior to his departure he had
also to fulfill his military duties. He could do this in
several ways: financial remission of his service; or
military license plus a 75,000 reis deposit; or sureties of
equal value by recognized fiat. When surety was given the
emigrant would later be reimbursed when answering his army
call.

Finally passports had one year validity and had to be
validated every year by a single tax of 500 reis. In sum,
to leave the country legally emigrants have to pay at least
3.5 times more than a non-emigrant.

---

54 Its text was reproduced in the Azorean daily newspaper, A
Uniao, Angra do Heroismo, May 13, 1907.

This legal apparatus for restraining emigration is commonly   seen as not having worked very effectively. After all, over half   a million people left the country clandestinely between 1891 and   1930. But the real question is not whether these regulations   stemmed the emigratory flow, but rather, how much did they help   to select it? By imposing legal restrictions, the Portuguese government in effect "favored" emigration of those able to raise the cost of obtaining a passport and to overcome a series of administrative difficulties, as well as those hardy enough to risk contravening such laws and able to pay the expenses of leaving the country clandestinely.

The overall aim of the Portuguese emigration policy seems to have been not the stoppage of the flow but a promotion of the family dispersion among the emigrant population necessary to maintain a regular flow of remittances (55). An analysis of the few surviving records of life stories of Portuguese emigrants indicate more clearly how these legal apparatus induced family dispersion and remittances (56). They indicated that the economic hardships imposed or induced by the emigration laws entailed

55 I wrote 'seems to have been' because the above evidence strongly indicates that the Portuguese elites did not deliberately follow a policy of no-exit; but there is no clear evidence that they deliberately followed a policy aimed to promote family dispersion. There is, however, too much regularity in the pattern followed by the Portuguese elites on emigration to make one suspicious that its overall result was simply the outcome of a fortuitous set of circumstances.
56 Eduardo Mayone Dias, Acorianos na California. Angra do Heroismo, 1982. This book is a collection of interviews of Portuguese immigrants in California, conducted by Mayone Dias.   It is relevant for the present discussion because a number of these immigrants interviewed came to the United States during the period under study.

family indebtedness or family networking in Portugal and in the country of destination. Such a situation tended to strengthen the links between those that left and those that remained, further insuring the flow of remittances while promoting at least initially family dispersion.

Anti-emigration regulations must not be seen as part of a failed policy of no-exit but as part of an economic policy aimed at protecting the country's labor supply while promoting remittances. This is also indicated by the fact that temporary labor emigration to Spain was overtly supported during this period. Emigration to Spain was a type of emigration that efficiently satisfied both goals-- protection of the country's labor supply and entry of foreign currency. Already in 1878 regulations were passed to allow Algarvian' fishermen to cross the border without passports. This legislation was reinforced in 1882; and in 1894 it was enforced by a treaty with Spain. Two years later (law of April 23, 1896) the privileges given to the seasonal migrants of the district of Algarve were extended to the whole country.

The period that followed is one of disruption with the past. The Republican Revolution of October 17, 1910 undermined the monarchic bureaucracy, defended liberal values, and attempted to re-rank hierarchically the dominant groups in favor of the small republican bourgeoisie. The republican struggle was soon lost but, while it lasted it disrupted the state apparatus and spread great administrative confusion. This situation was used to advantage by the emigrants. Between 1912 and 1920, they

left the country in unprecedented numbers (57). In the
mainland alone, the annual average number of departures, in
the two previous decades around 24 and 27 thousand per year,
jumped to 34 thousand between 1912 and 1920
(Evangelista,1971:91).

After the military coup of Sidonio Pais (1918)) the
odds became increasingly favorable to the conservative
groups; but only with the military dictatorship of Gomes da
Costa (1926) was power sufficiently consolidated in
conservative hands to allow for the reconstruction of the
state apparatus. By then, the American borders were already
closed and the international economic order was entering a
new phase. Given the new barriers in the receiving countries
to foreigners' entry emigration ceased to be an alternative
to the economic problems of the Portuguese elites.

The political and social instability that followed the
Republican Revolution never allowed time for the formulation
of a coherent new emigration policy by the republicans.
When the dictatorship began and the conservatives returned,
the use of emigration to help solve the socio-economic
problems of the country was no longer a viable alternative.

An interesting document of the early 1920's strongly
suggests that if the receiving countries had not drastically
changed their immigration policies, there would have been a
return to the emigration practices of the turn of the

---

57 It is necessary to be cautious about this migratory wave.
Two very different factors help to explain it: lack of
administrative enforcement due to political instability, and
political discontentment. Thus, at least part of the
migratory flow of this period is political not economically
motivated.

century. That document is the proposal of the commercial attache at Rio de Janeiro to Lisbon, in 1921, for a temporary hardening of the anti-emigration legislation in order to improve negotiations with Brazil on the wine trade. The rational of this government official was quite straight forward: the passage of anti-emigration legislation will give Portugal stronger bargaining power in the upcoming trade negotiations with Brazil. Given Brazil's labor needs, a temporary reinforcement of anti-emigration legislation in Portugal would induce the Brazilian government to make major concessions to the entry of Portuguese wines in its market in return for a loosen up of emigration regulations in Portugal.

Clearly it was not the reinforcement of a no-exit policy that the commercial attache had in mind. His main target was the protection of the interests connected with the production and exportation of the Portuguese wine. This would be in line with the interests of landowners and mercantile bourgeoisie, and therefore from the point of view of the commercial attache such interests were better protected if anti-emigration legislation was passed (58).

---

58 Text transcribed in Pereira, 1981:247-259.

BRIEF ACCOUNTING OF THE PORTUGUESE EMIGRATION POLICY

That selective migration was one of the final results of these legal provisions is proven by the fact that of the 27 thousand legal emigrants that left Portugual between 1898 and 1907, 74 percent were males of which 34 percent were married (59). That family dispersion was another final result was noticed by contemporary writers. Bento Carqueja, after analyzing emigration between 1909 and 1913, concluded that, "many families lost their head of the household" (Carqueja, 1916 :400), a remark confirmed by the low percentage of married women in the emigrant population (9 percent between 1898 and 1910). Likewise, Basilio Teles, while describing the harsh and deteriorating living conditions of the Portuguese peasantry, specifically refers to the fact that peasants saw the sending of their sons to Brazil as "their mutual funds, their life insurance, their savings" for old age or difficult times (Teles, 1904:79).

These two views on family dispersion are strongly confirmed by the answers of Portuguese representatives in Brazil to the official enquires about the Portuguese immigrants in that country (60). That these policies

---

59 All of the data coming from Portuguese representatives in Brazil indicate that male share in the migratory flow must have been much larger than that suggested by the official Portuguese statistics, and that the share of married females must have been much smaller -- see for example Emigração Portugueza - Documentos..., 1874: 226, 235). The percentages given here were computed from Emigração Portgueza, 1901-1910.
60 The data coming from the Portuguese representatives in Brazil are more dramatic than the literary sources and some specifically highlight the extension of human suffering associated with the emigration of minors (Emigração

maintained family dispersion is also indicated by Miriam H. Pereira's recent work. She writes:

> Most of the remittances were sent to men-- 59 percent of money orders and 80 percent of all the money sent. Given the dominant familial structure, we can infer that remittances for the male parents were more numerous than those sent to married women... However, in the district of Braga, the situation was absolutely different. Here, 80 percent of the money orders were addressed to women (Pereira, 1981:42,43).

Pereira's finding that remittances were mainly sent to men does not necessarily mean in the final analysis, that some of them were not addressed to wives. Although we know practically nothing of emigrants' families' living arrangements, recent anthropological works on northern Portugal (Trás-os-Montes) seem to suggest that married women and their children during at least their husband's absence were more likely to stay with their in-laws, their parents or even a relative than to head their own household, which would help explain the pattern of remittances referred to above (O'Neill, 1983:51-57). Likewise, Brettell's (1981, 1986) description of living arrangements for the Minho (Lanhezes), where female position within the household structure and the inheritance system seems to have been more favorable to women than in Tras-Os-Montes, is congruent with Pereira findings of a special pattern of remittances for Braga (a district also in the Minho province). In summary, there were two types of family dispersion-- one created by the departure of young males, the other created by the

---

Portuguesa, 1875, Documentos...,Relatorio de J.Andrade Corvo, in Pereira, 1981: 210-211).

departure of married males-- both mentioned by contemporary literary and governmental sources.

Recent research has indicated that emigration brings several gains to the sending country, including short-term relief for the government and substantial income in the form of remittances and other transfers. But Heisler argues that:

> To benefit fully from remittances, the sending country must be able to depend on the flow being consistent and reliable, not subject to fluctuations or secular decline. (Heisler 1985: 472)

What is known about Portuguese emigration around the turn of the century fits this optimal pattern. Pereira's research indicates that the supply of remittances provided a remarkably stable source of income and showed a constant upward trend between 1896 and 1924 (Pereira, 1981: 42).

While emigration remained vastly male dominated, it did not constitute a threat to the Portuguese elites, since periodic replacement of those that broke their links with Portugal-- and the dream of return-- would maintain the stability of the flow of remittances. What concerned the Portuguese elites was permanent emigration and, more concretely, permanent emigration of families. Familial emigration posed a real danger, since the settlement of entire families in receiving communities tends to produce permanent migration, and the cessation of close family ties to those in Portugal would also have cut the flow of remittances. If family reunification in the receiving community had been common, this would have decreased the need to send remittances; and that, we know, did not happen until the mid-1920's. In other words, the legal apparatus promoted a type of migration which can be considered most favorable to the dominant economic groups, regardless of whether or not this was achieved through a conscious effort (61). What economists and sociologists now claim to be effective strategy for the policy makers of sending countries, was-- perhaps fortuitously -- the strategy of the Portuguese elites in the period under analysis.

But if no policy is effective without administrative enforcement, by the same token no policy is effective without social sanctioning. The last part of this section deals precisely with the attitudes in Portugal towards emigration and with the images subscribed by the dominant social groups. In other words with the social controls that I see as complements of the legal controls just described.

---

61 Manuel VilaVerde Cabral (1976) wrote that massive emigration in this period was the result of the high expropriation rates of the small peasant, and offered as evidence the fact that, between 1888 and 1889, 35,000 small farmholdings disappeared (p.41), suggesting that the mechanisms at work were conscious and determined by the "visible hand" of capitalist development. Although powerful, his thesis has two main weaknesses. First, we do not know how much of these "expropriations" resulted in consolidation, and of what size. Moreover we do not know how many farmers left on account of these "expropriations"; and it can be argued that consolidation of small farmholdings in northern Portugal would lead to a wider job market. Second, as the author recognizes (p.42), small holdings were sustained and expanded, in this part of the country, by emigrants' remittances.   In other words, before we have further research on the structure and evolution of rural property, it is hard to foresee what caused what.

SOCIAL CONTROL - THE IDEOLOGY OF RETURN AND THE SOCIAL TYPE OF THE BRASILEIRO

For a long time, myths that were part of the Portuguese mentality favored a male exodus to Brazil. These had their roots in the auriferous period, and were related both to Brazil's former position as part of the empire and to the limited opportunities for social mobility within Portugal. That from 1870 on Portuguese emigrants increasingly replaced slave labor, and that Brazil had ceased to be a Portuguese colony in 1822 seem to have had no effect on the myth. Brazil remained in the popular imagination the "El Dourado"-- the place where everyone could quickly make a fortune and then return to climb to the top of the social ladder.

At its worst this myth contributed to the peasants' decision to alienate their sons. Sometimes these peasant's children were sent by themselves, more often they were "entrusted" to contractors or to distant relatives, which led to inhumane situations of child exploitation-- exploitation well documented in the official reports sent from Brazil to Lisbon, as well as in the press of the time (Benis, 1979:85-100). To understand these peasants' decisions, we must take into account the lack of ready cash of the majority of the Portuguese peasantry, their deeply rooted fear of conscription, the legal restrictions on the departure of young males, and the myth of the "torna-viagem". And we must also take into account the demagogic exploitation of these fears and hopes by agencies of contractors and shipping companies that sometimes went to the extreme of offering immediate financial benefits and "free passage" to the potential emigrant (Benis, 1979: 85-100).

The myth of the "torna-viagem" was so powerful that those who failed preferred to conceal the fact. As a member of the Portuguese Consulate at Rio de Janeiro testified in 1921:

> However, given the psychology of the emigrant who had not derived any benefit in Brazil and given his well-known habit of describing gains in wealth not enjoyed, resources not owned, and social importance that he is far from having, we must conclude that only vanity, self-pride, or the fear of an unfavorable opinion of his capacity as a worker, given the false but nevertheless deeply-rooted idea in Portugal that only the lazy do not make fortunes in Brazil, makes him hide with extreme care from his relatives and villagers, the extent of his privations and suffering. (Consular Report from the Consulate at Rio de Janeiro, Feb. 9, 1921, quoted in Pereira, 1981:29)

To admit one's failure was then seen as a sign of one's inability to work hard and save. There are great similarities between this popular Portuguese myth of the "torna-viagem" and the "self-made-man" myth of the United States in the nineteenth century, described by Stephen Thernstrom in Poverty and Progress (1964). Both had the same social function: to transfer guilt from society to the individual, and to deny that social mobility was inaccessible to the vast majority. In this sense, the popularization of the "torna-viagem" helped to maintain the Portuguese modus vivendi, and must be considered a powerful social control at the disposal of the dominant culture. But, after its creation by Camilo, the myth served other social functions more closely related to the dominant social groups in Portugal.

Nicola Chiaromonte (1985) has claimed that "nineteenth-century fiction meant to provide the true, not the official, history of the individual and society". As Chiaromonte, I am interested in capturing the social "truth". Thus I will concentrate on identifying the social type of the "Brasileiro" as it was channeled by fiction and political discourse. Specifically, I am focusing on what Y. Barel called a discourse's "mirror-function"-- that is the relation between the emigrant as a marginal and his native society. As Barel has remarked, fiction and political discourse are privileged sources for this type of analysis.

During the second half of the nineteenth century, Portuguese literature created a social type baptized the "Brasileiro," which enjoyed enormous popularity, and to which there was no coherent counter-image until the 1930's. Grotesque and negative allusions to the returned emigrant had existed prior to this creation (62). But these earlier versions were much less developed than the character sketched in 1868 by Julio Dinis, in A Morgadinha dos Canaviais. Eusebio Seabra was the beginning of a type both physical and psychological, of a half-real, half-fictional being that Camilo Castelo Branco would complete and transmit to posterity.

---

62 For example, during the eighteenth century, Antonio Jose da Silva (o Judeu) labelled him "mineiro" in his play Guerra do Alecrim e da Manjerona (staged for the first time in 1737).

Physically, the "brute" was forty-five to fifty years old, fat and short, with red skin; he was repulsive and constantly suffered from several diseases, preferably ridiculous. Bento in the Eusebio Macário, and Fialho in the Os Brilhantes do Brasileiro both share all these characteristics. Psychologically, he was devious and vain, happily parading both his wealth and his ignorance. His nucleus of friends was similarly corrupt; those who advised Fialho on questions of honor were a murderer, a smuggler, and a slave trader and modern contractor of emigrants. Upon their return to Portugal, these "brasileiros" formed the "clean class" or the "respectable corporation," claiming for themselves the right to judge anyone else's conduct. In 1879, Camilo described the qualities of the corporation in the following way:

> [...], the news spread through the parish, that the comendador Montalegre was coming . . . and would stay in the house of his sister, mistress of the priest. The brasileiro of the Big House thought that he must be a man without honor, a crook, a shameless person to accept the hospitality of such a house. This opinion was unanimously shared by the clean class. That no one would visit him was agreed. Gaspar, the proponent of avenging this affront, [who was] from the Brazilian class, or from the respectable corporation as he used to say, lived in concubinage with one of his sisters, and had already married off two other sisters --at two contos per head-- to farmers who were up to their ears in debt. Also participating in this proposal was the comendador Patricio, who married a weaver from Rochosa after having been the lover of her mother for four years; also applauding the idea [was] Guimaraes da Laje, who was enjoying the hospitality of his brother and the love of his sister-in-law. (in, Eusebio Macário, (1st ed. 1878), Porto, Lello & Irmao, 1957,p. 60-61)

Portuguese society welcomed the creation of this
Camilian character, since it sublimated its own
aggressiveness towards the brasileiro (63). Shaped outside
his own society, the emigrant remained in the same
marginalized situation, but the reasons had changed.
Initially, he was marginal due to the lack of economic
vacancies; upon his return, the absence which had secured
his fortune made him different from those who had remained
in the homeland. On foreign soil he had absorbed a new
culture, had acted, behaved, and thought differently, and
this made him an outcast from even the small group to which
he had once belonged.

If he nevertheless decided to stay and build a mansion at
the borders of the Lima river, or a house at Oporto or at
Lisbon , this was simply seen as an affirmation of his new
economic power-- power that would help him climb the
social ladder and obtain political influence.

Established first in the novel, the image was next
conveyed by the theater, and then absorbed into public
opinion. Finally, it was channeled by the political elites,
as the following extract from a speech, of Luis Palmeirim,
to the Camara dos Deputados (parliament), in 1882, and the
Camara reaction to it exemplifies:

> [...]
> the Portuguese capital was, and still is today, a
> capital of torna- viagem, and because I qualify it
> that way, I need to say to this house how the
> voyage is made.

---

63 Only with the romances of Ferreira de Castro, <u>A Selva</u>
(1930), and of Miguel Torga <u>Traço de União</u> (1955), does
Portuguese literature create a counter-image of the
"brasileiro".

I ... will call either finance or capital,
those men who represent one or the other, and who
deny their economic resources to the improvement
of the public good.
     The finance, formerly a simple emigrant,
left one day for Brazil, dressed ad hoc in a
jacket woven in this country [jaquetao de
saragoca nacional], and taking as his only
baggage an image of his village saint in his
pocket. Stays in Brazil the time necessary to
make a fortune and years after the humble shopboy
returns to his country, having impiously shifted
his veneration from the Bom Jesus do Monte to
the comenda da Conceição during his absence.
(**laughter from the house**)
     He arrived: his first concern is to
acknowledge his debt of gratitude, building at
the borders of the Lima river or the Minho river,
a mansion painted green and yellow, in tribute to
the colors of the Brazilian flag, in the shadow
of which the immigrant became a money-grubber.
(**laughter from the house**)
     Only afterwards does he become a patriot,
which is manifested by the eagerness with which
he buys bonds of credit, forgetting the
difficulty he will have, every six months, in
going to the public credit service to receive
the interest.
     (**laughter from the house**)
     Those more ambitious reserved in their safes
the necessary capital for an opportune time to
subsidize electoral agents, not with the noble
intent of propagating useful ideas, but already
with the thought in reserve of later adorning
themselves with the feudal ensignias of baron and
viscount.
     (**prolonged laughter from the house**)
[After congratulating the minister of finance for
capturing those men, Palmeirim concludes by
noting the] diplomatic finesse necessary to move
the paralytic whose name is capital and who does
not move without the spur of guaranteed interest.
(Diario da Camara dos Senhores Deputados, Lisboa,
Imprensa Nacional,1882, pp.1634-1635, in Benis,
1981:131,132)

The "Brasileiro" was thus, in the Camilian typification

a showy, morally corrupt, physically disgusting being who

had succeeded financially by more than devious means. He

spoke and wrote an atrocious kind of Portuguese that set him

apart as an alien in his homeland, as did his strange ideas

on business, religion, and art. But, worst of all, in the political discourse, he also was impious and unpatriotic. This "money-man" could not care less about the interests of the country, or more correctly, of its political elites. The only way the "lump" was moved was by the "spur" of definite interest (64).

Should we expect a more sympathetic image? Or more specifically, could the Portuguese elites subscribe to anything but a detrimental image of the emigrant? The most plausible answer is that unless it was stigmatized and restricted, emigration would have seriously interfered with the interests of the elites. Thus the "Brasileiro" must be seen as a device of social control and a coherent supplement to the legal restrictions.

Unrestricted emigration policies would probably in the long-run have created a lower level of remittances, since more of the emigrants' income would have been spent on family needs in the receiving country. And as we have seen, both the mercantile sector and the state depended heavily on those remittances. A non-pejorative image would have undermined the government's paternalistic rationale for regulating departures, and thus it would have undercut the selective nature of the migratory flow. Further, a more

64 We find also this same type described for the Azoreans emigrants with the particularity that in this case what it is stigmatized is their americanization. The emigrant is, in this case, portrait as promoting separatist ideas towards the mainland, of being unproductive and lustful and of being a bad influence on family circles. In sum, "he went bare foot, poorly dress without a cent, empty headed, and returned with western boots, overdressed, with 100 or 200 eagles [gold eagles], and with the tonic and grateful illusion that he thinks and that he knows".

positive image of the returnee would imply an obvious recognition of the elites' failure to integrate the surplus population. These consequences would have been unacceptable to a power structure that wished to reduce conflict and perpetuate itself. Thus, a detrimental image of the emigrant complemented the legal apparatus.

The "Brasileiro" image had one last social function: it sanctioned the high price for social integration paid by some upon their return to Portugal. At the national level, that price was to be the willing "capital" and "finance" for a state without creditors, and the purchaser of "newcomers" titles of nobility. At the local level, the price was to be the godfather, the head of charity, and the builder of exotic mansions dotting the northern landscape.

To conclude, social marginalization of the emigrant and the restrictive policies towards emigration, within the Portuguese context, did not just co-occur: they were logical complements. They maintained an anachronistic social structure and perpetuated the elites, since these social controls insured emigrants' remittances-- without which the social structure would hardly have held together. I mean by this that, by promoting, through legislative restrictions, a male-dominated migratory flow, government policies ensured the inflow of needed remittances, relieved social and demographic pressure, and maintained an adequate labor supply. By creating an unfavorable image of the emigrant, the dominant culture implied that those who had emigrated had made their fortunes unethically and sanctioned both its patriarchal role and the high price to be paid by those hoping to be socially absorbed upon their return.

I hope that this section has also shown that we cannot assume that the Portuguese political class was necessarily inept and incapable of fostering economic development. The capability to foster economic development depends upon the wish or the need to do so. And so far, no scholar, to my knowledge, has proved that the Portuguese elites desired or needed this. In fact evidence runs the other way around, as Salazar said, in a speech in March 16, 1933, "all advancement is not progress, and ... backwardness may simply mean that we have not departed too much from the principles of rational economy" (Salazar, 1939:168).

CHAPTER III - THE SENDING SOCIETY

Historians of the 1960's and the 1970's viewed Portuguese economic backwardness during the late nineteenth and early twentieth centuries as the result of its external dependency, its rural property structure, and its anachronistic social structure (Bairoch,1976; Sideri, 1978; Pereira, 1971; Cabral, 1976; Godinho, (1st ed. 1971) 1980).

Recently a number of Portuguese scholars have been revising these previous explanations. Even the extent of the country's economic backwardness has been contested (Justino,1988). In particular, the external dependency explanation has come under fire (Reis, 1984; Lains, 1986). To the explanations based on the country's rural property structure or its anachronistic social structure, the revisionists counterposed explanations based on the small size of the national market (Lains, 1986), or the paucity of human capital (Reis, 1984).

Prevailing explanations of Portuguese migratory determinants are consistent with the descriptions of the country's economic backwardness found in the historiography of the 1960's and 1970's. In fact, Portuguese historiography has never seriously contested the idea that emigration from the northern regions and the islands was based on the general poverty of the lower classes in these areas. This widespread poverty was the result of land fragmentation, low agricultural productivity, high birth rates, and lack of socio-economic opportunities (1).

Although they do not directly contradict the traditional stand of the Portuguese historiography on the determinants of emigration, the revisionists do raise some questions about its accuracy. After all, the country seems to have been much less backward than previously thought. Reis (1986), for instance, claims that Portugal experienced sustained industrial growth between 1870 and 1913. The growth rates for industry in Portugal paralleled those of such developed countries as France and Great Britain at the turn of the nineteenth century. In fact, industry is seen by this author as the dynamic sector of the Portuguese economy, with yearly growth rates varying between 2.5 and 2.8 percent between 1870 and 1913 (2). Industrial development was based since the 1870's on growing internal demand; it was associated after 1885 with preferential terms of trade with the colonies; and it was sustained after the 1890's by an internal process of import substitution (3).

Portuguese emigration attained its peak precisely during this period of industrial expansion, 1870-1913. We thus have to ask ourselves if the Portuguese were leaving because of the lack of job vacancies (as traditionally claimed), or

1 e.g. O.Martins (1894), 1956; A.Sampaio (1892), n.d.; A.Costa, 1911; M.Godinho,1978.
2 Between the 1860's and the 1900's agricultural production had a yearly rate of growth of .8 percent (Mateus, quoted in Reis, 1986:213).
3 Cabral, 1976; Serrão,1978; Reis,1984, 1986. It is important to remark that Lains' analysis of the export phases of growth are not in accordance with Reis' industrial phases of growth. This fact can be seen as a confirmation that the industrial development taking place was sustained by endogenous factors, namely growing internal demand.

regardless of job vacancies (as the new literature seems to suggest).

In other countries, as the work of A. Redford (1968) has shown, technological change and industrial development opened job vacancies and simultaneously led to emigration. What Redford found for Britain was that a segment of the working class which was unable to adapt to the new labor market conditions emigrated.

While the new stream of Portuguese historiography calls into question one set of determinants of emigration, it does not provide an alternative solution. One possibility would be to create a time-series regression model postulating that the changes in the migratory flow are a function of the changes in national industrial development. We could make our model more sophisticated by introducing some time lags to account for the period necessary for booms and crises in the industrial sector to have an impact on the labor market.

Such an approach would suffer, however, from the same weaknesses as the neoclassic and dependency models analyzed in chapter I of this work. The most that any of these models can tell us is whether there was a connection between the fluctuations in the volume of the migratory flow and in the volume of the country's industrial productivity. The establishment of a cause/effect relationship from aggregate national data does not take into account the regional disparities typical of the migratory movements.

To address the regional nature of migration, I present both a geo-economic description of Portugal, and an analysis of the Portuguese labor market between the 1880's and the

1920's. The main goal of the first part of this section,
the geo-economic description of the country, is to highlight
regional disparities that will later help to explain the
migratory flow. The main goal of the second part, the
evolution of the Portuguese labor market, is to see how
regional economic development affected job opportunities.
The basic sources for the following analysis were the Year
Books for 1894 and 1892 and the Portuguese Censuses of 1890,
1900, 1911, 1920, and 1930. For reasons of space,
discussion of methodological problems raised by the census
data, abbreviations, and some basic tables are presented in
Appendix 1 of this work.

GEOGRAPHICAL DESCRIPTION

Socio-political and cultural factors tend to interfere
with nature, creating unexpected outcomes. Still, the
geographic location of a country, its climate, and its
natural resources shape a country's economic structure.
These variables can be seen as setting limits on or offering
opportunities for economic development. Of course, the
level and type of development achieved depends on other
factors.

In 1890, over 60 percent of the economically active
population of Portugal was engaged in agricultural
activities. Knowing the limitations, or better yet the
predispositions, set by the climate and the morphology of
the soil is thus particularly useful.

According to the geographer Orlando Ribeiro, continental Portugal can be divided into four main geographical areas: the north-atlantic, which shows the influence of the Atlantic ocean; the north-transmontano "that the mountains isolate from maritime influences"; the south "where the meridional reveals itself by an increasing predominance of the mediterranean character"; and the center that shares characteristics of all three regions (Ribeiro,1955:235).

The boundaries of these four main geographical regions do not entirely agree with any traditional or administrative division of the country. The socio-economic data gathered by authorities use as units of reference either the traditional administrative division into provinces, or the modern administrative division into districts. I will use both the traditional and the modern administrative divisions, relating them as closely as possible to O.Ribeiro's geographic divisions (4).

During the period surveyed by this work, there were seven provinces and seventeen districts in continental Portugal (5), and four districts in the islands (see Map 1 and Table III:I). The geographical location of the districts and provinces is indicated on the accompanying map. The distribution of the population among provinces and districts

---

4 What Ribeiro terms North Atlantic corresponds roughly to the province of Minho and part of the Beira Alta province; Tras-Os-Montes province corresponds to the North Transmontano; the rest of the Beiras and the Extremadura mark the transition, incorporating traits of both north and south; and finally the Alentejo and the Algarve correspond to the South.
5 In 1926 a new district (Setubal) was formed from the partition of the district of Lisbon. Given the comparative purpose of this section, the new district (Setubal) is neither counted nor analyzed separately.

is summarized in Table III:I and the distribution of agricultural production is given in Table III:II.

FIGURE 2 - THE PORTUGUESE MAINLAND

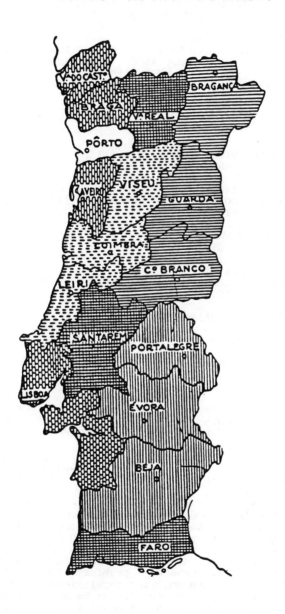

TABLE III:I –DISTRIBUTION OF THE POPULATION BY PROVINCE AND DISTRICT, 1890 - 1930

PROVINCE	DISTRICT	AREA (THOUSANDS KM2)	POPULATION (THOUSANDS) 1890	1930	DENSITY PER KM2 1890	1930
MINHO	VIANA BRAGA PORTO	7	1092	1465	153	206
TRAS-OS-MONTES	VILA REAL BRAGANÇA	11	417	439	39	41
BEIRA ALTA	AVEIRO COIMBRA VIZEU	12	995	1201	85	103
BEIRA BAIXA	GUARDA CAST.BRANCO	12	455	533	37	44
EXTREMADURA	LEIRIA LISBOA SANTAREM	18	1083	1833	60	102
ALENTEJO	PORTALEGRE EVORA BEJA	24	389	588	16	25
ALGARVE	FARO	5	229	301	45	59
ISLANDS						
AZORES	ANGRA HORTA P.DELGADA	2	256	254	113	113
MADEIRA	FUNCHAL	.8	134	212	159	251

Source: Census of 1890, Vol.I, p.LV, and p.34; Census of 1940, Vol.I, p.XII.

NOTE TO TABLE I -- According to the 1890 Census, vol.I, p.32, the size of Portugal was 92157 square kilometers. According to the Census of 1940, the size of the country was 92721 square kilometers. This discrepancy reflects improvements in measurement, not changes on the borders. This growing accuracy creates a problem. Every time there was a change in measurement, the population density of the country was computed with a different base. This makes the census information on population density meaningless for comparison. For this reason I chose the measurement reported in the 1940 census, theoretically the most perfect of those available to me, and reformulated the computations with this common base from 1890 to 1930.

TABLE III:II - AGRICULTURAL PRODUCTION REGIONAL DISTRIBUTION
1882-1884   (PERCENTAGE DISTRIBUTION)

PROVINCE DISTRICT	WHEAT	MAIZE	RYE	WINE	OLIVE OIL*
VIANA	0.97	8.04	2.08	2.73	0.52
BRAGA	0.51	14.26	4.87	6	0.05
PORTO	5.78	26.92	18.09	3.59	0.1
MINHO----------	7.26	49.22	25.04	12.32	0.67
V.REAL	0.58	3.21	7.42	9.74	1.44
BRAGANÇA	5.11	0.08	19.77	3.82	1.14
T.MONTES--------	5.69	3.29	27.19	13.56	2.58
AVEIRO	1.64	8.21	0.64	3.09	0.32
COIMBRA	0.96	6.56	0.69	3.35	1.61
VIZEU	2.32	6.88	7.07	8.85	0.58
B.ALTA----------	4.92	21.65	8.4	15.29	2.51
C.BRANCO	2.29	1.16	5.07	2.73	0.97
GUARDA	2.24	2.13	16.88	3.23	71.56
B.BAIXA----------	4.53	3.29	21.95	5.96	72.53
LEIRIA	3.44	2.65	0.28	10.27	0.79
LISBOA	11.8	1.69	0.69	25.72	0.55
SANTAREM	10.15	4.15	1.58	10.16	2.77
EXTREMADURA------	25.39	8.49	2.55	46.15	4.11
PORTALEGR	14.63	0.48	8.73	0.95	1.94
EVORA	10.52	0.34	4.8	2.52	1.29
BEJA	15.15	0.26	0.6	1.65	13.45
ALENTEJO---------	40.3	1.08	14.13	5.12	16.68
ALGARVE FARO	2.84	0.53	0.6	1.06	0.92
TOTAL - CONTINENT	90.93	87.55	9986	99.46	100
ANGRA	3.19	3.25	0.01	0.1	
HORTA	0.84	1.45	0.01	0.05	
P.DELGADA	3.43	7.68	0.03	0.2	
AZORES----------	7.46	12.38	0.05	0.35	
MADEIRA FUNCHAL	1.63	0.08	0.09	0.28	
TOTAL - ISLANDS	9.09	12.46	0.14	0.63	
TOTAL PRODUCTION (THOUSAND HECTOLITERS)	2194	5096	1707	2881	2134

Source : Year Book for 1884, 1886:341
* Olive oil only for 1884

THE MAINLAND

The northernmost province of Portugal is the Minho.
Orlando Ribeiro described Minho as a "vast amphitheater" of
7121 square kilometers facing the sea. The region is
particularly humid and green, and intensive farming
predominates. The most important product at the end of the
nineteenth century was maize. Minho's farmers produced 50
percent of Portugal's maize crop in 1882, and 43 percent in
1901-1903 (Pereira, 1971:403). Second in importance was
wine, with 10 percent of the country's wine produced here in
1881, and 29 percent in 1892 (Year Book for 1892, 1899:266-
283).

The land is extremely fragmented in this part of the
country. The average area of a farmholding was, in 1891, .76
hectares (Year Book for 1892, 1899:582). Such fragmentation
precluded extensive farming or sheep-farming.

For centuries this area has also been characterized by
the greatest population density on the mainland. With only
8 percent of the continental land area, Minho had in 1890 23
percent of the population, and a population density of 153
inhabitants per square kilometer. By 1930, the share of
the population living in this province had dropped to 21
percent, but the density per square kilometer had increased
to 206 inhabitants. The population was scattered on
separate farmsteads, rather than clustered in compact
villages.

The North Atlantic is divided from the North Transmontano
by the Minho mountains. Tras-Os-Montes was thinly populated

(see Table I). The region has two distinct geographic areas. In high lands, commonly known as the "Terra Fria" (Cold Land), here the soil is poor. Sheepfarming was the predominant activity, and rye, grown in biennial rotation, was the main agricultural product. The population lived agglomerated in villages sharing communal lands. The valleys or "Terra Quente" (Hot Land) had Mediterranean characteristics: fruit trees, olive trees, and vineyards. The vineyards of the Douro valleys produced a unique wine - "Oporto Wine" - particularly appreciated by the English consumer. "Oporto Wine" was the single most important export product of this region, and one of the most important of the country.

The center of the country, constituted by the provinces of Beiras and Extremadura, marks the transition from the North to the South. The Beiras resemble the Minho, but in the Beiras the "population is less dense, the property less fragmented, and the cohesion of the peopling is greater" (Ribeiro, 1955:243).

In the Beiras, maize is cultivated, but other products not characteristic of the Minho are also grown, notably olive trees. In 1884 a single district of this region - Guarda - produced 70 percent of the country's olive oil (see Table III:II).

The products of the Litoral Center (Beira Litoral, and Extremadura) are extremely varied (maize, wheat, grapes, rice, and olive trees). This region is particularly rich, especially the district of Lisbon. In 1882-1884, this district was the third wheat producer and the first wine producer of the country (see Table III:II). Moving southward, compact villages and specialized farming of olive trees and wheat become increasingly predominant.

The eastern part of the sparsely settled Extremadura (district of Santarem) marks the transition from the "polymorphism" of the north and center litoral to the "monotony" of the south (province of Alentejo) (O.Ribeiro,1955:249). If we take into account only geographic characteristics, the south covers about one-third of the mainland and includes part of the Beira Baixa, the meridional Extremadura, and the Alentejo province.

The south's meridional position and the lack of large mountains to condense humidity produce a climate with clear mediterranean and continental affinities (Ribeiro, 1955:250). The dry climate and poor water supply did not favor small plantations, and the area was dominated by extensive cultivation of wheat and olives. The average size of farmholdings in Alentejo was 16 hectares in 1891, 21 times the average for the Minho (Year Book for 1892, 1899:582). The three districts of the Alentejo province alone-- Portalegre, Evora, and Beja-- produced 41 of the country's wheat crop in 1882-1884, and 59 percent in 1902-1903 (Table III:II and Pereira,1971:403).

The smallest and southernmost province, the Algarve, had sparsely populated highlands and a densely populated litoral. Where water was abundant, intensive agriculture and small holdings predominated. In the drier lands, extensive cultivation of fruit trees was most common.

The waterway system for Portugal is centered around its three major rivers - Douro, Mondego, and Tejo. These flow east to west, crossing the whole country, and facilitate communication between the litoral and the interior along the navigable part of their courses. For centuries, the three rivers have served as major routes for the circulation of people as well as goods (6). At their mouths lie the three biggest cities-- Oporto, Coimbra, and Lisbon-- which dominated the North, Center, and South respectively.

Just as the river system links part of the interior regions, so does the seaboard tie together the coastal areas. The insecurity, the slowness, and the high cost of transport via the inland routes contributed to the maintenance of a very vibrant coastal life (Navarro,1887).

The coastal areas were also the locus of fishing activities. By the end of the nineteenth century, the value of the fishing catch represented a very small share of the total national product, equaling, for example, only 48 of the quarry production value, and 37 percent of the mining production value in 1889 (7).

Fishing was concentrated in a few districts, but only in Faro were activities connected with the sea-- saltpond extraction, sardine and tuna fishing, and in the early

---

6 The Douro is particularly known for its economic importance. Since the seventeenth century, it has been the waterway of international trade in Oporto Wine. This wine, which was produced in the Douro's valleys, was sent by special boats (Rebelo boats) to the warehouses of Gaya (a village facing the city of Oporto), and then distributed by the merchants of Oporto to the world. The river and the economy it supports inprint this whole region.
7 The value of the fish caught in 1889 was 3254.3 thousand contos.

1900's the seafood tinning industry-- the predominant economic activities.

Like fishing, quarrying and mining were concentrated in a few areas. In 1889, the district of Lisbon had 65 percent of the value of the quarrying production and 54 percent of this labor force, while Oporto had 20 percent and 22 percent respectively (8). Mining production was centered in the districts of Beja and Oporto (Year Book for 1884, 1886:382-392; Year Book for 1892, 1899:337). Although there was a significant change in the relative position of Oporto between 1882 and 1890 (Oporto's mining production share rose from 6 percent to 19 percent), the value of the mining production of the district of Beja remained four times that of Oporto.

THE ISLANDS

AZORES

The Azorean archipelago is in the Atlantic Ocean, 700 kilometers north of the archipelago of Madeira. It is 1400 kilometers from the Portuguese mainland and 3600 Kilometers away from North America.

The Azores consist of nine islands divided into three geographical sets: Western (S.Miguel and Santa Maria); Central (Terceira, Graciosa, S.Jorge, Pico, and Fayal); and Eastern (Flores and Corvo). The geographical division does not correspond to the administrative division. The

---

8 The total value of quarry extraction was 672567 contos in 1889. This activity engaged 4716 workers (Year Book for 1892, 1899: 328, 329)

three administrative districts of the Azores are as follows: district of Ponta Delgada (islands of S.Miguel and Santa Maria); district of Angra do Heroismo (islands of Terceira, Graciosa, and S.Jorge); and district of Horta (islands of Pico, Fayal, Flores, and Corvo).

During the nineteenth and early twentieth centuries, communication between the islands was irregular and depended on fishing vessels, which enhanced the isolationist characteristics of some of the islands (9). Communications with the mainland were assured on a monthly basis by ships of the Empresa Insulana, and communications with the American continent were maintained by ships en route to America. But such contacts were felt to be scarce, and complaints of isolation are quite common in the secondary literature (Maximo Pereira,1893:6,13: Lacerda,1902: X,XI).

The Azorean climate is mild with small temperature variations, but rain and storms are frequent. The Mediterranean-Atlantic climate favored the growth of fig and orange trees, along with the vineyards and other agricultural products typical of southern Europe. The volcanic origins of the soil make the landscape of the nine islands vary, with soil resources much more scarce in Fayal than in S.Miguel or Terceira (10).

According to Correia da Cunha (1963: 121,122), the type of island found in the Azores consists of a volcanic cone with a large base, gentle slope and jagged coast line. The

9 The isolation is frequently emphasized in travellers' accounts (e.g., Henriques, 1867; Walker, 1886, and Vermett,1984).
10 There were not volcanic eruptions during the period under consideration.

population is centered on the southern litoral, and on the
areas of lower altitude, up to 300 - 350 meters. This low
area is followed by a zone of dense vegetation or forest,
after which only pasture or non-cultivated areas are found.
The islands of Pico, Fayal, Terceira, and Corvo match da
Cunha's model. In the other islands-- S.Maria, Graciosa,
S.Jorge, and S.Miguel-- this pattern is not so obvious. In
Santa Maria, for example, the population was concentrated
in the interior and in the north. This population
distribution favored isolation, and the island was almost
totally self-sufficient until the Second World War (11).

The biggest and most densely populated island is
S.Miguel. According to Correia da Cunha, this island had the
most marked class differences, due to demographic pressure
and an anachronistic agrarian structure of large holdings in
the hands of a few owners (12). The situation was quite
different in Terceira, where more even land distribution
produced a smaller percentage of wage earners and a higher
and quite different standard of living (Correia da
Cunha,1963:126).

Agricultural production was unevenly distributed among
the islands, depending on how rocky the soil was and how
much the morphology of the terrain protected the crops from

---

11 The daily life and isolation of this island were vividly
described by Jacinto Monteiro (1982).
12 Bento Barcelos' (1987) description of Graciosa's property
structure suggests a similar agrarian structure for this
island. According to Ribeiro (1940:6,7), farmland in the
Azores is either too concentrated in a few hands or is too
subdivided into tiny holdings. Ribeiro concluded that small
farmers and agricultural laborers alike had no hope for
improvement in their homeland, and had to emigrate to
improve their prospects.

salty ocean winds. The major producers of cereals were the islands of Terceira, Graciosa, and S.Miguel. Wine production was centered in the islands of Pico, Graciosa, and Terceira. Also grown for local consumption were sugar beets, which were processed by a sugar factory founded in 1906 on the island of S.Miguel. Tobacco was grown in S.Miguel and Terceira for local consumption and for exportation to Madeira, where it was processed.

In S.Jorge, Pico, and S.Miguel, dairy products were produced for local consumption and for export to the mainland in insignificant quantities. After the blight on oranges in the mid-nineteenth century, orange production, which had brought to the islands a period of some prosperity, ended, although not without leaving behind a reminder in some "nouveau riche" houses on S.Miguel. The islands, particularly S.Miguel, tried to substitute pineapple exportation, but this crop brought in less revenue (Maximo Pereira,1893:25-27; Bruges,1915:44,45).

Lacking a major export crop and isolated on their respective islands, the Azoreans were extremely dependent on a subsistence economy that brought the peasantry to the brink of starvation in bad harvest years. In an interview, the Reverend Dr. João da Rosa (13) mentioned that in Fayal, during the worst famines of the nineteenth century, peasant women would try to sell their daughters from door to door. According to a recent Azorean monograph, "the whole

---

13 Interview with the Reverend Dr. João da Rosa, Horta, May 20, 1987.

nineteenth century was no more than a period of economic
decline" (Monograph for the Azores,1971:5).

Economic hardship in the Azores encouraged heavy
emigration that only stopped with the United States'
immigration restrictions in the 1920's. The closing off of
emigration induced a marked economic crisis in the Azores.
This crisis halted infrastructural improvements of the roads
and of the harbors of Ponta Delgada and Horta, a program
that had been funded largely by emigrants' remittances since
the First World War.

The scenario drawn by the monographs on the Azores is one
of isolation and poverty. An attachment to routine, small
average farm size, and the morphology of the terrain
discouraged modernization of agricultural practices. The
only prospects for the majority of the Azoreans who did not
migrate were as fishermen or as agricultural workers, both
at a subsistence level.

MADEIRA

The archipelago of Madeira is also in the Atlantic Ocean,
between the Azores and the Canaries. It is 510 nautical
miles from the mainland and has two populated islands,
Madeira and Porto-Santo.

Administratively the archipelago makes up a single
district, Funchal. In 1901, the government gave
administrative autonomy to the region. This law allowed
part of Madeira's tax revenues to be applied to local
infrastructural improvements, such as building roads,
bridges, a water-supply system, and other public works.

Emigrants' remittances and the savings of returned emigrants also underwrote the economic development of these islands at the turn of the century.

Regular communications between the islands of Madeira and Porto Santo were assured by small ships of the Empresa Funchalense de Cabotagem (weekly), and by small cargo vessels transporting goods and mail (twice a week). Regular communications with the mainland were assured by Portuguese ships on the islands routes (the Empresa Insular and Empresa Funchalense) and on the African route (Companhia National, and Companhia Colonial de Navegação). Foreign ships en route to Africa or America completed the network of communications with the exterior.

The climate of Madeira is Mediterranean-Atlantic, and sugar plantations, vineyards, and banana and orange trees are the principal agricultural sources of income. Dairy products were also produced, largely for home consumption. Wine, particularly "Madeira Wine," was exported to Northern Europe (14). Sugar production (15) or derivatives such as molasses or alcohol formed the core of the economy during the period of this study.

Two sugar factories, a tobacco factory, and an alcohol distillery created a small job market outside the primary sector. A network of craft-shops engaged in producing

---

14 An annual average of ten thousand barrels between 1910 and 1932.
15 Sugar production was estimated in 1861 to be 275800 kilograms; ten years later production had increased to almost 85000 kilograms, and by 1916 it attained approximately 5 million kilograms. From then until 1930, the average production was estimated to be between 2 and 3 million kilograms. The surplus after refining was exported to the mainland.

embroidery, inlaid wood, and cane furniture completed the secondary sector of Madeira's economy.(16)

In the tertiary sector, the tourist industry was the best resource of the island. During the period under study there were two big crises in this sector, caused by an epidemic of cholera-morbus (1910-1911) and by the bombardment of Funchal harbor by German submarines during the First World War.

In summary, Madeira was essentially a region which tried to profit from its natural resources, in terms of both soil and beauty. It developed manufacturing to complement its agricultural production, created a small job market for its population outside the primary sector, and put to good use the remittances of its emigrants. The economic resources available to Madeira's inhabitants were perhaps better than those available to the Azoreans, but the surprising feature to note is how advantageously Madeira's resources were employed (17).

---

16 Around 1940 there were 80 small shops dedicated to the production of cane furniture, employing 800 persons-- 350 males, 200 females, and 200 minors between 12 and 18 years of age.
17 The differences in natural resources alone do not explain the stagnation found in the Azores and the dynamism found in Madeira. The reasons for this outstanding difference between the two archipelagoes are not clear. I suspect that differences in the farmholding system, in the pattern of emigration, and, above all, in the pattern of investment of the emigrants' remittances in both communities were key, but these are just hypotheses. A comparative study of the economic development of both archipelagoes has not yet been done.

UNEQUAL INCOME DISTRIBUTION

The regional description of Portugal's natural endowments
reveals two essential traits of the country's socio-economic
structure that will be emphasized in the course of this
work: the extreme unevenness of resource distribution, and
the privileged position of two districts, Lisbon and Oporto.
The unevenness of resource distribution was a major trait of
other periphery or "deprived" European economies of the
time, such as Spain and Italy.

Unequal resource distribution is matched and exaggerated
by a "dramatic skewedness of income distribution"
(Trebilcock,1981). The extent of such inequality in the
Portuguese case is evident in such indicators as the
property, industrial, and income taxes (18).

Thirty-one percent of the property taxes paid during the
fiscal years of 1880-81 and 1890-91 came from the districts
of Lisbon and Oporto. Eighty-three percent and 58 percent
of the income taxes paid in 1880-81 and 1890-91 respectively
also came from these two districts. Finally, the two
districts contributed 68 percent of the industrial taxes of
the fiscal year of 1880-81 and 70 percent for 1890-91.
Whatever its source, the skewedness of income distribution
must have been very marked, given the gap between the wealth
(reflected in the taxes paid) of the districts of Lisbon and
Oporto and the rest of the country.

---

18 The following paragraphs were based on information
gathered from the Year Book for 1884,1886:665-670 and from
the Year Book for 1892, 1899:558-563.

Even more than the industrial taxes, information on labor, wages, and value of production for Portuguese industry in 1881 shows great regional gaps and highlights the predominance of Oporto and Lisbon in the country's economic and industrial structure (19). While paying only 68 percent of the country's industrial taxes in the fiscal year of 1880-81, these two districts had 82 percent of the nation's industrial labor force, paid 76 percent of its wages, and were responsible for 76 percent of the country's industrial production (20).

It must be said that fiscal revenue services (that collected property, income, and industrial taxes) were believed to be better organized than the new statistical services (that made the industrial inquiry), and that these services recognized that the inquiry did not completely cover the country's industry, due to lack of cooperation from the employers (21). But whatever the source, the indication is always the same-- a profound gap between the districts of Lisbon and Oporto and the rest of the country.

---

19 The following analysis is based on information contained on the Year Book for 1884, 1886:389,394-397,408-412,665.
20 There is no obvious correlation between number of workers, wages, and the value of production. Oporto had six times Lisbon's number of workers, but the average salary per worker in Lisbon was eight times higher than in Oporto (Oporto having the lowest per capita wages , and Lisbon the highest). The value of production for the two districts was very similar. The difference in the wage level for the two districts may be traceable to a higher proportion of female workers in the industrial sector in Oporto.
21   In the absence of regional estimates of income or net national product per capita for the nineteenth century, the fiscal values, even if "qui dit fisc dit fraude, ou illusion, ou les deux a la fois" (Braudel, 1979, v.I:23), and the not totally accurate results of the Industrial Inquiry of 1881 remain privileged sources for approaching the regional socio-economic disparities.

Countries with great economic regional disparities in development have been labelled by Trebilcock, following G. Myrdal, as having a "dual economy of backwardness." This type of backwardness has severe effects on economic development:

> The worst effects seem to be concentrated among ... the late developers attempting industrial growth but carrying the incubus of large, geographically defined, regions of immiserization. This is the dualism of backwardness...and it is probable that its ill-effects may intensify rather than diminish as growth is achieved in the modern sector....as the modern sector grows, so it sucks capital and labor away from the traditional sector, intensifying both its own development and the pauperization of the primitive region, stretching the gap from both sides.... Perhaps the most considerable ... cost of this economy fracture lay in the small size of the viable market which dualism imposed.... Primitive sectors could retaliate for their accelerating pauperization at the hands of the industrial regions by denying to the latter significant shares of the "national market". (Trebilcock, 1981:317,318)

The Portuguese economy at the turn of the nineteenth century is best described as a dual economy of backwardness. The country's G.N.P. could have been growing at rates much higher than the ones previously proposed (22), and Portuguese industrial development could have been paralleling the industrial development of other advanced economies (Reis,1987:213,214), without either of these factors affecting entire regions of the country. In other words, growth could have been occurring in some regions while others were suffering recession.

---

22 David Justino (1987) revised Bairoch's (1976, 1976) estimations of the Portuguese GNP. Justino estimated that between 1870 and 1910 the yearly growth rates of the GNP was .66 instead of .2 as estimated by Bairoch, that is, three times higher.

Such a possibility raises a hypothesis: in the pauperized regions, lack of job vacancies was leading to out-migration (emigration and internal migration), while in the advanced regions, in-migration was occurring due to new job opportunities. In the next section, I look at mobility, urbanization, and labor market evolution by age, sex, and district between 1890 and 1930, in order to test this hypothesis.

INTERNAL MOBILITY

The Portuguese censuses (1890 to 1930) do not give any direct information about population mobility. The date for enumeration, December 1st, was especially chosen for being in "a period of the year when the population fluctuates less" (Census of 1890, Vol.I,p.XV).
It is known that northern populations traditionally transversed the country for the southern harvests and crossed the Spanish border in search of seasonal agricultural work (e.g. Brettell, 1981,1986). The censuses lack information for measuring this type of seasonal migration. Given the time span between enumerations, the censuses also provide little data on "short-term temporary migration" lasting one to five years.

There are, however, some crude indicators in the censuses that shed some light on internal mobility trends for this period. The first indicator is the place of birth by district, given in all the censuses under consideration. According to this variable, more than 90 percent of the

Portuguese population lived in their district of birth. The
country's share of those "resident in their districts of
birth" was respectively 94 percent in 1890, 93 percent in
1900, 92 percent in 1911, and 92 percent in 1930 (23). Only
two districts, Lisbon and Oporto, consistently had more than
the national average share of residents living outside their
districts of birth. The two cities of Lisbon and Oporto
alone (in the districts of the same name) had, in 1890,
respectively 37 percent and 29 percent of the national
population residing outside their native districts. Clearly
those cities were the greatest poles of attraction during
the whole period.

The share of the resident population born outside their
district of residence, for the whole country, increased from
5.7 percent to 8.2 percent between 1890 to 1930. From 1890
to 1900, 19 districts experienced an increase in their share
of residents born outside their borders. There were only
four districts-- Oporto, Lisbon, Portalegre, and Evora--
where this share exceeded the national average, however.
Lisbon had 25 percent of its residents born outside the
district, which was more then twice the figure for second-

---

23 See Table A:4 in Appendix 1. Although the administrative
unit "concelho" is outside the scope of my analysis, it is
interesting to note that the percentage of the population
born in their concelhos of residence was extremely high --
90 percent in 1890, 87 percent in 1900, 86 percent in 1911,
and 87 percent in 1930. Since the average size of the
concelho (316 square kilometers) was 1/14 of the average
size of districts (4388 square kilometers), such high
percentages further substantiate my claim that the bulk of
the population remained in their native areas (when not
abandoning the country entirely). Moreover, the range of
movement for the bulk of the population remained quite
restricted during the period, 316 square kilometers on
average.

ranking Oporto. From 1900 to 1911 the number of districts with an increasing proportion of residents born outside the borders dropped to 13. Only Oporto, Lisbon, and Evora remained above the national average, and the gap between Lisbon and Oporto widened. In the last period, 1911-1930, only seven districts increased their share of residents born outside their borders (24), and only Lisbon remained above the national average.

Summing up, we can say that, quite apart from Lisbon, the country experienced some increase in internal mobility between 1890 and 1900. From 1911 to 1930, the movement contracted, and even areas of great attraction earlier, such as Oporto, suffered major decreases in their shares of non-native residents. This information points to a restricted demand for labor outside the districts of Lisbon and Oporto, and a decline in the initially slight internal movement, particularly from 1911 on.

Still, we need at least a crude measure of what happened to that small segment of the population that did move. To determine which districts were experiencing net in- and out-migration, I estimated the expected population (total or "de facto" and active) for 1900, 1911, and 1930, holding all other factors constant. The expected population was then subtracted from the existing population to determine which districts lost or gained population, relative to other areas.

---

24 This increase was, both in absolute and relative terms, quite insignificant (except in Lisbon). The Census of 1930 (Vol. 5, p.12) remarks that internal mobility was decreasing.

The formula used is as follows: All things being equal, $[(P_{DN} - P_{DO}) / P_O * P_N]$ must equal zero if there were no population movement, where:

P_{DN} = population of each district at the end of the period;

P_{DO} = population of each district in the beginning of the period;

P_N = total population of the country at the end of the period;

P_O = total population of the country in the beginning of the period.

The full results are given in Tables A:5 in Appendix 1. The results can be briefly summarized. Throughout the whole period, the provinces of Minho (with the exception of Oporto district), Tras-Os-Montes, Beiras, and Algarve, and the archipelago of the Azores "lost" expected population; the provinces of Extremadura and Alentejo, and the archipelago of Madeira, gained population. Given the magnitude of the difference between its expected and actual population (54688; 75016; 166706 respectively), the district of Lisbon probably received population from all the other districts. The more modest gains found for Oporto (12081; 22124; 33374 respectively) can probably be attributed to the northern surrounding districts alone. The even more modest gains of the districts of Leiria, Santarem, Portalegre, Evora, and Beja were the combined result of an exodus from the neighboring districts and, at least in part, a transformation of the traditional seasonal migrants from the north into permanent settlers (25).

If we accept that the population shifts taking place were labor oriented, then the different levels of attraction found must be connected to economic differences between the receiving districts. In other words, the level of attraction of a district is primarily a function of its job market.

O.Ribeiro argues that the single most powerful human factor in the distribution of the Portuguese population was rural life (O.Ribeiro,1955:113). Such an hypothesis would explain the population shift from the northern districts towards Leiria, Santarem, Portalegre, Evora, and Beja, since there was an higher labor demand for agricultural workers in these areas. At the same time, there was another movement going on in the direction of Oporto and Lisbon, which was associated with urban job opportunities or urban attraction rather than agriculture.(26). The obvious next step is to

---

25 I will return to this point later. Briefly I believe that the explanation of the movements for these districts must be along the following lines: the agricultural development of these districts after the protectionist tariffs of the 1890's and the use of chemical fertilizers in the beginning of the twentieth century created a higher demand for labor.
26 I am using the word attraction to refer to the dislocation to the cities based more on rumor that on the real creation of job opportunities. Michael P.Todaro put the problem the following way:"Field studies and econometrics analyses indicate the importance of the economic motive in the decision to migrate. Econometrics estimates of migration functions have also demonstrated that the probability of urban employment, independent of the differences in actual rural and urban wages, contributes significantly to the explanation of variance among time periods and subgroups of the rural population in rates of urban migration."
(M.Todaro, 1985: 181)

look at the urban movement, in an attempt to clarify this point further.

URBAN POPULATION

Information on the urban population is given in the censuses of 1890, 1900, and 1911, under two headings: "urban population by district" and "population living in cities." Figures for the two categories do not agree, for the size of the "urban population" is about twice that for "population living in cities". There is no indication of what criterion was used to create each category. (27)   I decided to base my analysis on the "people living in cities" because that enables me to control for city size.

Scholars differ on what should be considered an urban setting.   The number of people necessary to assure the existence of urban functions is one of the most controversial topics; common choices for lower limits range from 1000 to 5000 inhabitants. (28)   A reasonable breakdown suggested by the Portuguese data is as follows: small cities (20 cases in 1890) between 2.9 thousand and 10 thousand inhabitants; medium sized cities (11 cases in 1890) between

27 If we compare the share of the urban population to the total population for 1890, according to both sources of information (Census of 1890, vol.I, p.LXXXIV and p.30), the results are: for "urban population" 32 percent, and for "people living in cities" 15 percent.
28 A. Ferrin Weber's choice is one thousand inhabitants for the lower limit.   P.Bairoch prefers five thousand, and Ch.Pouthas three thousand inhabitants. (Adna Ferrin Weber,The Growth of Cities in the Nineteenth Century. N.Y.,1969 (1899); and B. Lepetit and J.Royer, Croissance et taille des villes:contribution a l'etude de l'urbanization de la France au debut du XIXieme siecle. Annales E.S.C.,#5,1980,p.987/1010).

10 and 30 thousand inhabitants; and big cities (2 cases in 1890) over 100 thousand inhabitants.(29) It seems that the cut-off points indicated by the data make more sense than any other grouping.

Information on the population and location of the thirty-three Portuguese cities in 1890 and 1911 is given in Table A:6 in Appendix 1. Table III:III summarizes Table A:6 by city size.

TABLE III:III - POPULATION RESIDENT IN CITIES OVER TWO THOUSAND INHABITANTS BY CITY SIZE

CITY SIZE	1890	1900	1911
BIG CITIES TOTAL (N=2)	447945	523964	629368
PERCENTAGE OF TOTAL URBAN	8.9	9.6	10.5
MEDIUM CITIES TOTAL (N=11)	172291	183137	194056
PERCENTAGE OF TOTAL URBAN	3.4	3.3	3.2
SMALL CITIES TOTAL (N=20)	140786	151669	162107
PERCENTAGE OF TOTAL URBAN	2.8	2.8	2.7
URBAN POPULATION TOTAL	761022	858770	985531

Source: Censuses of 1890, 1900, 1911

The figures in Table III:III show that the urban population grew in absolute terms from 1890 to 1911 in all classes of cities. This would be expected, since the total population was also growing in absolute terms during this period.

29 There was one city listed with a population below one thousand inhabitants in 1890, but it was clearly not representative and was disregarded. The breakdown suggested by the data differs from Charles Pouthas' categories only in the last cut-off point. This author considers urban settings with more than twenty thousand inhabitants to be big cities. For Portugal in 1890, this would include Braga (23,089 inhabitants) and Lisbon (301,206 inhabitants) in the same category and exclude Funchal (18,778 inhabitants) (in B.Lepetit and J.Royer, 1980:899).

More important are differences in the pattern of growth
by city size. It is clear from Table III:III that large
cities (Lisbon and Oporto) were growing faster than the
medium-sized and small cities. Moreover, the share of the
total population in medium and small cities slightly
declined (for the medium 3.4, 3.3, 3.2 percent respectively
and small 2.8, 2.8, 2.7 percent respectively), while it
increased for Lisbon and Oporto (8.9, 9.6, 10.5 percent
respectively). In other words, the country's urban growth
can be largely attributed to the growth of the two big
cities, Lisbon and Oporto. Outside the largest cities,
urbanization per se did not attract population, particularly
from 1900 to 1911. In relative terms, by 1900, medium and
small cities had ceased to grow, and they even experienced a
slight decrease in their percentage of the total population
from 1900-1911.

Computation of the difference between expected and actual
urban population by district (1890 - 1911) indicates that
over two-thirds of the districts suffered losses in their
expected urban populations. They also show that four
districts in 1890-1900, and five in 1900-1911, had negative
rates of growth. Eleven of the districts experienced
decreases in their rates of urban growth between 1890-1900
and 1900-1911. Moreover, except for Lisbon and Oporto
districts, all the other districts' urban growth rates were
below the national rate in at least one period.

The pattern of urban growth in Portugal between 1890 and
1911 is consistent with my earlier findings on internal
mobility and economic structure. The gap between Lisbon and

Oporto and the rest of the country is clear. My hypothesis
that population movements were due to the attraction of
Lisbon and Oporto and to the new opportunities in
agricultural work in the south (particularly from 1900 to
1911) receives further confirmation.

These findings also raise an interesting methodological
problem. When analyzing economic development, scholars tend
to use the total urban growth of a country to measure
economic development. This neglects the asymmetries of
development and can conceal the fact that urban growth could
be attributed mainly to one or two cities. Often during the
Old Regime, one city (generally the capital) or two cities
were growing disproportionately, relative to the country's
overall level of urbanization. The asymmetries these major
cities created mirrored the general imbalances of Old Regime
political and socio-economic structure. As Braudel
remarked, big cities were primarily the locus of state
formation and centralization, and were sometimes
international emporiums for goods and money. Smaller cities
were where the industrial revolution took place
(Braudel,1979, V.I:453-491).

In sum, I would stress the general lack of vitality of
the Portuguese urban network, and the disproportionate
weight that the cities of Lisbon and Oporto had within it.
Both facts confirm my contention in the previous section
that the Portuguese economy at the turn of the nineteenth
century was a typical "dual economy of backwardness."
Furthermore, the gap between the advanced poles (the South)

and the pauperized areas (the North and the Islands) was widening (30).

GENERAL DESCRIPTION OF THE PORTUGUESE LABOR FORCE

Between 1890 and 1930, the Portuguese labor force decreased at an annual rate of -.01 percent, while the population at risk-- here considered to be those age 10 and over (31)-- showed a positive annual growth rate of .76 percent. Labor force participation rates indicate that the decrease in the gainfully employed population was constant and marked throughout the whole period. Table III:IV summarizes this evolution.

---

30 While I was finishing the revision of this work, I came across Nunes' (1989) work on Portuguese urbanization. Nunes based her analysis in a demographic criterium (places with five thousand inhabitants) while I used an administrative/demographic criterium. Given the differences of criteria, our results are not readily comparable, however, and except for small size cities, her findings support the above conclusions.
31 I have considered 10 years of age as the lower limit. Earlier calculations, with a lower limit of 14 years of age, gave a surplus for the active population in the age group under 20. Only in 1915 was industrial labor for minors less than 12 years of age forbidden by law (Carqueja, 1916:218).

TABLE III:IV - **LABOR FORCE 1890 - 1930**

POPULATION	1890	1900	1911	1930
LABOR FORCE	2530450	2457253	2544964	2516693
POP.AT RISK	3905426	4175972	4550597	5294048
LABOR FORCE PARTICIPATION RATES (%)	65	59	56	48
LABOR FORCE RELATIVE TO 1890	100	97	101	99
POP.AT RISK RELATIVE TO 1890	100	107	117	136

Source: Portuguese censuses at given year

Between 1890 and 1930, the labor force participation rate for both sexes combined dropped 17 percentage points. The decline was particularly marked between 1890 and 1900 (6 percentage points) and between 1911 and 1930 (8 percentage points). Moreover, in every enumeration year except 1911, the absolute size of the labor force fell below that of 1890. This contraction of the labor force can be attributed to drop-out from the job market, since the size of the population of working age was increasing.

The main reason for the decrease of the active population was a major decline in the female labor force. Between 1890 and 1930, the female labor force had a negative annual growth rate of -.71 percent. This decrease was due not to a drop in the female population age 10 and over (32), but rather to women's increasing exclusion and departure from the labor force. As Table III:V illustrates, over 200,000

---

32 Female population of 10 years of age and over grew at an annual rate of .78 percent between 1890 - 1930.

fewer women were in the labor force in 1930 than in 1890. The labor force participation rate for women age ten and older fell from 45 percent to 25 percent over that period.

TABLE III:V - LABOR FORCE BY SEX   1890 - 1930

YEAR	MALES	PARTIC. RATE	FEMALES	PARTIC. RATE
1890				
POPULATION	1849333	100	2056093	100
LABOR FORCE	1609250	87	921200	45
1900				
POPULATION	1957971	100	2218001	100
LABOR FORCE	1726293	88	730960	33
1911				
POPULATION	2113218	100	2437379	100
LABOR FORCE	1848119	87	696845	29
1930				
POPULATION	2479214	100	2814834	100
LABOR FORCE	1823805	74	692888	25

Source: Portuguese censuses at given year

Although the male labor force had a positive overall annual growth rate of .31 percent, this did not keep pace with the overall annual growth rate of .74 percent for the male population of working age. In relative terms, the male labor force participation rate remained almost stable from 1890 to 1911, and then dropped 14 percentage points by 1930.

One possible explanation for the decrease in female labor force participation is modern economic development. It has been noted that during the process of modernization, female participation in the labor force tends to decline. This tendency has been explained by the decreasing importance of "traditional" occupational activities (such as female-

oriented service in the household) in favor of "new"
occupational activities (such as male-oriented metalworking
and transportation). But when we compute the annual growth
rate for the female labor force between 1890 and 1930 for
all occupational groups except household servants, the
decrease is even greater, -1.02 percent, indicating that
other factors were at work in the Portuguese case.
Moreover, this explanation does not account for the decline
in male labor force participation noted above.

Another common explanation for the decline in labor force
participation rates during this period is the increasing
importance of schooling. In the Portuguese case, however,
this explanation can be rejected. Illiteracy rates did not
change significantly during this period. Furthermore, the
younger age groups of the labor force do not present a
pattern of behavior different from the older age groups.

A more plausible explanation is a deterioration of labor
market conditions between these 1890 and 1930. This
deterioration forced women out of the job market and
precluded entry of an important segment of female cohorts
reaching working age. This deterioration had a similar but
less marked impact on males of working age, especially from
1911 to 1930.

Analysis by age and by sex of both the national
population at risk and the active population (33) indicates
that female participation rates decreased throughout the

---

33 Such an analysis is restricted by the fact that the 1930
census does not indicate age by occupation, and that the
previous ones do not furnish the age distribution for
servants in the household.

whole period, and for all age groups (see Table A:7 in
Appendix 1). The drop was more accentuated for the age
group 60 and older (20 points), and slightly less
accentuated for those age 20-39 (15 points).

The analysis also indicates that the slight increase,
from 1890 to 1900, of male participation in the active
population (2 points), was due to a slight increase in the
participation rate of two age groups, 20-39 and 40-59 years
of age. From 1911 to 1930 male overall participation rates
dropped markedly (14 points). The specific age pattern for
the 1920's cannot be identified, but, given the magnitude of
the fall, all male age groups must have been affected.

In conclusion, it seems that the deterioration of the job
market from 1890 to 1930 reduced female participation in all
active age groups throughout the whole period. At least
from 1900 to 1911, declining opportunities also affected all
male active age groups, except those 20-39 years of age.
Clearly job opportunities were not keeping pace with the
growth of the male population at risk. From 1911 to 1930
the drop in male participation rates was so marked that all
age groups must have been affected.

CHANGES AT THE DISTRICT LEVEL

Between 1890 and 1930, we verified a major decrease in
the active population of Portugal (see Tables A:8 to A:10 in
Appendix 1) (34). The loss, which was essentially due to

---

34 The decrease was not homogeneous across the country. The
biggest increases occurred in the district of Lisbon:

females leaving the labor force, covered almost the whole country. The exceptions were really very few. Two districts in 1900 show some increase in the female labor force relative to 1890 (Braga, and Aveiro); one district marked an increase in 1911 (Lisbon); and two districts registered gains in 1930 (Lisbon, and Funchal). The major decreases occurred in the districts of Vila Real, Angra do Heroismo, and Horta (35).

During the whole period from 1890 to 1930, only the Azores consistently lost male population relative to 1890, for both the working ages and the gainfully employed. The mainland districts do not present such a clear pattern. By 1930 the Northern districts (Vila Real, Bragança, Vizeu, Guarda, and Castelo Branco) had lost male population, while the Southern districts (Leiria, Santarem, Lisbon, Portalegre, Evora, and Beja) had gained.

The mainland districts that lost active male population do not show a corresponding decrease in their male population at risk, except in the districts of Vila Real and Bragança where the male population 10 years of age and over also decreased in absolute terms relative to 1890. We already documented (in the section on internal mobility)

---

relative to 1890, the employed population was 9 percentage points higher in 1900, 28 in 1911, and 52 in 1930.
These figures are consistent with the findings on internal mobility: except for the insular district of Funchal, and the northern districts of Braga and Oporto, the North and the islands lost active population relative to 1890, while the South gained.
35   The decrease in female gainfully employed in these three districts is associated with a decrease (or the smallest increase recorded) in female population at risk, thus it is probably connected with the migratory trends of these districts.

that spatial relocation of the male active population from
the North to the South occurred during this period. We now
have further evidence that this shift, particularly marked
for the male labor force, was more related to the job market
opportunities than to demographic trends.

CHANGES IN PARTICIPATION RATES AT THE DISTRICT LEVEL

The national decrease in participation rates for males
from 1911 to 1930, and for females throughout the whole
period, affected all of the districts. But male
participation rates were much more homogeneous than female
participation rates.

Male participation rates present small ranges and great
concentration, while female participation rates show wide
ranges and great dispersion. In over two-thirds of the
cases,(36) the male participation rate for the district was
identical to the national rate, while the female
participation rate for the district was below the national
female participation rate in at least half of the cases.

The wide range found for female participation rates can
be attributed to marked regional dualism. In the seven
northernmost districts (Viana, Braga, Oporto, Vila Real,
Bragança, Aveiro, and Vizeu), female participation rates
were very high, relative to the country's overall female
participation rate, while in the South and the islands they
were very low. It is tempting to attribute this dualism to
emigration, common denominator of all the seven northern

36 Each district in each census year equals one case.

districts.   But their dissimilarity from the participation rates for the islands suggests that emigration did not produce the same outcome in all regions.

The traditional sexual division of labor was certainly one of the reasons for the regional dualism found between the North and the South of the mainland. A second reason was the existence of two different rural property structures, each with complementary labor demands.

The traditional engagement of women in agricultural activities in the northern part of the country was related to male emigration and to male seasonal migration to other areas of the country. The small size of the landholdings in the North, particularly in the Minho province (less than one hectare in 1891), was one of the reasons why men emigrated or migrated, thereby increasing female labor force participation. Even when men stayed, the average farm size was so small that a great number of these farmholdings were insufficient to sustain the household on their production, obliging men to look for other activities and women to attend to the family farmland. Moreover, land fragmentation and the low productivity associated with it must also have driven a significant number of women to look for work outside their family unit, which would explain the overrepresentation of older age groups in the labor force of this region and the disproportionate number of females in personal service during the whole period. The fact that textiles were centered in the northern part of the country also opened up job opportunities for women, reinforcing the pattern just described (37).

But emigration was equally affecting the islands without producing similarly heightened female participation rates. The reason for the difference in female participation in the labor force in the two migratory areas (the North of the mainland and the islands) can be explained by the higher female participation in the migratory flow from the islands. Since the 1850's at least (see the following chapter) there were two migratory patterns in Portugal. The exodus from the mainland was constituted almost entirely (over 75 percent) by young adult males, while in the islands the corresponding figure was less than 60 percent. Literary evidence suggests that propertyholding was concentrated in a small number of hands in the Azores (Bento,1987 and Correia da Cunha,1963). The landless peasantry must thus have been comparatively larger in the islands than in the Northern regions of the mainland, which would explain a weaker attachment to the land and the lack of a marked sexual division of agricultural labor in the islands. Furthermore, these differences in property structure would explain higher female participation in emigration from the islands than from the northern regions of the mainland.

Male labor force participation rates show much less regional variation. 1930 is the first year in which we find districts falling below the national male participation rate by 5 or more percentage points. These districts were Horta

---

37 Brettell's (1986) analysis of the parish of Lanhezes (Minho province) supports the above description.

in the Azores, and Guarda and Castelo Branco on the
mainland. Given the earlier homogeneity of male
participation rates, these districts were probably the most
affected by the marked deterioration of the job market that
took place from 1911 to 1930.

The influence of emigration is also revealed in the age
structure of the labor force by district. In the non-
migratory districts-- Santarem, Lisboa, Portalegre, and
Evora-- men in the younger and the older age groups made up
a slightly smaller share of the male labor force than was
the case for the rest of the country (38). In the Azorean
islands and in Viana, the older group had a higher
proportion active than in the rest of the country. For
females, two distinct patterns merit note. The districts of
Oporto and Lisbon had a much younger female labor force than
the rest of the country; the Azorean districts of Angra and
Horta had much older active populations than the rest of the
districts.

To sum up, the Portuguese labor force contracted between
1890 and 1930. Lack of job opportunities increasingly
displaced a growing segment of the population of working
age. Although both sexes were affected, the female labor
force suffered the most severe blow. The age structure of
the labor force, when compared to the country's age
structure, shows overrepresentation for both sexes in the
most active years in life (20-59 years of age), and
underrepresentation for those under 20 years of age. Among

38 This finding substantiates my claim that the shift of
population from the northern regions to the southern regions
occurred preferentially in the most active age groups.

those 60 years and over, we found that female labor force, when compared to the population at risk, was consistently overrepresented, while in the male labor force in this age group kept pace with the population.

The regional distribution of the labor force by district presents distinctive traits for each sex. The female labor force varied more by region and was disproportionately centered in the northern districts. For women, the two main forces at play were the attraction of cities and emigration. For men, regional shifts in agriculture and emigration were key. The contraction of the younger and older age group in the male labor force of some districts was due to the redistribution of the male active population from North to South, and the overrepresentation of the older groups in the Azorean districts can be explained by emigration.

Most of the disparities in the sex composition and regional distribution of the Portuguese labor force by district can be attributed to the country's economic structure. The following analysis of the Portuguese labor force by economic sector will clarify the most striking disparities uncovered so far.

LABOR FORCE BY ECONOMIC SECTOR

Up to 1930 the character of the Portuguese labor force was determined by the primary sector. In 1890, this sector engaged 62 percent of the Portuguese labor force, and in 1930 it still engaged 51 percent of the working population. The relative importance of the primary sector declined between these two dates, but not enough to give the Portuguese labor force a modern appearance. In the 1880's France, Germany and Great Britain already had a smaller share of the labor force engaged in the primary sector than Portugal had in 1930 (39).

Until 1930 the Portuguese census gave a breakdown by occupation within economic sectors for the primary and tertiary sectors; for the manufacturing sector only the total was furnished. This aggregation reduces the possibilities for analysis, especially of the development of key "modern" activities, such as chemicals and heavy industry. The data do, however, allow us to address changes in the volume of the labor force by economic sector and by age, sex, and region. I aggregated the activities by sector as follows: for the primary sector, all activities connected with extractive industries; for the secondary sector, all activities connected with the transformation of raw materials or production of goods; for the tertiary sector, all activities connected with distribution and services.

---

39 In Great Britain in 1881 the share of the active population in the primary sector was 18 percent; in Germany in 1882 it was 50 percent; and in France in 1886 it was 49 percent (Bairoch, 1968:84-107).

A summary of the distribution of the Portuguese labor force by sector and activity is give in Table III:VI.

TABLE III:VI - DISTRIBUTION OF THE PORTUGUESE LABOR FORCE BY ECONOMIC SECTOR, 1890 - 1930 (IN PERCENTAGE)

SECTOR	1890	1900	1911	1930
PRIMARY	61.95	62.40	57.80	51.16
AGRICULTURE	60.72	61.35	56.68	49.15
FISHING	1.05	0.87	0.76	1.57
MINING AND QUARRYING	0.18	0.18	0.36	0.44
SECONDARY	17.69	18.53	21.52	18.59
INDUSTRY	17.69	18.53	21.52	18.59
TERTIARY	20.36	19.06	20.68	30.27
TRANSPORTATION	2.07	2.70	3.02	2.86
COMMERCE	4.08	5.77	6.06	5.78
PROTECTIVE FORCES	1.62	1.52	1.51	2.17
PUBLIC ADMINISTRATION	0.67	0.60	0.63	1.34
LIBERAL PROFESSIONS	1.16	1.43	1.62	1.53
DOMESTIC WORK	5.82	2.69	1.61	9.09
SERVANTS	4.94	4.35	6.23	7.50
TOTAL	100	100	100	100
LABOR FORCE IN THOUSANDS	2530	2457	2545	2517

Source: Basic Tables A:11 to A:14 in Appendix 1

Table III:VI will be the reference point for the following analysis of the Portuguese active population by economic sector.

PRIMARY SECTOR

Throughout the period from 1890 to 1930, the primary sector predominated in terms of its share of the active population. Within this sector, fishing and mining activities were of little importance, never encompassing more than 2 percent of the country's labor force.

Agricultural activities engaged the great majority of the Portuguese labor force.

FISHING AND MINING ACTIVITIES BY DISTRICT

Fishing and mining activities had a marked regional pattern. Fishing was particularly centered in four districts: Oporto, Aveiro, Lisbon, and Faro. The primacy of the first three districts can be explained by their geographical location and their proximity to the country's major urban concentrations, Lisbon, Oporto, and Coimbra. Faro's position was the result of a growing specialization according to the natural resources of this region. A foodstuff industry, based on sardines and tuna, grew significantly in this region, which was the ideal location for catching both types of fish (40).

Like fishing, mining had strong regional concentrations. The population engaged in this activity was centered in four districts: Oporto, Aveiro, Lisbon, and Beja (particularly the last). Mining offered job opportunities to less than 1 percent of the Portuguese labor force.

AGRICULTURAL WORKS

The share of the active population engaged in agriculture in Portugal was much greater than that in any other activity during our period. By 1930 the agricultural labor force of

40 In 1890 there were 5.3 thousand people gainfully employed in fishing activities in Faro's district. In 1930 their number had jumped to 8.5 thousand-- representing 8 percent of the total active population of this district.

the country still incorporated 49 percent of the country's
total labor force.

The population engaged in agriculture dropped in both
relative and absolute terms from 1890 to 1930. Its annual
rate of growth, from 1890 to 1930, was -.54 percent, and
all intercensal periods examined exhibit negative rates of
growth: 1890-1900 (-.19 percent); 1900-1911 (-.40 percent);
1911-1930 (-.81 percent). But in relative terms the share
of the country's overall labor force engaged in agriculture
increased between 1890 and 1900 (see Table III:III). This
finding is absolutely at variance with that anticipated.
As A.Miller has stated:

> That the share of agriculture in a country's work
> force goes down in the course of economic
> development appears to be one of the very few
> eternal verities uncovered by the social
> sciences. (A. Miller,1971:1)

Undermining, even slightly, one of the "eternal verities"
of the social sciences has its costs, since it leaves us
with the question-- how did this happen? Two possible
explanations are regional specialization and changes in age
structure. We can begin to test the first hypothesis by
comparing the regional distribution of the agricultural
labor force by district in 1890 and 1930 (41).

---

41 Another possibility is that the inclusion of female labor
force is biasing my results. But excluding female
participation would be hard to defend. In 1930, for
example, over 120 thousand females were hired workers in
agriculture. To exclude them from the analysis would be to
disregard 15 percent of the labor force engaged in
agriculture.

REGIONAL PATTERN

On the basis of agricultural predominance, Portugal was clearly divided into two parts: the districts of Oporto and Lisbon (with a very low proportion of their labor force in agriculture), and the rest of the country (with proportions in agriculture similar to or higher than the national share in agriculture). If Lisbon and Oporto are left aside, the rest of the country could also be divided between the north and the south, for the northern districts consistently had higher proportions of their population in agriculture. But this North-South gap was closing, at least in terms of the relative share of the labor force engaged in agricultural work. Still, only in the northern districts was more than half of the labor force found in agriculture by 1930.

The annual rates of growth of the economically active population in agriculture by district suggest that, not only were the northern districts losing their agricultural labor force, but also the rate of decrease was accentuating over time. These figures also give us the first real indication of why the relative share of the total active population engaged in agriculture rose between 1890 and 1900. Between these censuses, twelve out of twenty-one districts had a positive annual rate of growth of their active population in agriculture. In other words, in a period marked by decrease in the total labor force in agriculture, more than half of the districts registered increases in the absolute number of workers engaged in agriculture. The predominance of the agricultural sector, relative to the country's labor force, reached its peak in 1900, when eighteen districts had over 60 percent of their labor force in agriculture, compared to 15 districts in 1890, 16 in 1911, and 9 districts in 1930.

The analysis by district indicates that, until 1900, we can speak of a shift away from the agricultural sector only for the north of Portugal. After 1900, the Azorean islands joined the north in the movement away from agriculture, but neither the south nor Madeira experienced any major change from 1900 to 1930.

For the period 1890 to 1930, seven northern districts (Viana, Braga, Porto, Vila Real, Bragança, Aveiro, and Vizeu) consistently had a larger share of the female population in agriculture than did the rest of the country. Five districts (Coimbra, Guarda, Castelo Branco, and Santarem) had an intermediate position between the seven northern districts and the five southern and the three insular districts. In the southernmost and the insular districts, the female share in agriculture dropped even more markedly than in the rest of the country.

Between 1890 and 1911, there were some changes in the age structure of the agricultural labor force, when compared with the age structure of the country's total labor force (42).

In 1890, males were overrepresented in agriculture in all age groups, except 20-39 years of age, when compared to the age structure of the total male active population. A more distinct pattern had emerged by 1900 and 1911, when the male

42 As noted, an analysis of age by occupation can only be carried out for the years of 1890, 1900, and 1911.

labor force in agriculture was clearly overrepresented in the younger and the older age groups (under 20 and 60 and older).

For women the pattern was quite different. Between 1890 and 1911, the female labor force in agriculture shifted from an overrepresentation of the youngest age group (under 20 years of age) to a overrepresentation of the two older age groups (40-59 and 60 and older), relative to the age structure of the total female labor force.

The male labor force engaged in agriculture was younger than the female agricultural labor force, and this difference became more pronounced in each succeeding period. While the share of the male agricultural labor force aged 40 years and older dropped from 44 percent in 1890 to 41 percent in 1911, the corresponding female share rose from 41 percent to 49 percent.

More than half of the female agricultural labor force in all age groups was concentrated in seven northern districts (Viana, Braga, Oporto, Vila Real, Bragança, Aveiro, and Vizeu). Between 1890 and 1930, five southern districts (Santarem, Lisboa, Portalegre, Evora, and Beja) were gaining an increasing share of the country's female agricultural labor force. They were doing so by an accentuated growth in the younger age group, even as young women were constituting a smaller share of female agricultural workers nationally.

The age structure of female agricultural labor changed in Portugal according to two different patterns. In the districts where the female active population in agriculture was diminishing, older women made up an increasing share of the female agricultural labor force. In the districts gaining an increasing share of the country's female agricultural labor force, younger women in particular were being hired.

The explanation for the aging of the female active population engaged in agriculture in those districts that were losing agricultural female labor force is probably complex, and related to deteriorating labor market conditions. Changes in the female population engaged in agricultural work in the islands, on the other hand, was linked to familial emigration. In addition, competing demand for young female workers in the secondary sector, both in the north and in Madeira, produced low agricultural participation rates for women under 40.

Were differential in the age structure of men and women workers, found in agriculture, also evident in other sectors? The answer is yes, as Table III:VII shows:

TABLE III:VII -   AGE STRUCTURE IN AGRICULTURE, INDUSTRY AND
    SERVICES   1890 - 1911 IN PERCENTAGE BY SEX AND AGE GROUP

MALES

YEAR/SECTOR	M<20	M20-39	M40-59	M>60
1890				
AGRICULTURE	22.68	33.84	28.09	15.39
INDUSTRY	19.78	44.21	27.02	8.99
SERVICES	11.30	51.59	28.11	9.00
1900				
AGRICULTURE	23.39	35.61	26.82	14.18
INDUSTRY	21.12	44.44	26.31	8.13
SERVICES	12.76	50.24	28.52	8.49
1911				
AGRICULTURE	22.78	36.76	26.08	14.39
INDUSTRY	21.79	44.91	25.26	8.03
SERVICES	14.03	49.74	28.27	7.95

FEMALES

	F<20	F20-39	F40-59	F>60
1890				
AGRICULTURE	23.75	35.31	27.03	13.91
INDUSTRY	22.05	42.23	24.86	10.85
SERVICES	10.84	29.36	33.59	26.21
1900				
AGRICULTURE	21.79	34.63	27.88	15.71
INDUSTRY	28.05	46.44	18.75	6.77
SERVICES	7.55	30.64	33.72	28.09
1911				
AGRICULTURE	16.76	34.20	29.53	19.51
INDUSTRY	25.71	48.09	19.76	6.45
SERVICES	12.38	38.05	31.41	18.16

Source: Table A:15 in Appendix 1
Note: Servants in the household not included

Table III:VII indicates that the age structure for males in
industry tended to be older than that for females in the
same sector, but the inverse was true in the tertiary sector
(43).

---

43 Servants in the household not included. As noted, the
censuses do not give information on age for this group.

We can also compare the age structure in agricultural work with the age structure in industry and services for each sex. Males in both the youngest and the oldest age groups were consistently overrepresented in agriculture throughout the period from 1890 to 1930. This finding is in accordance with a hypothesis suggested by A. Miller:

> Our hypothesis with regard to the age structure is that expanding -- or modern -- sectors will tend to have disproportionate numbers of young adults, while more traditional activities will engage the youngest entrants, or the older workers, or both, in greater than the average proportions. (Miller, 1971:9)

For females, this hypothesis seems not to hold so well. Using the age structure of women agricultural workers as a basis of comparison, we find, from 1900 on, an overrepresentation of the youngest age group (under age 20) in industry, and an overrepresentation of the oldest age group (age 60 and older) in the tertiary sector. Apart from the influence of emigratory trends of the period (44), the discrepancy between Miller's hypothesis and the Portuguese data can be attributed to the peculiarities of the regional distribution of the female labor force, and to the small range of activities open to women outside the agricultural sector.

Work opportunities for women in both agriculture and industry were centered in the northern part of the country. The drop in the female agricultural labor force resulting from marked withdrawal by young women can be explained partially by alternative job opportunities in the textile

---

44 Emigration tended to drive out of the country the most active age groups.

industries of this area. During this period, a growing
share of female population under 20 years of age was drawn
into this industry. Servants in the household, another job
category that absorbed preferentially young women, was
growing simultaneously, particularly in the northern
districts. The overrepresentation in services found for the
female population age 60 and older (compared to their share
in agriculture and industry) was due to the concentration of
older females in retail trade and domestic work in the
tertiary sector.

In conclusion, it is not Miller's hypothesis that is
unsound. Rather, Portuguese women workers were concentrated
in regions where the most active members were leaving the
country in increasing numbers, or were entering a small
number of activities outside agriculture.

THE MANUFACTURING SECTOR

Between 1890 and 1930, the yearly rates of growth of the
active population engaged in manufacturing and the yearly
rates of growth of the total active population followed
different paths. As noted, the Portuguese labor force
diminished at an annual rate of -.29 percent between 1890-
1900, but the industrial labor force grew at an annual rate
of .17 percent. Between 1900-1911 the active population
grew .32 percent annually, while the industrial labor force
increased much faster, 1.69 percent annually. Finally,
between 1911 and 1930 the active population diminished
again, at an annual rate of -.06 percent, while the

industrial active population decreased at a much higher speed, -.83 percent annually.

This lack of synchronism is not surprising. We have seen how overwhelmingly agricultural was the country's labor force until 1930, and how the weight of this primary activity shaped the country's occupational structure. There is, however, a second reason for the dissimilarity-- the high regional concentration of manufacturing. Two districts, Lisboa and Oporto, contained 39 percent of the country's industrial labor force in 1890. By 1930, their share of the total manufacturing workers had risen to 45 percent.

The regional industrial pattern had other notable characteristics. The concentration of the industrial labor force in the north, observed in 1890, began to dissipate after 1900. In absolute terms, and relative to 1890, the southern districts and the insular district of Funchal gained more industrial workers than did the rest of the country in the succeeding periods. The greatest decreases occurred in the northern mainland districts of Vila Real, Bragança, Vizeu, and Guarda, and in Angra and Horta in the Azorean islands. The biggest increases in the industrial labor force occurred in Lisbon, Faro, and Funchal.

The privileged position of the districts of Oporto and Lisbon, the dominant factor in unequal regional development during the whole period, tended to increase with time. The relative position of these two districts changed during the period, however; Oporto, which until 1900 had the highest share of the country's industrial labor force, lost its position as frontrunner to Lisbon after 1911. Differences in the sex and age composition of the labor force-- specially when occurring between the north and the rest of the country, or between Oporto and Lisbon--, help explain these changes in the manufacturing sector.

SEX COMPOSITION OF THE MANUFACTURING LABOR FORCE

The changes occurring in the industrial sector, and especially the big drop in industrial workers between 1911 and 1930, was predominantly due to women's withdrawal from the industrial sector. The male industrial labor force also decreased in both absolute and relative terms from 1911 to 1930. But the change for men was of much less magnitude than the transformation of the female industrial labor force (45).

Over time, the regional distribution of the industrial labor force for each sex tended to became concentrated in a smaller, but not totally overlapping, number of districts. For males these districts were, by order of concentration, Lisbon, Oporto, and with a wide gap from the first two, Braga and Aveiro. For females they were Oporto, Lisbon, and, again with a wide gap from the first two districts, Braga, Funchal, and Aveiro.

The four districts of the mainland-- Oporto, Lisbon, Braga, and Aveiro -- already had over 50 percent of the industrial labor force in 1890. By 1930 these districts had

---

45 There were 25 thousand fewer males employed in industry in 1930 than in 1911. The comparable figure for women was 55 thousand.

increased their share by more than 10 percentage points.
Funchal's industrial labor force is interesting for its
disproportionate share of the country's female labor force
(2.38 percent in 1890 and 9.36 percent in 1930), rather
than for its total share of the country's manufacturing
sector (2.11 percent in 1890 and 2.55 percent in 1930). By
contrast, Lisbon had a larger share of the total
manufacturing workers but a lower female industrial share
than the other four districts.

The findings match the expected course for a country's
economic development. This is, female labor force
participation tends to drop when traditional industries,
such as textiles, give away to modern industries, such as
metallurgy or chemicals.

At the same time a redistribution of the country's
industrial labor force is expected to occur when the
"domestic system" gives away to the "factory system". The
rationalization of the economy affects the place of work and
the forms of ownership, with both becoming more
concentrated. The development of capitalism produces areas
of specialization that supposedly later will come together
in a national market, spreading the benefits of a more
rational utilization of each region's potentialities
throughout the whole country.

The first part of this scenario-- female exodus from the
industrial labor force-- did take place. Their place was
taken by male workers, for the total industrial labor force
continued to grow between 1900 and 1911. When the
industrial labor force shrank (between 1911 and 1930), the

contraction was much more dramatic for females than for males. This fact would seem to indicate changes in the type of industrial activities, with greater expansion of those demanding preferentially male workers. Unfortunately the first census to give a breakdown of industrial activities is that of 1930.

Comparing the information from the 1930 census and the First Industrial Inquiry of 1881 (abstracts of this Inquiry were published in the Year Book for 1884, 1886:389-412) indicates that there were no major changes in the nature of industrial activities. The vast majority of the labor force in the manufacturing sector was in 1881 concentrated in textiles (54 percent), followed by construction trades (7 percent), and by clothing, metallurgy, and foodstuff industries (6 percent). The cotton textile industry, the dominant element in textiles (80 percent), still largely consisted of labor working in the domicile (84 percent) centered in the district of Oporto, where 87 percent of the labor force in textiles was also concentrated. This industry employed predominantly female workers (58 percent). In the other industrial activities Oporto held the overwhelming share of the labor force (70 percent) in 1881, followed by the district of Lisbon as a distant second (12 percent) (46).

While the structure of industrial activities had not changed markedly by 1930, their ranking had. Building was now the leading activity (27 percent of the industrial labor

46 It is important to remark that these indications of the Inquiry of 1881 are in accordance with the information given in the 1890 census.

force), followed by clothing (24 percent), metallurgy and textiles (both with 10 percent), and foodstuff industries (7 percent). By 1930 Lisbon had the biggest share of the country's industrial labor force (24 percent), followed by Oporto (22 percent). Women represented only 22 percent of the total industrial labor force (versus 58 percent in 1881), a decline reflecting the marked fall in women's jobs in textiles.

This brief comparison suggests changes of huge magnitude in the ranking of the industrial activities, according to their relative weight in manpower employed. But the nature of the new leading activities (building and clothing), plus their higher concentration in the two districts of Lisbon and Oporto, seems to indicate that changes in the industrial sector were more related to the needs of the two urban settings (the cities of Lisbon and Oporto) than to any real modernization of the productive structure of the country. The share of the active population engaged in modern industries such as chemicals (.63 percent), industries related to means of transportation (1.12 percent), or production of physical force (1.25 percent) remained quite insignificant, and were centered mainly in the district of Lisbon.

The progressive contraction of the textile industry reduced job opportunities for females. Such contraction was partially offset by the expanding clothing industry, but the reallocation of the places of work probably led to a different type of demand for labor. In any case female workers never enjoyed the preponderance in the clothing trade that they had had in textiles.

Comparing the distribution of industrial activities for Lisbon and Oporto reveals a major difference between the two districts. Building and clothing had similar relative weights in both districts. But the relative importance of textiles in Oporto corresponded to the importance of metallurgy in Lisbon.

To sum up, the population engaged in the manufacturing sector grew in absolute and relative terms between 1890 and 1911, and decreased between 1911 and 1930. Between 1890 and 1911, the growth of the manufacturing share (relative to the country's labor force) came at the expense of both the tertiary and the primary sector. The contraction of the industrial sector from 1911 to 1930 favored only the growth of the relative share of the population engaged in services.

Changes in the sex and the age composition of the industrial labor force, from 1890 to 1930, suggest a change in the size of working places. This hypothesis is supported by several findings: first, the loss of importance in the industrial population of the rural districts of Guarda, Covilhã, and Bragança; second, the increased concentration of industrial workers in the urban districts of Lisbon and Oporto; and, third, the increased weight of the youngest age group (less than 20 years of age) in the industrial labor force (47).

47 The end of the outwork system and domestic system that characterized previously the productive structure of textiles allowed this activity to survive until the late nineteenth century in the rural districts. Its progressive replacement by the factory system led to a concentration of

The two centers of industrialization, the districts of Lisbon and Oporto, were developing quite differently. Lisbon's growth rates were higher than Oporto's. In addition, the breakdown for 1930 indicates that the industrial structure of Lisbon had a more modern outlook (with higher concentration in heavy industry, chemicals, and industries related to means of transportation) than the district of Oporto, where industry was heavily centered in textiles. The overall concentration of the Portuguese industrial labor force in Lisbon and Oporto, where all economic development was occurring, increased the gap between these two districts and the rest of the country. The widening of this gap further reduced the possibilities for the creation of a national market. Job opportunities and thus purchasing power, which had been scarce outside the districts of Lisbon and Oporto, decreased further during this period (48).

THE TERTIARY SECTOR

Economic analysts disagree on whether certain activities should be included in the primary or the secondary sector. For example, mining, as an extractive activity, seems to belong to the primary sector. Yet it is also clear that the development of mining can be more connected to the growth of the manufacturing sector than to the development of the

the work force in the urban areas and to a lower age for the female workers engaged in this activity (the more mobile elements).
48 Pereira's (1975) analysis of working class diets between 1874 and 1922 supports this point.

other primary activities (49). By the same principle, quarrying is more easily connected to the building trades than to the other primary activities, agriculture and fishing. In practice, the final choice of the composition of the primary and the secondary sectors depends on the questions the researcher wants to answer (50).

Unfortunately, this type of reasoning is hard to defend when we leave the primary and secondary sectors. Does it make sense to encompass in a single category all the activities usually included in the tertiary sector? What shall we conclude from the grand totals of this sector? Do they represent primarily the tertiary sector of the transport, commerce and liberal professions that when "s'agrandit porte toujours temoignage sur une societe en voie de developpement" (Braudel, 1979,V.III:519) ? Or the tertiary of the protective forces and public administration that tell us about state bureaucracy? Or the tertiary of domestic service that is "unlikely to [be chosen] ... in the presence of more attractive opportunities" (A.Miller, 1971:7) ?

The tertiary is a residual group of activities whose aggregation tends to be more misleading than informative. The problem was clearly seen by A.Miller when she wrote:

> From the point of view of development, probably the division for which it is most important to

---

49 The Year Book for 1884 (1886: 384,385) states that 99 percent of the country's production of metallic minerals was exported. It would be a mistake to consider developments in this activity related to the country's economic development if the situation in this activity did not change after the 1880's.
50 For a discussion of the concept of economic sectors, see: Martin Wolfe, 1955: 402-420.

> show some breakdown is services, an extremely
> heterogeneous category, encompassing both the
> simplest and the most advanced types of activity
> and workers at the very lowest and at the very
> highest levels of any earnings scale.
> (A.Miller,1971:6)

The problem is compound by the fact that the three subsets
of tertiary activities referred to above are responsive to
quite different stimuli. The first subset of activities
(transport, commerce, and liberal professions) tends to grow
with economic development. The last group (domestic service
and servants in the household) tends to contract with
economic development. And the middle group (protective
forces and public administration) has a dynamic of its own.
In sum, the tertiary sector not only encompasses activities
representing totally different levels of skill and wages,
but also combines groups of activities that react in inverse
ways to the same stimulus.

The development of the Portuguese tertiary sector between
1890 and 1930 is a good example of this analytic problem
(2). Between 1890 and 1900, the tertiary sector contracted,
and between 1911 and 1930, it expanded. What does this
decrease and this increase mean? Does the first period
indicate a phase of economic recession, and the second, a
phase of economic expansion?

Such an inference would be quite premature. The first
period, from 1890 to 1900, registered increases in
activities connected with distribution and professions,
simultaneously with a contraction in total tertiary jobs.
The increase in the tertiary sector from 1911 to 1930 can be
attributed to an increase in personal services, and was a

symptom of economic deterioration. Thus, for the national economy, the contraction of the tertiary sector between 1890 and 1900 can be considered a more favorable sign than the expansion registered between 1911 and 1930 (51).

One more point merits attention. We have seen that, except for agriculture, all primary and secondary activities were extremely unevenly distributed regionally. This regional imbalance was even more pronounced for activities in the tertiary sector, for services were particularly centered in urban areas. Except for domestic service and servants in the household, the share of all tertiary activities located in the districts of Lisbon and Oporto experienced a marked increase throughout the period from 1890 to 1930. Most notably, the state bureaucracy was increasing and becoming more and more centered in the capital, Lisbon, and the city of Oporto. Similarly, the concentration of activities connected with distribution and the professions indicates a huge gap between Lisbon and Oporto and the rest of the country, and confirms the extreme imbalance of the country's development. These findings are consistent with other evidence pointing to accentuated growth in these two cities and stagnation or even decline in

---

51 The reason for the different behavior and meaning of changes in the tertiary sector lies, in the Portuguese case, in the changing relative weight of each subgroup of activities within the tertiary sector. The outlook of the tertiary sector was, in 1890 and 1930, mainly determined by personal services (domestic service and servants), which represented 53 and 55 percent of the tertiary sector respectively. In 1900 and 1911, however, the outlook of this sector was mainly determined by activities connected with distribution and the professions (transportation, commerce, and liberal professions), which represented 52 percent of the tertiary sector.

the other urban areas (52). A marked decrease in the growth
rates of distribution and professional activities between
1911 and 1930 confirms the economic deterioration of the
country between these two dates.

The two last activities, domestic service and servants,
are hard to analyze (53). They were the least urban
activities of the tertiary sector. They were also the two
activities where the elasticity to absorb female labor was
largest throughout our period. In periods like that between
1890 and 1900, when the job market was relatively favorable,
the share of domestic service and servants in the household
decreased; when the job market was unfavorable, as it was
between 1911 and 1930, the opposite happened.

TRENDS AND COMPOSITION OF TERTIARY SUBSECTORS

The tertiary sector is composed of three very different
sets of activities, with only two characteristics in common:
all the population engaged in these activities performs some
kind of service; and all these activities are located
disproportionately in cities. But the similarities end
here, and each set of activities considered separately
reveals much more than the aggregated totals.

---

52 These findings also seem to verify Braudel's assertion
that this group of activities can be used fruitfully as an
indicator of economic development.
53 The main difference between the two categories is that
servants live in the household they worked for, while
domestic service was performed by nonresident workers. This
situation implied that servants were usually single.

The first group of occupations-- transportation, commerce, and liberal professions-- experienced growth rates indicating some economic prosperity between 1890 and 1900. From 1900 on, the yearly growth rates for this subgroup increasingly slowed, becoming negative between 1911 and 1930, except in the districts of Lisbon and Oporto. This set of activities is the only one within the tertiary sector with a clear mixed sex composition. Although the sex ratio was throughout the whole period unfavorable to women, it was much less so in commerce and liberal professions than in transportation. The age structure of the labor force engaged in these three activities was biased towards those over forty years of age, as was likely to happen in activities demanding skills more than physical strength.

The second group of activities, protective forces and public administration, is more important in terms of the structure of the governmental apparatus than in terms of the structure of the labor force. This set of activities was entirely constituted by men in the most active age groups (20 to 40 years of age). The major point to note here is that the considerable level of governmental centralization already in place during the last decades of the monarchy (when my analysis begins) was further strengthened during the First Republic and the dictatorship.

The last set of activities, domestic service and servants in the household, were almost entirely composed of women. Understanding labor force contraction and redistribution between 1890 and 1911 greatly depends on our understanding of female labor force behavior in the several activities women were engaged in between these two dates. We face, however, two great limitations in the attempt. The first is lack of information on age for servants in the household; the second is probable errors in numbers for domestic service recorded in the censuses (54).

We have seen that the country's economic situation between 1890 and 1900 was much better than it was in the subsequent periods. Between 1890 and 1900, a modest increase in the absolute numbers of the male labor force engaged in such occupations as agriculture, industry, commerce, and transportation took place. It might be argued that the opening of these job opportunities for males reduced the need for female earnings in a small number of households, but this line of reasoning is utopian. Wages were close to subsistence level for the vast majority of the Portuguese labor force, making it unreasonable to presume that the households dependent on earnings from unskilled work were the first to give up female earnings. More

54 The recorded numbers of females engaged in domestic services during the period under study were as follows: in 1890, 139920; in 1900, 58912; in 1911, 34718 ; and in 1930, 228835. There is no logical explanation for these enormous fluctuations except for the period between 1911 and 1930, when the losses in agriculture and industry were of similar magnitude to the gains in domestic service and servants. For the period between 1890 and 1900, the numbers are puzzling, as can be seen from a comparison of the female labor force engaged in the five activities where unskilled female labor was likely to be found:

OCCUPATION	1890	1900	CHANGE
AGRICULTURE	481964	380293	-
INDUSTRY	157747	135292	-
COMMERCE	31070	45773	+
DOM.SERV	139920	58912	-
SERVANTS	97326	94897	-
TOTAL	908027	715167	-
		192860	

reasonable is a recording error for the female population engaged in domestic services, either in 1890 and 1930, or in 1900 and 1911.

Even with these limitations, it is worth looking at the redistribution of female labor between 1900 and 1930 in those activities women's participation was highest (see Table III:VIII).

TABLE III:VIII - **FEMALE LABOR FORCE IN SPECIFIC OCCUPATIONS**

OCCUPATION	1900	1911	1930	CHANGES	
				1900-1911	1911-1930
AGRICULT.	380293	334416	164329	−	−
INDUSTRY	135298	155197	100503	+	−
DOM.SERV.	58912	34718	228835	−	+
SERVANTS	94897	128566	158939	+	+

These figures suggest that losses in agriculture tended to be mainly absorbed by servants, while losses and gains in industry tended to be mainly absorbed by domestic services. That would be in accordance with our finding that industry moved to urban areas during this period and that domestic services were preferentially urban activities, while servants in the household was a category centered preferentially in rural areas.

To use this information, we must briefly recall some of our earlier findings. First, we know that the female labor force in all activities was centered in the northern regions of the country. In particular, textiles were mainly centered in the northern districts where opportunities for female work were greater than in other industries. Second, industry and thus industrial jobs were heavily concentrated in the city of Lisbon and its suburbs, while industry and industrial jobs were scattered over the district of Oporto (Carqueja, 1916: 218,219). Third, we assumed that servants in the household tended to be young and single, while domestic workers we know were mostly over forty and married. Fourth, we have seen that agricultural work engaged fewer and fewer women under twenty years of age, particularly in the northern part of the country. Finally, we know that the majority of the peasants' households were poverty-stricken (Basilio Teles, 1904, Poinsard,1912).

We can now begin to hypothesize with a certain plausibility about job opportunities for women during our period. The most relevant issue seems to be the movement of young females from peasant households in the northern part of the country (55).

The three positions more likely to be open to a young girl from a peasant family were as industrial worker, servant, and agricultural worker. The chance of entering each of these jobs was far from equal, however. We must remember that in Portugal there was never anything similar to the English boarding houses or poor houses to accommodate factory workers (56). Thus we can assume that openings in Portuguese industry for young girls could only be fulfilled by young females whose family or relatives were in nearby

---

55 This topic should be considered under the assumption that as soon as a child was able to be accepted in the job market (in this work 10 years of age was considered the lower limit), her parents would force her to do so.
56 There was also nothing similar to the Lowell boarding houses of the early nineteenth century where American farmers would send their single daughters to work in the mills.

shops or factories needing child or young female labor.
This situation was most likely to occur in Oporto district
and in Lisbon and its suburbs, where we know a great number
of residents were born outside the district. For the vast
majority of the young women entering the labor force from a
peasant household, to be a domestic servant was the only
real possibility for easing the burden of feeding a
household of quite meager resources. Contrary to
agricultural work, household service offered board, food,
clothing, and usually some money.

If the domestic servant married, her ability to enter the
labor force depend on other factors-- particularly the
location of her new household and her family size. We also
know that job opportunities in industry tended to diminish
with age, and that between 1890 and 1930 there was a
regional redistribution of the working places in industry,
that clearly favoring the centralization of this sector in
the districts of Oporto and Lisbon. This movement reduced
further the chances of a growing number of married females
to find an industrial job, particularly in some of the
northern districts where textiles were traditionally
centered. In sum, for a women over forty the real
alternative to agricultural labor seems to have been
domestic services.

The main conclusion to be derived from this reasoning is
that young female workers movements from the primary sector
(agriculture) could be absorbed by either the tertiary
sector (as servants) or the secondary sector depending on
the location of the entrant's household and on the

industrial demand for young labor in the region. Movements
from the tertiary sector (domestic services) to the
secondary sector were also likely to occur if demand for
female labor in industry increased. Movements from the
secondary sector to the tertiary sector (domestic service)
were more likely to occur in times of economic recession or
at older ages. These female intersectoral movements were
taking place in Portugal between 1900 and 1930.

We can now relate our findings and construct concluding
hypotheses on the development and redistribution of the
Portuguese labor force between 1890 and 1930. This is the
topic of the next section.

CONCLUSIONS

Three goals guided the research questions I tried to
answer in this section. The first goal was to see if
revisionist scholars' contention of higher levels of
Portuguese economic development (57) are reflected in the
evolution of the Portuguese labor market. The hypothesis
being tested was whether job opportunities were rising
during the late nineteenth and early twentieth centuries
given the extent of economic growth claimed by the new
literature (Reis,1986; Justino, 1988). The second goal was
to see if the favorable economic evolution of the national
industrial index and G.N.P. resulted from (or promoted)
integrated growth, or if this economic growth was so
regionally centered that its benefits never spread over

57 Namely, Reis, 1984, 1986; Lains, 1986; and Justino, 1988.

certain areas of the country. The last goal was to link the results from the first two queries with determinants of emigration. This last focus was intended to complement the analysis of such determinants presented in the first two chapters.

My findings can be summarized as follow, Portuguese economic structure around the 1890's can be characterized as a typical dual economy of backwardness. To the country's uneven distribution of natural resources corresponded a still more uneven distribution of the country's wealth. By 1930, the scenario was darker. The rich regions of the 1890's had grown richer, the poor regions had become more impoverished.

Five factors were largely responsible for the widening gap between the developing regions and the stagnating areas. The first was the disproportionate economic and political weight of the capital, Lisbon. The second was that, except in agriculture, all economic development during this period was centered in two districts, Lisbon and Oporto. The third was the lack of a dynamic urban network. The fourth was the lack of internal mobility. And the final factor was the lack of a national labor market sufficiently dynamic to make people move from the pauperized regions to the developing areas. Obviously, these three last factors were as much a result of, as a reinforcement of the two first factors.

Between 1890 and 1911, the Portuguese labor force did not keep pace with the growth of the population of working age. In absolute terms, the gainfully employed population decreased from 1890 to 1900. But the findings by economic sector lend support to the claim that the period from 1890 to 1911 was a period of economic growth. Between 1890 and 1900, industrial growth did not produce significant increases in the industrial labor force. Yet, during the same decade, the expansion of activities connected with distribution and the professions attest to the existence of a certain prosperity. Between 1900 and 1911, we find a significant number of new entrants in manufacturing and a small increase in the activities connected with the distribution of goods and the professions. Both changes point to expanding job opportunities in the secondary and the tertiary sectors.

To claim that Portugal registered economic growth between 1890 and 1911 is misleading because this statement neglects the most striking characteristic of the Portuguese economic structure: enormous regional asymmetries. Certainly, economic expansion did not characterize northern Portugal (except for Oporto) or the Azorean islands. For these regions I find overwhelming evidence of severe economic recession. The labor market there was markedly contracting in all activities, except servants and domestic services. The end point to the claims of Reis (1986) and Justino (1988) and my findings is a well-known story. It goes more or less like this: my neighbor ate two chickens, and I did not eat any. On average, we both ate a chicken, but I am starving. Simply put, in Portugal, part of the country was eating, but the rest had to emigrate to do so (58).

---

58 Regional economic imbalances do not necessarily led to international migration. In fact, they can have several outcomes. In France during the nineteenth and early

The areas where the labor market was contracting overlapped with the migratory areas. The severe decrease of job opportunities for women in the northern regions of the mainland and in the Azorean islands helps to explain increasing female participation in the migratory flow after the 1900's.

Because the Portuguese population grew at annual rates that could not be absorbed by the job market, we can reasonably presume that the emigrants who left Portugal between 1890 and 1930 were a surplus population. The fact that those leaving were overwhelmingly young adults without any particular skill further substantiates the view that emigrants were marginal. If the "safety valve" mechanism had not been at work during this period, the retention of a surplus population of working age, plus their offspring, might well have ruined the Portuguese social fabric.

---

twentieth centuries they induced the rural exodus to the big cities (Chatelain, 1976). In England during the first half of the nineteenth century they were responsible as much for international outflows as for inflows from neighboring Ireland (Redford, 1968).

CHAPTER IV - PORTUGUESE EMIGRATION TO THE UNITED STATES
1820-1930

INTRODUCTION

GENERAL CHARACTERISTICS OF THE PORTUGUESE EMIGRATION
1855-1930

Over one million emigrants left Portugal between 1885 and 1930. How many came legally and illegally? What were their characteristics and socio-economic backgrounds? From what regions of Portugal did they come? This chapter addresses these questions.

The general characteristics of Portuguese emigrants have already been described by several scholars. The best syntheses available on the topic are: in the nineteenth century, Rodrigues de Freitas (1867), A.de Figueiredo (1873), and Oliveira Martins (1891); in the early twentieth century, Afonso Costa (1911) and Bento Carqueja (1916); and, more recently, Sousa Bettencourt (1961), João Evangelista (1971), Joel Serrão (1st ed. 1972, 1977), and Magalhães Godinho (1978).

The nineteenth-century writings are still the best available sources for some periods (e.g.1855-1865). More recent syntheses present some inconsistencies that led me to prefer, whenever possible, to redo the computations from the original sources. The following description of the general characteristics of the Portuguese emigration between 1855 and 1930 is based on Portuguese official statistics published during this period.

AN EDUCATED GUESS ON THE VOLUME OF PORTUGUESE EMIGRATION BETWEEN 1855 AND 1930

THE PROBLEM

Portuguese statistics on emigration are as flawed as any other migration statistics from this period with which I have worked (e.g.American and Brazilian). Recording is unsystematic and poor until the 1900's; information for the period before 1866 is largely limited to the total number of emigrants per year. The records are often inconsistent. For example, in Movimento da População for 1901-1905 the abstracts on emigration by motivation and destination indicate that 129776 Portuguese emigrated during those five years, while the abstracts on emigration by district and destination indicate that 128341 emigrants left during the same period. There are temporal gaps in the information registered (1), and changes in the recorded population (e.g. after 1907, neither emigration to Europe nor emigration to Brazil and the United States via first and second class were recorded). Finally, we lack information on the conceptual basis for compilation and aggregation.

Missing or inconsistent information is, of course, quite common in nineteenth and early twentieth centuries statistics of all types. But there is usually a way to compensate for some gaps. Lacunae in the Portuguese statistics on emigration are particularly serious, however, because the records leave out a whole segment of the migrant population, the clandestine. In other words, official

---

1 For example, the Year Book for 1923 and the Year Book for 1929 did not publish departures from the district of Guarda for 1923, nor from the district of Viana for 1925 to 1927.

statistics on Portuguese emigration are biased because they record only the legal emigrants, i.e. emigrants leaving the country with a passport.

To estimate the total volume of Portuguese emigration, we must adjust the official information to account for those departing without passport (clandestine emigrants). The underregistration of departures would not constitute a serious problem if we had reliable information on births and deaths during this period. Unfortunately, vital events are also known to be underrecorded (2).

Two demographers, L.Bacci (1971) and J.Evangelista (1971), have analyzed the structure of the Portuguese population between 1864 and 1930. Although, they have not surveyed quite the same universe (Bacci's numbers and estimations concern the entire country (mainland and islands) and Evangelista's figures concern only the mainland), their results are consistent. A summary of their findings for 1890 to 1900 is given in Table IV: I.

---

2 Still if it was only deaths or only births that were under registered we could use one of the several technic available to solve the problem (on the techniques available see for example Barclay, 1966 and United Nations, Manual x, 1983).

Table IV: I - CHARACTERISTICS OF THE PORTUGUESE POPULATION
1890 - 1900

CHARACTERISTICS	ENTIRE COUNTRY (THOUSANDS)	MAINLAND (THOUSANDS)
Population 1890	5049.7	[4660.1]
Population 1900	5423.1	[5016.3]
Pop. Mid Period	5236.4	[4838.2]
Live births (1891/900)	1601	[1423]
Deaths (1891/900)	1112.9	[982]
Natural increase	488.1	441
Net migration	-114.7	
Birth rate	30.57	30.3
Death rate	21.25	21.1
Net Migration rate	-2.19	

Source: Bacci, 1971:36 for the entire country; Evangelista,
1971: 43, 54, and 72 for the mainland.
Note: the figures in brackets are the official figures that
we can infer were used by Evangelista.

We can test the consistency of the figures in Table IV: I
by using the balance equation $P_n = P_o + N - E + I$ where

P_n = population at the end of the period
P_o = population at the beginning of the period
B = live births between o and n
D = deaths between o and n
N = natural increase (B - D)
E = legal emigration (E_l) + clandestine emigration
(E_c)
I = immigration (I).

Substituting with Bacci's figures for Table IV:I, and
given that legal emigrants were during this period 258.4
thousand, we have:

$5423.1 = 5049.7 + 488.1 - 258.4 - E_c + I$

or

$114.7 = 258.4 + E_c - I.$

The only way this equality is satisfied is by assuming that
the number of immigrants (I) (presumably primarily returning
emigrants) not only totally canceled out the clandestine
emigrants (E_c) but also counterbalanced at least 56 percent
(143.7 thousand) of the legal emigrants (E_l).

Bacci was aware that births were underregistered for this period, and he put the error at 4.1 percent. He thus estimated that the true number of live births between 1891 and 1900 was 1669.6 thousand (Bacci,1971:29). Incorporating this correction of registered births into our formula produces a net migration figure of 183.3 thousand. Given that the number of legal emigrants during the period was 258.4 thousand, the immigrants (return migrants) still cancel out clandestine emigration and account for 29 percent (75.1 thousand) of the legal emigration. In sum, Bacci's figures-- whether adjusted or not for birth underregistration-- are only plausible if we assume that the level of return migration in Portugal between 1891 and 1900 was so high that it canceled out all clandestine emigration and also accounted for a minimum of 29 to a maximum of 56 percent of the legal emigration (3).

Bacci's numbers and estimates are contradicted by all available information on emigration and return migration for this period. It is beyond dispute that Portuguese emigration during the nineteenth century had a significant clandestine component and an insignificant number of returns (4). Bacci's figures are thus unacceptable. Clearly,

---

3 There is no need to test the consistency of Evangelista's figures because this demographer was fully aware that the available official figures on population size, births, deaths, and emigration yield an error of 131 thousand persons (Evangelista, 1971:72).
4 All scholars who have addressed Portuguese emigration during the nineteenth century agree that clandestine emigration was very high (e.g Evangelista, 1971:123 estimated that between 1891 and 1960 the clandestine stream was equivalent to 33 percent of the legal flow; O.Martins, 1891:226 estimated the clandestine component for the 1880's to be at least 13 percent of total emigration). Returns were on the other hand very low (e.g. O.Martins,1891:226

estimating the volume of migration from the demographic
balancing equation given above and official statistics is
unworkable, and an alternative method is needed (5).

AN ESTIMATION OF THE TOTAL VOLUME OF EMIGRATION

The method described on the next pages uses the age
structure of the Portuguese population and the birth and
death rates implied by a life table for a stable population
with the same type of age structure (6). My approach also
uses sex-specific figures, for two reasons. First,
emigration is a sex-specific phenomenon (with more men than

considered them insignificant; Serrão, 1977:39 estimated
them to be 3.5 percent of the legal departures between 1919
and 1930). Another problem connected with return migration
should be addressed at this point. It is unknown the extent
to which the same individuals (individuals making several
trips) were counted more than once in the official
statistics. Given the economic limitations of the
Portuguese population involved, and the small number of
returns, it is very unlikely that the error introduced by
this limitation is of any significance.
5 Evangelista acknowledges the existence of inconsistencies
in the available information but does not purpose any
alternative to solve the problem.
6 I have also tried to estimate total net emigration using
the census survival ratios technique (see Lee, 1957:9-106
for a detailed description of this technique). I used the
intercensal period of 1890 to 1900 for my computations.
Census survival ratios techniques were designed to estimate
internal migration in a population closed to migration. The
total Portuguese population is far from being a closed
population, but we can treat those regions with an
insignificant emigration rate as a closed population. I
assumed that, in the absence of emigration, the areas of
Portugal with high emigration would have behaved like the
nonmigratory areas.
    I then computed the census survival ratios for the
nonmigratory areas (the South), and used these ratios to
estimate population losses by age group and sex for the
migratory areas (North and islands). The results were,
unfortunately, quite unrealistic. I presume that was due to
the fact that this technique is extremely sensitive to age
misreporting.

women emigrating). To use aggregate figures for the whole population would thus introduces a major source of error into the computations. Second, the life tables and stable population models that were used to determine birth and death rates are sex-specific.

My estimates of the total emigration are for the intercensal period of 1890- 1900. This was a period of heavy out-migration, and other data are available for testing the validity of my results. The age structure used to determine birth and death rates was computed from the 1900 census, rather than the 1890 census, for the following reasons: 1) the age structure at the end of the period reflects the influence of births, deaths, emigration and immigration throughout the period of interest; and 2) the 1900 census is considered more accurate than the 1890 census.

To determine the appropriate birth and death rates for the Portuguese population, I compare the age structure of the Portuguese population, in 1900 (given in Table B:1 in Appendix 2)-- considering separately both for the mainland and the islands-- with the age structures given for stable populations models for South Europe (in, A.Coale et al., Regional Model Life Tables and Stable Populations, 2d ed., 1984). The age structure of the Portuguese female population in 1900 corresponds best to a female stable population for model south at level 12, with a birth rate of 29.02 and a death rate of 19.02 for the mainland, and a birth rate of 30.8 and a death rate of 18.8 for the islands. Repeating the operation for males I relied on a male stable population for model south at level 12 with a birth rate of 34.79 and a death rate of 19.79 for the mainland, and a birth rate of 37.7 and a death rate of 19.7 for the islands.

Stable population models assume that births and death rates are constant and that there is no migration for any age group. We must thus assume for now that the Portuguese population was a stable population between 1890 and 1900.

A stable population can be pictured at two different points in time using the following compound growth rate formula: $P_n = P_o * (1 + B_r - D_r)^{n-1}$

where:

P_n= population at the end of the period
P_o= population at the beginning of the period
B_r= birth rate during the period
D_r= death rate during the period
n = number of years

It follows that the number of births in any year (t) during the period will be given by the expression

$$B_r * P_o * (1 + B_r - D_r)^{t-1}$$

Consequently, the total number of births during a decade will be given by the expression

$$B_r * P_o \sum_{n=1}^{10} (1 + B_r - D_r)^{n-1}$$

or

$$B_r * P_o * \frac{(1 + B_r - D_r)^{10} - 1}{B_r - D_r}$$

Similarly, the number of deaths occurring during the same period will be given by the expression

$$D_r * P_o * \frac{(1 + B_r - D_r)^{10} - 1}{B_r - D_r}$$

Using these expressions, I estimated the births and deaths occurring between 1890 and 1900.

With my new estimates of births and deaths, I could return to the population balancing equation

$$P_n = P_o + N - E + I$$

and recompute the volume of permanent emigration (E-I) between 1890 and 1900.

Bringing together these estimates yields the following summary of the Portuguese population for the period between 1890 and 1900 (7).

TABLE IV: II - CHARACTERISTICS OF THE PORTUGUESE POPULATION
1890 - 1900 (THOUSANDS)

Character- ristics	Portugal		Mainland		Islands	
	Males	Females	Males	Females	Males	Females
Pop.1890	2430.4	2619.4	2251.3	2408.8	179	210.6
Pop.1900	2591.6	2831.5	2402.1	2614.2	189.5	217.4
Live Births	911.7	799.3	838.5	730.8	73.2	68.5
Deaths	515.3	520.6	477.1	478.8	38.3	41.8
Nat.Incr.	396.4	278.7	361.4	252	34.9	26.7
Net Migr.	235.2	66.6	210.6	46.6	24.5	19.9

Although total departures cannot be estimated from official Portuguese statistics my indirect estimation suggests that a net of 301.8 thousand people left Portugal permanently between 1890 and 1900. Given that the legal departures between 1891 and 1900 amounted to 258.4 thousand,

---

7 The results of Table IV:II have some problems. The most questionable data are male births and deaths for the mainland. The problem arises from my choosing for the base of my estimations the age structures of 1900 instead of 1890. The anomalies introduced by emigration, particularly in the male age structure of the mainland, would have been much smaller if I had used 1890. But problems with the ages recorded are much greater for 1890 than for 1900, so much so that previous estimations using the age structures of 1890 yield totally unacceptable results.

the clandestine flow was 14 percent of the legal departures,
assuming that between 3 to 3.5 percent of the emigrants
returned to Portugal (8). The next question is, are these
estimates consistent with other data ?

TESTING THE RESULTS

In 1891, the Portuguese sociologist O. Martins estimated
the volume of the Portuguese clandestine flow to be at 13
percent of the legal emigration (O. Martins, 1891:226).
This contemporary estimate is reassuringly close to my own
indirect estimate (9).

O. Martins was of the opinion that all the Portuguese
clandestine emigration of his time (1880's) was "constituted
by adults of military age." A variety of evidence supports
this claim. Certainly this is consistent with literary
evidence from the period (10). The Azorean newspapers leave

---

8 Serrão, 1977:39.
9 Based on scattered information, J. Evangelista estimated
that, between 1891 and 1960, the number of clandestine
departures could not have exceeded 33 percent of the legal
departures (Evangelista, 1971:123). Evangelista's estimate
of illegal emigration covers too long a period of time to be
a useful check on my results. There were marked differences
between emigration in the period 1890 to 1900 and emigration
in subsequent decades. For example, the high level of
returns during the economic crisis of the late 1920's and
early 1930's was unprecedented. Further, the level of
clandestine emigration to Western Europe from the 1950's on
was doubtless higher than the level of clandestine
emigration to the United States and Brazil around the turn
of the century. Clandestine emigration was much easier in
the recent decades, due to the proximity of the receiving
society and the extension of the border with Spain.
10 E.g., Dabney, 1884, Guerreiro, 1891, Sequeira, 1891, and
Peck, 1904. Also of the four case records that I uncovered
on clandestine emigration for the 1890's for the court of S
João Novo in the city of Oporto three concern men accused of
trying to emigrate illegally to avoid the draft. One for
1893, court record n.530; one for 1896, record n.2372; and
two for 1897, records n.2908 and 2787.

no doubts on this matter. A Persuasão of Ponta Delgada (1522, March, 1891) states that of those drafted that year more than 80 percent had already emigrated. O Açoriano of Horta (39, November, 1890) comments: "this year not even recruitment can be blamed for emigration, because they all emigrate, even the exempted".

Other sources that I analyzed support both O. Martins' claim that clandestine emigration was mainly constituted by males of military age and his estimate of the volume of clandestine migration. My survey of the passports issued by the district of Angra between October 1890 and December of 1891, both for Brazil and the United States, indicates that not a single passport was issued to a male between 14 and 19 years of age, which implies that emigration by this subgroup was all illegal. And according to my survey of the Manifest Ship Lists for the ports of Boston and New York between July 1890 and December 1891, males between 14 and 19 years of age comprised 14.39 percent of the total Portuguese arrivals in the United States. This proportion is consistent with O. Martin's and my own estimates of the volume of clandestine emigration. Furthermore, the discrepancy between the number of legal departures to the United States (reported in the Portuguese passport registers and aggregated published statistics) and the total number of Portuguese arrivals in the United States (reported in the American annual reports on immigration), indicated that clandestine departures amounted to 15 percent of the legal departures between 1897 and 1910. In sum, all the evidence that I gathered for the late 1880's and the 1890's show a similar proportion of clandestine.

There is no reason for the clandestine emigration to be different when directed to Brazil instead of the United States, at least until American anti-immigration policies were enforced after 1917. In fact, that is precisely what the results presented on the preceding pages indicate (11). I have thus assumed that the proportion of clandestine emigration was basically the same for Brazil and the United States.

With this plausible assumption, we can finally estimate the total volume of Portuguese emigration between 1855 and 1930. Portuguese emigration will be equal to legal emigration inflated by the estimated proportion of clandestine emigrants (i.e., legal departures to the United States divided by arrivals to the United States, minus one). The results are given in Table IV:III.

The figures on Table IV:III are based on the following specific adjustments. For the period 1855 and 1878, I assumed that 5 percent of the Portuguese emigrants were clandestine. This figure is based on two pieces of information. According to R. de Freitas (1867: 10), 5010 emigrants left for United States between 1855 and 1865; according to the American official statistics (Young, 1871:XII-XIV), 5291 immigrants arrived from Portugal (Cape Verdians not included). These figures suggest 5 percent of the Portuguese emigrants between 1855 and 1865 were

---

11 The proportion found for clandestine emigrants is quite similar in both migratory streams (i.e., flow from the mainland; flow from the islands).

clandestine. For lack of alternative information, I used these figure of 5 percent found for 1855 to 1865 to adjust emigration between 1855 and 1878. For 1879 to 1890, I used O.Martins estimation of 13 percent. For 1891 to 1910, I used 15 percent, which is the ratio of clandestine obtained by comparing legal departures from Portugal and registered arrivals in the United States for 1897 to 1910. For 1911 to 1930, I used 7 percent, obtained by the same method.

TABLE IV:III   PORTUGUESE EMIGRATION 1855-1930

YEAR	POPULATION AT CENSUS	YEARLY	EMIGRATION LEGAL	WITH CLANDESTINE
1854	3844000	3844000		
1855		3877124	11557	12135
1856		3910533	10288	10802
1857		3944230	9861	10354
1858		3978217	8963	9411
1859		4012498	9309	9774
1860		4047073	6524	6850
1861		4081947	5945	6242
1862		4117121	5674	5958
1863		4152598	4411	4632
1864	4188410	4188410	4517	4743
1865		4213302	4175	4384
1866		4238341	6469	6792
1867		4263530	7150	7508
1868		4288868	7127	7483
1869		4314357	8380	8799
1870		4339997	9655	10138
1871		4365790	12728	13364
1872		4391735	17284	18148
1873		4417836	12996	13646
1874		4444091	14835	15577
1875		4470502	15440	16212
1876		4497070	11035	11587
1877		4523796	11057	11610
1878	4550699	4550699	9917	10413
1879		4590326	13211	14928
1880		4630299	12597	14235
1881		4670620	14637	16540
1882		4711291	18272	20647
1883		4752317	19251	21754
1884		4793701	17518	19795
1885		4835444	15004	16955

1886		4877551	13998	15818
1887		4920025	16992	19201
1888		4962868	23981	27099
1889		5006085	20614	23294
1890	5049729	5049729	29427	33253
1891		5085885	23585	27123
1892		5122300	21074	24235
1893		5158976	30383	34940
1894		5195914	26911	30948
1895		5233117	44746	51458
1896		5270586	27680	31832
1897		5308323	21334	24534
1898		5346331	23604	27145
1899		5384611	17774	20440
1900	5423132	5423132	21235	24420
1901		5469879	20646	23743
1902		5517030	24170	27796
1903		5564587	21611	24853
1904		5612553	28304	32550
1905		5660934	33610	38652
1906		5709731	38093	43807
1907		5758949	41950	48243
1908		5808591	40145	46167
1909		5858661	38223	43956
1910		5909162	39515	45442
1911	5960056	5960056	59661	63837
1912		5968102	88929	95154
1913		5976159	77645	83080
1914		5984227	25730	27531
1915		5992306	19314	20666
1916		6000395	24897	26640
1917		6008496	15825	16933
1918		6016607	11853	12683
1919		6024730	37138	39738
1920	6032991	6032991	64783	69318
1921		6107921	24597	26319
1922		6183781	39795	42581
1923		6260584	40171	42983
1924		6338340	29710	31790
1925		6417062	22884	24486
1926		6496762	42067	45012
1927		6577452	27674	29611
1928		6659144	34297	36698
1929		6741851	40361	43186
1930	6825883	6825883	23196	24820

SOURCES: For column 1 - Census at given year
For column 3 - 1855-1865, R. Freitas, 1867
1866-1884, Year Book for 1884, 1886:54,55 and
A.Figueiredo,1873
1885-1890, Movimento da População for 1887 to
1890
1890-1896, Afonso Costa,1911:77
1897-1921, Movimento da População for 1900 to
1921
1917-1930, Year Book for 1917 to 1930
NOTE: Column 2: assumes constant intercensal growth rate
Column 4: see text for explanation

Plotting the emigration estimates given in column 4 above yields the picture of the Portuguese emigration between 1855 and 1930 shown in Figure 3.

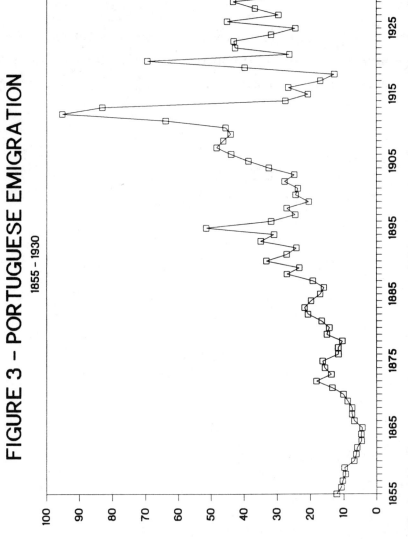

FIGURE 3 – PORTUGUESE EMIGRATION

1855 – 1930

The curve of the Portuguese emigration shows first, a cycle with a phase of expansion during the 1850's, followed by a phase of contraction until 1865. Thereafter, the curve presents a clear exponential trend up through 1912. The long phase of expansion was followed by a sudden and marked drop between 1912 and 1918. From 1918 to 1930, the curve shows well-defined cycles of three to four years.

The general pattern of emigration over time is presented in different form in Table IV:IV, which aggregates the detailed information from Table IV:III by intercensal intervals.

TABLE IV:IV - PORTUGUESE EMIGRATION BY INTERCENSAL PERIODS

INTERCENSAL PERIOD	TOTAL DEPARTURES	EMIGRATION RATE PER THOUSAND (12)
1855-1864	80901	20.1
1865-1878	155660	35.6
1879-1890	243517	50.7
1891-1900	294492	56.2
1901-1911	432239	75.9
1912-1920	380759	63.5
1921-1930	337742	52.5

From an emigration rate of 20.1 emigrants per thousand population between 1855 to 1864, the Portuguese emigration rate rose continuously to a peak of 75.9 emigrants per thousand population between 1901 to 1911. In the following two intercensal periods (1912-1920; 1921-1930), emigration

12 The intercensal emigration rates are not readily comparable to the emigration rates usually published. To make my results more easily comparable, I am including the yearly average emigration rates per thousand. They are respectively: 2.01; 2.54; 4.23; 5.62; 6.90; 7.06; and 5.25.

rates decreased markedly, attaining between 1921 and 1930 a lower rate (52.5) than that (56.2) observed during the 1890's.

GEO-DEMOGRAPHIC CHARACTERISTICS OF THE MIGRANTS

MIGRATORY AREAS

Emigration never has the same impact in all areas of a country, and Portugal is no exception to this rule. The regional selectivity of the migratory phenomenon is the direct result of migration determinants. It is not enough for a community to face economic hardship for migration to occur; the population also has to view migration as an acceptable alternative, and the necessary channels must be open, for migration to take place. Until after the Second World War, these three conditions were met in only some areas of Portugal, which were well-defined and fairly consistent. These peak migratory areas were the provinces of Minho, Tras-os-Montes, and Beira Alta, and the islands of Azores and Madeira (13). Between 1855 and 1930, these regions were the source of over 85 percent of the Portuguese legal migratory flow. Table IV:V synthesizes the evolution of the regional distribution of the Portuguese emigration.

---

13 These areas included the following districts: in the mainland seven northern districts-- Viana, Braga, Oporto (Minho), Vila Real, Braganca (Tras-Os-Montes), Aveiro, Vizeu, and Coimbra (Beira Alta); in the islands-- Angra, Horta, Ponta Delgada (Azores), and Funchal (Madeira).

TABLE IV:V - REGIONAL DISTRIBUTION OF LEGAL EMIGRATION
1855-1930 (IN PERCENTAGE)

PROVINCE	1855-1930
MINHO	28.10
TRAS-OS-MONTES	10.91
BEIRA ALTA	26.54
BEIRA BAIXA	4.96
EXTREMADURA	7.46
ALENTEJO	0.49
ALGARVE	1.08
AZORES	14.79
MADEIRA	5.66
TOTAL	100
EMIGRANTS	1216250

SOURCE: TABLE B:2 IN APPENDIX 2
NOTE: SELECTED YEARS

The share of the migratory areas never fell below 80 percent
prior to the 1920's (see Table B:2 in Appendix 2 for
detailed information of the regional distribution). In that
decade the relative importance of emigration from the
islands dropped markedly. The anti-immigration legislation
passed by the United States during this period (particularly
the Immigration Acts of the 1920's) explains the change.
Azorean emigrants, who tended to chose the United States as
their destination, were seriously affected by the closing of
the American door, while their counterparts from the
mainland, who favored emigration to Brazil, were much less
so.

A second obvious change over time in the source of
emigrants was the steady rise after 1890 in the proportions
from the province of Beira Baixa (particularly the district
of Castelo Branco). This was attributable to worsening
economic conditions in the area, most notably the
progressive collapse of artisanal textile industry.

The participation of the district of Lisbon was erratic and less symptomatic of regional discrepancies. We must remember that over 90 percent of the Portuguese population lived in the districts where they were born (see section on internal mobility), with two great exceptions, Lisbon and Oporto. The probability that emigrants holding passports issued at Lisbon and Oporto, were temporary migrants from another region, was much higher than the probability for any other district. Elsewhere, the probability that an emigrant holding a passport from a district he was not a native of is less than 3 percent.

The regional distribution of the migratory areas is in perfect accord with the dual economic structure of backwardness that characterized the Portuguese economy (see Chapter III). In other words, migratory areas corresponded to the economically stagnant regions, that is the northern part of the country and the islands. Moreover, as labor market conditions deteriorated over a larger share of the country, the number of regions sending out emigrants expanded, encompassing almost the whole country (14) by the 1920's. This pattern supports my claim in the previous chapter, that Portuguese emigration between 1890 and 1930 was connected to the growing lack of job vacancies.

We have seen why and from where the Portuguese emigrated. My next focus is on who emigrated: the profile of the Portuguese emigrant.

---

14 The exception is the province of Alentejo.

SOCIO-DEMOGRAPHIC CHARACTERISTICS OF THE MIGRANT

It is a well-established fact that Portuguese emigration
was individual (rather than familial) and male-dominated.
In Chapters 1 and 2, I noted that both the lack of cash
among the rural peasantry and Portuguese emigration policy
favored and perpetuated this outcome. A national sex ratio
biased in favor of females, noted by census takers from 1864
on (e.g. 1864 Census,1868:XIII, 1878 Census,1881:XVIII) is
just one piece of evidence supporting the predominance of
male emigration.

After 1900, contemporaries complained that these
traditional characteristics of the Portuguese emigration
were changing. Emigration was going "from temporary to
permanent and from individual to familial" wrote A.Costa in
1911 (A.Costa, 1911:84). More recent writers (e.g. Serrão,
1977:123) subscribe to the same idea of a marked change in
the composition of the migratory stream after the turn of
the century. This is, however, a dangerous generalization,
because it lumps together two different types of emigration
going on simultaneously.

As O. Martins noted (1891:228,229), the sex, age, and
marital status distributions of Portuguese emigration
differed markedly between regions. For as far back as the
records extend, the mainland and the islands were points of
departure for different types of emigration that persisted
into the twentieth century. Emigration from the mainland
was overwhelmingly dominated by adult males; emigration from

the islands incorporated a significant number of children
and women.

Even without correcting for clandestine (15), the
differences in the sex, age, and marital status composition
of the migratory flows from the two regions are eloquent
enough (Tables B:3 to B:6 in Appendix 2). Between the
1860's and the 1920's, the female share of the migratory
flow was 21 percent for the mainland, compared to 44 percent
for the Azores and 35 percent for Madeira. Minors (those
under age 14) share represented only 15 percent of the
migratory stream of the mainland, versus 26 and 25 percent
for the Azores and Madeira. Furthermore, for each one
hundred married men leaving between 1897 and 1906 there were
21 married females departing from the mainland and 67 from
the islands.

In sum, Portuguese emigration from the mainland was
consistently an individual and male-dominated phenomenon,
initially sought as a "temporary" (16) move. From the
beginning Portuguese emigration from the islands included a
much higher share of children and females. Although
individual male departures also dominated Madeira and Azores

---

15 The clandestine emigrant of this period was a young
adult male. Thus, the simple fact that there were much more
men departing legally from the mainland than from the
islands means that mainland numbers favor much more female
participation than the corresponding numbers for the
islands.
16 The myth of return (see chapter I, and Brettell, 1985)
was extremely strong in Portugal. particularly in the North.
The high share of married males among emigrants from the
mainland (46 percent between 1897 and 1927) suggests that a
great majority must have left with the idea of returning.

migratory streams, emigration from these islands was more permanent and familial than the mainland exodus (17).

As Bacci (1971:35) has remarked, from the 1890's on Portugal had one of the highest rates of net emigration (Ireland excluded) in Western Europe. This fact, coupled with the demographic selectivity of emigration noted above, produced an anomalous population structure compared to the population structure of other European countries. Portugal had an exceptionally high proportion of females in its population (18). In terms of age structure, males under 15 were overrepresented; females over 15 years of age predominated; and males between 15 and 60 years of age were underrepresented. Indeed, this last group (males 15 to 60) comprised a smaller proportion of the Portuguese population than it did in other European countries (e.g., Carqueja, 1916:105,113,143,184,287, and Mitchell, 1982:28-56).

In two respects, however, the migratory flows from the mainland and the islands were almost identical. Regardless of their region of origin, Portuguese emigrants were overwhelmingly illiterate and unskilled. As the Portuguese Consul in Boston noted in 1874:

> Almost all [Portuguese immigrants] are laborers. Very few have a craft before they arrived to this country. The majority do not know how to read or write. (Emigração Portugueza, Doc...., 1874:248)

---

17 In chapter 1 we saw that family emigration both to Brazil and the United States could only be done in stages due to economic constraints.
18 In 1920 the Portuguese population was constituted by 52 percent of females. Only countries of heavy emigration like Poland had a female proportion so high at this time (Mitchell, 1982).

Thirty years later the situation had not improved much. Between 1901 and 1908, more than half of the Portuguese emigrants legally departed were either unskilled or without occupation, and more than 60 percent were illiterate (A. Costa, 1911:84, 85).

The country of destination for emigrants also exhibited marked regional divergencies. Between 1897 and 1927 the mainland exodus took essentially (81 percent) the direction of Brazil, while the migratory flow from the Azores was massively (85 percent) directed to United States. The migratory stream from Madeira was much more evenly distributed: 50 percent went to Brazil, and 34 percent went to the United States. Earlier in the nineteenth century, regional disparity had been even more pronounced. Of the 5010 emigrants that left for United States between 1855 and 1865, 5008 departed from the Azores and the remaining 2 from Madeira (R. de Freitas, 1867:10).

The connection between the type of emigration and the country of destination for Portuguese migrants will be further explored in the remainder of this chapter, which focuses on the nature of Portuguese emigration to United States.

SOURCES FOR PORTUGUESE EMIGRATION TO THE UNITED STATES 1820-1930

Portuguese immigration to the United States can be studied adequately only by combining information from both the sending and the receiving countries. Both sources have serious but dissimilar gaps, although the American sources are superior overall.

In Portugal, two main sources are available on emigration: official statistics containing aggregate data on emigration, and the registers and case records of passports containing individual-level data. We have seen previously, how seriously incomplete are the Portuguese official aggregated statistics. To the shortcomings already noted we must add that until the 1880's, the United States was not specified as a country of destination in Portuguese statistics.

The second source, the passport registers give for each emigrant (individual passport) or group of emigrants (collective passport) the following information: name, age, marital status, and place of birth. For males the register added occupation (19), and for minors, father's and mother's name and surname. Collective passports also indicated the relationship of each person to the primary passport holder.

Portuguese passport registers have never been systematically studied (20), for three reasons: the records are scattered throughout Portugal; most of the older record have been destroyed; and the data require lengthy demographic and quantitative analysis. The systematic study of this source would, however, greatly enhance our understanding of Portuguese emigration to both Brazil and

---

19 Occupation for females was not consistently recorded in the shiplists.
20. That does not mean that they are totally unexplored. Lagos Trindade (1976), for example, surveyed the passport registers for Azores. She seems to have also surveyed the registers for Madeira, but as far as I know only some preliminary results for Azores were published.

the United States. When linked to American and Brazilian sources, the passport registers can help us measure the clandestine flow (21). Furthermore, these registers are the only surviving source to record the place of residence of legal emigrants. Linkage of these records to the American shiplists can help us to measure the demographic impact of emigration in the communities of origin, and the extent and functioning of the migratory network in specific communities in both Portugal and the United States. Unfortunately, like the aggregate statistics, the passport registers cover only legal emigrants.

Two American sources can be used to draw the profile of Portuguese immigration to the United States, the <u>Annual Report on Immigration</u> (1820 to date), and the Manifest Shiplists (or Passengers' Shiplists).

THE U.S. ANNUAL REPORTS ON IMMIGRATION

Congress tried to determine who was arriving to the American shores by passing the Act of March 2, 1819 "regulating passenger ships and vessels"; under this act, collectors of customs recorded information on the number of foreign passengers entering American seaports. The Secretary of State presented to Congress an annual report on immigration based on this information. These reports were sometimes lengthy appraisals of immigration trends and problems, and sometimes just statistical summaries of

21 Passport registers list the legal migratory flow the American and at least some of the Brazilian sources list arrivals regardless of the way the departure was made.

foreigners entering the United States. The reports were published as Congressional Executive Documents and describe immigration to the United States from 1820 on.

Over time, the official entities issuing the annual statistics on immigration changed. The Department of State published annual series on immigration between 1820 and 1870; the Bureau of Statistics Series, between 1868 and 1891); and the Bureau of Immigration (later renamed the Bureau of Immigration and Naturalization, and the Immigration and Naturalization Service) from 1892 to the present. Soon after publication had begun, contemporaries criticized some of the deficiencies of the annual reports (e.g.Tucker, 1846; Brownell, 1856). For example, Jesse Chickering, in 1848, wrote the following critique of the Secretary of State's annual report on immigration:

> These returns are imperfect. There are omissions in the printed reports for whole quarters....
> It appears that the number of foreign passengers arriving at New York, during the nine months, commencing Oct. 1, 1845 and Oct. 1, 1846, as shown by the books of the health officer, and for whom bonds were given, was greater by nearly 11 per cent. in the last period, than the number registered at the custom-house....
> Besides the foreign passengers who arrive in the collection districts, many are landed elsewhere,..., without being so reported.... In ordinary years, we may suppose that 50 per cent. is to be added to the number returned by the collectors, in order to obtain the probable number of foreign emigrants who have settled in the United States. (J.Chickering, 1848: 2-4)

To amend some of these deficiencies, in 1853, the Department of State begun distributing uniform schedules for reporting passenger arrivals to custom collectors: nonetheless many ambiguities still remained.

Several scholars (e.g. Willcox, Vol.I, 1929:194; Vol.II, 1931:86; Gould,1979:597,598)) have noted these and other deficiencies in the reports.   Even official entities connected with immigration acknowledged some major flaws. For example, the Report of the Immigration Investigating Commission of 1895, remarks that reentries were not distinguished from new arrivals, although in New York alone reentrants comprised 14 percent of the migratory flow in 1894.   Hutchinson (1958:963-995), who studied immigration series carefully, pointed out the following main problems:

A. For the Department of State series, 1820-1867

1.lack of information on compilation practices;
2. coverage of the foreign-born rather than
aliens; 3. ambiguity about whether the data refer
to country of citizenship, country of last
permanent residence, or country of birth; 4.
inclusion of those who died on board; 5.changes in
the reporting period; 6. no reference to arrivals
by land until 1853, and only irregular information
afterwards.

B. For the Bureau of Statistics series, 1868-1891

1. exclusion of temporary visitors (estimated to be 1.5 percent of totals) and deaths on board; 2. ambiguity about whether the data referred to country of nativity, citizenship or last permanent residence; 3. incomplete and irregular reporting of land arrivals; 4. and failure to isolate reeentrant aliens.

C. For the Bureau of Immigration or INS series, 1892 to 1932

1. inclusion only of steerage passengers until 1902 (cabin passengers estimated to be 12 percent of the total); 2. no systematic reference to entrants by land borders; 3. inclusion of aliens in transit until 1904; 4. failure to specify reentries until 1906 (estimated to be between 9 and 19 percent of the total); 5. after 1908, and for statistical purposes, immigrants were defined as incoming emigrants who intended to reside permanently in the United States.

After his exhaustive analysis, Hutchinson concluded that the following will never be known: the number of cabin class passengers from 1892 to 1904; the number of arrivals by land; and the number of illegal entrants. For the remaining problems, some adjustments can improve year to year comparability.

In my research, I became aware of another major problem in these series not noticed previously. The numbers given in these annual reports are aggregated by country of origin. What this heading means concretely (i.e., country of birth, country of last residence, or country of citizenship) is uncertain, but that is not the only problem. I found that the disaggregation of emigrants from a particular country into their region of origin in the reports yields entirely misleading results. Let me be more specific. Until the 1890's Portuguese arrivals are listed on the annual reports disaggregated into three groups: arrivals from Portugal,

arrivals from the Azores, and arrivals from Madeira (22).
Supposedly, this would mean that there were three different
regions of origin for the incoming Portuguese-- the
mainland, Azores, and Madeira. That is, in fact, true.
What is not true are the published numbers associated with
each of these areas of origin.

The point is easily proven. The Annual Report for 1860
recorded 90 Portuguese from Portugal, and 268 from Azores
and Madeira. According to the headings, these 90 Portuguese
should have come from the mainland, and the remaining 268
should have come from the islands. My survey of the
Manifest Shiplists for Boston for 1860 indicates that only
7 of these 90 Portuguese came from the mainland, while the
remaining 83 came from the Azores (more concretely from the
island of Flores).

The source of the problem is simple: during the
nineteenth century nationality was frequently confused with
native region. Based only on the annual reports, we would
have assumed that 25 percent (90 emigrants) of the
Portuguese migratory flow to the United States in 1860
departed from the mainland, while 75 percent departed from
the islands. Such an inference would be wrong because, as
the shiplists indicate, only 2 percent (7 emigrants) came
from the mainland. Furthermore, my survey of the Manifest
Shiplists for the 1890's and 1900 indicate that the same
problem of misleading information persisted at least through
1900.

---

22 I am excluding arrivals from Cape Verde.

In sum, the information on place of origin given in the
annual reports must be used with great caution. In
particular, the reported figures pose especially serious
problems for researchers dealing with immigration from
countries like Portugal, Italy, and Spain. I noticed in my
survey of the manifest shiplists that immigrants from
regions like the Azores, Sardinia, and the Canary Islands,
could be attributed to Portugal, Italy, Spain, the Azores,
Sardinia, or the Canary Islands. The confusion arises from
the way immigrants perceived themselves or were perceived by
the ship's clerk when they entered the vessel bringing them
to the United States. The registration of these immigrants
under different headings in the annual reports suggests,
however, precise criteria for defining the emigrants' region
of origin.

The only practical solution to this confusion in the
annual reports is to aggregate the figures for each region
of the countries under study, and use only the national
totals. Any inferences about regions of origin from this
source are bound to be seriously wrong.

Given the inaccuracy of the values shown under the
heading "country of origin", no time series for Portugal
based on the official statistics can be trusted
(particularly for the period before the 1870's), unless the
figures aggregated under separate headings (Portugal,
Azores, and Madeira) are combined. A good example of the
serious distortions contained in these time series is given
on Table IV:VI, where I tabulated Portuguese emigration to

the United States between 1848 and 1870 according to three different American official sources.

TABLE IV:VI PORTUGUESE EMIGRATION TO THE UNITED STATES 1848-1930, ACCORDING TO THREE DIFFERENT SOURCES

YEAR	SOURCES		
	(1)	(2)	(3)
1848	87	87	67
1849	74	74	26
1850	539	546	366
1851	153	161	50
1852	238	246	68
1853	272	359	95
1854	324	340	72
1855	342	381	205
1856	480	488	128
1857	768	771	92
1858	475	480	177
1859	343	453	46
1860	447	445	122
1861	304	310	47
1862	229	229	72
1863	313	313	86
1864	694	700	240
1865	897	897	365
1866	692	695	344
1867	585	511	126
1868	580	555	174
1869	704	714	507
1870	771	852	697
TOTAL	10311	10607	4172

SOURCE: 1. Young, 1871:XII-XIX
2. Annual Reports for the given years
3. Immigration Commission Report, 1910. Vol.I, 1911:66-88

In the first and second source, (Young, 1871:XII-XIX, and the annual reports for the given years) I aggregated the several headings covering Portuguese emigrants, in the third source only the total is given. Comparing the series in Table IV:VI we find, for example, that Young's (1871:XII-XIX) series (column 1) indicate that 10311 Portuguese emigrants entered the United States between 1848 and 1870 while the corresponding figure given by the Immigration

Commission Report, 1910 (Vol.I, 1911:66-88) (column 3) is
4172 (i.e, 40 percent of the Portuguese arrivals). Sometimes
the distortions in the last source are extremely large; in
1858, for example, Young (1871) indicates 475 Portuguese
arrivals, the Annual Report for 1858 indicates 480, and the
Immigration Commission Report, 1910 indicates for the same
year 177 (i.e., only 37 percent of the Portuguese arrivals).

Despite the problems arising from different criteria for
compilation, ambiguous definitions (23), and misleading
categories, there are official series on immigration to the
United States from 1820 until the present. The information
contained in these series has been published in Ferenczi and
Willcox (1929) and republished and updated in Historical
Statistics of the United States, Colonial Times to 1970
(1976). The first publication, by Ferenczi and Willcox, can
only be used, in the Portuguese case, for the period after
1893. Until that date (see, for example Table I and II
"Distribution by Nationality", Ferenczi and Willcox,
1929:377-385), only a small part of the Portuguese flow to
the United States is given (i.e., the elements that the ship
clerk recorded as Portuguese in the manifest shiplists and
that the customs collectors copied to their own lists). The
second publication is useless for the study of Portuguese

---

23 The definition of an immigrant for statistical purposes
was, over time, as follows: until 1867-- all steerage
passengers entering the United States; from 1868 to 1891 --
all travellers that declared their intention to remain in
the country; from 1892 to 1907-- aliens officially admitted
who had previously resided in a foreign country and who
declared their intention of residing in the United States;
from 1907 on, both the declaration of intention to reside in
the United States and previous residence in a foreign
country were essential to the definition of immigrant
(Willcox, Vol.II,1931:86)

immigration. The Portuguese flow is included in a residual category labelled "Southern Europe".

THE MANIFEST SHIPLISTS

The second American source available for studying Portuguese immigration to the United States are the manifest shiplists, many of which are deposited at the National Immigration Archives (Balch Institute, Philadelphia) and at the National Archives (Washington, D.C.). This source furnishes individual-level data and provides more information than the annual reports. In the earlier lists (e.g., for the port of Boston in 1860), the following information is usually available for each incoming passenger: name, age, sex, occupation ("trade or profession"), "country to which they severally belong", "country of which they intend to become inhabitants", deaths on board, and the part of the vessel occupied during the crossing. The lists from the 1890's and 1900's are even more inclusive. They give, for each passenger, the following: name, age, sex, occupation, country of citizenship, country of birth, place of destination, number of pieces of luggage, location of the compartment or space occupied, date and cause of death, and whether the emigrant was, by self-declaration, only visiting or intending permanent settlement.

The specific reliability of these shiplists varies, depending on the care taken by the particular ship clerk. For the most part, internal evidence points to reliability

(24). The lists for Boston for 1860 are second-generation documents, and none was signed by the captain of the vessel. The lists for New York and Boston for 1890/1891 are first generation-documents and are all signed by the captain of the vessel. The manuscripts deposited at the National Immigration Archives (Philadelphia) are usually well preserved and easy to read. The shiplists for Boston and New York for 1890, 1891, and for Boston and San Francisco for 1900 that I collected at the National Archives (Washington, D.C.) are less detailed, and extremely difficult to read.

The manifest shiplists are undoubtedly superior to any other available source on immigration. Unfortunately, their systematic use by individual researchers studying particular immigrant groups is seldom a feasible task (25). For example, there are 1987 manifests for 1891 for New York deposited at the Balch Institute. Some of these lists record over 800 passengers, and only occasionally does one encounter a Portuguese passenger. To collect the data on

---

24 Some entries are less carefully done then others. E.g., name, sex, and age are quite reliable. Very few times did I find a female name attributed to a male or vice versa, and ages are not rounded to the nearest five or zero. Occupation and pieces of luggage are the less reliable entries. Many times luggage is not given, and some times occupation, particularly for women, is not given or the same occupation is given for all women passengers.
25 Swierenga (1981, and 1982) has extensively used these manifests in his study on Dutch immigration; Erickson (1982) presented a paper on the relevance and superiority of the manifests for the study of British and Irish immigrants, and Ira Glazier, who currently directs an ongoing project on immigration to the United States based on these manifests, has published several studies on Italian immigration (e.g., DiComite and Glazier, 1985).

incoming Portuguese in that year, I had to review
individually each of these 1987 shiplists.

TESTING THE SOURCES

As noted earlier in this chapter, Portuguese sources on
emigration registered only legal departures.   The data from
Portuguese sources necessarily differs from that in the
American sources on immigration since the latter recorded
aliens/passengers arrivals regardless of the manner of
departure from the sending country.   But as we have seen,
even the American sources (i.e., the annual reports and
manifest shiplists), yield dissimilar results.   We have thus
to ask if these sources can be indiscriminately used, and
which of them is closest to the "true" population,
Portuguese emigrants to the United States.

Comparing the socio-demographic profile of the Portuguese
emigrants implied by the shiplists for the port of Boston in
1860 and by Azorean passport registers for that same year
(Lagos Trindade, 1976:270-276) yields the following results

TABLE IV:VII - SOCIO DEMOGRAPHIC PROFILE OF PORTUGUESE
EMIGRANTS IN 1860 FROM SHIPLISTS (U.S.) VERSUS PASSPORT
REGISTERS (AZORES)

A. PERCENTAGE DISTRIBUTION BY SEX

SEX	MANIFESTS	PASSPORTS
MALE	58	49
FEMALE	42	51
TOTAL	100	100
N	280	249

B. PERCENTAGE DISTRIBUTION BY SEX AND AGE

SEX/AGE	MANIFESTS	PASSPORTS
MALE	50	36
FEMALE	36	38
CHILDREN	14	19
UNKNOWN	0	7
TOTAL	100	100
N	280	249

C. PERCENTAGE DISTRIBUTION FOR MALE OCCUPATIONS

OCCUPATION	MANIFESTS	OCCUPATION	PASSPORTS
MARINER	56	SEAMAN	32
LABORER	17	WORKER	39
FARMER	6	LANDOWNER	8
CARPENTER	0	MERCHANT	13
UNKNOWN	21	ARTISAN	2
OTHER	0	OTHER	3
TOTAL	100	TOTAL	100
N	141	N	90

As Table IV:VII indicates, the manifests and the passports paint a different portrait of the Portuguese emigration in 1860. For example, while, the shiplists describe a predominantly male population, the passports indicate a female majority. The age distribution and the predominant occupations of the migrants also differ for the passport registers and shiplists.

If we add 20 percent to the male population recorded in the passports, we obtain a similar sex ratio from both sources. We may hypothesize that the difference observed is the result of male clandestine emigration. But this hypothesis would not explain the differential occupational structure for males in the two sources (26).

---

26 If clandestine emigrants were all young adult men, and occupation differed for young and older men, the omission of illegal could hypothetically account for the observed occupational differences.

When comparing the characteristics of populations recorded in two different sources, we are likely to find slight differences that can derive simply from random errors in the recording process. We must thus test whether the differences in the characteristics of the migrants found in the Portuguese and the American sources are indeed significant. This problem corresponds to the statistical problem of testing whether two samples came from the same mother population.   In this case we ask, can the differences between the results from the two sources be attributed to random error, and do the two sources belong to the same mother population ?

Among the several statistical tests available, the chi-square test is an adequate procedure for the present case because it takes into account the distribution of nominal characteristics to be tested. First, I assumed that the differences found, for the male distribution, in the two sources were due to random error. Thus, a good estimate of the true value is the mean of the two values given by the sources. The results of the chi-square test reject this assumption at .01 level of significance (27).

I next assumed that the distribution from the shiplists was the correct one, and tested the hypothesis that the sex distribution indicated by the passport registers came from

27   RESULTS OF THE CHI-SQUARE TEST FOR THE FIRST HYPOTHESIS: MALES 1860

	Manifests	Passports		
Observed	140	90		
Estimated	115	115	α =.01	c.v. =6.63
O - E	25	-25		
$(O-E)^2/E$	5.43	5.43 = 10.86	x^2 =10.86	

the same population. Based on the results of the chi-square test (28), I also reject this hypothesis at the .025 level of significance.

To confirm the results obtained for 1860, I repeated the test using data for 1904, taken from the annual report on immigration and the Portuguese official statistics on emigration. Again, I reject the hypothesis that the values indicated by the two sources for the male distribution, the sex distribution, and the age distribution came from the same population, at the .01 level of significance (29).

Next, I compared the information from the shiplists for the port of Boston for 1860 with the data given in the annual report on immigration for that year. The totals differ slightly; 353 incoming Portuguese are listed on the shiplists, versus 359 in the annual report. This discrepancy indicates either a slight over recording error in the annual report or a missing shiplist for the port of Boston. The differences in the sex of the migrants are not statistically significant, however (30).

Finally, I compared the sex and age distribution for 1890/1891 given in the shiplists for Boston and New York and the annual reports. The differences in the sex distribution and the age for women migrants are not statistically significant (31). The results of the chi-square test for the age distribution of the male migrants indicate that the

---

28 α=.025; c.v.=5.02; x^2=5.68.
29 For the male distribution: α=.01; c.v.=6.63; x^2=258.6.
For the sex distribution: α=.01; c.v.=6.63; x^2=80. For the age distribution: α=.01; c.v.=6.63; x^2=26.1.
30 Tested sex distribution: α=.01; c.v.=6.63; x^2=.051.
31 Tested sex distribution: α=.01; c.v.=6.63; x^2=.559. For female age distribution: α=.01; c.v.=6.63; x^2=1.31.

two sources give significantly different age structures (32). It is possible that this discrepancy is due to the fact that I only surveyed the ports of New York and Boston which include only 67 percent of the total male population arrived (33).

Based on the results obtained for 1860 and 1890/1891, I decided to accept the numbers from the annual reports on the sex, age, port of arrival, and occupation of Portuguese migrants. I reject the data on country of origin in this source, however. As pointed out above the published figures confound country of origin and native region.

The data and the results of the chi-square tests for the Portuguese case, point to a larger generalization: the use of sources containing only data on legal emigration do not accurately portray the "true" migratory flow from countries that have large clandestine streams. When combined, the peculiar characteristics of the clandestine flow and of the legal stream create a new migratory current. This "true" migratory flow may have characteristics diverging from both the legal and the clandestine streams.

In conclusion, a critical appraisal of the sources for studying Portuguese emigration to the United States generated by the sending and the receiving society shows that they actually refer to different migratory flows. American sources on Portuguese emigration into the United States prove to be superior. Furthermore, the annual report

---

32 Tested male age structure: $\alpha=.01$; c.v.$=6.63$; $x^2=59.5$.
33 I was unable to locate the shiplists for New Bedford where 29 percent of the Portuguese migrants arrived in 1891. It is possible that these lists would solve the discrepancy noted above in the male age structure.

on immigration provides an accurate description of the characteristics of the Portuguese migrant population (apart from the data on country of origin), although the total numbers of annual entrants and probably the age distribution for males may not be completely reliable.

NAME LINKAGE:PORTUGUESE NAMES,TRADITION, ILLITERACY AND ANGLICIZATION.

To address some research questions like regions of departure and the dynamics of migrant networks, we need to link the American shiplists to the Portuguese passports registers. But longitudinal linkage of migrants on multinational records poses serious methodologic problems. Even when theoretically linkable records of international migrants survived in both the sending and in the receiving society, a host of problems have to be solved before linkage is done (34).

Records that were made for different purposes (and were created by different clerks with different degrees of accuracy) have minimal overlapping information. The different contents provide the primary justification for linking multinational records: to gather information that no national record alone can give. But, the critical overlapping information upon which the linkage has to be based, the common individual identifier, is frequently

---

34 The unique legal character of international migration and the wide variation in national policies leads frequently to recording problems. As Heisel (1979:4) noted the migrant and the two countries concerned may describe and record the move differently.

reduced to a distorted or truncated name associated with a sex and an age.

This section addresses the problems in linking passport registers to American passenger shiplists created by name changes and incomplete information on names. It also indicates the solutions I relied on, and the limitations of analysis based on linked records from the data sets used here.

In her study of Norwegian-American names, M. Kimmerle stated that:

> When foreign surnames are exchanged for American surnames or entirely lose their foreign character, the very loss of the alien element points to a parallel loss in the immigrant's native social heritage. Because surnames reflect both the old and the new culture of the immigrant in a very personal way, they serve as an excellent index to the social problems of immigration. (Kimmerle, 1941:1, quoted in, Pap, 1949:124)

Kimmerle's statement implies that name-changing occurred in tandem with assimilation. According to this paradigm, linkage of the Portuguese recorded in the United States censuses would reveal that the more time an immigrant had spent in United States, the greater his probability of having an anglicized name.

We know that some name-changing due to adjustment needs occurred among Portuguese immigrants. For example, in the 1873 Report of the Protestant North End Mission (a charitable institution that assisted Azorean women in the Boston area), name-changing among Portuguese immigrant females was clearly noted and attributed to environmental pressure. The Report states:

> They find their Portuguese names useless
> because we cannot pronounce them, and so rename
> themselves for our accommodation. Sometimes they
> give the translation of the Portuguese name. (The
> North End Mission Magazine, II,3, July 1873:66,
> quoted in, Pap,1949:132)

Assimilation was perhaps the primary factor in the process
of name-changing among Norwegian immigrants, and no
doubt assimilation pressured a significant number of
Portuguese immigrants to anglicize their names. But name-
changing among Portuguese immigrants also occurred for
reasons other than adjustment needs, and the process often
began even before emigrants reached the United States.
Shiplists reveal that name-changing tended to occur as soon
as the Portuguese emigrant set foot on the vessel going to
the United States and his/her presence was recorded by the
ship clerk.

In the shiplists for the port of Boston, only
occasionally did I find Portuguese emigrant names that had
the correct Portuguese orthography and that observed the
main Portuguese conventions of name-giving. By contrast the
shiplists surveyed for the port of New York recorded
Portuguese emigrant names with great accuracy. The
outstanding difference between these two sets of records is
that the shiplists for Boston belonged almost entirely to
American vessels manned by captains of nationalities other
than Portuguese, while the shiplists for New York were
mainly written by Portuguese captains manning Portuguese
emigrant ships.

Exogenous factors, such as the native language of the
vessel's clerk and the literacy level of the emigrant

involved, seem to have been at least as relevant for
maintaining or changing emigrant names as were later
adjustment needs. Illiterate emigrants certainly could not
notice changes in their names made either by the ship's
clerks or by the American authorities on arrival, since they
did not know how to spell them anyway. Clerks, who were
native English speakers could do no more than register
sound-alike names if only verbal information was given.

Leo Pap (1949), a linguist who studied Portuguese-
American speech, was also of the opinion that name-changing
occurred from the beginning of the migratory process. He
contended that alterations in Portuguese names and surnames
were in some cases motivated by assimilation or adjustment
needs, but other factors were also at play, particularly the
education level of the emigrant and the traditions in name-
giving in Portugal (Pap,1949:125-127).

Pap found that the first flow of Portuguese emigrants to
the United States, in the eighteenth century, were more
likely to maintain their family names than were emigrants
coming in the last decades of the nineteenth century (35).
This different behavior in the two migratory waves, Pap
attributes to differences of education and social status.
The first group was constituted by Jews fleeing religious
persecution. The majority of these people were educated and
upwardly mobile and they were able to maintain their roots

---

35 According to Leo Pap, in the forties it was still
possible to identify the American Jews of Portuguese
ancestry, who formed the first wave of Portuguese
emigration, since they still maintained their surnames
uncorrupted by Anglicization. The most frequent names were:
Cardoza, Seixas, Pinto, Carvalho, Silva, Moraes, da Costa,
and Madeira (Pap,1949:3).

through generations since they could keep records (36). The
second group was constituted by mainly poor and illiterate
rural Azoreans, who were often unable to spell their names
and ashamed of their low social status. This group was both
unable to notice the changes in their names perpetrated by
the vessel's clerk or the American authorities, and was
willing to accept or to promote the Anglicization of their
names.

The effects of low education and social status were
compounded by Portuguese freedom in name-giving. The
Portuguese law of the time allowed a child to be given,
after his christian name(s), either his father's surname(s),
her mother's surname(s), or a mixture of both in non-
discriminated order. Most commonly, children added to their
given name(s) the mother's family name(s), followed by their
father's surname(s). A married woman could choose between
the name of her family of origin and her husband's family
name(s), but most added the latter. In rural areas a
nickname was very often added as well (37). The final
result of this combinatory freedom in the use of family
names was that, even in official documents (e.g., passport
registers, wills, death certificates, and court records), a

---

36 According to Celestino Soares (1939:56) during the 1930's
Jewish families descended from this first emigratory wave
still celebrated religious service in ancient Portuguese at
the Portuguese Sisterhood Synagogue in New York.
36 An observer writing on the Portuguese immigrants in
United States in the last decades of the nineteenth century
noticed the preference among Azoreans immigrants for
nicknames instead of given names (Lang, 1892: 17). This is
in accordance with the fact that the majority were in fact
from rural areas.

person could be identified in the same document by one, two, or more full names (38).

To sum it up, Leo Pap identified the following types and methods of name-changing:

> 1. The spelling of the name is changed, either
> a) in an attempt to insure the original native pronunciation of the name by persons used to conventional English spelling, or
> b) to the extent and for the purpose of Anglicization the name while still retaining close similarity with the original form.
> 2. The name is shortened or lengthened for Anglicization without its original form being completely abandoned.
> 3. The name is translated into English, in the case of surnames which have also a generic meaning, or is replaced by its English cognate in the case of Christian given names.
> 4. The native name is dropped in favor of an American (English -looking) name which has neither phonetic nor semantic similarity with the former. (Pap,1949:126)

Problems raised by some of these name-changing methods are, to a certain extent, soluble. If the changes were made using the first, the second, or the third method, alternative lists of names can be drawn for linkage purposes, to take into account the most common alterations. In such a list, Joe Perry in an American record will stand for José or João Pereira in a Portuguese record; John Marshall will stand for João Machado; and Manuel or Manny Wood will stand for Manuel Silveira (see Appendix 2, List of Names and Alternates in American and Portuguese sources).

When the fourth method was used (i.e., a dissimilar American surname was adopted) the problem has no practical

---

38. In the Passport Register for the district of Angra, we find for example, a record of a Luis Machado Trindade also known as Luis Machado Mancebo (passport number 430 of 1890) and a Guillhermina Augusta de Brito Moraes also known as Guillhermina Augusta Moraes d'Azevedo and Guilermina Augusta de Brito Moraes d'Azevedo.

solution even when only surnames were modified. It is impossible to trace back to a Portuguese record (birth certificate, passport register, census record, will, etc.) on the bases of a person christian name(s) alone. For example, when a Portuguese crew member named Joaquim, was given by the American skipper the full name of Joe King-- which actually corresponds to the two phonemes a native English speaker perceives in the Portuguese name (Joa-quim)- -, this man is obviously lost for linkage purposes. Similarly, Manuel Morgan stands for Manuel plus the vessel's name (Morgan) where Manuel was employed; and Manny Snow stands for Manuel plus the surname of the captain's vessel taking in Manuel. Although there is some possibility that the departures of such emigrants were recorded in Portuguese records, these individuals are nevertheless impossible to link (39).

The frequency with which certain names and surnames reappear, among the Portuguese immigrants further complicates the linkage process. The surname Silva was so frequent that "Portuguese immigrants in general are sometimes called *Silvy's* (sg., *a silvy*) by American neighbors" (Pap, 1949:137). In the same vein, the 1873 Report of the Protestant North End Mission, remarked that:

> The Azoreans have a curious fashion concerning
> names, causing much perplexity in keeping records
> of them. They have a name for us -- another for

---

39 The above examples are given by Pap, 1949:130,131. Lang explains the frequent alteration of Joaquim into Joe King in the following way: "The Portuguese Christian name Joaquim, quite common among Azoreans, is by the practical English mind interpreted as representing the two English names Joe King, an appellation readily adopted by our Portuguese colonists" Lang, 1892:17.

the employer -- still another for the Chardon
Street Committee of Relief. *Mary Joseph* is a
favorite name. *Mary Rose*, or *Rosa Mary*, another.
It is not uncommon to hold a dialogue after this
manner: "What is your name ?" "*Mary Joseph.*"
Perhaps I do not hear distinctly and say, "What is
it ?" "Well, *Mary Joseph, or Mary Rose, or Rosa
Mary, or Rosa Joseph*; anything you like to write;
it shall be my name for you." (The North End
Mission Magazine, II, 3, July, 1873:66, quoted in
Pap, 1949:132)

Name-changing is only one of the difficulties encountered
when trying to follow the Portuguese emigrants, particularly
if they are females or children. In the passenger
shiplists surveyed women and children were frequently
registered by only their christian name(s). When these
women or children travelled in the company of a man and it
was possible to identify them as a group, the family name of
the male associated with the group was added under the
assumption that they all used the same surname. Such an
assumption is, for reasons indicated above, quite a broad
one; even if the male associated with the group was a
father, a husband, or a brother, we can never be totally
sure that the whole family used the same surname(s). Still,
this is the best approach, since it is likely that they all
adopted or, entering together, were given the same
surname(s) in the United States.

For the remaining males, females or children listed in
passenger shiplists-- who cannot be assumed to travel in a
group and that were not registered by more than their
christian name(s)-- we have no more than sex, age, and
sometimes an occupation. Any attempts to use this limited
information for linkage with Portuguese records are
worthless.

The data on Portuguese immigration to the United States contained in the annual reports and the manifest shiplists have not, to my knowledge, been fully explored previously. This does not imply that Portuguese immigration has not been addressed for some periods, but the elements are scattered and the analysis lacks depth (40).

What I propose to do now is to describe the Portuguese emigration to the United States based on the numbers in the American series from 1820 to 1930, with particular focus on the period after 1850. In order to accomplish my goal I searched for yearly information from the annual reports on immigration presented to Congress until 1895 and from 1897 to 1932 on the <u>Annual Report of the Immigration Commissioner</u>. I completed this information with the manifest shiplists for Boston (1860, 1890, 1891, 1900), for New York (1890, 1891), and for San Francisco (1900) and the passport registers of the three Azorean districts (Angra do Heroismo, Horta, and Ponta Delgada) for the same years.

The data on Portuguese immigration contained in these sources, manifest shiplists and passport registers, whose strengths and weaknesses I have just reviewed, has never to my knowledge been systematically explored and linked. The story that unfolds from my research is told in the following text and tables.

---

40 For example, Taft (1967) published statistical information on Portuguese immigration to the United Sates between 1899 and 1919, and Bannick (1917) did the same for 1908 to 1916. A recently published, synthesis of the Azorean immigration to the United States by Williams (1982) also contains some statistical material, particularly for the period after 1870.

GENERAL CHARACTERISTICS OF THE PORTUGUESE EMIGRANTS TO THE
UNITED STATES

HOW MANY CAME ?

Beginning with a few dozen immigrants and increasing to a
few hundred by the mid-nineteenth century, the Portuguese
migratory flow to the United States had become a sustained
and growing movement by the 1870's. An average of four
thousand Portuguese arrived in the United States each year
between 1870 and 1919. Over thirty-four thousand came in
1920 and 1921. After that point, the flow receded markedly,
curtailed by American anti-immigration policies.

Portuguese annual arrivals into the United States (1820-
1930), and the totals of the Portuguese emigration (1855-
1930) and American immigration (1820-1930), are given in
Table IV:VIII.

TABLE IV:VIII PORTUGUESE EMIGRATION TO U. S. 1820 - 1930

YEAR	PORT. EMIGR. TO U.S.	TOTAL PORT. EMIGRATION	TOTAL U.S. IMMIGRATION
1820	38		8385
1821	19		9127
1822	34		6911
1823	25		6354
1824	13		7912
1825	16		10199
1826	17		10837
1827	12		18875
1828	26		27382
1829	56		22520
1830	11		23322
1831	2		22633
1832	10		60482
1833	638		58640
1834	73		65365
1835	46		45374
1836	34		76242
1837	39		79340

1838	32		38914
1839	26		68069
1840	25		84066
1841	10		80289
1842	19		104565
1843	40		52496
1844	40		78615
1845	21		114371
1846	17		154416
1847	29		234968
1848	87		226527
1849	74		297024
1850	546		310004
1851	161		439442
1852	246		371603
1853	359		368645
1854	340		427833
1855	381	12135	200877
1856	488	10802	195857
1857	771	10354	112123
1858	480	9411	191942
1859	453	9774	129571
1860	445	6850	133143
1861	310	6242	142877
1862	229	5958	72183
1863	313	4632	132925
1864	700	4743	191114
1865	897	4384	180339
1866	695	6792	332577
1867	511	7508	303104
1868	555	7483	282189
1869	714	8799	352768
1870	852	10138	387203
1871	887	13364	321350
1872	1311	18148	404806
1873	1194	13646	459803
1874	1659	15577	313339
1875	1958	16212	227498
1876	1333	11587	169986
1877	2364	11610	141857
1878	1332	10413	138469
1879	1375	14928	177826
1880	810	14235	457257
1881	1223	16540	669431
1882	1464	20647	788992
1883	1586	21754	603322
1884	1973	19795	518592
1885	2092	16955	395346
1886	1260	15818	334203
1887	1374	19201	490109
1888	1648	27099	546889
1889	2130	23294	444427
1890	2650	33253	455302
1891	3002	27123	560319
1892	3884	24235	579663
1893	4258	34940	439730
1894	2600	30948	285631
1895	1529	51458	258536

1896	2766	31832	343367
1897	1874	24534	230832
1898	1717	27145	229299
1899	2096	20440	311715
1900	4241	24420	448572
1901	4176	23743	487918
1902	5309	27796	648743
1903	8433	24853	857046
1904	6338	32550	812870
1905	4855	38652	1026499
1906	8729	43807	1100735
1907	9648	48243	1285349
1908	6809	46167	782870
1909	4606	43956	751786
1910	7657	45442	1041570
1911	7469	63837	878587
1912	9403	95154	838172
1913	13566	83080	1197892
1914	9647	27531	1218480
1915	4376	20666	326700
1916	12208	26640	298826
1917	10194	16933	295403
1918	2319	12683	110618
1919	1574	39738	141132
1920	15174	69318	430001
1921	18856	26319	805228
1922	1867	42581	309556
1923	2802	42983	522919
1924	3892	31790	706896
1925	720	24486	294314
1926	793	45012	304488
1927	843	29611	335175
1928	844	36698	307255
1929	853	43186	279678
1930	780	24820	241700

SOURCE: For 1820 to 1870: Young, 1871:XII-XIX.
For 1871 to 1930: Annual Report for the given year.

If we plot the data given in column 1 of the above table, we obtain the picture of Portuguese emigration to the United States between 1820 and 1930 shown in Figure 4.

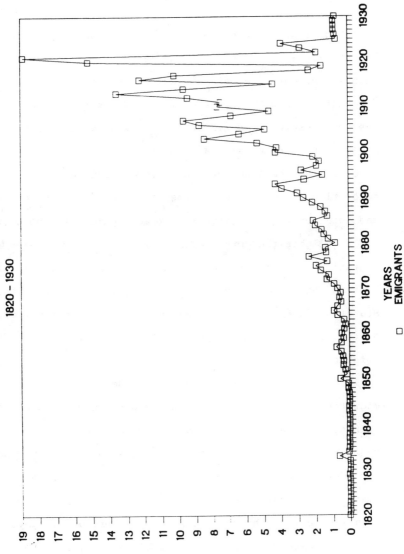

FIGURE 4–PORTUGUESE EMIGRATION TO U.S.

1820 – 1930

Until the 1850's the curve of the Portuguese emigration is practically a flat line. In the late 1860's and early 1870's, the curve takes off, indicating a tendency to exponential growth until the First World War. Thereafter, the curve exhibits marked cycles and wide variances until 1924, when it returns to a flat line.

Comparing the shape of the curve for Portuguese emigration to the United States to the shape of the curve of the total Portuguese emigration (see Figure 5 in Appendix 2), highlights the very similar pattern for Portuguese migration streams. If we now repeat the exercise comparing instead the curve for Portuguese emigration to the United States and the curve for total immigration to the United States (see Figure 6 in Appendix 2) quite different emigratory patterns are obvious.

In the 1920's, Jerome (1926) contended that swings in the migratory flow to the United States were determined by the swings of the American economy. Jerome backed up his contention by pointing to the homography of the curves of the American business cycles and of the cycles of the American immigration flow.

The idea that the evolution of the American economy directly shaped the behavior of the migratory flow to that country has been favored in some of the most influential writings on intercontinental migration. Among others, Brinley Thomas, Simon Kuznets, and Richard Easterlin have been instrumental in diffusing and substantiating this hypothesis. Thomas (1954) claimed that capital investment

in the United States was followed by human capital flows
into the United States. Kuznets (1958) argued that it was
unreasonable to presume that the several economies from
which immigrants were drawn shared a similar economic
evolution; thus we had to accept that swings in the American
economy were the main determinant of fluctuations in the
migratory flow to the United States. Easterlin (1968, 1982)
contended that increases in job opportunities in the United
States were followed by migration flows into the country.
The general argument did not go unchallenged (Bodnar, 1985;
Kamphoefner,1986), but it still remains an arena of sharp
controversy.

Given this theoretical background, the dissimilarity
between the curve of Portuguese emigration to the United
States and the curve of the total immigration flow into the
United States is particularly interesting. The similar
pattern for Portuguese emigration to the United States and
total Portuguese emigration is also notable in this context.
Portuguese emigration to the United States never accounted
for more than 18 percent of the total migratory flow from
Portugal. Thus, the similarity of behavior of these two
curves cannot be the result of the relative weight of the
Portuguese migratory flow to the Unite States in determining
the shape of the total Portuguese migratory stream.
Instead, the outlook of the Portuguese migratory flow is
essentially determined by the current from the mainland to
Brazil; at least 80 percent of all Portuguese emigrants
chose Brazil as their country of destination between the
1850's and the 1920's. Given these two facts, the

homography of the two curves (the total migratory flow from Portugal and the Portuguese migratory stream to the United States) suggests that home conditions were more important in determining the level of Portuguese emigration to the United States than were conditions in the United States. After all, that two economies as different as the Brazilian and the American had coinciding "pull" factors, over such a long period of time is hard to believe (41).

A summary of Portuguese emigration to the United States, its relation both to the total Portuguese outflow and American inflow, is given in Table IV:IX.

TABLE IV:IX - PORTUGUESE EMIGRATION TO THE UNITED STATES AS A PERCENTAGE OF THE TOTAL PORTUGUESE EMIGRATION AND THE AMERICAN IMMIGRATION   1820 - 1930

YEARS	PORTUGUESE EMIGRATION TO THE U.S	PORTUGUESE EMIGRATION AS % TOTAL PORT. EMIGRATION	PORTUGUESE EMIGRATION AS % TOTAL AMERICAN IMMIGRATION
1820-1829	256		.20
1830-1839	911		.17
1840-1849	362		.03
1850-1859	4225		.15
1860-1869	5369	8.47	.25
1870-1879	14265	10.52	.52
1880-1889	15560	7.97	.30
1890-1899	26376	8.62	.71
1900-1909	63144	17.83	.77
1910-1919	78413	18.16	1.24
1920-1929	46644	11.90	1.09

SOURCE:TABLE IV:VIII

Table IV:IX indicates that Portuguese emigration to the United States almost tripled between the 1860's and the following decade. The 1880's were a period of slow growth,

---

41 For a discussion of the determinants of the Portuguese emigration see Chapter I.

however. The following three decades again registered marked increases, particularly during the 1900's. But only in the following decade the Portuguese emigration to the United States account for more than 1 percent of the total number of incoming emigrants to the United States. In terms of the total Portuguese emigration, the flow to the United States attained its peak during the same decade, the 1910's, when a significant number of Portuguese from the mainland came to the United States.

FROM WHERE WERE THEY COMING?

As noted above, the annual reports do not provide reliable information on the regions of departure of Portuguese emigrants coming to the United States, and we must then rely on Portuguese sources and on the shiplists for this topic (42). It has often been stated without dispute that the vast majority of Portuguese emigrants to the United States came from the Azores (O. Martins,1891; Bannick, 1917; Taft,1967; Lagos Trindade, 1976; Williams, 1982). I believe that such a statement needs periodization. Table IV:X yields the material for such periodization which indicates the percentages of the Portuguese legal emigrants to the United States coming from specific regions between the 1890's and the 1920's,

---

42 The implicit assumption made here is that clandestine emigration was randomly distributed by place of origin.

TABLE IV:X - DISTRIBUTION OF THE LEGAL PORTUGUESE EMIGRATION
          TO THE UNITED STATES BY REGION OF ORIGIN

REGION	1897-1899	1901-1905	1912-1916	1923-1927
MAINLAND	.59	1.25	30.75	53.79
AZORES	98.00	95.65	54.91	23.88
MADEIRA	1.24	3.10	14.34	22.30
TOTAL	100	100	100	100
EMIGRANTS	5112	25776	46725	6470

SOURCE: Table B:7 in Appendix 2

Until the 1900's, the Portuguese migratory flow to the
United States was clearly dominated almost entirely by
Azoreans (over 95 percent). The composition of the
migratory flow by region of origin changed drastically after
1910, however. Between 1912 and 1916, emigration to the
United States from the mainland and Madeira accounted
respectively for 31 percent and 14 percent of the migratory
flow, a not insignificant share. Between 1923 and 1927
emigration from the mainland alone accounted for 54 percent
of all the legal departures to the United States, and the
Azorean share dropped to 24 percent.

Given the respective percentages, the Azoreans obviously
constituted the largest share of the Portuguese migratory
stream, to the United States between 1820 and 1930, but this
dominance should not be overstated. The Azoreans almost
entirely dominated the migratory flow from the 1820's to the
1900's. On the other hand, almost half of all Portuguese
arrivals between 1820 and 1930 took place between 1910 and
1930, when the Azoreans did not dominate the migratory flow
(43).

43 Cape Verdians were excluded from this computation, but if
they were included the Azorean share would be smaller,

1900 is the last year for which I have individual-level data that allow me to trace the Portuguese emigrants to the United States back to their communities of origin. As we have just seen, until that date the Portuguese departing to the United States were almost entirely drawn from the Azores. I will thus center the remaining analysis on these nine islands.

As Chapter I demonstrated Portuguese emigration to the United States was initiated by direct recruitment of crews for American whaling and merchant fleets. Not surprisingly, we have abundant literary evidence that the vast majority of Azoreans who first came to the United States departed from Faial and soon after from Pico (44). Faial is the Azorean island closest to the United States and the island with the best natural harbor. Faial's harbor was naturally frequented by vessels on both the whaling and Baltic routes, and fishing and whaling were typical occupations for the inhabitants of Faial and Pico. This familiarity with marine activities made of the islanders of the two islands a ready-made labor source for the American whaling and merchant fleets. The two islands are not only within easy reach of each other via small fishing boats but also are at eyesight distance. Pico's population could see vessels coming to Faial. Finally, an important American merchant house, the

particularly after 1900. From the Annual Reports, it is possible to gather the following information on Cape Verdian's arrivals: for 1820-1889, 565 arrivals (1 percent of incoming Portuguese); for 1890-1896, 947 arrivals (5 percent of incoming Portuguese); for 1903-1913, 12522 arrivals (10 percent of incoming Portuguese).
44 E.g., Rodrigues de Freitas, 1867:10; L. Trindade, 1976:240.

Dabney family, was based on this island. The Dabneys recruited men both to their own vessels and as agents for other American ship owners.

Lagos Trindade (1976), who analyzed the passport registers of the Azores between 1775 and 1900, maintains that until 1896 the Portuguese migratory flow to the United States was first based on Faial and Pico, and then spread by "a process of diffusion" to the islands under Faial's influence, Flores and Corvo (L. Trindade, 1976:254). She published the results of her research for these four islands (45) for the period 1860-1867. Her main conclusion is that, during this period, 75 percent of the passport holders (1350) that left from the district of Horta were natives of Faial (46 percent) or Pico (29 percent) (L. Trindade, 1976:252 and 276).

The contention of L. Trindade that the vast majority of the Portuguese emigrants during the 1860's were coming from Faial and Pico seems reasonable. Less plausible is this author's contention that: "at this time there was no significant clandestine emigration from those islands" (L.Trindade, 1976: 253). The 1979 emigrants that she found had left legally the district of Horta between 1860 and 1867 represent only 48 percent of the Portuguese arrivals registered in the American annual reports. Either there was a huge clandestine migratory flow from Faial and Pico to the United States, or there are many more passport registers to be found. I think, contrary to L. Trindade, that

---

45 The islands of Faial, Pico, Flores, and Corvo constitute the district of Horta. Horta is also the capital city of Faial.

clandestine emigration was very high during this period. As the comparison of the 1860 passport register and the shiplists for the port of Boston indicated earlier illegal accounted for at least 20 percent of the male migration.

The shiplists for 1860 for the port of Boston can also be used, with some precaution, to infer place of origin. Of the 353 Portuguese passengers recorded, we know for certain that 7 came from the mainland and 1 from Madeira. For the remaining 345 Portuguese arrived to Boston in 1860, I inferred from the port of embarkation and stated nativity that 143 came from Faial (i.e., 41 percent), 126 came from Flores (i.e., 36 percent), 4 came from Graciosa (i.e., 1 percent), and 72 came from non specified areas of the Azores (i.e., 20 percent). Faial was undoubtedly the main source of Portuguese emigration to the United States, as L. Trindade claimed. But L. Trindade was not correct in claiming that only after 1896 did emigration to the United States spread to other islands. It is obvious from the shiplists that this process must have begun earlier.

For the 1890's we can be more precise about the regions of origin of Azoreans departing to the United States. The shiplists for the ports of Boston and New York for 1890/1891 indicate the nativity of the passengers. The way the register of nativity was done looks, however, suspiciously similar with the register of port of embarkation.

To test the accuracy of the information on nativity I linked the two largest shiplists (Manifests 358 and 702 for New York for 1891) for the first semester of 1891 with the passport registers for the districts of Angra and Horta

(46). There were registered from Terceira 59 passengers in the shiplists, of whom I identified 57 in the passport registers for Angra. All these 57 passengers had their nativity correctly recorded in the shiplists.

There were 352 passengers in the shiplists recorded as boarding at Faial island of whom I linked to the passport registers for Horta 322 (91 percent). Of those 322 cases linked, 108 cases (34 percent) had the passengers' nativity incorrectly attributed to Faial. The most common error was to attribute to natives of Pico a nativity from the island of Faial.

The distribution of the 241 cases with nativity recorded as Faial in the shiplists was according to the passport register as follows: Faial .552; S.Miguel .012; Graciosa .071; S. Jorge .062; St. Maria .008; Pico .253; Terceira .042. Adjusting the information on nativity from Faial in the shiplists by the distribution suggested, by the linkage of the shiplists and the passport registers is given in Table IV:XI,

---

46 I was unable to locate the registers for 1890/1891 for the district of Ponta Delgada.

TABLE IV:XI - NATIVITY OF PORTUGUESE PASSENGERS 1890-1891

	ORIGINAL RECORDING		ADJUSTED	
REGIONS	EMIGRANTS	PERCENTAGE	EMIGRANTS	PERCENTAGE
FAIAL	1167	36.7	644	20.4
S.MIGUEL	853	26.8	867	27.4
FLORES	467	14.7	467	14.8
S.JORGE	278	8.7	351	11.1
TERCEIRA	128	4.0	177	5.6
PICO	77	2.4	372	11.8
GRACIOSA	25	.8	108	3.4
S.MARIA	22	.7	31	.9
MAINLAND	87	2.8	87	2.8
N.I.(*)	55	1.7	55	1.7
TOTAL	3159	100	3159	100

SOURCE:SHIPLISTS FOR NEW YORK AND BOSTON 1890/1891 AND
PASSPORT REGISTERS FOR THE DISTRICTS OF HORTA AND ANGRA
NOTE: (*) NO INFORMATION OR UNSPECIFIED AREA

S. Miguel was now the place from whence the largest share of
Azoreans departed to the United States, but emigration to
the United States was well spread among all the islands
(47).

---

47 This is a preliminary linkage. I am convinced that if I
locate the passport registers for Ponta Delgada new
adjustments will be made this time more favorable to Faial.
Ch. Dabney (1884) American Consul in the Azores and a major
agent of emigrant ships on route to the United States stated
in his report to the Secretary of State that S. Miguel was a
region of low emigration to the United States. It is thus
hard to believe that only 7 years later it was the island
sending the largest stream.

THE CROSSING

Browsing through the Azorean newspapers (48), I
frequently came across advertisements for emigrant ships,
both to Brazil and the United States. By 1890
advertisements for ships on route to the United States had
become much more frequent. For example, O Açoriano (Horta)
included 87 such advertisements in 1890, 72 of which (83
percent) were for vessels travelling to the United States.

The content of these advertisements was usually sober,
like the following:

> To New Bedford in early July the well known
> American [vessel] Mose B. Tower, captain Narciso
> d'Azevedo. For cargo and passengers contact the
> agents Bensaude & C.o (O Açoriano, Horta, June 13,
> 1886)

The exceptions to this rule came from the agents Ch. Dabney
& Sons. The advertisements of this agency were more
spectacular, promising:

> To California great reductions, prices without
> competition in the bark Sarah (O Açoriano, Horta,
> June 1,1890)

> Magnificent ships with excellent accommodations.
> Unexpensive passages... (O Açoriano, Horta,
> February 20, 1887)

The American destinations most frequently advertised in the
Azorean newspapers were Boston and New York, but smaller
ports like New Bedford, Fall River, Providence, and Taunton
were also mentioned.

According to the American annual reports on immigration,
between the 1850's and the 1880's, 60 to 80 percent of the

48 I surveyed O Açoriano published in Horta, for 1887 to
1890, and A Persuasão published in Ponta Delgada for 1891.

Portuguese emigrants arriving in the United States landed at
the port of Boston. The other two ports receiving
significant numbers of Portuguese were New Bedford and New
York. Small sailing vessels (i.e., brigs, schooners, and
barks) were used for the crossing at this time (49).

The shiplists for Boston in 1860 (50) indicate that the
353 Portuguese arriving there had departed predominantly
from Azorean ports. They came on sailing vessels with an
average tonnage of 221 tons and an average capacity of 38
passengers (51). These vessels cleared from two main areas:
Northern Europe (Liverpool and Halifax), and the Azores
(Faial, Flores, and Azorean harbors not specified). All the
vessels clearing from Northern Europe belonged to the
British merchant fleet; all those departing from the Azores
belonged to the Bostonian merchant fleet.

The Azorean ports of embarkation were of much greater
relative importance than the Northern European ports, in
terms of Portuguese emigration to the United States. Only
11 of the Portuguese emigrants (3 percent) arriving in
Boston in 1860 crossed on steamers, and only 8 (2 percent)

49 For further details on this topic see: Eugene Smith
(1963), F.Bowen (1930), Samuel Morison (1961).
50 During 1860 80 percent of the 447 Portuguese emigrants
arrived at the United States landed at Boston (Annual
Report, 36th Congress, 2d Session, Doc.# 81, Vol. 10, 1860)
51 At the Balch Institute I found thirteen shiplists with
Portuguese passengers registered. These thirteen crossings
were done by nine different vessels. The Brig Medford of
Boston did three trips between Flores and Boston, and the
Bark Azon from Boston did two trips between Faial and
Boston. Three were steamers, and the remainder were sailing
vessels. The tonnage of the sailing vessels varied between
106 tons (Brig Medford of Boston) and 231 tons (Bark Azon of
Boston). The tonnage of the steamers varied between 750
tons (Ship Josephus of Boston) and 2097 tons (Steamer Europa
of Glasgow).

embarked at Liverpool or Halifax. In the vessels coming from Northern Europe, Portuguese passengers (8 persons) comprised only 2 percent of all passengers carried. By contrast, on the vessels coming from Azorean ports, individuals born in Portugal accounted for 79 percent of the passengers, and second generation or naturalized Portuguese made up much of the remainder.

In sum, in 1860 the vast majority of the Portuguese emigrants to the United States landed at Boston. They travelled on small sailing vessels that specialized in transporting Portuguese emigrants to the United States and that cleared directly from Azorean ports.

Thirty years later, Portuguese arrivals in Boston showed similar characteristics. The primary change was that the sailing vessels had become bigger with larger passenger capacity. The average tonnage of sailing vessels more than doubled between 1860 and 1890/1891. (The average tonnage for 1860 was 221 tons; the average for 1980/1891 was 463 tons). The average carrying capacity almost tripled over the same period. (The average number of passenger carried per ship in 1860 was 38; the average for 1890/1891 was 100 passengers).

The evidence from thirteen shiplists for the port of Boston for 1890 and 1891 [filed in the National Immigration Archives (Philadelphia) and the National Archives (Washington, D.C.)] points to the continued importance of specialized vessels departing from the Azores (52). Of the

---

52 These thirteen shiplists corresponded to eight different vessels, since two of them, Bark Sarah and Schooner Kennard,

thirteen crossings, nine (69 percent) left from Azorean ports. Ninety-nine percent of the 907 Portuguese emigrants arriving in Boston had boarded in Azorean ports. They represented 92 percent of all passengers carried by vessels clearing from Azorean ports.

The vessels clearing from the Azores were sailing vessels, barks and schooners, with an average tonnage of 463 tons. The smallest, the Schooner Augusta E. Herrick, had 95 tons, and the largest, the Schooner Kennard, had 592 tons.

Of the four remaining trips, three departed from Liverpool, and one left from Cuba. I have detailed information on only two of the three ships departing from Liverpool. Eight of the ten Portuguese who embarked outside the Azores came via these ships (the Steamship Kansas and the Steamship Catalonia). These Portuguese emigrants comprised only 3 percent of the passenger load. The ships clearing from Liverpool were much larger than those leaving the Azores (3455 tons and 3093 tons).

By 1890/1891, the importance of Boston as port of arrival had greatly diminished (53). During the fiscal years

---

made respectively four and three trips between Azores and Boston during these two years.
53 I found for the port of Boston for 1901 only four shiplists registering Portuguese passengers. These four shiplists corresponded to four different ships departing from Northern Europe, and they brought 10 Portuguese to Boston. During the fiscal year of 1901, 4176 Portuguese arrived in the United States.In 1889 and 1890, 4780 Portuguese emigrants arrived in the United States. Of these, only 18 percent entered via New York. In 1891 and 1892, 55 percent of the 6886 Portuguese emigrants entered via New York. Even those Portuguese emigrants intending to go to California landed first at Boston or later at New York. My survey of the shiplists for San Francisco for 1901 indicates that only 10 Portuguese arrived directly in San Francisco, on board nine different vessels, and two of these ten

1890/1891, over five thousand Portuguese arrived in the
United States, and less than a fifth entered via Boston. By
1891, the port of New York and Ellis Island had become the
main gate of entry of all immigrants, including the
Portuguese (54).

Portuguese emigrants entering New York travelled on
larger vessels than Portuguese emigrants entering via
Boston. And like their counterparts entering Boston, most
of the Portuguese coming to New York had boarded in
Portugal. Of the 2737 Portuguese who arrived in New York
between June 1890 and December 1891, 97 percent embarked
from Portuguese ports. Two vessels alone, the steamers Vega
and Olinda, made 12 of the 16 trips between Portugal and the
United States. Seventy-two percent of all Portuguese
arrivals to New York had come on the Vega.

The emigrant ships clearing from Portuguese ports had on
average 1535 tons, and nearly all stopped at the Azores.
Most of the passengers were either Portuguese (49 percent)
or natives of Portugal with American citizenship and
second/generation immigrants.

A few of the Portuguese arriving in New York in 1890/1891
(3 percent) had left from Northern European and Latin
America ports. The ships departing from Northern Europe
were very large, having on average 4743 tons. They brought,
on their seven voyages, 4072 passengers, of whom only 7

Portuguese were sailors who were returning from Japan and
Sydney.
54 For the period between June 1890 and December 1891, I
found fifty-eight manifest shiplists for the port of New
York registering Portuguese passengers. The number of ships
was in fact much smaller than the number of shiplists, since
a considerable number of the vessels made several trips.

(.002 percent) were Portuguese. The ships clearing from Latin America had on average 1416 tons. They made 35 trips and brought 1848 passengers, 63 of whom (.03 percent) were Portuguese.

The ship that brought over 70 percent of the Portuguese arrivals to New York, the Vega was divided into two parts: cabins on deck and steerage below deck (55). Steerage was in turn divided into three parts: forward steerage for single men, steerage amidships for married couples and families, and afterwards steerage for single women (56).

According to the Immigration Investigating Commission of 1910, the majority of immigrants arriving in the United States were still carried on vessels using the "old" type of steerage. The "new" type of steerage was available only on emigrant lines from Northern Europe (57). The old steerage was succinctly described in this report as follows:

> Considering this old-type steerage as a whole, it is a congestion so intense, so injurious to health and morals that there is nothing on land to equal it. That people live in it only temporarily is no justification of its existence. The experience of a single crossing is enough to change bad standards of living to worse. It is abundant opportunity to weaken the body and emplant there germs of disease to develop later. It is more than a physical and moral test; it is a strain. (Senate Documents, 61st Congress, 3d Session, Vol.19, 1911:10)

---

55 Mendes Guerreiro (1894:4), who boarded the Vega from New York to Azores in 1894, described the Vega as a comfortable ship. The Vega did not have the accommodation or the service of the big European liners, but it had inferior prices. Guerreiro also remarked that the crossing took only eight days.
56 This configuration characterized almost all emigrant ships during this period. See Figure 6 in Appendix 2)
57 Senate Documents, 61st Congress, 3d Session, Vol.19, 1911:10. On this topic see also Hyde, 1975 and footnote 4.

This was a strain that almost all Portuguese emigrants endured.

As far as I know, the only surviving diary (58) describing a crossing by Portuguese emigrants to America is an account of an emigrant British vessel, the Thomas Bell, that brought contract laborers from Madeira to the Sandwich Islands, between November 8, 1887 and April 14, 1888. Hawaii was not yet part of the Union then, but the daily experiences of other Portuguese emigrants to the States must have been similar to those of the 394 human beings trapped on this emigrant vessel. Indeed, apart from their musical instruments (e.g., Machetes (59)), and religious rituals (e.g., Lapinha (60)), the passengers of the Thomas Bell could have been of any nationality.

The Portuguese diarist travelled in steerage, and he referred only once to cabin passengers (noting the bad fall of a lady). These two worlds, cabin and steerage, had nothing in common, and their inhabitants did not share the same space on board.

The voyage of the Thomas Bell took 156 days. During this time, three marriages took place, twenty-five persons died, and six children were born. One month before arriving in Hawaii, the diarist João Baptista d'Oliveira wrote:

---

58 I did find some succint descriptions of other crossings (e.g. Pereeira, 1964: 483-485), but, as far as I know, only Rodrigues Miguéis' fictional account "Steerage" (Rodrigues Miguéis, 1983: 155-176) is conmparable in detail to the source I am using.
59 Machetes are small guitars.
60 Lapinha is a celebration of nativity. An altar with a nativity scene is built and songs and prayers are offered between Christmas and the Epiphany.

> My God, what a long trip ! Here I am out of
> tobacco; the water is salty; they are already
> cutting down on my soup; when will we ever arrive
> at the Sandwich Islands ? They must be at the
> other end of the world. (Baptista d'Oliveira,
> 1970:38)

There was not much to do on board. The daily routine was
marked by the time of meals: at 8 a.m., breakfast,
consisting of seabiscuits and coffee; at 12 a.m., lunch,
with the usual menu white beans with meat and potatoes, or
codfish with potatoes, or horse beans with codfish; at 6
p.m., supper, invariably composed of bread with tea. In
special occasions, like Christmas, the menu departed from
the dull routine, to incorporate small livestock (chickens
and pigs) and other foodstuffs brought on board by some
passengers. There was a special diet for the sick
consisting of fine flour, condensed milk and sugar. These
last items could also be obtained, according to the diarist,
by males who bribed the cook with brandy, and by women who
were "close enough to the stewart to allow him to hug and
kiss them" (d'Oliveira, 1970:25).

Most of the time was passed on deck playing cards and
chatting if the weather was good, and being seasick if the
weather was bad. From time to time there was dancing on the
deck.

Baptista d'Oliveira was a single man and one of his
favorite topics was female behavior. One of his remarks on
a female passengers' group goes this way:

> Some of them were proud old women who had gotten
> the crazy notion that they were Cupid's daughters.
> Others, who were charming, fell so easily into the
> trap that was set for them that it seemed as if
> they had never seen a man before. (d'Oliveira,
> 1970:7-8)

The diary is full of details of the personal lives of the passengers and crew, for gossip was one of the main entertainments available. We learn, for example, the story of João d'Ornellas, who brought on board his wife, his five children, and his mistress. Ornellas had convinced his wife to sell her own house, by promising that he would leave his mistress if they moved to Hawaii. During a short stop at Chile, Ornellas jumped ship, despite armed vigilance from the crew, and left behind the wife, the children, and a pregnant mistress. We are not told what happened to the deserted wife and children, but the mistress married one of the passengers, one month after her former lover left the ship.

Tensions between the crew and the steerage passengers led to open confrontation more then once. The most common grounds for confrontation were food rations, food preparation, and harassment of female passengers. Fights among passengers were also frequent. The provocation for these fights varied considerably, ranging from an accidental spill of coffee, to a jealous wife beating and being beaten by her husband, to disputes over children's behavior.

Steerage passengers had assigned duties, such as cleaning their dishes, their linens, and, on rotation their quarters. The refusal by a male passenger to clean his quarters, on the grounds that he had paid for his trip, led to his imprisonment on the captain's orders. The rules on board were strict. For example, on Sundays the passengers were forbidden to play the guitar or engage in card games. Brutality was not uncommon. A kitchen helper, Francisco da

Silva, who threw his food into the sea in the presence of the steward was punished by the captain as follows:

> [The captain] hit da Silva on his head and slapped him. Leaning against the mast, he lassoed da Silva with a rope about his waist, and tied him to the mast. The mate appeared with irons to fetter the prisoner, after which the latter was handcuffed and ordered to remain on deck. (d'Oliveira, 1970: 12)

Baptista d'Oliveira seems to have viewed corporal punishments, like this, as deserved, or at least accepted them as fair. For instances, three days after departure from Madeira, two boys were found by the captain "satisfying their desires with a certain young women" (d'Oliveira, 1970:7). The captain made it known that future cases would be punished by binding the hands and feet of the males involved. Several similar incidents were reported to the captain, and the man involved was sometimes beaten as well as imprisoned. The punishment imposed by the captain was simply recorded, without further comment.

The most serious occurrence on board took place at Iquique (Chile). During the night the crew, armed with revolvers, guarded the deck with orders to shoot if any passenger tried to jump ship. As might be expected, this incident aroused resentment among the passengers. The steerage passengers on board the Thomas Bell were contract laborers, and it is possible that such extremes did not take place with free emigrants. Still, between 1878 and 1909 over sixteen thousand Portuguese, most of whom were under contract, crossed the sea to Hawaii under conditions that were probably as bad as the ones described in d'Oliveira.

SOCIO-DEMOGRAPHIC CHARACTERISTICS OF THE PORTUGUESE
MIGRANTS TO THE UNITED STATES 1820-1930

SEX, AGE, AND MARITAL STATUS

The sex ratio for the Portuguese migratory flow to the
United States was imbalanced throughout the whole period,
with males predominating. From 1850 on, however, the female
share was substantial and increasing (see Table B:9 in
Appendix 2).

As Table B:9 indicates, between 1820 and 1849, women
accounted for only 13 percent of the Portuguese migratory
stream. In the following decades this proportion rose (to
31 percent between 1850 and 1874; to 34 percent between 1875
and 1889; to 41 percent between 1890 and 1914). Between
1915 and 1930, the share of women emigrants dropped to 36
percent.

The female share of the migratory stream peaked in 1924,
when women accounted for 68 percent of all Portuguese aliens
admitted to the United States. This peak was the temporary
result of conjunctural events, the Immigration Acts of 1921
and 1924, which favored family reunification (see chapter
II). More revealing is the female share (41 percent)
between 1890 and 1914. Because no particular exogenous
stimulus can account for this figure, this high proportion
of females in the Portuguese migratory flow indicates either
growing family emigration or increasing job opportunities in
United States for Portuguese females.

The sex ratio for the total Portuguese emigration and the sex ratio for the Portuguese emigration to the United States are quite different. This difference reflects the greater weight of the migratory stream to Brazil, and the overwhelmingly predominance of young adult males from the mainland in the migratory current to Brazil (see Table B:3 and 7 in Appendix 2).

The sex ratio for Portuguese emigrants to the United States differed from that for the so called "new" immigrants. For example, between 1899 and 1910, the Greek and Italian migratory streams had a female share of only 5 percent and 21 percent respectively, while the Portuguese had 41 percent. The sex composition of the Portuguese migratory current is, in fact, more similar to that of the "old" immigration. Between 1899 and 1910, the German migratory flow had a female share of 41 percent, and the English had a female share of 39 percent (Reports of the Immigration Commission, 1910, Vol.I, 1911:97).

The available information on the age structure of Portuguese migrants to the United States is not internally comparable. Between 1870 and 1930, when age was systematically published in the annual reports, three different age groupings were used to aggregate incoming immigrants (61).

Despite these changes, some general points can be made. Between 1873 and 1930, the age structure of incoming

---

61 These age groups were as follows: between 1873 and 1898, 14 and under, 15 to 39, and 40 and over; between 1899 and 1917, under 14, 14 to 44, and 45 and over; and between 1918 and 1930, under 16, 16 to 44, and 45 and over.

Portuguese migrants to United States was dominated by the
most active age group (see Table B:10 in Appendix 2);
namely, those 15 to 40 years of age (in 1873-1898), those 1
to 45 years of age (in 1899-1917), and those 16 to 45 (in
1918-1930). This broad age group represented at least 61
percent of all Portuguese arrivals.

We can be even more accurate and say that the Portuguese
migratory flow was dominated by young adult migrants betwee
16 and 29 years of age between 1860 and 1930. My survey of
the shiplists for 1860 and 1890/1891 indicate that 56
percent and 50 percent respectively of all incoming
Portuguese migrants were between 16 and 29 years of age.
The annual reports for 1925 to 1930, which give age by five
years groups, indicate that this age group accounted for 5
percent of all Portuguese aliens admitted at the end of the
period under study.

Two other general remarks can also be made. First, over
time the oldest age group represented an ever-shrinking
share of the total migratory flow. The second point is tha
the relative weight of the youngest age group varied
considerably, falling into four different phases. Until
1895, this age group constituted about 13 percent of the
migratory flow; between 1897 and 1908, their share rose to
24 percent; between 1909 and 1927, the proportion of
children emigrants diminishes to 16 percent; and after 1927
their share rose again to 25 percent.

To summarize, as expected the migratory flow was
dominated by young adults (between 16 and 29 years of age)
throughout the whole period (1873 to 1930). The relatively

high proportion of child and female emigrants between 1899
and 1910 indicates that familial emigration or family
reunification peaked during these years (62).   The renewal
of this tendency after 1927 was due to American immigration
policy.

The available information on the age structure of the
Portuguese migrants by sex, aggregated by decades is given
in Table IV:XII.

TABLE IV: XII - SEX AND AGE DISTRIBUTION OF THE PORTUGUESE
        MIGRANTS TO THE UNITED STATES 1873 - 1930
                (IN PERCENTAGE)

MALES

SELECTED YEARS	0-14	15-39	40 AND OVER	TOTAL
1873-1879	8.3	81.4	10.3	100
1880-1889	11.5	79.6	9.0	100
1890-1895	11.8	80.0	8.2	100
1910-1917	14.2	79.0	6.9	100
1920-1930	8.8	86.8	4.4	100

FEMALES

SELECTED YEARS	0-14	15-39	40 AND OVER	TOTAL
1873-1879	18.2	70.1	11.7	100
1880-1889	19.9	68.7	11.3	100
1890-1895	14.9	75.9	9.2	100
1910-1917	21.6	70.4	8.1	100
1920-1930	20.6	70.6	8.8	100

SOURCE: TABLE B:11 IN APPENDIX 2.
NOTE: SEE FOOTNOTE #2 IN TABLE B:11

---

62 It is possible that the same pattern of family emigration
went on from the Azores after 1908/1910. The familial
component from the Azores may get lost in the aggregated
numbers on Portuguese emigration, due to the fact that from
1910 mainlanders dominated the Portuguese migratory flow to
the United States. These aggregate figures are, however,
the only type of information available for this period.

These figures show that the age structure of the Portuguese male migrants remained more or less constant between the 1870's and the 1890's. The most noticeable change is that the share of males over 40 years (or 45 after 1899) of age decreased slightly over time, and these decreases were absorbed by the youngest age group. The group 15-39 years of age (or 14-44 after 1899 and 16-44 after 1918) represented at least 80 percent of all male migrants and varied very little during the whole period.

During the final two decades (1910 to 1930), the age group 14 to 44 years of age (or 16 to 44 after 1918) absorbed even larger share of the male emigrant pool. In the 1910's, this gain came at the expense of the oldest age group, and in the 1920's, by a contraction in both the youngest and the oldest male age groups.

Between the 1870's and 1930, female migrants' age structure varied a little more than did male age structure. During the 1870's and the 1880's there was a slight (2 percentage points) contraction of the age group 15 to 39 years of age in favor of the youngest age group. In the following period, the 1890's, a change of equivalent magnitude in the opposite direction occurred. In the 1910's (particularly between 1910 and 1914), the youngest age group gained again. In the last period, 1920-1930, the age structure of Portuguese female migrants remained similar to that observed by the 1910's.

Comparing the age structure of male and female migrants shows that females were less concentrated in the age group 15 to 40 years of age (or 14 to 44 after 1898 and 16 to 44

after 1918), and had larger proportion than males in both
the youngest and the oldest age groups.

This age structure by sex is consistent with my
contention that familial emigration or familial
reunification peaked between the 1899 and 1910.
Unfortunately information on marital status is available
only after 1910, and thus cannot clarify whether the
persistent differences in the age structure of males and
females were the result of familial emigration and familial
reunification (63). The data on conjugal condition after
1910-- particularly the high ratio of married females to
married males-- also indicates (see Table B:12 in
Appendix 2) that the Portuguese migratory flow, after 1922,
had a much higher number of married females than in the
previous decade, suggesting family reunification (64).

---

63 The linkage of the passport registers for the district
of Horta and Angra and the shiplists for Boston and New York
for 1890/1891 indicates that those travelling in group were
usually related but seldom completely nuclear families.
Delayed family emigration was not uncommon among other
migrant groups. MacDonald and MacDonald noted that Southern
Italian emigration to the United States was marked by serial
migration of breadwinners and delayed family emigration.
64 By the 1920's American Immigrantion law was decidely
promoting family reunification. It is thus difficult to
know if the relevance attained, after 1922, by family
reunification is the natural result of an unfolding
migratory process or a by-product of the new American
immigration policies of the period.

LITERACY, OCCUPATION, AND FINANCIAL RESOURCES OF INCOMING PORTUGUESE MIGRANTS

Portuguese migrants to the United States at the moment of their arrival had fewer financial resources, lower literacy rates, and greater concentration at the bottom of the occupational scale than almost any other migrant group.

Between 1899 and 1910, over eight million aliens over 14 years of age were admitted into the United States. Overall, twenty-seven percent were illiterate. In comparison, the proportion illiterate among Portuguese aliens admitted was 68 percent, the highest registered for any immigrant group. The next most disadvantageous alien group, were the Turks who registered 60 percent of illiterate (65).

During the same period, seven million immigrants declared their occupation. The Greek migratory flow was overwhelmingly comprised of laborers and farm laborers (86 percent), and the Southern Italian flow also had a very high proportion of these groups (77 percent). The corresponding percentage for the Portuguese between 1897 and 1917 was 70 percent. But because females composed a much higher proportion of the Portuguese migratory flow than was the

---

65 The data for the period of 1899-1910 is given on Reports of the Immigration Commission, 1910. Vol. I, 1911:97-104. Although 41 percent of the Portuguese immigrants were females, illiteracy rates are not raised by their presence. Portuguese census' takers registered the anomalous fact that in the islands (Azores and Madeira) illiteracy was higher among males then among females (Censo de 1911. vol.I:XXIII). The data on Portuguese immigrants in the Annual Report on Immigration for 1910 confirms this previous statement. In fact, of the 4092 Portuguese males over 14 years of age registered, 69 percent were illiterate, while of the 2039 Portuguese females, in the same conditions, only 66 percent were illiterate. More detailed data for literacy, occupation and financial resources at entry is given in Appendix 2.

case for the Southern Italians and the Greeks, we must add in servants when analyzing the Portuguese occupational structure (66). Servants, laborers, and farm laborers accounted for 88 percent of all these with stated occupations among Portuguese aliens (67). This situation had improved slightly by the 1920's, but still three-quarters of the Portuguese who reported an occupation were either servants or laborers (see Table B:14 in Appendix 2).

Two types of information given in the annual reports after 1893 have been generally used to rank emigrants' financial resources at arrival in the country: the minimum sum of money that they were required to carry, and the total amount of money shown at entry. This latter information has been used by several researchers (e.g., Bannick, 1916:42; Taylor, 1971:97) for comparison among emigrants groups. Such inferences are, however, of arguable value. As the General Commissioner of Immigration stated in 1897:

> The amount of money brought into the country can not be accurately given,... our statistics do not pretend to ascertain it. By the Act of March 1893, it was determined that if an immigrant could exhibit $30 in money it would be sufficient for practical purposes, and if he possessed more he

---

66 The sex ratio for Portuguese immigrants differs from the sex ratio of the so called "new" immigrants. For example, between 1899 and 1910, the Greek and Italian migratory streams had a female share of only 5 and 21 percent respectively, while the Portuguese had 41 percent. The sex composition of the Portuguese migratory current is, in fact, more similar to that of the "old" immigration-- e.g., German migratory flow had a female share of 41 percent, and the English had a female share of 39 percent (Reports of the Immigration Commission, 1910, Vol1, 1911:97).
67 Occupation for females is not given in the passport registers for Angra. The passport registers for Horta give occupation for females. There is not a single dress maker registered in the passport registers of Horta travelling to the United States. The above proportion for the unskilled underestimates the true proportion of this group.

should not be required to disclose it. An
immigrant is, therefore, only asked to exhibit $30
or less. Annual Report ..., 1897:4

I will thus rely only on the information on the minimal
amount of money shown at entry. Taking again the same
period (1899-1910), we find that 18 percent of all aliens
had at least thirty dollars when entering the country,
between 1899 and 1903, and 14 percent had at least fifty
dollars between 1904 and 1910. Fewer Portuguese had such
in-pocket resources (see Table B:15 in Appendix 2). Some
alien groups, such as the Southern Italians, carried even
less money, but the Portuguese were certainly toward the
bottom of the scale.

Although the overwhelming majority of the Portuguese who
arrived in the United States had a similar lack of skills
and financial resources, the different economic
opportunities in their places of settlement in the United
States produced in the long run considerable diversity in
the resident immigrant population. Specifically, the
socio-economic conditions of receiving communities offer
different opportunities for economic success and
integration. The main areas of destination as well as the
socio-economic conditions of the Portuguese immigrants in
Massachusetts, California, and Hawaii will be my next focus
of analysis.

THE RECEIVING SOCIETY - PORTUGUESE IMMIGRANTS IN THE UNITED STATES

According to their declared destination at the moment of arrival, between 1901 and 1910, 61 percent of the Portuguese emigrants intended to settle in Massachusetts, 15 percent in California, 10 percent in Rhode Island, 6 percent in New York, and 5 percent in Hawaii (68). After 1913, Hawaii lost completely its earlier importance as a major area of destination for Portuguese emigrants (69). Hawaii's place was taken by New Jersey, where 9 percent of the Portuguese arrivals between 1920 and 1930 intended to settle (see Table B:16 in Appendix 2). Massachusetts continued to be the major area of destination (with 41 percent of the arrivals declaring their intention of settling there), followed by California (13 percent) and New York (12 percent).

The declarations of intended destination and the actual settlement pattern for the Portuguese do not agree, however. Table IV:XIV indicates that between 1870 and 1900 the Portuguese settled preferentially in California, but only a small minority of the declarations of intended destination referred to that state (70).

---

68 The remaining 3 percent had as their intended destination other states.
69 In 1913 sugar prices dropped, and Hawaiian employers decided to reduce costs by substituting Japanese contract labor for Portuguese contract labor (Estep, 1941:6).
70 At the two main ports of arrival, New York and Boston, only 5 percent of the Portuguese declared as final destination California in 1890 and 1891 (shiplists for Boston and New York for 1890 and 1891). During the 1890's the majority of the Portuguese emigrants did not sailed directly to California.

TABLE IV:XIII - **MAIN PORTUGUESE SETTLEMENTS IN THE CONTINENTAL UNITED STATES 1850 - 1930 (PERCENTAGE)**

STATES	1850	1860	1870	1880	1890
MASSACHUSETTS	22.8	25.9	29.8	22.9	31.2
RHODE ISLAND	4.6	2.0	2.5	2.5	5.4
NEW YORK	15.2	8.2	3.9	2.8	3.0
CALIFORNIA	8.6	28.8	38.4	51.5	48.4
N =	651	3560	6704	12470	22630
TOTAL IN U.S	1274	5477	8973	15650	25705

STATES	1900	1910	1920	1930
MASSACHUSETTS	44.2	50.6	50.3	41.2
RHODE ISLAND	7.1	9.3	11.3	10.8
NEW YORK	2.0	1.8	2.3	5.4
CALIFORNIA	38.5	32.8	29.4	32.9
N =	37156	73308	106652	98895
TOTAL IN U.S	40431	77634	114321	109453

Source: U.S. censuses at given year
Note: figures for 1850 do not include the Atlantic Islands

Given the high percentage of Portuguese immigrants who settled in California (see Table IV:XIII), it is clear that a great number of Portuguese arrivals declared to officials only their first intended destination, not their final destination.

Table IV:XIII indicates that for most of the period between 1850 and 1930 two areas in the continental United States were the main regions of attraction for Portuguese migrants (71). Outside the continental United States only Hawaii had a sizable Portuguese community. Table IV:XIV gives the number of Portuguese residents in the main areas of Portuguese settlement in the continental United States.

---

71 Rhode Island's importance only becomes comparable to that of Massachusetts and California after 1910.

TABLE IV:XIV - **YEARLY GROWTH RATES OF THE MAJOR PORTUGUESE SETTLEMENTS IN THE UNITED STATES 1850 - 1930**

MASSACHUSETTS   CALIFORNIA

YEAR	PORTUGUESE	YEARLY GR. RATE	YEAR	PORTUGUESE	YEARLY GR. RATE
1850	290		1850	109	
1860	1421	17.22	1860	1580	30.65
1870	2678	6.54	1870	3450	8.12
1880	3582	2.95	1880	8061	8.86
1890	8024	8.40	1890	12446	4.44
1900	17885	8.35	1900	15583	2.27
1910	39253	8.18	1910	25437	5.02
1920	57485	3.89	1920	33566	2.81
1930	45053	-2.41	1930	36029	0.71

RHODE ISLAND   HAWAII (72)

YEAR	PORTUGUESE	YEARLY GR. RATE	YEAR	PORTUGUESE	YEARLY GR. RATE
1850	58				
1860	110	6.61			
1870	227	7.51			
1880	395	5.70			
1890	1380	13.33	1890	8602	
1900	2865	7.58	1900	7668	-1.14
1910	7217	9.68	1910	8498	1.03
1920	12949	6.02	1920	5982	
1930	11850	-0.88	1930	3713	

Source: U.S. censuses at given year
For Hawaii for 1890: Estep,1941; and for 1900-1930: U.S. censuses at given year
----

Table IV:XIV shows that there was great temporal diversity in the size and the relative importance of the Portuguese settlements in the United States. The size of the Portuguese settlement in Hawaii remained at around eight thousand people until 1910 and then dropped markedly. Migration to Hawaii was marked from the start by a great number of departures to the continental United States. As soon as Portuguese immigrants fulfilled their initial contracts, many left for California. These departures are

---

72 According to Freitas (1930:151) 11649 Portuguese contract laborers arrived in Hawaii between 1878 and 1889.

estimated to have been around half of the arrivals (Freitas, 1930:151). After 1913, when the Hawaiian government and sugar planters decided to substitute Japanese labor for Portuguese labor, the number of Portuguese residents in Hawaii fell, reaching less than four thousand by 1930.

The three preferential areas of Portuguese settlement (Massachusetts, California, and Hawaii) offered quite different economic opportunities to newcomers. New England was in the late nineteenth and early twentieth centuries the core area of the American textile industry. Irish and French Canadians at mid nineteenth-century, Poles, Italians, Greeks, and other eastern European immigrants after the 1880's, all came to New England industrial cities (e.g., Lowell, and Taunton) in search of the unskilled industrial jobs that industrialization had opened up in this region. Textile manufacturers had at their disposal a changing but reliable and cheap pool of labor to choose from, and migrants had job opportunities that did not demand skill or special knowledge of the native language.

The Portuguese come initially to Massachusetts (73) as crew members for the whaling and merchant fleets in the early nineteenth century. By the 1880's the Portuguese were profiting, like the other "new" immigrant groups, from the opening of low skill job opportunities in the textile mills of the region.

The Portuguese went to California in the mid-nineteenth century to be gold miners, but they soon became farmers. As

---

73 The creation and development of the Portuguese migratory stream to Massachusetts, California, and Hawaii have already been described in chapter I.

early as 1860, the census indicated that the majority of the

Portuguese settled in that state were engaged in whaling and

fishing, and in farming. Twenty years later, whaling had

lost its importance in the California economy; although the

Portuguese still dominated that activity, they were now

centered in farming (Brown, 1944:58, 59). The available

land, even at low prices, was not immediately affordable for

the majority of Portuguese immigrants. Still, through a

process of renting followed by buying, the Portuguese

succeeded in establishing a niche for themselves in two

branches of agriculture, market gardening and dairy

production. The fictional description of this process by

Jack London in The Valley of the Moon (1913) is well

grounded historically (74);

> Forty years ago old Silva come from the Azores.
> Went sheep-herdin' in the mountains for a couple
> of years, then blew into San Leandro. These five
> acres was the first land he leased. That was the
> beginnin'. Then he began leasin' by the hundreds
> of acres, an' by the hundred-an-sixties. An' his
> sisters an' his uncles an' his aunts begun
> pourin' in from the Azores-- they're all related
> there, you know; an' pretty soon San Leandro was a
> regular Porchugeeze settlement. (London,1913:309)

The Portuguese stream to the last main area of settlement

analyzed here, Hawaii, was stable from 1878 to 1913. It was

based on a contract labor system reflecting both the needs

of the sugar economy and the desire of the Hawaiian

political elite to stop the growth of the oriental element

in the islands (Freitas, 1930:148; Estep,1941:6). From the

beginning, this Portuguese migratory flow differed

---

74 Several of the interviews referred to in chapter I
described exactly the same pattern.

substantially from the migratory streams to the continental United States. The movement to Hawaii was subsidized by sugar planters and the government, and usually the contract involved the entire family unit (75). Job opportunities in Hawaii were also substantially different from those in the other areas. As in California, most of the available jobs were connected with agriculture. But unlike California, where uncultivated land was available for purchase, in Hawaii established sugar plantations had taken up the best land by the time the Portuguese arrived.

In sum, there were three main concentrations of Portuguese communities in the United States between 1850 and 1930: Massachusetts, California, and Hawaii. The Portuguese immigrants living in these communities had from the start quite different economic opportunities, due to the different job markets in these regions.

The contrasting social structures of Massachusetts, California, and Hawaii offered different opportunities for integration to new arrivals. In Massachusetts the social niche available to the Portuguese was as part of the "inferior new immigration" (Taft, 1967, Lauck, 1912, Lang, 1892). The social placement of the Portuguese in Hawaii was also well determined from the start. Viewed as ethnically superior to the oriental element and inferior to the caucasian (haole) element, the Portuguese immigrants belonged to neither, but were set apart as a distinct racial

---

75 Documentos...Emigração Portugueza Para as Ilhas Hawaiianas,1885:34-38,and KuyKendall, in Felix and Senecal, 1978:34.

group labelled the "Portuguese" (76). As late as 1940 a third-generation Portuguese still would refer to this special treatment as follows (77):

> It is a shame that just because our ancestors came here as laborers, with low economic status, that their children, for generations, have been made to feel keenly inferior through prejudicial practices in the Islands. (in Estep, 1941:12)

In economic terms the Portuguese in Hawaii were like the oriental imported labor, even if they remained socially distinct. California, on the other hand, was a "frontier" region when the Portuguese began flocking to the area. The social structure of that region was much less well-defined, and the Portuguese created from the start socio-economic niches to which no special social stigma was attached (78).

The contrasts in the socio-economic characteristics of the Portuguese residing in Massachusetts, Hawaii, or California are sufficiently great to support the hypothesis that migratory streams drawn from the same pool can be differently shaped by the socio-economic conditions of the receiving areas. Migration studies have tended to center on a single preferential area of settlement of the migrant group under analysis and to extrapolate from there to the general characteristics of the group (e.g. Morawska, 1985).

---

76 According to the Hawaiian censuses the Portuguese were a distinct race separate from the orientals and the whites (Estep, 1941; U.S. Census 1910).
77 In the 1940's social stigmatization was still so vividly felt by the Portuguese living in Hawaii, that Estep (1941:12) described it as "a group inferiority complex".
78 The Report of the Immigration Investigating Commission of 1908 (1911) includes a description of the Portuguese community in San Leandro (California). Comparing the description for California with contemporary descriptions of the Portuguese in New England, (e.g. Lauck, 1912) is extremely revealing of the different attitudes towards the Portuguese.

It would be hard to generalize about the Portuguese immigrants in United States based solely on an analysis of just those residing in California, or in Massachusetts, or in Hawaii.

To capture the diversity of Portuguese immigrant communities in different regions, I compared the socio-economic characteristics of first generation Portuguese households in the three main areas of settlement, Massachusetts, California, and Hawaii. Previous scholarship has addressed both the socio-economic placement and the assimilation of the Portuguese element in these three regions (79), but to my knowledge no one has focused on the influence of available economic opportunities on residence patterns. Specifically, I focused on living arrangements in Milpitas (Santa Clara county, California), Hilo (Hawaii county, Hawaii), and Taunton (Bristol county, Massachusetts), using a random sample of the first

---

79 The bibliography on Portuguese settlements in the United States is scarce. Thus, for example, all that Caroline Brettell's Annotated Bibliography (1978) mentions, on Portuguese emigration to the United States, are 8 articles, 9 books or parts of books, and a research project in progress. Obviously, not even these few items are all on Portuguese settlements in the U.S.. Although not as poor as the example just referred may suggest, and regardless of a few more bibliographic items that may be gathered from Hansen (1975), Pap (1976), Kettenring (1984), and Viera et al. (1989), the fact remains: there is a true bibliographic paucity on this topic. Of the existent literature, some is quite open to debate (e.g., Soares, 1939, Cunha et al.,1985), and some, the most useful for this work, has already been referred. To this last group, I would add: 1.unpublished and published dissertations-- Leder,1968, and Graves, 1977 (on the Portuguese settlement in California); Ferst, 1972 (on Portuguese settlement in Providence); 2. articles written by contemporaries-- Caswell, 1873; Lang, 1892; Peak, 1904; Lauck, 1912-- revealing of the perceptions Americans had of the Portuguese as an immigrant group; 3. and the following books -- Cumbler, 1979; Felix et al., 1980; and Williams, 1982.

generation Portuguese households in these areas collected from the manuscript census of 1910 (80).

In 1910, Taunton was a typical New England textile city with thirty-four thousand inhabitants (81). Like the Irish and the French Canadians before them, the Portuguese came to Taunton because the textile mills of the city constantly opened up new job opportunities for unskilled labor. The occupations and the economic sectors of activity of the Portuguese male household heads in this city were quite restricted and clearly determined by the labor market of the receiving community. The occupations of Portuguese male household heads in Taunton in 1910 are given in Table IV:XV.

---

80 I considered as a Portuguese household a household headed by a first-generation Portuguese who, if married, was married either to a first or to a second generation Portuguese. From this pool I drew a 10 percent random sample for Taunton, a 50 percent sample for Hilo, and I took the whole population for Milpitas.
81 The abstracts of the 1910 census only give the number of Portuguese (829), therefore all the Portuguese that indicated as place of birth the Atlantic Islands are not included.

TABLE IV:XV - TYPES OF OCCUPATION AND ECONOMIC SECTORS OF
ACTIVITY OF THE PORTUGUESE MALE HOUSEHOLD HEADS IN TAUNTON,
IN 1910

TAUNTON

SECTORS	UNSKILLED	SEMISKILLED	SKILLED
AGRICULTURE	6	1	
MANUFACTURING	18	4	4
TRANSPORTATION	3		
CONSTRUCTION	2		
TRADE	2	1	2
SERVICES	4		2
NO INF	7		
TOTAL	42	6	8
PERCENTAGE	75.0	10.7	14.3

N IN SAMPLE   61
N IN CENSUS   605

Source:U.S. manuscript census of 1910

The overwhelming majority of the Portuguese male heads in
Tauton were wage earners (82). Of these workers the majority
were unskilled laborers in manufacture.

The situation was quite different in Milpitas, in the San
Francisco-Oakland Bay area, where 55 percent of all the
Portuguese immigrants in California lived. This was a rural
region dedicated to general farming (Graves, 1977:86). The
Portuguese in Milpitas were connected with market gardening;
as in the case of Taunton, the market economy of the
receiving region determined their occupational structure.

---

82 Of the 58 male household heads in the sample, 2 cases
have no stated occupation. Of the remaining 56 cases, 53
(91 percent) were wage earners.

TABLE IV:XVI - **TYPES OF OCCUPATIONS AND ECONOMIC SECTORS OF ACTIVITY OF THE PORTUGUESE MALE HOUSEHOLD HEADS IN MILPITAS, IN 1910**

MILPITAS

SECTORS	UNSKILLED	SEMISKILLED	SKILLED
AGRICULTURE	76	2	
MANUFACTURING			
TRANSPORTATION	2	2	
CONSTRUCTION			
TRADE			
SERVICES			
TOTAL	78	4	
PERCENTAGE	95.2	4.8	

N IN SAMPLE   94
N IN CENSUS   94

Source:U.S. manuscript census of 1910

Table IV:XVI, which shows the occupational structure of Portuguese male household heads in Milpitas, needs some explanation because it can be misleading, and it is not readily comparable with the figures for Taunton in Table IV:XV. Three-quarters of the Portuguese in Milpitas were farmers and as such are classified as unskilled, but they were not unskilled agricultural laborers. The overwhelming majority of those in agriculture (87 percent) were either employers or self-employed. If level of skill is used for comparison, the Portuguese in Taunton appear to be better placed economically than the Portuguese in Milpitas. But opportunities for self-employment in agriculture actually produced greater success for the Milpitas group.

Hilo, the last community analyzed, was the second largest city of the island of Hawaii. The majority of the city's inhabitants were still connected to sugar plantation work. The Portuguese were no exception to this rule, more than half of the Portuguese households heads in the city

were, as Table IV:XVII indicates, connected to sugar

plantation works.

TABLE IV:XVII - **TYPE OF OCCUPATION AND ECONOMIC SECTORS OF ACTIVITY OF THE PORTUGUESE MALE HOUSEHOLD HEADS IN HILO, IN** 1910

HILO

SECTORS	UNSKILLED	SEMISKILLED	SKILLED
AGRICULTURE	20	1	1
QUARRY	1		1
MANUFACTURING			
TRANSPORTATION	2		1
CONSTRUCTION			
TRADE		6	
SERVICES	2	1	1
NO INF	1		
TOTAL	25	9	4
PERCENTAGE	67.6	24.3	10.8

N IN SAMPLE   50
N IN CENSUS   125

Source:U.S. manuscript census of 1910

In Hilo, as in Milpitas, the Portuguese were centered in

agricultural activities. But, the Portuguese in Hilo were,

unlike in Milpitas, predominantly wage-earners (83), rather

than independent farmers or agricultural employers. On the

next section, the work status of the Portuguese male

household heads and the living arrangements promoted by this

same status are further analyzed.

_____

83 There were 34 workers (92 percent) in the 37 stated
occupations.

GENERAL CHARACTERISTICS OF THE PORTUGUESE IMMIGRANT
HOUSEHOLDS IN MILPITAS, TAUNTON, AND HILO IN 1910

The distribution of households types and the mean size of

Portuguese immigrant households in Milpitas, Taunton, and

Hilo are given in Table IV:XVIII (84).

TABLE IV:XVIII - **PORTUGUESE IMMIGRANT HOUSEHOLD TYPES AND
HOUSEHOLD MEAN SIZE IN MILPITAS, TAUNTON, AND HILO IN 1910**

MILPITAS

HOUSEHOLD TYPE (85)	PERCENTAGE	MEAN SIZE
SOLITARY	9.2	1
NO-FAMILY	3.2	2.7
NUCLEAR FAMILY	51.1	6.1
EXTENDED FAMILY	10.6	7
MULTIPLE FAMILY	4.3	6.8
WITH BOARDER(S)	5.3	8.6
WITH EMPLOYEE(S)	16.0	5.8
TOTAL	100	5.69
N =	94	

N IN CENSUS   94

---

84 The 1910 Census has an entry where all the members of the
household are listed in accordance with their relation to
the household head (e.g. wife, nephew, uncle, cousin, father
in law, boarder, employee, etc). Based on this information,
I constructed a grid for types of household based on
Laslett's household typology (see for example Laslett,
1983). Because I was interested in finding differences in
the living arrangements of the Portuguese immigrants derived
from the economic conditions of the areas they lived in, I
added two categories to my grid of household types. These
two categories are households with boarders and households
with employees.
85 Solitaries - one-person households; No-family households
- co-residents amongst whom no conjugal family unit can be
discerned; Nuclear-family households - conjugal family units
only; Extended-family households - conjugal units having
kin-linked individuals; Multiple-family households - two or
more kin-linked conjugal units (Laslett, 1983:519).

TAUNTON

HOUSEHOLD TYPE	PERCENTAGE	MEAN SIZE
SOLITARY	4.9	1
NO-FAMILY	0	–
NUCLEAR FAMILY	60.7	4.92
EXTENDED FAMILY	3.3	5
MULTIPLE FAMILY	4.9	8.67
WITH BOARDER(S)	26.2	6.44
WITH EMPLOYEE(S)	0	–
TOTAL	100	5.31
N =	61	

N IN CENSUS   605

HILO

HOUSEHOLD TYPE	PERCENTAGE	MEAN SIZE
SOLITARY	8.0	1
NO-FAMILY	0	–
NUCLEAR FAMILY	72.0	5.2
EXTENDED FAMILY	10.0	6.2
MULTIPLE FAMILY	2.0	9
WITH BOARDER(S)	8.0	6.5
WITH EMPLOYEE(S)	0	–
TOTAL	100	5.16
N =	50	

N IN CENSUS   125

Source: United States manuscript census of 1910

Table IV:XVIII shows substantial differences in the
distribution of household types and in household mean size
for Portuguese immigrant households according to place of
settlement. In Taunton two household types dominated,
nuclear families (61 percent) and households with boarders
(26 percent), and other types of living arrangements were of
relatively small importance. In Hilo nuclear family
households represented 72 percent of all households, but

extended family households (10 percent) and households with boarders (8 percent) were also not uncommon. In Milpitas, nuclear family households represented a much smaller proportion of all households (51 percent), and both extended family households (11 percent) and households with employees (16 percent) had considerable weight.

The mean size of Portuguese immigrant households was also different in the three areas. The difference was greatest between Hilo (mean household size of 5.1 members) and Milpitas (mean of 5.7 members), with Tauton in an intermediate position (mean of 5.3 members). The differences were particularly marked in some household types. Nuclear family household, for example, had on average 4.9 members in Taunton and 6.1 members in Milpitas.

In sum, when compared to those in Taunton and Hilo, the Portuguese immigrant households in Milpitas were larger and less dominated by nuclear families. The high proportion of households with employees and of extended family households suggests that the Portuguese immigrant households in Milpitas relied on both extended family members (86) and wage-earners to satisfy their labor demands. The fact that all the employees in Portuguese households (20 cases) were themselves Portuguese (87) and that a substantial number of the extended family members were males who had arrived after the household head indicates that Portuguese employers in Milpitas relied on kinship and informal migrant networks

86 Extended family households in Milpitas were frequently extended laterally, while extended family households in Hilo and Taunton tended to be extended either downwards or upwards.
87 Includes one second-generation Portuguese.

active at both ends of the trajectory (in this case, the
Azores and California) to supply their labor demands (88).
As one of the Immigration Commissioners of 1908 (1911)
remarked referring to another Portuguese settlement in this
area (San Leandro):

> There is one noteworthy difference between these
> Portuguese and the American farmers, which may be
> indicated at this point. It lies in the fact that
> the former employ their countrymen practically to
> the exclusion of other races, whether as regular
> or as temporary hands. These they pay from $20 to
> $25 per month if regularly employed, or from $1 to
> $1.25 per day if temporarily employed during the
> harvest season, always with board and lodging.
> These wages are about $5 per month and from 25 to
> 30 cents per day less than laborers are paid by
> native farmers in other neighboring
> localities.(Reports of the Immigration Commission,
> Doc. #33, 1911:490,491)

In Taunton, the high proportion of households with
boarders suggests that a significant share of Portuguese
immigrant households in that city took in lodgers to
supplement their incomes. Referring to the "new"
immigration and particularly to the Portuguese operatives in
the cotton-mills of New England, Lauck remarked in 1912:

> The households of the southern and eastern
> European operatives are marked by low standards of
> living. The preponderance of males, together with
> low wages and the general desire to live on the
> basis of minimum cheapness and to save as much as
> possible, has led to boarding-groups instead of
> independent family-living arrangements.... Owing
> to the comparatively small number of children
> among the recent immigrants, they depend mainly
> upon the payment of boarders or lodgers for family
> income supplementary to the earnings of the
> husband. (Lauck, 1912:712)

---

88 On Azorean's network dynamics, both for Brazil and United
States, see Baganha, 1988. I am using the concept of
migrant networks in a broad sense, encompassing both what
MacDonald and MacDonald (1964) called chain-migration and
impersonal structures of information and support and what
Tilly and Brown (1976) called auspices of kinship.

Boarders (28 cases) in the Taunton sample were all first-generation Portuguese, indicating that the strategy to complement household earnings with boarders could be achieved within the Portuguese migrant network active in the region (89).

In Hilo, unlike Milpitas, extended family households were only extended upwards or downwards rather than laterally (90). Unlike in Taunton, where boarders were Portuguese, in Hilo households that needed to supplement the family wages with boarders could not rely on Portuguese immigrants for their supply (91). The majority of the boarders of the Portuguese households in the sample for Hawaii were Japanese. Together, these two facts suggest that there was no active migrant network in Hilo connected to areas in Portugal.

GENERAL CHARACTERISTICS OF THE PORTUGUESE HOUSEHOLD HEADS IN
TAUNTON, MILPITAS, AND HILO IN 1910

Table IV:XIX summarizes the general characteristics of the Portuguese household heads in Taunton, Milpitas, and Hilo.

---

89 In this case the migrant network may or may not have been active at both ends; we just have no information.
90 In the sample for Hilo there were 3 extended families, none laterally. In Milpitas there were (regardless of having employees or not) 13 extended families, of which 69 percent (9 cases) were extended laterally.
91 In Hilo in 1910 there was only one first generation Portuguese boarder, and he lodged in a household headed by a non-Portuguese.

TABLE IV:XIX - GENERAL CHARACTERISTICS OF THE PORTUGUESE
HOUSEHOLD HEADS IN TAUNTON, MILPITAS, AND HILO IN 1910

INDIVIDUAL CHARACTERISTICS	TAUNTON	MILPITAS	HILO
HOUSEHOLD HEADS	61	94	50
MALE	58	89	42
FEMALE	3	5	8
MARITAL STATUS			
MARRIED FEMALE	0	1	3
WIDOW FEMALE	1	4	5
SINGLE FEMALE	2	0	0
MARRIED MALE	54	74	36
WIDOWER MALE	2	8	2
SINGLE MALE	2	7	4
FEMALE MEAN AGE	52.3	46.8	54.4
MALE MEAN AGE	36.5	46.6	41.6
PERCENTAGE ILLITERATE	66	63	56
FAMILY CHARACTERISTICS			
WIVES' MEAN AGE	32.9	37.6	35.6
CHILDREN UNDER 16	163	126	150
N IN CENSUS	605	94	125

Source: U.S. census manuscript of 1910

The individual and familial characteristics of the
Portuguese household heads differed significantly in
Taunton, Milpitas, and Hilo. The most striking contrasts
are in the mean age of male household heads (there was a ten
years difference between Milpitas and Taunton and a five
years difference between Milpitas and Hilo), in wives' mean
age (a two year difference between Milpitas and Hilo, and a
five year difference between Milpitas and Taunton), and in
the proportion of children who were under 16 years of age

(larger in Taunton then in Milpitas or Hilo). These
differences can be attributed to a multitude of factors, in
the present case date of arrival being the most obvious of
all.

Date of arrival of the Portuguese household heads, their
immigration status, and their work status (92) are given in
Table IV:XX.

---

92 Work status is only given for male household heads. Only
occasionally does the 1910 census give information on female
occupation.

TABLE IV:XX - DATE OF ARRIVAL, IMMIGRANT STATUS, AND WORK
STATUS OF THE PORTUGUESE HOUSEHOLD HEADS IN MILPITAS,
TAUNTON, AND HILO IN 1910 (IN PERCENTAGES)

DATE OF ARRIVAL	MILPITAS HOUSEHOLD HEADS	TAUNTON HOUSEHOLD HEADS	HILO HOUSEHOLD HEADS
THROUGH 1880	30.9	8.2	8.0
1881-1890	27.6	14.8	62.0
1891-1900	16.0	27.9	18.0
1901-1910	21.3	49.2	12.0
UNKNOWN	4.3		
TOTAL	100	100	100
N =	94	61	50
IMMIGRANT STATUS			
ALIEN	54.3	80.3	70.0
NATURALIZED	34.0	8.2	12.0
PAPERS	4.3	3.3	6.0
UNKNOWN	7.5	8.2	12.0
TOTAL	100	100	100
N =	94	61	50
WORK STATUS			
WORKER	15.7	90.2	68.0
OWN ACCOUNT	23.6	1.6	4.0
EMPLOYER	52.8	3.3	2.0
UNKNOWN	7.8	4.9	26.0
TOTAL	100	100	100
N =	94	61	50
N IN CENSUS	94	605	125

Source: U.S. census manuscript of 1910

Table IV:XX indicates that the majority of Portuguese
heads of households in Milpitas had arrived prior to 1891
(58.5 percent), but there was a much more uniform
distribution in Milpitas by date of arrival than in any
other area. In Taunton, household heads by date of arrival
were concentrated in the period between 1891 and 1910, and
in Hilo in the period between 1881 and 1901.

If we assume that there were no striking differences in
the mortality rates for Portuguese immigrants in these three

communities, then we may infer that the migratory flow to Milpitas was well-established from the 1870's and was continually replenished by the inflow of new arrivals. The Portuguese settlement in Taunton was the newest of the three, and Portuguese immigrants were flocking to that city in unprecedent numbers after 1901. After a major inflow between 1881 and 1890, the settlement in Hilo was losing vitality, and arrivals were insufficient or departed too rapidly to renew the community.

The differences in the date of arrival of the Portuguese immigrants in the three communities are in accordance with the age differences noted above. As a comparatively new area of settlement for the Portuguese, Taunton had a younger population with an higher proportion of small children in the household than both Hilo and Milpitas.

The information on immigrant status confirms once more the existence of striking differences in the three communities. In Milpitas, 38 percent of the Portuguese male household heads were either naturalized or were in the process of becoming so. The corresponding figure was 12 percent for Taunton and 18 percent for Hilo. One possible explanation for the great predominance of aliens in Taunton is the higher proportion (49 percent) of new arrivals (immigrants resident in the United States for less than ten years). The hypothesis loses power, however, when we look at the low percentage (18 percent) of those already naturalized or becoming naturalized in Hawaii, where 70 percent of the Portuguese household heads had arrived prior to 1891. For Hawaii the low percentage of naturalizations

could be connected to the social stigmas against Portuguese
that scholars (e.g.,Estep,1941) have identified in this
region. But if we look to Table IV:XXI another factor--
work status-- can be related to the decision to become
American in all three areas.

In Taunton and Hilo, regardless of their date of arrival,
the overwhelming majority of Portuguese household heads were
alien wage-earners; in Milpitas, where a sizable proportion
was naturalized, the majority of the immigrant household
heads were either self-employed or employers. It is
reasonable to presume that with economic achievement came
the desire to adopt the nationality of the receiving
society, particularly if upward mobility was connected to
fixed property (as was the case in California). Literary
evidence also suggests that the economic niches the
Portuguese were able to occupy in California were highly
profitable. The diary industry, for example, to which the
Portuguese appear successfully connected after 1880 was a
quite lucrative business. As the San Francisco Chronicle
remarked in 1904:

> The dairy industry is especially inviting to the
> progressive settler of moderate means, as a few
> acres intelligently and industrially handled will
> afford a good and sure income. (in Graves, 1977:
> 125)

In other words there were obvious motivations for the
Portuguese to remain attached to California. These
motivations were at their lowest in Hawaii, where we know a
great number of immigrants abandoned the islands as soon as
they finished they contracts, and are difficult to judge in
Taunton, where the reduced number of immigrants arrived

prior to 1900, may be attributed either to a young migratory flow, or to a transient immigrant population, or to both (93).

Table IV:XXI gives the proportion of Portuguese household heads who owned (either free or mortgaged) some kind of property (farm or house), by date of arrival. The percentage of the Portuguese household heads who owned some kind of fixed property was similar (25 percent) in Hilo, Taunton, and Milpitas. The pattern of ownership was, however, quite different in these three communities.

TABLE IV:XXI - PORTUGUESE HOUSEHOLD HEADS WHO OWNED FIXED PROPERTY, BY DATE OF ARRIVAL, IN MILPITAS, TAUNTON, AND HILO IN 1910 (IN PERCENTAGES)

DATE OF ARRIVAL	MILPITAS	TAUNTON	HILO
PRIOR TO 1881	54.5	25.0	14.3
1881-1890	31.8	18.8	85.7
1891-1900	13.6	25.0	-
1901-1910	-	31.3	-
TOTAL	100	100	100
N =	22	16	14
N IN SAMPLE	94	61	50
N IN CENSUS	94	605	125

Source: U.S. manuscript census of 1910
Note: N equals number of cases for which both variables (property and date of arrival) are known
----

In Milpitas, the percentage of owners decreased smoothly as the date of arrival became more recent; in Hilo, property owners had nearly all arrived in one decade (1881-1890); in

---

93 My data supports both hypothesis. Return migration to Portugal was heavier from Massachusetts than from any other state. In the sample for Taunton 31 percent of the household heads arrived after 1900.

Taunton, the percentage of property owners showed little variance from period to period. In other words, the temporal pattern of ownership suggests that in Milpitas newcomers would in time attain some kind of property as the majority of their predecessors had done. In Hilo, only the household heads who arrived between 1881 and 1890 seem to have enjoyed that opportunity; in Taunton, regardless of their date of arrival, only a fourth of the immigrants could expect to become property owners. This pattern is quite similar to the one found for naturalization, suggesting that property (here used as a proxy for economic achievement) was more important in the decision-making about naturalization than were temporal or social considerations.

There were many more Portuguese aliens in Taunton and Hilo than in Milpitas. The disproportionate number of aliens in these two areas suggests the hypothesis that Portuguese immigrants in Massachusetts and Hawaii were much more likely to return to their homeland than Portuguese immigrants in California. Return migration will be my next focus of analysis.

RETURN MIGRATION 1908 - 1930

Whatever were the initial dreams of the Portuguese emigrants at the moment of departure, the fact is that the vast majority of them never returned home. Prior to 1908 we do not have direct information on return migration (94).

94 While the character and determinants of return migration to Portugal is of considerable interest, the direct information on this topic covers only a very limited period

But comparison of the yearly growth rates of the Portuguese enumerated in United States censuses and of Portuguese arrivals in the intercensal periods (given in Table IV:XXII) suggests that until the First World War, and except for the period from 1870 to 1880, returns must have been insignificant.

TABLE IV:XXII - PORTUGUESE-BORN RESIDENTS IN THE
CONTINENTAL U.S. 1850 - 1930 AND PORTUGUESE ARRIVALS BETWEEN
CENSUSES

YEAR	PORTUGUESE	YEARLY GROWTH RATE	YEAR	PORTUGUESE ARRIVALS	YEARLY GROWTH RATE
1850	1274		1840/1849	362	
1860	5477	15.70	1850/1859	4225	27.85
1870	8759	4.81	1860/1869	5369	2.43
1880	15650	5.98	1870/1879	14265	10.27
1890	25735	5.10	1880/1889	15560	0.87
1900	40431	4.62	1890/1899	26376	5.42
1910	77634	6.74	1900/1909	63144	9.12
1920	114321	3.95	1910/1919	78413	2.19
1930	109453	-0.43	1920/1929	46644	-5.06

Source: U.S. censuses at given year
        For Portuguese arrivals, Table IV:IX
        Note: Hawaii not included.

The net increases in the Portuguese population resident in the United States are of such magnitude that we may infer that the majority of the arrivals became permanent settlers.

The change from a tendency for permanent emigration to a tendency for temporary migration is evident in the proportion of departures prior to and post the First World War. Between 1908 and 1913, Portuguese departures from the United States (7338 individuals) equaled only 15 percent of

(after 1908) when the geographic origins of the migratory stream differed significantly from the earlier flow. For this reason, return migration is discussed only briefly in this work.

the arrivals (95). These 7338 Portuguese immigrants left especially from Massachusetts (59 percent), and almost all of them (69 percent) had arrived in the previous five years. During the same period only 11 percent of the departures were from California.   In other words, at least from 1908 to 1913 the Portuguese migratory flow to Massachusetts was less oriented to permanent settlement than was the case in California (96).

After the First World War, anti-immigration policies and the economic crises of the late 1920's drove home a considerable number of Portuguese (see Table B:18 in Appendix 2). But by this period the composition of the Portuguese migratory flow had also changed. Rather than coming from the Azores, the largest segment was coming from the mainland, where there was a much greater tendency for individual male migration (see Table IV:IV). Probably due to the combination of these three factors, between 1920 and 1930 departures (34973 individuals) equaled 74 percent of the arrivals. Departures still occurred preferentially from Massachusetts (53 percent), but, unlike the previous period, a significant number of the departing immigrants had been in the United States for more than five years (97). Migration

---

95 Reports of the G.C.I. for 1908-1913. See Table B:17 in Appendix 2. Note that these returns include the Cape Verdeans who were known to have a seasonal pattern of emigration to the United States during this period (Bannick, 1917:62-67.
96 This tendency was also remarked by the Portuguese representatives in United States. The Portuguese Consul in San Francisco observed in 1912: "Unfortunately the Portuguese immigration to California...has become permanent" (in Graves, 1977:69). See Table IV:XVII for the distribution of the Portuguese population in these two states.
97 Twenty-nine percent had been in the United States between five and ten years.

from California remained comparatively small (10 percent), suggesting that the hardships of the Depression were felt less severely in California than in Massachusetts.

The Portuguese emigrants who came to America at the turn of the century seem irrational decision-makers. Judging from their socio-economic achievements in Taunton, Milpitas, and Hawaii, they should all have gone to California. In fact, the Portuguese emigrants did not make the "rational" decision; they made the "possible" decision.

We have seen in chapter I that the majority of the Portuguese emigrants did not have the readily available cash to make the trip on their own. They relied on kin members in the United States, on family savings or indebtedness in Portugal to pay the initial cost of their move. Still, when the last method was used, they needed the support of the Portuguese migrant network in the United States to find a job to support themselves. They arrived in total ignorance of the English language and with just the necessary minimum to get to their place of destination. Connections in the United States were thus absolutely necessary for the move to take place, and they determined the destination of the Portuguese immigrants. Bodnar's insightful statement:

> Work, shelter, and order would be secured in industrial America...through an intricate web of kin and communal associations. The immigrant would not enter America alone. (Bodnar, 1985:57)

is certainly applicable to the Portuguese case as it is to other migrant groups. Dependence upon the migrant network

increases in proportion to ignorance of the English language
and the lack of economic resources of the immigrant. In
consequence, the Portuguese probably entered America with
greater dependence than other southern and eastern Europeans
on their migrant network (98).

Without the necessary cash family emigration could only
be done in stages (99). The most easily available
alternative, and one that a considerable number chose (over
eleven thousand between 1878 and 1889), was to come as a
contract laborer, since this contract usually included the
whole family unit. That alternative was open only to

---

98 A more detailed analysis of this topic was done in
Chapter I. Parallel machanisms existed, however, in almost
all migrant groups -- see for example: Namias, 1982
(immigrants' auto-biographical accounts); and Ratti, 1931,
MacDonald and MacDonald, 1964, and Briggs, 1978 (on the
Italians, a migrant group with great similarities with the
Portuguese). These mechanisms seem, in fact, to cross time
and space. Noticeable similarities, can be easily detected
on the descriptions of the Portuguese migrant networks
contained in Silva Santos, 1977, and Penido Monteiro, 1985
(both dealing with Portuguese immigrants in Brazil at the
turn of the 19th century); and Brettell, 1978, and Brettell
and Callier-Boisvert, 1977, Minga, 1985, and Monteiro, 1987
(dealing with contemporary Portuguese immigrants in France,
Switzerland, and the United States respectively).
99 The linkage of the passport registers for the district of
Horta and Angra and the shiplists for Boston and New York
for 1890/1891 indicates that those travelling in group were
usually related but seldom completely nuclear families.
Delayed family emigration was not uncommon among other
migrant groups. MacDonald and MacDonald (1964) noted that
Southern Italian emigration to the United States was marked
by serial migration of breadwinners and delayed family
emigration.

Hawaii.   The fact that in the sample for Hawaii there was not a single household with a family extended laterally, nor Portuguese boarders in a single household headed by a Portuguese, seems to indicate that Portuguese immigrants in Hawaii did not establish an active migrant network with links to their home communities.   In sum, contract labor does not seem to produce chain migration.

CONCLUSION

In this work I take for granted that international labor migration is economically determined and politically sanctioned. Further, I accept that there is an international labor market in which some countries produce and sell labor that other countries consume. What I debated were the dynamics and specificities of that market. I was particularly interested in two questions: To what extent is the international labor market a free or a regulated market? Who controls the flow within the market, the sending country, the receiving country, or the emigrants themselves?

Using Portuguese emigration to the United States from 1820 to 1930 as a case study, I tested the explicative power of the neoclassic and dependency/marxist models on international migration determinants. I found that, although Portugal had a large economically marginal population and the American economy demanded the inflow of unskilled labor, Portuguese emigration to the United States was only initiated after direct recruitment from the American economy. Migration models based on the economic advantages of the receiving society, and models based on deteriorating economic conditions in the sending society, performed poorly for the Portuguese case. When political change was also taken into account, however, these same models performed much better.

For the Portuguese case, after adjustment for political control of the migratory flow, the dependency/marxist model performed better than the neoclassic model. But after migratory movement takes off, its main determinant and the most powerful filter of the direction the movement takes seem to be the dynamics of the networks active at both ends of the trajectory. Embodying in its functioning the economic conditions of both of the societies involved, the bitterness of those leaving, and the achievements of the departed, networking has a pace of its own which did not necessarily match the fluctuations of either the Portuguese or the American economy.

Because international labor movements occur between nation states, governments are active and integral parts of the migratory process. In fact, it seems misleading to address individual or community decision-making processes in emigration without first taking into account the political parameters within which such decisions could be made. I was thus interested in analyzing American and Portuguese migration policies, and the extent to which government controls shaped the Portuguese migratory flow to the United States. I found that these parameters were at times extremely limiting, as in the case of the Portuguese wishing to emigrate to the United States after the American anti-immigration policies of the 1920's. The Portuguese policymakers were also more than bystanders. By promoting a male-dominated flow, the Portuguese elites insured the flow of remittances and relieved social and demographic pressure, without endangering their labor supply. It is perhaps debatable whether or not the Portuguese political elite consciously used emigration to promote family dispersion to insure the flow of remittances, but the outcome certainly served their interests.

After defining the political parameters within which Portuguese emigration to the United States took place, I considered the economic parameters. Specifically, I asked were the Portuguese migrating because of the lack of job vacancies in their own country, or regardless of job opportunities? Analysis of the Portuguese economic structure, and particularly of the labor market, indicates that Portugal was, between 1880 and 1930, a country with a typical dual structure of backwardness. Economic development was taking place in some very specific and limited areas, but the majority of the country was stagnating. Further, I verified that the areas that were developing did not have the potential to absorb the economically marginal population of the deteriorating areas. Internal migration remained very limited in scope throughout the whole period. The peripheral regions, where the economy was deteriorating, were the same regions from which emigration was taking place.

One of the main results of Portugal's economic backwardness was that an increasing number of people of working age were left out of the job market. After 1900 a growing share (although only a small fraction of the total flow) of females emigrated. It has been assumed that such change was the result of family emigration/family reunification. The extent of deterioration in the country's job market, particularly for women, strongly suggests that a significant part of the change in the composition of the

migratory flow was connected with adverse labor conditions
in Portugal during the period.

Over a quarter of a million Portuguese emigrated to the
United States between 1820 and 1930. Men came first,
tentatively and in small numbers. In time, women and
children followed. The reconstruction of their stories was
the focus of the remainder of my work. I began by making
some educated guesses on the volume of the Portuguese
emigration. I called my estimates educated guesses because
with the uncertain numbers nineteenth-century statisticians
left us, the end result is never truly satisfactory.

Analysis of the general characteristics of the Portuguese
emigration revealed the main differences between the
migratory flows of the mainland and the islands. Emigration
from the mainland was essentially directed to Brazil, and
had a much stronger male component than emigration from the
islands, which was primarily to the United States. The
individual characteristics of the emigrants to the United
States were my next focus of analysis. Through linkage of
surviving records in Portugal and the United States, I was
able to follow the migrants from their communities of origin
to their receiving communities. The individual data at my
disposal (passport records and passenger shiplists) allowed
me not only to describe the socio-demographic
characteristics of the migrants, but also to test and
correct the aggregate data published on Portuguese
emigration in both Portugal and the United States.

I ended my work by analyzing three Portuguese communities
in the United States in the main areas of Portuguese

settlement, to find out how economic conditions in the receiving society shaped migrants lives in their new settings. Although drawn from the same pool, Portuguese immigrants had very unequal opportunities for upward mobility in the United States. If a migrant chose (or rather his network directed him to) Massachusetts, his chances for economic betterment were considerably worse than if he went to California. His chances to move upward were seriously compromised if he had signed a contract and went to Hawaii.

In other words, opportunities were greatly a function of the destination, or more specifically they were a function of the job vacancies and land availability of the receiving area. Clearly, in the three cases observed, the socio economic structure of the region determined the employment structure of the Portuguese. This last structure was remarkably simple, because the majority of the Portuguese male heads were, in the three communities, concentrated in a single economic activity: as unskilled workers in manufacture, in Tauton; as unskilled laborers in sugar plantations, in Hilo; and as farmers, in Milpitas. It was not the level of skill that obviously distinguished the members of these Portuguese settlements, but their work status. In fact, while in Milpitas 83 percent of the Portuguese household heads (males and females) with a stated occupation were either employers or self-employed, in Tauton and in Hilo their percentage dropped drastically to 5 and 8 percent respectively.

The work status attained by the Portuguese immigrants in the structure of the Californian labor market was, as we saw, directly linked to the land availability and more generally to the available socio-economic niches (particularly in market gardening, general farming, and diary production) existent in the region. The Portuguese, however, were able to profit fully from these opportunities because an active network at both ends of the trajectory allow them to fulfill their labor demands within their own ethnic network at lower cost than the prevailing rates in the area, while insuring, in due time, an upward process of socio-economic mobility to a sizable part of the group.

The living arrangements of the Portuguese households in Milpitas, particularly when compared to those in Taunton and Hilo, reflect the mechanisms just noticed. In fact, we have seen that first generation Portuguese lodgers, in Portuguese households were, in Milpitas, employees of the household head. In Taunton, they were boarders, and in Hilo they didn't existed. Obviously, the presence of first generation Portuguese, without family ties to the household head, in Milpitas and Taunton, corresponds to the different needs of the Portuguese household in these two regions. In the Californian case, their presence was an answer to the labor demands of the household while in Massachusetts case their presence was a way to supplement the income needs of the household. The percentage of households extended laterally, larger in Milpitas than in Taunton and again inexistent in Hilo, reinforces this same idea. This is, that in California, Portuguese households relied heavily on their own network to supply their labor demands. No similar process was open to those that went to Massachusetts or Hawaii, because in none of these regions did the Portuguese control a socio-economic niche that they could reinforce based on their own ethnic network.

The migrant network was active in both Massachusetts and California, but I found no evidence of its functioning in Hawaii. The functions performed by the migrant network varied from place to place, but in all cases it functioned partly because it was economically advantageous to those involved. In California, where I found clear evidence of upward mobility over time, newcomers were employed by the already established elements of the Portuguese community, albeit at lower wages than the current rates. In return, newcomers received board, information, and the certitude of a job as soon as they arrived in California. In Massachusetts, where the Portuguese immigrants did not control any economic niche, the established Portuguese could still rely on the newcomers to supplement their incomes by offering them board, and the newcomers could more easily adapt to their new setting by lodging in a Portuguese household.

In sum, the Portuguese emigrant to the United States at

the turn of the nineteenth century was an unskilled laborer who became an industrial worker in Massachusetts or a farmer in California. The Portuguese that went to Hawaii largely entered sugar plantation work. Economically the Portuguese show greatest upward mobility in California and lowest in Hawaii. There, only the second-generation made it out of the plantations.

TABLE A:1 - DECISION MODELS OF EMIGRATION TO THE UNITED
STATES

MODEL I $EMIGR_T = \alpha + \beta GNPRATE_T$

RESULTS:
Model R^2 = .0691

Coefficient	Estimate	St. Error	Prob (T)
α	.00126	.00023	.0001
β	-.00005	.00003	.1014

MODEL II $EMIGR_T = \alpha + \beta GNPAVG_T$

RESULTS:
Model R^2 = .0674

Coefficient	Estimate	St. Error	Prob (T)
α	.00125	.00023	.0001
β	-.00005	.00003	.1058

MODEL III $EMIGR_T = \alpha + \beta AGRDEP_T$

RESULTS:
Model R^2 = .0006

Coefficient	Estimate	St. Error	Prob (T)
α	.00102	.00081	.2142
β	-.00009	.00061	.8808

MODEL IV $EMIGR_T = \alpha + \beta USA_T$

RESULTS:
Model R^2 = .3499

Coefficient	Estimate	St. Error	Prob (T)
α	.00110		
β	-.00088	.00019	.0001

MODEL V

$$EMIGR_T = \alpha + \beta USA_T + \mu AGRDEP_T$$

RESULTS:
Model R^2 = .6250

Coefficient	Estimate	St. Error	Prob (T)
α	-.00231		
β	-.00116	.00021	.0001
μ	.00270	.00052	.0001

MODEL VI

$$EMIGR_T = \alpha + \beta USA_T + \mu AGRDEP_T + \tau GNPRATE_T$$

RESULTS:
Model R^2 = .6512

Coefficient	Estimate	St. Error	Prob (T)
α	-.00200		
β	-.00192	.00027	.0001
μ	.00212	.00062	.0015
τ	.00008	.00005	.1083

MODEL VII

FOR MALES

$$Log(EMIG) = \alpha + \beta GR1 + \Gamma GR3 + \mu PASS + \tau MEXP + \theta AG1 + \Omega AG2 + \delta AG3 + \sigma MST + \pi OCC$$

FOR FEMALES

$$Log(EMIG) = \alpha + \beta GR1 + \Gamma GR3 + \mu PASS + \tau MEXP + \theta AG1 + \Omega AG2 + \delta AG3 + \sigma MST$$

TABLE A:2 - NOTATION TO VARIABLES IN TABLE A:1

$EMIGR_T$ - ratio of the number of emigrants arrived to United States to population at risk, in period T..

$GMPRATE_T$ - ratio of the United States' G.N.P. per capita to Portugal's G.N.P. per capita, in period T.

$GNPAVG_T$ - ratio of the average of the United States' G.N.P. per capita in T-1, T and T+1 to Portugal's G.N.P. per capita in period T.

$AGRDEP_T$ - ratio of agricultural dependents to gainfully employed population in agricultural activities in period T.

USA_T - American immigration policy; 0 if 1891 ≤ T ≤ 1920 and 1 if 1921 ≤ T ≤ 1930.

EMIG - Emigrants from Terceira in 1901; 1 = to US, 0 = to Brazil.

GR1 - Parishes with a migratory flow over 60 percent of which went to Brazil.

GR2 - Parishes with a mixed migratory flow.

GR3 - Parishes with a migratory flow over 60 percent of which went to the United States.

PASSP - Type of passport; 1=individual, 0=collective.

MEXP - Migrant experience; 1=passport holder or one of his or her dependents was born either in US or Brazil, 0=passport holder and dependents were born in Portugal.

AG1 - Emigrants less than 14 years of age (child).

AG2 - Emigrants between 14 and 25 years of age (young).

AG3 - Emigrants between 26 and 40 years of age (middle).

AG4 - Emigrants over 40 years of age (old).

MST - Marital status; 1=single, 0=married or widowed.

OCC - Occupation; 1=laborer, 0=otherwise.

TABLE A:3 - NOTES ON THE VARIABLES IN TABLE A:1

EMIGR$_T$ - the probability of emigrating to the United States from Portugal was computed as follows. First, I estimated the Portuguese population between censuses. This, was added to the legal emigration adjusted for clandestines (12 percent after returns). I considered the results of this estimation to be the population at risk. Second, I adjusted the American Immigration Reports' information on Portuguese arrivals to stand for calendar years instead of fiscal years, by averaging the arrivals in T-1 and T. I then computed the yearly ratio of the Portuguese arrivals in the United States to the population at risk
    The sources used to construct this series were: for the population at risk -- the Portuguese Censuses of 1890, 1900, 1911, 1920, and 1930; for the emigration to United States -- Annual Immigration Report presented to the House of Representatives from 1885 to 1895, and Annual Report of the Commissioner-General of Immigration from 1897 to 1931.

GNPRATE$_T$ - the sources used to construct this series were: for the Portuguese gross national product per capita-- Mata, 1984; for the American gross national product per capita-- Historical Statistics of the United States, 1976; for the conversion of the Portuguese series in dollars-- Mata, 1984, and Butler, 1986.

GNPAVG$_T$ - the same sources as GNPRATE$_T$.

AGRDEP$_T$ - Portuguese Censuses for 1891, 1900, 1911, and 1930.

FIGURE 1 - TERCEIRA MIGRANT NETWORK 1901

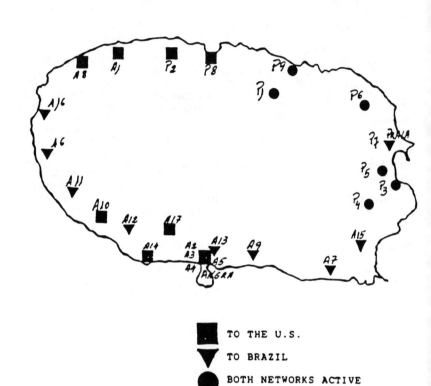

LEGEND TO FIGURE 1: TERCEIRA'S PARISHES

CODE	PARISH
A1	ALTARES
A2	NOSSA SENHORA DA CONCEICAO – ANGRA
A3	SANTA LUZIA – ANGRA
A4	S. PEDRO – ANGRA
A5	SE – ANGRA
A6	DOZE RIBEIRAS
A7	PORTO JUDEU
A8	RAMINHO
A9	RIBEIRINHA
A10	NOSSA SENHORA DO PILAR
A11	SANTA BARBARA
A12	S.BARTOLOMEU – REGATOS
A13	S. BENTO
A14	S. MATEUS DA CALHETA
A15	S. SEBASTIAO
A16	SERRETA
A17	TERRA CHA – BELEM
P1	AGUALVA
P2	BISCOUTOS
P3	CABO DA PRAIA
P4	FONTE DO BASTARDO
P5	FONTINHAS
P6	LAGENS
P7	PRAIA DA VICTORIA – SANTA CRUZ
P8	QUATRO RIBEIRAS
P9	VILLA NOVA

NOTES ON THE PORTUGUESE CENSUSES

The gathering and homogenization of information in order
to create a data bank for future treatment always raises
problems that impose subjective choices on the researcher,
even when the data come from similar sources (as is true in
this case). This section deals with the problems I
encountered with the census data on occupations, and the way
I dealt with them.

THE CHOICE OF A OCCUPATIONAL GRID

1864 was the first year in which information on
occupations was gathered by the Portuguese census-takers.
But the occupational data collected for the censuses of both
1864 and 1878 were never analyzed, and later, with the
destruction of the census bulletins, any chance of doing so
completely vanished. Thus, my analysis of Portuguese
occupational structure could only begin in 1890, the first
year that information was not only collected but also
published.

The first problem I faced with those censuses that did
publish information on occupations was to decide which
occupational grid to use throughout the whole work. As the
introduction to the 1911 census makes clear, the censuses of
1890, 1900, and 1911 all followed common rules for
aggregating the data. The three censuses present the same
kind of abstracts, rely on the same geo-administrative
units, list the same twelve occupational categories, and

divide the population between those <u>de facto</u> practicing an occupation and those dependent on the practitioners.

The census of 1930 uses the familiar geo-administrative units for its abstracts. But this census differs from the preceding ones by dividing the population into three groups -- those practicing an occupation, family helpers, and those dependent on those practicing an occupation -- and by listing fifty-eight occupational categories. A close look at these fifty-eight categories of the 1930 census seems to indicate that a reaggregation into the twelve categories of the previous censuses is possible, allowing comparative analysis without subverting the underlying reasoning of the 1930 document. Given this possibility, the basis for my grid of occupations had to be the census of 1890, clearly the archetype for three of the four censuses analyzed in this work.

Unfortunately, the census of 1890 tells much less than I would like to know about the reasoning behind the aggregated numbers printed in its abstracts. Even so, in vol.I, p.XX, the following useful information is given:

> 1. among the major concerns of the Bureau of Statistics were: a) to separate clearly those who actually practiced an occupation from those who depended directly or indirectly on it; b) in cases where the respondent practiced several occupations, to determine the principal one; c) within an occupation, to specify clearly the rank of the respondent (for example, to distinguish **landowner** [either absent or not] from **tenant**);
> 2. when the respondent described himself with a vague designation (such as **merchant, employed,** or **apprentice**), the sector of activity was to be asked (for example, **trade, industry,** or **craft**) by the census taker;
> 3. the grid of occupations of the printed abstracts was constructed a <u>posteriori</u> by the

Bureau of Statistics, after taking into account
other countries' past experience and the
resolutions of the **International Institute of
Statistics** in its sections of Paris (1889), Vienna
(1891) and Chicago (1893);
    4. for further details, the reader is referred to
Bulletin de l'Institute de Statistique and to <u>Cours
elementaire de statistique,</u> p.194 by Jacques
Bertillon, author of the project on nomenclatures of
occupation presented to the Institute.

To find more information on the reasoning behind the
creation of the occupational abstracts of the 1890 census, I
surveyed Bertillon's work, <u>Cours Élémentaire De Statistique
Administrative</u> (Paris,1895).(1)

In his work, Bertillon stressed the need to standardize
internationally the methodology used and the information
collected by census takers (Chapter XII). To solve this
dual problem of standardization, Bertillon constructed the
grids for occupations presented in his work. These grids
were a refinement of the author's original proposal to the
international meetings of the Institute, held in the
previous year, and Bertillon took into account the
criticisms and the procedures of other directors of Bureaus
of Statistics in Europe. He made careful revisions to
ensure that the grids could be adopted by any Western
country.

Bertillon proposed three grids for aggregating
occupations, which differ solely in their degree of detail.
The first grid included 61 occupational categories; the
second, 206; and the third, 499 occupations. Both the

1 Bertillon was the director of the Statistics Bureau in
Paris and a member of the Superior Committee of Statistics,
a position that gave him both contact with the other
Bureaus of Statistics and access to detailed information on
the work being done in the field.

criterion of standardization and the grids proposed are

important for understanding the Portuguese censuses.

Bertillon began by laying out what he called the **"Major**

occupational groups," and the logic behind them:

"Si l'on compare les differentes nomemclatures
actuellement en usage, on voit que'elles sont assez
concordantes sur les divisions generales qu'il convient
d'adopter. On les met a peu pres d'accord en inscrivant les
grandes divisions professionelles suivantes:

A) PRODUCTION DE LA MATIERE PREMIERE:
   I. Agriculture;
   II. Extraction de matieres minerales.
  B) TRANSFORMATION ET EMPLOI DE LA MATIERE
PREMIERE:
   III. Industrie;
   IV. Transport;
   V. Commerce;
  C) ADMINISTRATION PUBLIQUE ET PROFESSIONS
LIBERALES:
   VI. Force publique;
   VII. Administration publique;
  VIII. Professions liberales;
   IX. Personnes vivant principalement de leur
revenu.
  D) DIVERS:
   X. Travail domestique;
   XI. Designations generales sans indication
d'une industrie determinee;
   XII. Improductifs. -Profession inconnue.
Ces divisions sont tellement logique, qu'il est a
peine besoin de les justifier:
A) L'homme se procure les matieres premieres
necessaires a toute professions, soit par
l'exploitation du sol (I.Agriculture), soit par
l'exploitation du sous-sol (II.Extraction de
matieres minerales);
B) Ces matieres premieres sont ensuite
transformees par l'industrie (III.Industrie),
portees a l'endroit ou elles sont demandees par les
moyens de transport (IV. Transport) et distribuees
entre les consommateurs (V.Commerce);
C) Pour veiller au bon ordre et a la securite des
professions qui precedent, chaque pays possede une
armee et une gendarmerie (VI. Force publique), une
administration publique (VII). Les professions
liberales (VIII) et les personnes vivant de leurs
revenus (IX) trouvent tout naturellement leur place a
la suite des professions que nous venons de passer
en revue.
D) Enfin, il convient d'etablir trois divisions
professionelles pour les individus non classes ou
sans profession. (Bertillon, op.cit.,p.196-97)

The underlying logic of Bertillon's schema was that demand, rather than technology, should be the basis of division. The reasoning can be summarized as follows. Nature was the point of departure of all activity, allowing men to survive and furnishing them with the raw materials to be transformed in order to obtain industrial goods. The primary extractive group had two subgroups: agriculture and mineral extraction. The next step was the transformation of the raw materials into consumable goods and their distribution. This group had three subgroups: industry, transport, and commerce. The next occupational group, public administration and protective forces, found its "raison d'etre," in Bertillon's reasoning, in the preceding occupations; the protective forces and public administration existed to ensure order and security for the previous occupations. The liberal professions and people living off their own income came next. Although Bertillon did not explain why these subgroups came **"naturally next,"** it seems, following the author's logic, that the liberal professions existed to provide services demanded by the preceding groups. In the same vein, people living off their own income appeared next as consumers of the raw materials, goods, and services furnished by the other groups. Finally, a residual group, "divers," encompassed occupations not included elsewhere.

If we examine the detailed grid, another key feature emerges. Bertillon's grids were intended to cover the total population, not just those who were economically active.

This becomes clear when we note that the group "domestic workers" includes "members of the family (married women, etc.) doing housework," and that the "nonproductive and unknown occupations" group includes "children without occupation, students, sick people, mentally ill people, inmates, and vagrants."

Although the Bureau of Statistics, which supervised and organized the Portuguese census of 1890, referred the reader to Bertillon's work for further explanation of its occupational grid, major differences are apparent when the two grids are compared. The first major difference is the distribution of the population. As we have seen, Bertillon intended to cover all the population with his occupational grid. The Portuguese census divided the population into three main categories: people with an occupation; dependent people; and servants doing domestic work in the household. These main entries seem to conform to one of the major concerns expressed by the Bureau -- distinguishing those who in fact practiced an occupation from those who lived directly (dependents) or indirectly (servants in the household) from it. These three main entries were disaggregated by administrative divisions (kingdom, district, and concelho), and for each geographical unit the following occupational groups were presented:

    I.Agricultural work
   II.Fishing and hunting
  III.Mineral extraction
   IV.Industry
    V.Transportation
   VI.Commerce
  VII.Protective forces
 VIII.Public administration
   IX.Liberal professions
    X.People living off their own income
   XI.Domestic work
  XII.Nonproductives and unknown occupations

This ordering might seem to follow the same logic
followed by Bertillon in his specification of the "major
occupational groups," but there are subtle differences.
Bertillon included fishing and hunting under "agriculture";
in the Portuguese census, fishing and hunting were put in a
separate category. Bertillon's group "general occupations
not well defined" does not appear in the Portuguese census.
While this might seem to imply that the Portuguese census-
takers succeeded in solving the problem of missing data and
poorly defined occupations, it is more likely that the
problem could only be reduced, not totally solved. It is
reasonable to assume that, after the experience obtained
with the censuses of 1864 and 1878 (in which information on
occupations was collected but not published), more precise
directives were given to the 1890 enumerators, to ensure
better recording of occupations. Because a priori
directives were given to the census-takers on the subject,
such missing information was perhaps reduced to the point
where persons in this category could be relegated to the
residual group, "nonproductives and unknown occupations."
In fact, such a practice would account for the size of this

group, which comprised 4 percent of the total population and 7 percent of the active population of Portugal in 1890.

Because I was working with aggregated data (the printed abstracts of the census), I did not attempt any social classification based on the census material; too little was known to justify such classification. But if actual practice conformed to the written description, it should be possible to rearrange the census entries in a more meaningful way, to show more clearly the active population of Portugal in 1890. Looking for models, I surveyed recent works on the subject. But either because my data were aggregated into fewer categories or because I did not agree with the proposed grids, I decided to maintain the entries of the census with some alterations. I subtracted two groups, "people living off their own income" and "nonproductives and unknown occupations," from "people practicing an occupation," and I added to the last group "servants in the household." After these alterations, the distribution of the total population by district (the geo-administrative unit chosen for my study) was as follows:

ACTIVE POPULATION

1.Agriculture
2.Fishing and hunting
3.Mineral extraction
4.Industry
5.Transportation
6.Commerce
7.Armed forces
8.Public administration
9.Liberal professions
10.Domestic work
11.Servants in the household

NON-ACTIVE POPULATION

1.Living off own income
2.Non-productive
  and unknown occupations
3.Dependents

The 1930 census (in vol.V, pp.8-10) provides some sketchy information on the criteria followed for aggregating the active population into fifty-eight occupational categories, and for dividing each category into four main columns, according to the source of income. The three first columns -- "employed by the state," "employed by a firm," and "self-employed" -- are self-explanatory. The same cannot be said of the fourth column, "family members helping the respective head of the household" (hereafter referred to as "family helpers" or "helpers").

Unlike earlier censuses, the 1930 census clearly defines a cut-off point dividing the active from the non-active population: " All those having any kind of profitable occupation were considered part of the active population." This statement would seem to imply that "family helpers" were limited to those family members who were remunerated for their work. But the stated principle is contradicted a few paragraphs later, when the 1930 census report specifies that "Married women taking care of their households were included in the active population, but counted separately in each occupational category and considered as helpers of the head of the household" (1930 Census, Vol. V:9). This information, which I later put to use in reaggregating the entries for analysis, suggests the wisdom of including "helpers" in the non-active population.

The seemingly definitive principle for classifying the non-active population was further violated in the 1930 census, as the following statement indicates:

> (...) for technical reasons... the unemployed, the
> inmates in prisons or in hospitals were listed as
> actives, although they did not have any profitable
> occupation at the time the census was taken. In the
> same way persons who do not practice any activity,
> such as those living off their own income and the
> retired, were qualified professionally as actives,
> since they live off the income or pensions they
> receive, maintaining their families, exactly like any
> other person considered to be active.
> (1930 Census, V.V:9)

This statement reinforces my decision to exclude these

persons from the active population in the censuses of 1890-

1911, and obviously supports a similar procedure for the

1930 census.

So far, all the information given seems to indicate that

reaggregating the entries in the 1930 census according to

the entries I intended to use for the censuses of 1890-1911

would be possible. The 1930 census report testifies to

other problems, however. For example:

> "All persons working in a firm or shop were
> aggregated, independently of the character of the
> function they practice, in the professional group to
> which the firm or shop belongs.... for example, under
> the label agricultural works were counted not only
> persons directly occupied in agricultural works,
> but also the administrative personnel and the
> clerks, because their remuneration is dependent on
> the respective agricultural exploration they work
> for. Similarly ... a carpenter ... when
> practicing his activity on an auto-repair shop would
> be classified differently than if he worked for a
> building trade. In the first case he would be
> classified in the group industries related to
> the construction of means of transportation,
> and in the second case, in the group industries
> related to building construction."(1930 Census, Vol.V,
> p.9)

There is a clear difference between Bertillon's reasoning

for the placement of the active population (followed in the

occupational grids of the 1890, 1900, and 1911 censuses) and the reasoning of the designers of the 1930 census. For Bertillon, the determining factor for classifying a person's place in the occupational grid was his/her position in the productive process; for the designers of the 1930 census, the determining factor was the source of income.

These different criteria would certainly produce serious problems if we had a detailed occupational grid for the earlier censuses. Yet while comparison between the 1930 census and the previous censuses is necessarily imperfect (because the censuses were not constructed under precisely the same guidelines), I believe that my eleven major occupational categories will absorb the major discrepancies resulting from the application of different criteria. The use of broad categories does not solve cases like the clerk working for an agricultural firm, but the number of persons in such circumstances was certainly so insignificant that their inclusion should not affect the comparison.

As first steps in reducing the matrix given in the 1930 census to a matrix comparable to the one used for the earlier censuses of 1890, 1900, and 1911, three major changes were made:

First, I equated "family helpers" -- column four of the active population on the original matrix -- with "dependents," and moved them to the non-active population. This decision seems to be the only logical one. Consider the following example. In the category "people definitively without an occupation," the abstracts for the whole country in 1930 show 15,854 males and 1,289 females who were helped by 4 males and 14,196 females. Since the female share in the category "helpers" for this group is one of the highest registered, it would seem that you need many more women helping you to do nothing than you need to help you to to do something. More seriously, this example raises the problem of the meaning of "family helpers" and what to do with them.

The appropriate resolution is implied by other examples. In the category "protective forces," 54,585 males were listed for the whole country, along with 2,179 female "helpers." Since women were forbidden to enter the army, it seems reasonable to assume that the 2,179 females were the wives of married army men. Given the low ratio of females to males here, these "helpers" were probably officers' wives. Similarly, in the category "teachers," we find 5 males and 3,941 females listed as "helpers." The most logical explanation is that the label "helpers" was sometimes (as the census discussion suggests) a euphemism for spouses.

Based on the examples mentioned, it is hard to justify including "helpers" in the active population. Rather, it would seem that persons included in the category "family helpers" should be moved to the non-active population -- particularly since even the designers of the census acknowledged including mainly non-active population under this entry.

This solution seems less appropriate when we think of other categories such as retail trade or agriculture. Here "family helpers" could take a very active role and substitute for hired labor. Still, even for these cases I contend that the reclassification discussed above should be

maintained. Consider the figures given in the 1930 census
for agriculture and retail trade nationally:

AGRICULTURE AND RETAIL TRADE - 1930 CENSUS

HAVING AN OCCUPATION		FAMILY HELPERS		DEPENDENTS	
MALES	**FEMALES**	**MALES**	**FEMALES**	**MALES**	**FEMALES**
			AGRICULTURE		
1072678	164329	10875	588698	587006	783772
			RETAIL TRADE		
13975	1744	27	8325	7782	11186

Except for the very old and the very young, is it reasonable
to argue that the work of the nearly six hundred thousand
"family helpers" in agriculture differed greatly from the
work of the 1.37 million dependents? Were the tasks
performed by the eight thousand helpers in retail trade
truly unlike those of the eighteen thousand dependents?
Given what is known about daily life in this period (I am
referring especially to literary descriptions), the answer
ought to be no. Any division of this population into active
and nonactive groups has to be totally arbitrary, since it
is impossible to determine how many were too old or too
young to participate.

There is one more reason why I decided to move "family
helpers" into the non-active population. Composed largely
of women (1,156,355 females versus 13,146 males), this
group's inclusion in the active population would raise
female relative participation in the active population from
27 percent to 47 percent. This last level of participation
is totally out of line with female relative participation in

the active population in previous censuses (respectively 37 percent in 1890, 28 percent in 1900, and 26 percent in 1911). Including this group in the active population would undermine the validity of comparisons over time.

The second step I took was to move the category "people living off their own income" to the non-active population. This practice was in accordance with the reaggregation done for the previous censuses.

For the last preliminary step, the categories "people definitively without occupation" and "professions, jobs, crafts or occupations not mentioned in any of the previous categories" were considered to correspond to the category "nonproductive and unknown occupations" of the previous censuses; as such, this group was also moved to the non-active population. In 1930 these two groups represented 5 percent of the active population (before any reaggregation), and with dependents included they represented 6 percent of the total population. This percentage is slightly below that found for "nonproductive and unknown occupations" in the 1890 census (7 percent). But the figures are close enough to support the inference that the two categories of 1930 correspond to the one of 1890, and must be treated as a residual category. As we have seen from the description given in the 1930 census, this residual group was overwhelmingly composed of the non-active population. Thus, as was done for the other censuses, these persons were removed from the active group.

Following these changes, the fifty-eight categories of the 1930 census were converted to the eleven categories of the preceding censuses in the following way:

<u>1930 CATEGORIES</u>   <u>NEW CATEGORIES</u>

1. Agricultural works   1. Agriculture
2. Fishing and hunting   2. Fishing & hunting
3. Mining   3 to 5   3. Extraction of
4. Quarrying   minerals
5. Saltpond extraction
6. Textile industries   6 to 23   4. Industry
7. Leather and fur industries
8. Wood industries
9. Metallurgy industries
10. Ceramic industries
11. Chemical industries
12. Food related industries
13. Shoes and clothing industries
14. Furnishing industries
15. Building related industries
16. Industries related to the construction
    of means of transport
17. Industries related to the production and
    transmission of physic forces
18. Industries related to literature, art,
    and science
19. Rag industries
20. Cork industry
21. Tobacco industry
22. Paper industry
23. Industries not specified in the previous
    groups
24. River and sea transport   **24 to 29**   5. Transport
25. Railways
26. Transport by automobile
27. Urban bus transport
28. Mail, telegraphs, and telephones
29. Transport industries not specified
30. Banks, credit institutions,   **30 to 47**   6. Commerce
    and insurance
31. Commissions
32. Textiles trades
33. Wood trades
34. Leather and fur trades
35. Metal trades
36. Ceramic products trade
37. Chemical products trade
38. Hotels, restaurants, and taverns
39. Foodstuff trade
40. Trade of shoes and clothing
41. Furnishing trade
42. Building trade
43. Small local mixed trade
44. Fuel trade

45. Trade related to literature, arts, and science
46. Trades not specified in any of the other groups
47. Armed forces   7. Protective forces
48. Public administration   8. Public administration
49. Religion   **49 to 53**   9. Liberal professions
50. Justice
51. Public health
52. Teachers
53. Liberal professions related to literature, arts. and science
54. Persons living off own income   **(removed to non-active)**
55. Domestic services   10. Domestic services
56. Servants in the household   11. Servants
57. Persons definitively without occupation   **(removed to non-active)**
58. Professions, positions, arts, crafts or occupations not cover in any of the previous groups   **(removed to non-active)**.

THE CHOICE OF REGIONAL UNITS

The geographical unit chosen for the core of the analysis was the district. This geo-administrative unit presented advantages in terms of homogeneity over time, average size for comparative purposes, and feasibility that made its choice an obvious one.

The choice of macro geographical units was not so obvious. Portugal has traditionally been divided in several ways, all of which have a certain rationality. The geographical description in Chapter 3 of this work illustrates these main divisions, and clearly suggests that they all were meaningful. The geographical description also indicated an additional macro division -- the districts of Lisbon and Oporto versus the rest of the country-- that was at the very least as meaningful as the traditional divisions of the country.

Because I was particularly interested in the structure of the labor force, I did a statistical analysis testing for significant differences in the distribution of the active population for 1890 using two traditional macro divisions - North, Center, South, and Islands; and Littoral, Interior, Islands-- and a nontraditional division -- the districts of Lisbon and Oporto, Mainland, and Islands. My goal was to determine whether, in terms of labor force distribution, one of the macro divisions was statistically more significant than the others.

The results (F-test at the .01 level of significance) show that all the macro divisions isolate statistically significant differences in the labor force and population. I thus decided to use both a traditional division-- North, Center, South, Islands-- and my own division-- districts of Lisbon and Oporto, Mainland, Islands. This exercise raised one last point of interest that is worth remarking. Contrary to what seems to be the view of O.Ribeiro (O.Ribeiro,1955:113), there is more than one right way of dividing the Portuguese land according to its population distribution.

ERRORS

For the period under analysis, 1890 to 1930, it is reasonable to expect to find several errors in aggregate data published by the state. Since I had information on several variables referring to the same population, computational errors in the census materials were easy to

identify. It was less easy to decide at what level of
aggregation necessary corrections should be made.

I found that the grand totals for the census at the
national level always added up correctly, regardless of the
variable considered. For this reason, needed corrections
were made at the lower level of aggregation of the data.
This procedure at least guaranteed that coherence would be
maintained between the several subsets of data.

ABBREVIATIONS

1. ACTIVITIES

agric = agriculture
commerc = commerce
dom.work = domestic services
lib.prof. = liberal professions
prot.forc. = protective forces
publ.adm. = public administration

2. DISTRICTS

Angra = Angra do Heroismo
C.Branco = Castelo Branco
P.Delgada = Ponta Delgada
Portalegr = Portalegre
V.Real = Vila Real

3. PROVINCES

Beira A. = Beira Alta
Beira B. = Beira Baixa
Extrem = Extremadura
T.Montes = Tras-Os-Montes

4. Sex

f = female
m = male

TABLE A:4 - "DE FACTO" POPULATION BORN OUTSIDE THE DISTRICT OF RESIDENCE
1890 - 1930

DISTRICT	POPULATION "DE FACTO" BORN OUTSIDE THE DISTRICT OF RESIDENCE				PERCEWNTAGE BY DISTRICT			
	1890	1900	1911	1930	1890	1900	1911	1930
VIANA	3725	4609	6010	6808	1.81%	2.15%	2.66%	2.84%
BRAGA	6041	11732	12893	10434	1.79%	3.29%	3.38%	2.52%
PORTO	57308	71280	79023	62895	10.63%	12.06%	11.75%	7.81%
V.REAL	4702	9350	8918	8712	2.00%	3.90%	3.65%	3.44%
BRAGANCA	2498	4384	4700	4402	1.40%	2.39%	2.46%	2.38%
AVEIRO	5909	9658	11906	17874	2.06%	3.19%	3.55%	4.69%
VIZEU	4464	8616	10060	10249	1.14%	2.15%	2.42%	2.38%
COIMBRA	7260	13640	16290	20799	2.30%	4.12%	4.55%	5.37%
GUARDA	4869	6143	7629	4363	1.95%	2.35%	2.81%	1.63%
C.BRANCO	5729	7315	8299	4702	2.80%	3.38%	3.44%	1.77%
LEIRIA	6843	10813	12228	12627	3.15%	4.53%	4.66%	4.02%
SANTAREM	14374	18321	25772	16848	5.65%	6.48%	7.92%	4.45%
LISBOA/SETUBAL	130742	172349	224946	338895	22.10%	24.97%	26.97%	30.14%
PORTALEGRE	6305	10022	9595	5314	5.63%	8.11%	6.82%	3.20%
EVORA	9979	13637	14069	12000	8.49%	10.71%	9.52%	6.65%
BEJA	5975	6067	10583	9545	3.81%	3.73%	5.52%	3.98%
FARO	2662	3779	4538	5702	1.17%	1.49%	1.67%	1.90%
ANGRA	2463	2496	1955	1377	3.44%	3.43%	2.82%	1.97%
HORTA	1656	1526	1679	1202	2.84%	2.79%	3.40%	2.47%
P.DELGADA	994	2566	1206	2771	0.80%	2.02%	1.00%	2.08%
FUNCHAL	485	1476	1063	2075	0.36%	0.99%	0.63%	0.99%
PORTUGAL	284983	389779	473362	559594	5.69%	7.24%	8.00%	8.23%
DIST.AVG.	13570.61	18560.90	22541.04	26647.33				
MIN	485	1476	1063	1202				
MAX	130742	172349	224946	338895				
STD	28617.90	37204.77	47988.17	70978.58				

SOURCE: CENSUSES ABSTRACTS FOR THE GIVEN YEARS

TABLE A:5 - "DE FACTO POPULATION AND DIFFERENCES BETWEEN OBSERVED AND EXPECTED 1890 - 1930
(FOREIGNERS EXCLUDED)

DISTRICT	POPULATION RESIDENT IN THE DISTRICT				DIFFERENCES BETWEEN "DE FACTO" AND EXPECT		
	1890	1900	1911	1930	1890-900	1900-1911	1911-930
VIANA	205838	214044	226221	239863	-7124	-9200	-19861
BRAGA	337530	356088	381208	414170	-6581	-10443	-23495
PORTO	538945	591165	672330	805276	12081	22124	33374
V.REAL	235342	239456	244321	253367	-13414	-19050	-27138
BRAGANCA	178258	183813	191353	184861	-7721	-10818	-34831
AVEIRO	286986	302522	335128	381013	-5838	2392	-3747
VIZEU	390223	401087	415599	430573	-18199	-25546	-46576
COIMBRA	315954	331441	358243	387180	-8045	-6300	-24119
GUARDA	249767	261229	271085	267375	-7140	-16234	-43858
C.BRANCO	204617	216362	240932	265394	-3494	2961	-11220
LEIRIA	217113	238584	262340	314280	5301	-72	13088
SANTAREM	254407	282889	325520	378337	9534	14378	4608
LISBOA/SETUBAL	591475	690215	834165	1124411	54688	75016	166706
PORTALEGRE	111987	123559	140785	166020	3231	4886	4385
EVORA	117600	127356	147758	180482	997	7683	10841
BEJA	156759	162822	191641	240005	-5612	12558	19982
FARO	227892	254287	271944	300238	9422	-7739	-11981
ANGRA	71703	72862	69207	69796	-4181	-10932	-9661
HORTA	58308	54728	49322	48739	-7923	-10872	-7888
P.DELGADA	124247	127211	121169	133505	-6290	-18747	-5609
FUNCHAL	133439	149684	168588	210555	6307	3955	16999
PORTUGAL	5008390	5381404	5918859	6795440	0	0	0
DIST.AVG.	238494.7	256257.3	281850.4	323592.3			
MIN	58308	54728	49322	48739			
MAX	591475	690215	834165	1124411			
STD	135317.1	153434.4	181892.3	237331.2			

SOURCE:CENSUSES ABSTRACTS ACCORDING TO PLACE OF BIRTH

TABLE A:6 - POPULATION RESIDENT IN CITIES OVER TWO THSOUSAND INHABITANTS
1890 - 1911

DISTRICT	CITIES	1890	1900	1911
LISBON	LISBON	301206	356009	435359
OPORTO	OPORTO	146739	167955	194009
	BIG CITIES	447945	523964	629368
BRAGA	BRAGA	23089	24202	24647
FUNCHAL	FUNCHAL	18778	20844	24687
LISBON	SETUBAL	17581	22074	30346
C.BRANCO	COVILHA	17562	15469	15745
COIMBRA	COIMBRA	16985	18144	20581
P.DELGADA	PONTA DELGADA	16767	17620	16179
EVORA	EVORA	15134	16020	17901
PORTALEGRE	ELVAS	13291	13981	10645
FARO	TAVIRA	11558	12175	11665
ANGRA	ANGRA DO HEROISMO	11012	10788	10057
PORTALEGRE	PORTALEGRE	10534	11820	11603
	MEDIUM SIZE CITIES	172291	183137	194056
VIANA	VIANA DO CASTELO	9682	9990	10486
FARO	FARO	9338	11789	12680
AVEIRO	AVEIRO	8860	9979	11523
VIZEU	LAMEGO	8685	9471	8696
BRAGA	GUIMARAES	8611	9104	9550
BEJA	BEJA	8394	8885	10113
FARO	SILVES	8362	9687	9919
FARO	LAGOS	8259	8291	9673
SANTAREM	SANTAREM	8210	8628	9897
VIZEU	VISEU	7996	8057	8167
HORTA	HORTA	6879	6575	6099
CAST.BRANCO	CASTELO BRANCO	6728	7288	7798
GUARDA	GUARDA	5990	6124	6635
VILA REAL	VILA REAL	5920	6716	6822
BRAGANCA	BRAGANCA	5840	5535	5787
SANTAREM	TOMAR	5816	6888	8054
COIMBRA	FIGUEIRA DA FOZ	5676	6221	6926
OPORTO	PENAFIEL	4631	5065	5573
LEIRIA	LEIRIA	3932	4459	4697
GUARDA	PINHEL	2977	2917	3012
	SMALL SIZE CITIES	140786	151669	162107
	URBAN POPULATION	761022	858770	985531

SOURCE: CENSUS AT GIVEN YEAR

TABALE A:7 - POPULATION AGE 10 AND OVER AND LABOR FORCE BY SEX AND AGE 1890 - 1930

AGE	BOTH SEXES				MALES				FEMALES			
	1890	1900	1911	1930	1890	1900	1911	1930	1890	1900	1911	1930
10 - 19												
POPULATION	986326	1096244	1206447	1329046	495609	546231	602473	668191	490717	550013	603974	660855
LABOR FORCE	495517	497658	489926		325899	367334	384175		169618	130324	105751	
20 - 39												
POPULATION	1403608	1513856	1674293	2012603	653817	704959	761769	943380	749791	808897	912524	1069223
LABOR FORCE	895719	907353	959604		604173	675756	740513		291546	231597	219091	
40 - 59												
POPULATION	992362	1036179	1087091	1285932	459940	474095	494482	584457	532422	562084	592609	701475
LABOR FORCE	672481	633926	630921		441160	462130	476925		231321	171796	153996	
60 AND OVER												
POPULATION	523130	529693	582766	666467	239967	232686	254494	283186	283163	297007	328272	383281
LABOR FORCE	341947	311343	305995		210258	208996	216554		131689	102347	89441	
PORTUGAL												
POPULATION	3905426	4175972	4550597	5249048	1849333	1957971	2113218	2479214	2056093	2218001	2437379	2814834
LABOR FORCE	2405664	2350280	2386446	2328008	1581490	1714216	1818167	1774059	824174	636064	568279	533949

NOTE: SERVANTS NOT INCLUDED

SOURCE: CENSUSES ABSTRACTS FOR AGES

TABLE A:8 - POPULATION AGE 10 AND OVER AND LABOR FORCE BY DISTRICT
1890 - 1930

DISTRICT	1890		1900		1911		1930	
	POP.	L.FORCE	POP.	L.FORCE	POP.	L.FORCE	POP.	L.FORCE
VIANA	163610	124815	169413	119105	176672	113903	185007	98873
BRAGA	262762	176016	274155	191064	291012	178359	311715	167769
PORTO	416576	286982	454403	282809	515221	303237	623978	308988
V.REAL	183388	146382	186464	114172	185890	112037	193248	92644
BRAGANCA	138292	97142	141246	82798	144537	84802	139580	67197
AVEIRO	219331	148099	231303	152373	251557	141847	290958	145979
VIZEU	299632	204755	308695	192189	315309	183945	331086	156896
COIMBRA	246880	158698	258262	144188	276492	147109	306153	141777
GUARDA	189365	120874	197783	109456	203982	107661	204236	87155
C.BRANCO	156311	104060	163646	86419	180289	96249	203824	89009
LEIRIA	166137	102427	181281	101124	199003	104085	239611	103107
SANTAREM	195703	117495	216781	117902	251505	136956	293504	137479
LISBOA	490085	290012	565982	315586	678358	371212	924870	441784
PORTALEGRE	87773	53769	95176	52830	106368	57950	128974	61371
EVORA	92392	57908	99988	57055	112188	63962	139046	69715
BEJA	121538	76787	127690	75187	145078	81876	186258	86184
FARO	172414	95210	195456	104270	206213	103117	237143	101556
ANGRA	57070	31250	57442	28940	53994	24849	56183	22775
HORTA	46571	26452	44529	22205	39339	18174	39465	15888
P.DELGADA	96966	50834	97222	48085	93480	45503	100935	44039
FUNCHAL	102630	60583	109055	59496	124110	68131	158274	76508
PORTUGAL	3905426	2530450	4175972	2457253	4550597	2544964	5294048	2516693
DISTR. AVG.	185972.6	120497.6	198855.8	117012.0	216695.0	121188.7	252097.5	119842.5
MIN	46571	26452	44529	22205	39339	18174	39465	15888
MAX	490085	290012	565982	315586	678358	371212	924870	441784
STD	108477.0	71325.66	122750.5	74611.28	145253.7	82908.01	192725.5	94129.97

SOURCE: CENSUSES ABSTRACTS ACCORDING TO AGE

TABLE A:9 - MALE POPULATION 10 AND OVER AND MALE LABOR FORCE BY DISTRICT
1890 - 1930

MALES

DISTRICT	1890		1900		1911		1930	
	POP.	L.FORCE	POP.	L.FORCE	POP.	L.FORCE	POP.	L.FORCE
VIANA	68761	61477	70874	62940	73212	64846	75922	58813
BRAGA	114924	98513	119446	106540	127834	112409	140028	103044
PORTO	189084	162819	204064	174396	230793	199707	283343	207281
V.REAL	86403	78735	88386	79281	84894	74407	91329	65658
BRAGANCA	68853	60835	69386	59462	70072	60874	68347	50604
AVEIRO	96395	82580	100302	85759	108188	93475	127359	95881
VIZEU	135546	114602	138754	127049	137416	118814	147624	109630
COIMBRA	112487	97943	114717	99485	120819	103818	136468	100844
GUARDA	90067	77788	93130	82623	93656	80967	92959	64545
C.BRANCO	77228	72664	78928	66840	86688	76325	97505	68201
LEIRIA	80833	71706	86643	78889	93581	82582	114187	81636
SANTAREM	96593	84230	105571	93888	121970	108762	142459	109720
LISBOA	255152	217321	287799	251533	340168	296597	452223	325190
PORTALEGRE	44817	39544	47841	43190	52970	47166	65488	50659
EVORA	47789	42307	51397	45213	57108	51580	70187	57155
BEJA	62612	54592	64724	57543	73857	66364	94735	69326
FARO	86325	74516	97062	85599	99337	86728	113029	82211
ANGRA	24625	21206	25411	22711	23818	20415	26259	18565
HORTA	19037	16262	18864	17279	16662	14455	18546	12956
P.DELGADA	44116	37927	44186	40164	42653	37992	47215	35152
FUNCHAL	47686	41683	50486	45909	57522	49836	74002	56734
PORTUGAL	1849333	1609250	1957971	1726293	2113218	1848119	2479214	1823805
DISTR. AVG.	88063.47	76630.95	93236.71	82204.42	100629.4	88005.66	118057.8	86847.85
MIN	19037	16262	18864	17279	16662	14455	18546	12956
MAX	255152	217321	287799	251533	340168	296597	452223	325190
STD	53117.33	45089.54	59323.26	51508.81	69902.84	60677.51	92145.15	66381.16

SOURCE: CENSUSES ABSTRACTS ACCORDING TO AGE

TABLE A:10 - FEMALE POPULATION AGE 10 AND OVER AND FEMALE LABOR FORCE BY DISTRICT
1890 - 1930

FEMALES

DISTRICT

	1890		1900		1911		1930	
	POP.	L.FORCE	POP.	L.FORCE	POP.	L.FORCE	POP.	L.FORCE
VIANA	94849	63338	98559	56165	103460	49057	109085	40060
BRAGA	147838	77503	154709	84524	163178	65950	171687	64725
PORTO	227492	124063	256339	108413	284428	103530	340635	101707
V.REAL	96985	67647	98578	34891	100996	37630	101919	26986
BRAGANCA	69439	36307	71860	23336	74465	23928	71233	16593
AVEIRO	122936	65519	131001	66614	143369	48372	163599	50098
VIZEU	164086	90153	169541	65140	177893	65131	183462	47266
COIMBRA	134393	60755	143545	44703	155673	43291	169685	40933
GUARDA	99298	43086	104653	26833	110326	26694	111277	22610
C.BRANCO	79083	31396	84718	19579	93601	19924	106319	20808
LEIRIA	85304	30721	94638	22235	105422	21503	125424	21471
SANTAREM	99110	33265	111210	24014	129535	28194	151045	27759
LISBOA	234933	72691	278183	64053	338190	74615	472647	116594
PORTALEGRE	42956	14225	47335	9640	53398	10784	63486	10712
EVORA	44603	15601	48591	11842	55080	12382	68859	12560
BEJA	58926	22195	62966	17644	71221	15512	91523	16858
FARO	86089	20694	98394	18671	106876	16389	124114	19345
ANGRA	32445	10044	32031	6229	30176	4434	29924	4210
HORTA	27534	10190	25665	4926	22677	3719	20919	2932
P.DELGADA	52850	12907	53036	7921	50827	7511	53720	8887
FUNCHAL	54944	18900	58569	13587	66588	18295	84272	19774
PORTUGAL	2056093	921200	2218001	730960	2437379	696845	2814834	692888
DISTR. AVG.	97909.19	43866.66	105619.0	34807.61	116065.6	33183.09	134039.7	32994.66
MIN	27534	10044	25665	4926	22677	3719	20919	2932
MAX	234933	124063	278183	108413	338190	103530	472647	116594
STD	56217.99	30298.05	64178.13	28056.79	76074.84	25758.22	101015.5	29193.07

SOURCE: CENSUSES ABSTRACTS ACCORDING TO AGE

351

TABLE A:11 - ACTIVE POPULATION BY SECTOR AND DISTRICT 1890

DISTRICT	AGRIC.	FISHING	MINING	INDUSTRY	TRANSP.	COMMERC	PROT.FORC	PUBL.ADMI	LIB.PROF	DOM.WORK	SERVANTS	TOTAL
VIANA	98678	561	20	11520	1185	3126	1159	525	1225	2586	4230	124815
BRAGA	119002	207	124	31558	1138	5867	1189	554	2102	2662	11613	176016
PORTO	116881	5590	1381	96805	6479	19412	4081	2192	4089	13873	16099	286882
V.REAL	122515	18	7	11162	1048	3168	1586	322	1085	574	4897	146382
BRAGANCA	75565	21	36	10029	417	2691	1293	291	949	1811	4039	97142
AVEIRO	97308	6394	502	24135	2037	5915	528	461	1325	3156	6338	148099
VIZEU	153538	21	13	26541	1569	5406	1570	541	1825	4336	9395	204755
COIMBRA	100178	1558	217	26178	2183	4672	1011	888	1541	12236	8036	158698
GUARDA	81353	11	2	21321	957	3751	1736	366	1153	5510	4714	120874
C.BRANCO	67091	28	36	22286	1080	2651	1679	317	859	4649	3384	104060
LEIRIA	67749	897	7	13282	1871	3222	935	307	911	8873	4573	102427
SANTAREM	78023	219	2	16004	2353	3733	1643	541	1023	9106	4848	117495
LISBOA	86786	3738	262	78159	15856	25759	12846	6975	6302	30351	22978	290012
PORTALEGR	32405	20	5	7933	1187	1842	2422	336	660	4171	2788	53769
EVORA	35633	11	0	7940	1316	2222	1583	329	855	4619	3400	57908
BEJA	51711	47	1790	10635	1343	2315	1752	344	610	3506	2734	76787
FARO	56710	5268	47	11952	4331	3109	2111	426	719	6810	3727	95210
ANGRA	16270	202	0	4398	909	762	553	256	498	5997	1405	31250
HORTA	12851	77	0	2635	1168	556	227	217	346	7389	986	26452
P.DELGADA	26834	894	0	6431	2539	1662	708	316	756	8408	2286	50834
FUNCHAL	33293	978	0	6716	1521	1413	474	398	516	6658	2616	60583
SUM	1536374	26560	4451	447620	52487	103254	41086	16902	29349	147281	125086	2530450
AVG	73160.66	1264.761	211.9523	21315.23	2499.380	4916.857	1956.476	804.8571	1397.571	7013.380	5956.476	120497.6
MIN	12851	11	0	2635	417	556	227	217	346	574	986	26452
MAX	153538	6394	1790	96805	15856	25759	12846	6975	6302	30351	22978	290012
STD	37281.92	2016.476	465.8057	23035.56	3261.063	5994.425	2567.081	1438.081	1346.609	6145.758	5173.003	71325.66

SOURCE:PORTUGUESE CENSUS FOR 1890, ABSTRACTS FOR OCCUPATIONS

TABLE A:12 - ACTIVE POPULATION BY SECTOR AND BY DISTRICT 1900

DISTRICS	AGRIC.	FISHING	MINING	INDUST.	TRANSP.	COMMERCE	PROT.FOR.	PUBL.ADM	LIB.PROF	DOM.WORK	SERVANT	TOTAL
VIANA	94543	569	35	12085	1355	3255	878	339	1403	1546	3097	119105
BRAGA	127307	131	202	40651	1201	7932	892	446	2814	2543	6945	191064
PORTO	111798	4046	956	95627	8585	26186	4399	1959	5044	7257	16972	282809
V.REAL	91418	22	24	9789	1008	3500	858	273	1344	1729	4207	114172
BRAGANCA	63759	14	172	8669	489	3082	966	301	977	1735	2634	82798
AVEIRO	96296	4921	804	27398	3747	8064	594	419	1497	3599	5034	152373
VIZEU	146204	20	59	22622	1581	5975	1605	466	2019	4480	7158	192189
COIMBRA	95002	1811	268	23575	1995	5833	818	668	1677	6255	6286	144188
GUARDA	79064	43	13	16537	859	3757	1134	347	1256	3845	2601	109456
C.BRANCO	57418	24	67	16663	1153	2864	1065	253	921	2686	3305	86419
LEIRIA	70624	892	3	14130	1812	3892	692	275	895	3743	4166	101124
SANTAREM	80603	291	4	18380	2644	4724	1166	461	1261	3591	4777	117902
LISBOA	98574	4153	297	85006	21840	43525	14798	6226	8619	9919	22629	315586
PORTALEGR	34678	172	54	7667	1263	2308	1820	330	687	1560	2291	52830
EVORA	36605	12	145	8050	1367	3267	1318	264	934	1942	3151	57055
BEJA	54377	28	1195	9007	1146	3250	743	282	659	1604	2896	75187
FARO	67784	1369	39	14354	8324	3696	1650	348	866	2905	2935	104270
ANGRA	18308	270	0	4063	1116	1116	625	255	517	1519	1151	28940
HORTA	15030	624	0	2491	701	814	157	168	320	1200	700	22205
P.DELGADA	28530	1194	0	8503	2329	2644	541	347	712	1221	2064	48085
FUNCHAL	39639	868	0	10029	1869	2111	701	246	734	1325	1974	59496
SUM	1507561	21474	4337	455296	66364	141795	37420	14673	35156	66204	106973	2457253
AVG	71788.61	1022.571	206.5238	21680.76	3160.190	6752.142	1781.904	698.7142	1674.095	3152.571	5093.952	117012.0
MIN	15030	12	0	2491	489	814	157	168	320	1200	700	22205
MAX	146204	4921	1195	95627	21840	43525	14798	6226	8619	9919	22629	315586
STD	34712.81	1462.638	335.1283	23886.68	4694.155	9675.902	3025.833	1287.159	1844.077	2208.826	5135.181	74611.28

SOURCE: PORTUGUESE CENSUS OF 1900. ABSTRACTS FOR OCCUPATIONS

TABLE A:13 - ACTIVE POPULATION BY SECTOR AND BY DISTRICT 1911

DISTRICT	AGRIC.	FISHING	MINING	INDUST.	TRANSP.	COMMERCE	PROT.FOR.	PUBL.ADM	LIB.PROF	DOM.WORK	SERVANT	TOTAL
VIANA	84691	552	109	14596	1392	3605	1531	353	1498	877	4699	113903
BRAGA	106146	105	239	42898	1669	7906	2122	560	2950	2226	11538	178359
PORTO	102809	2823	907	114041	8873	29071	5086	2050	6062	5395	26120	303237
V.REAL	85881	22	246	11240	1104	3390	1393	339	1395	629	6398	112037
BRAGANCA	61417	22	151	11150	658	3384	1102	258	1120	1059	4481	84802
AVEIRO	83419	3298	954	30637	2951	7862	609	398	1814	2214	7691	141847
VIZEU	136021	9	144	24758	1573	5079	767	497	2302	1811	10984	183945
COIMBRA	91637	1988	259	26974	2537	6843	893	618	2128	3547	9685	147109
GUARDA	76723	19	145	17427	1037	3339	840	380	1443	959	5349	107661
C.BRANCO	62427	30	438	19851	1195	3333	673	280	1069	1712	5441	96249
LEIRIA	70397	1160	7	16605	2026	4317	509	326	1052	825	6861	104085
SANTAREM	94796	277	15	21641	2846	5483	1401	441	1399	1715	6942	136956
LISBOA	96952	4561	439	116868	27717	51326	15774	7367	10940	9385	29883	371212
PORTALEGR	36098	33	153	10331	1610	2410	1124	299	798	1227	3867	57950
EVORA	39071	10	77	9853	2138	2993	1362	294	914	3052	4198	63962
BEJA	54738	62	4934	11116	1677	2822	673	285	820	1258	3491	81876
FARO	62282	1109	28	17089	9753	3866	1248	400	1098	1407	4837	103117
ANGRA	15752	410	0	4368	963	1146	307	210	487	291	915	24849
HORTA	12192	214	0	2630	929	661	158	124	365	433	468	18174
P.DELGADA	28345	1117	1	7848	2209	2362	279	275	769	522	1776	45503
FUNCHAL	40570	1581	1	16030	1943	3116	464	278	780	474	2894	68131
SUM	1442364	19402	9247	547751	76800	154314	38315	16032	41203	41018	158518	2544964
AVG	68684	923.9047	440.3333	26083.38	3657.142	7348.285	1824.523	763.4285	1962.047	1953.238	7548.476	121188.7
MIN	12192	9	0	2630	658	661	158	124	365	291	468	18174
MAX	136021	4561	4934	116868	27717	51326	15774	7367	10940	9385	29883	371212
STD	31338.07	1246.171	1039.264	30360.75	5856.772	11347.51	3276.611	1524.341	2330.579	2043.510	7246.426	82908.01

SOURCE: POTUGUESE CENSUS FOR 1911. ABSTRACTS FOR OCCUPATIONS

TABLE A:14 - ACTIVE POPULATION BY SECTORS AND BY DISTRICT 1930

DISTRICT	AGRIC.	FISHING	MINING	INDUST.	TRANSP.	COMMERCE	PROT.FOR.PUBL.ADM	LIB.PROF	DOM.WORK	SERVANT	TOTAL
VIANA	63706	645	210	10651	892	2556	1102	628	1081	11897	5505	98873
BRAGA	92155	145	640	37534	1625	6412	1291	1034	2522	10759	13652	167769
PORTO	85828	6190	2748	101074	10948	28254	5621	5122	5939	25495	31769	308988
V.REAL	65007	43	170	6808	911	1900	1166	534	1045	10094	4966	92644
BRAGANCA	46219	28	147	6187	626	1652	868	607	985	5114	4764	67197
AVEIRO	72254	2198	818	31591	4192	6590	1118	856	1867	13072	11423	145979
VIZEU	102236	42	361	15579	1177	3939	1112	932	1807	21024	8687	156896
COIMBRA	75011	2010	485	20294	3117	6231	2013	1450	2274	18424	10468	141777
GUARDA	51878	41	148	11844	830	2913	855	727	1320	11791	4808	87155
C.BRANCO	50928	28	519	16246	1243	2900	1468	516	992	8317	5852	89009
LEIRIA	60191	2561	207	14850	1526	3880	1045	866	980	10798	6203	103107
SANTAREM	84065	376	238	18831	4190	5403	3656	866	1319	11559	6976	137479
LISBOA ‡	103525	11282	1673	110069	30322	54129	24385	14478	11160	33187	47574	441784
PORTALEGRE	38584	44	90	7577	980	1988	2312	659	547	3697	4893	61371
EVORA	43296	39	111	8891	1691	2538	2307	614	732	3922	5574	69715
BEJA	58663	88	1940	9783	1551	2573	937	439	669	5255	4286	86184
FARO	53761	8478	174	14995	2822	4316	1676	970	958	8231	5175	101556
ANGRA	13678	582	88	2679	214	904	487	465	362	2648	668	22775
HORTA	8996	625	37	1721	532	629	269	347	308	1982	442	15888
P.DELGADA	24347	1553	143	5257	1007	2091	400	830	661	5695	2055	44039
FUNCHAL	42679	2416	71	15344	1509	3570	497	698	905	5874	2945	76508
SUM	1237007	39414	11018	467805	71905	145368	54585	33638	38433	228835	188685	2516693
AVG	58905.09	1876.857	524.6666	22276.42	3424.047	6922.285	2599.285	1601.809	1830.142	10896.90	8985	119842.5
MIN	8996	28	37	1721	214	629	269	347	308	1982	442	15888
MAX	103525	11282	2748	110069	30322	54129	24385	14478	11160	33187	47574	441784
STD	25618.51	2996.079	701.9765	28350.78	6422.935	11930.00	5015.642	3035.810	2391.468	7734.104	10723.78	94129.97

SOURCE: PORTUGUESE CENSUS FOR 1930. ABSTRACTS FOR OCCUPATIONS

NOTE: SINCE 1926 THE DISTRICT OF LISBON WAS DIVIDED INTO TWO (LISBON AND SETUBAL)

TABLE A:15 - AGE STRUCTURE BY SEX IN AGRICULTURE INDUSTRY
        AND SERVICES 1890 - 1930

MALES

YEAR/SECTOR	M<20	M20-39	M40-59	M>60	MTOTAL
1890					
AGRICULTURE	239131	356800	29621	162260	787812
INDUSTRY	57333	128158	78314	26068	289873
SERVICES	23837	108863	59324	19002	211026
TOTAL	320301	593821	167259	207330	1288711
1900					
AGRICULTURE	263680	401402	302383	159803	1127268
INDUSTRY	67595	142196	84200	26007	319998
SERVICES	31025	122197	69357	20649	243228
TOTAL	362300	665795	455940	206459	1690494
1911					
AGRICULTURE	252342	407233	288923	159450	1107948
INDUSTRY	85546	176303	99167	31538	392554
SERVICES	40669	144141	81935	23050	289795
TOTAL	378557	727677	470025	214038	1790297

FEMALES

1890					
AGRICULTURE	114484	170158	130289	67033	481964
INDUSTRY	34791	66623	39220	17113	157747
SERVICES	19480	52735	60334	47084	179633
TOTAL	168755	289516	229843	131230	819344
1900					
AGRICULTURE	82850	131709	106008	59726	380293
INDUSTRY	37951	62832	25362	9153	135298
SERVICES	8940	36274	39919	33251	118384
TOTAL	129741	230815	171289	102130	633975
1911					
AGRICULTURE	56062	114364	98758	65232	334416
INDUSTRY	39902	74628	30663	10004	155197
SERVICES	9640	29634	24465	14148	77887
TOTAL	105604	218626	153886	89384	567500

NOTE: FISHING, QUARRYING, AND SERVANTS IN THE HOUSEHOLD NOT INCLUDED

SOURCE: CENSUS AT GIVEN YEAR

APPENDIX 2

TABLE B:1 - AGE STRUCTURE OF THE PORTUGUESE POPULATION IN 1900

ISLANDS - 1900   MAINLAND - 1900

AGE GROUPS	MALES	CUM.PERC	FEMALES	CUM.PERC	AGE GROUPS	MALES	CUM.PERC	FEMALES	CUM.PERC
0 - 4	26.2	0.138551	25.1	0.115774	0 - 4	297.6	0.124165	288.1	0.110450
5 - 9	24.3	0.267054	23	0.221863	5 - 9	285.5	0.243282	277.4	0.216799
10 - 14	20.6	0.375991	20	0.314114	10 - 14	274.7	0.357893	265.1	0.318432
15 - 19	18	0.471179	19.6	0.404520	15 - 19	232.9	0.455065	245.3	0.412475
20 - 24	15	0.550502	17.2	0.483856	20 - 24	202	0.539344	231.2	0.501111
25 - 29	11.5	0.611316	14.2	0.549354	25 - 29	172.7	0.611398	194.2	0.575563
30 - 34	10.8	0.668429	13.6	0.612084	30 - 34	151.2	0.674482	174.9	0.642616
35 - 39	9.8	0.720253	12.3	0.668819	35 - 39	132.1	0.729597	151.3	0.700621
40 - 44	10.1	0.773664	11.8	0.723247	40 - 44	135	0.785922	156.8	0.760734
45 - 49	8.4	0.818085	10.5	0.771678	45 - 49	110.4	0.831984	128.6	0.810035
50 - 54	8.7	0.864093	11.9	0.826568	50 - 54	115.2	0.880048	138.6	0.863172
55 - 59	6.6	0.898995	9	0.868081	55 - 59	79.7	0.913301	94.9	0.899555
60 <	19.1	1	28.6	1	60 <	207.8	1	262	1
TOTAL	189.1		216.8		TOTAL	2396.8		2608.4	

SOURCE: PORTUGUESE CENSUS FOR 1900

TABLE B:2- LEGAL EMIGRATION 1855 - 1930 REGIONAL DISTRIBUTION

PROVINCE	LEGAL EMIGRANTS								
	1855-65	1866-71	1872-79	1880-89	1890-99	1900-08	1911-16	1923-27	1855-930
MINHO	71.36%	47.82%	40.34%	26.66%	24.48%	22.51%	17.29%	24.70%	28.10%
TRAS-OS-MONTES	0.00%	4.28%	5.98%	7.83%	11.42%	9.96%	18.97%	11.24%	10.91%
BEIRA ALTA	0.00%	18.71%	22.98%	26.25%	31.04%	29.44%	28.25%	34.43%	26.54%
BEIRA BAIXA	0.00%	0.43%	0.51%	1.64%	4.86%	4.88%	9.36%	7.20%	4.96%
EXTREMADURA	0.00%	0.84%	9.66%	6.25%	8.17%	8.22%	7.44%	11.43%	7.46%
ALENTEJO	0.00%	0.59%	0.02%	0.19%	0.84%	0.18%	0.89%	0.88%	0.49%
ALGARVE	0.00%	0.03%	0.15%	0.62%	0.63%	0.62%	1.42%	3.40%	1.08%
AZORES	20.51%	20.50%	15.09%	21.55%	12.73%	19.12%	11.84%	2.67%	14.79%
MADEIRA	8.13%	6.81%	5.27%	9.01%	5.83%	5.06%	4.53%	4.05%	5.66%
TOTAL	100.00%	100.00%	100.00%	100.00%	100.00%	100.00%	100.00%	100.00%	100.00%
EMIGRANTS	81224	51508	105775	157521	92036	270077	295946	162163	1216250

SOURCE: PORTUGUESE OFFICIAL STATISTICS ON EMIGRATION
R. FREITAS, 1867; A.FIGUEIREDO, 1873; A.COSTA, 1911
NOTE: SELECTED YEAR. NOT INCLUDED 1885, 1891, 1896

TABLE B:3 - SEX DISTRIBUTION OF LEGAL EMIGRANTS 1866-1930

	1866-71			1872-79			1880-84			1897-99		
REGION	MALE	FEMALE	TOTAL	MALE	FEMALE	TOTAL	MALE	FEMALE	TOTAL	MALE	FEMALE	TOTAL
MAINLAND	35077	2366	37443	77232	7010	84242	49910	4997	54907	41527	11079	52516
AZORES	6611	3946	10557	9702	6257	15959	13134	9315	22449	3444	3624	7068
MADEIRA	3508	0	3508	3277	2297	5574	2763	2098	4861	1612	1087	2699
TOTAL	45196	6312	51508	90211	15564	105775	65807	16410	82217	46583	15790	62773

PERCENTUAL DISTRIBUTION

	1866-71			1872-79			1880-84			1897-99		
REGION	MALE	FEMALE	TOTAL	MALE	FEMALE	TOTAL	MALE	FEMALE	TOTAL	MALE	FEMALE	TOTAL
MAINLAND	93.68%	6.32%	100.00%	91.68%	8.32%	100.00%	90.90%	9.10%	100.00%	78.94%	21.06%	100.00%
AZORES	62.62%	37.38%	100.00%	60.79%	39.21%	100.00%	58.51%	41.49%	100.00%	48.73%	51.27%	100.00%
MADEIRA	100.00%	0.00%	100.00%	58.79%	41.21%	100.00%	56.84%	43.16%	100.00%	59.73%	40.27%	100.00%
TOTAL	87.75%	12.25%	100.00%	85.29%	14.71%	100.00%	80.04%	19.96%	100.00%	74.68%	25.32%	100.00%

	1901-05			1912-16			1923-27	TOTAL OF PERIOD	1866-927			
REGION	MALE	FEMALE	TOTAL	MALE	FEMALE	TOTAL	MALE	FEMALE	TOTAL	MALE	FEMALE	TOTAL
MAINLAND	75232	18105	93337	134595	63340	197935	117670	33612	151282	531243	140509	671752
AZORES	14992	13162	28154	13753	13512	27265	2746	1590	4336	64382	51406	115788
MADEIRA	3719	2380	6099	6820	4283	11103	4521	2044	6565	26220	14189	40409
TOTAL	93943	33647	127590	155168	81135	236303	124937	37246	162183	621845	206104	827949

PERCENTUAL DISTRIBUTION

	1901-05			1912-16			1923-27	TOTAL OF PERIOD	1866-927			
REGION	MALE	FEMALE	TOTAL	MALE	FEMALE	TOTAL	MALE	FEMALE	TOTAL	MALE	FEMALE	TOTAL
MAINLAND	80.60%	19.40%	100.00%	68.00%	32.00%	100.00%	77.78%	22.22%	100.00%	79.08%	20.92%	100.00%
AZORES	53.25%	46.75%	100.00%	50.44%	49.56%	100.00%	63.33%	36.67%	100.00%	55.60%	44.40%	100.00%
MADEIRA	60.98%	39.02%	100.00%	61.42%	38.58%	100.00%	68.87%	31.13%	100.00%	64.89%	35.11%	100.00%
TOTAL	73.63%	26.37%	100.00%	65.66%	34.34%	100.00%	77.03%	22.97%	100.00%	75.11%	24.89%	100.00%

SOURCE: PORTUGUESE OFFICIAL STATISTICS ON EMIGRATION

NOTE: SELECTED YEARS

TABLE B: 4 - AGE DISTRIBUTION OF LEGAL EMIGRANTS 1866-1930

REGION	1866-71			1872-76			1880-84			1897		
	<14	14>	TOTAL	<14	14>	TOTAL	<14	14>	TOTAL	<14	14>	T
MAINLAND	5498	31946	37444	9313	49668	58981	4044	50923	54967	9691	41856	5
AZORES	2293	8264	10557	2310	8097	10407	6473	15974	22447	2026	5341	
MADEIRA	0	3508	3508	535	1660	2195	1754	3107	4861	818	1866	
TOTAL	7791	43718	51509	12158	59425	71583	12271	70004	82275	12535	49063	6

PERCENTUAL DISTRIBUTION

REGION	1866-71			1872-79			1880-84			1897		
	<14	14>	TOTAL	<14	14>	TOTAL	<14	14>	TOTAL	<14	14>	T
MAINLAND	14.68%	85.32%	100.00%	15.79%	84.21%	100.00%	7.36%	92.64%	100.00%	18.80%	81.20%	10
AZORES	21.72%	78.28%	100.00%	22.20%	77.80%	100.00%	28.84%	71.16%	100.00%	27.50%	72.50%	10
MADEIRA	0.00%	100.00%	100.00%	24.37%	75.63%	100.00%	36.08%	63.92%	100.00%	30.48%	69.52%	10
TOTAL	15.13%	84.87%	100.00%	16.98%	83.02%	100.00%	14.91%	85.09%	100.00%	20.35%	79.65%	10

REGION	1901-05			1912-16			1923-27			TOTAL OF PERIOD		1866
	<14	14>	TOTAL	<14	14>	TOTAL	<14	14>	TOTAL	<14	14>	T
MAINLAND	16175	77162	93337	42516	148555	191071	7075	144207	151282	65766	369924	43
AZORES	7922	20232	28154	6371	19514	25885	619	3707	4326	14912	43453	5
MADEIRA	1920	4179	6099	2634	7377	10011	1028	5537	6565	5582	17093	2
TOTAL	26017	101573	127590	51521	175446	226967	8722	153451	162173	86260	430470	51

PERCENTUAL DISTRIBUTION

REGION	1901-05			1912-16			1923-27			TOTAL OF PERIOD		1866
	<14	14>	TOTAL	<14	14>	TOTAL	<14	14>	TOTAL	<14	14>	T
MAINLAND	17.33%	82.67%	100.00%	22.25%	77.75%	100.00%	4.68%	95.32%	100.00%	15.09%	84.91%	10
AZORES	28.14%	71.86%	100.00%	24.61%	75.39%	100.00%	14.31%	85.69%	100.00%	25.55%	74.45%	10
MADEIRA	31.48%	68.52%	100.00%	26.31%	73.69%	100.00%	15.66%	84.34%	100.00%	24.62%	75.38%	10
TOTAL	20.39%	79.61%	100.00%	22.70%	77.30%	100.00%	5.38%	94.62%	100.00%	16.69%	83.31%	10

SOURCE: PORTUGUESE OFFICIAL STATISTICS ON EMIGRATION

NOTE: SELECTED YEARS

TABLE B:5
MARIATAL STATUS DISTRIBUTION OF LEGAL EMIGRANTS 1890-1930

		1897-89			1901-05	
REGION	SINGLE	MARRIED	TOTAL	SINGLE	MARRIED	TOTAL
MAINLAND	26971	24186	52606	47143	42794	93337
AZORES	4283	2447	7068	17452	9635	28154
MADEIRA	1514	1103	2699	3420	2526	6099
TOTAL	32768	27736	62373	68015	54955	127590

PERCENTUAL DISTRIBUTION

		1897-89			1901-05	
REGION	SINGLE	MARRIED	TOTAL	SINGLE	MARRIED	TOTAL
MAINLAND	51.27%	45.98%	100.00%	50.51%	45.85%	100.00%
AZORES	60.60%	34.62%	100.00%	61.99%	34.22%	100.00%
MADEIRA	56.09%	40.87%	100.00%	56.07%	41.42%	100.00%
TOTAL	52.54%	44.47%	100.00%	53.31%	43.07%	100.00%

		1897-1927	
REGION	SINGLE	MARRIED	TOTAL
MAINLAND	255930	225910	495160
AZORES	40110	23812	66814
MADEIRA	13865	11830	26466
TOTAL	309905	261552	588440

PERCENTUAL DISTRIBUTION

		1897-1927	
REGION	SINGLE	MARRIED	TOTAL
MAINLAND	51.69%	45.62%	100.00%
AZORES	60.03%	35.64%	100.00%
MADEIRA	52.39%	44.70%	100.00%
TOTAL	52.67%	44.45%	100.00%

SOURCE: PORTUGUESE OFFICIAL STATISTICS

NOTE: SELECTED YEARS

TABLE B:5 (CONT.)
MARIATAL STATUS DISTRIBUTION OF LEGAL EMIGRANTS 1890-1930

REGION	1912-16			1923-27		
	SINGLE	MARRIED	TOTAL	SINGLE	MARRIED	TOTAL
MAINLAND	110528	83220	197935	71288	75710	151282
AZORES	16299	9701	27256	2076	2029	4336
MADEIRA	5812	4962	11103	3119	3239	6565
TOTAL	132639	97883	236294	76483	80978	162183

PERCENTUAL DISTRIBUTION

REGION	1912-16			1923-27		
	SINGLE	MARRIED	TOTAL	SINGLE	MARRIED	TOTAL
MAINLAND	55.84%	42.04%	100.00%	47.12%	50.05%	100.00%
AZORES	59.80%	35.59%	100.00%	47.88%	46.79%	100.00%
MADEIRA	52.35%	44.69%	100.00%	47.51%	49.34%	100.00%
TOTAL	56.13%	41.42%	100.00%	47.16%	49.93%	100.00%

MARRIED FEMALES TO MARRIED MALES
1897 -1906 (1)

	MALES	FEMALES	TOTAL	MALES	FEMALES	TOTAL
MAINLAND	71831	14988	86819	82.74%	17.26%	100.00%
ISLANDS	12982	8643	21625	60.03%	39.97%	100.00%
TOTAL	84813	23631	108444	78.21%	21.79%	100.00%

	MALES	FEMALES	TOTAL	MALES	FEMALES	TOTAL
MAINLAND	71831	14988	86819	84.69%	63.43%	80.06%
ISLANDS	12982	8643	21625	15.31%	36.57%	19.94%
TOTAL	84813	23631	108444	100.00%	100.00%	100.00%

NOTE: ALL YEARS INCLUDED

TABLE B:6
COUNTRY OF DESTINATION OF LEGAL EMIGRANTS 1890-1930

REGION	BRAZIL	1897-89 U.S.	TOTAL	BRAZIL	1901-05 U.S.	TOTAL
MAINLAND	47668	30	52606	83364	323	93337
AZORES	1916	5010	7068	3274	24655	28154
MADEIRA	1671	72	2699	3618	798	6099
TOTAL	51255	5112	62373	90256	25776	127590

PERCENTUAL DISTRIBUTION

REGION	BRAZIL	1897-89 U.S.	TOTAL	BRAZIL	1901-05 U.S.	TOTAL
MAINLAND	90.61%	0.06%	100.00%	89.32%	0.35%	100.00%
AZORES	27.11%	70.88%	100.00%	11.63%	87.57%	100.00%
MADEIRA	61.91%	2.67%	100.00%	59.32%	13.08%	100.00%
TOTAL	82.17%	8.20%	100.00%	70.74%	20.20%	100.00%

REGION	BRAZIL	1897-1927 U.S.	TOTAL
MAINLAND	402988	18200	495160
AZORES	8398	56868	66814
MADEIRA	13123	9015	26466
TOTAL	424509	84083	588440

PERCENTUAL DISTRIBUTION

REGION	BRAZIL	1897-1927 U.S.	TOTAL	BRAZIL	1897-1927 U.S.	TOTAL
MAINLAND	81.39%	3.68%	100.00%	94.93%	21.65%	84.15%
AZORES	12.57%	85.11%	100.00%	1.98%	67.63%	11.35%
MADEIRA	49.58%	34.06%	100.00%	3.09%	10.72%	4.50%
TOTAL	72.14%	14.29%	100.00%	100.00%	100.00%	100.00%

SOURCE: PORTUGUESE OFFICIAL STATISTICS

NOTE: SELECTED YEARS

TABLE B:6 (CONT.)
COUNTRY OF DESTINATION OF LEGAL EMIGRANTS 1890-1930

		1912-16			1923-27	
REGION	BRAZIL	U.S.	TOTAL	BRAZIL	U.S.	TOTAL
MAINLAND	174762	14367	197935	97194	3480	151282
AZORES	1389	25658	27256	1819	1545	4336
MADEIRA	3868	6700	11103	3966	1445	6565
TOTAL	180019	46725	236294	102979	6470	162183

PERCENTUAL DISTRIBUTION

		1912-16			1923-27	
REGION	BRAZIL	U.S.	TOTAL	BRAZIL	U.S.	TOTAL
MAINLAND	88.29%	7.26%	100.00%	64.25%	2.30%	100.00%
AZORES	5.10%	94.14%	100.00%	41.95%	35.63%	100.00%
MADEIRA	34.84%	60.34%	100.00%	60.41%	22.01%	100.00%
TOTAL	76.18%	19.77%	100.00%	63.50%	3.99%	100.00%

TABLE B:7 - LIST OF ALTERNATIVE NAMES FOR LINKAGE USE
    NAME-CHANGING AMERICAN - PORTUGUESE NAMES

AMERICAN	PORTUGUESE
AGNES	IN(G)ES
AGUSTINA	AGOSTINHA(O)
ALMADA	ALMEIDA
ALMY	ALMEIDA
ANDREW(S)	ANDRADE
ANNIE	ANNA
ANTHONY	ANTONIO
ARUDE	ARRUDA
BARROWS	BARROS
BENNETT	BERNARDO
BETTY	ISABEL
BILL	GUILHERME
BOTELIO	BOTELHO
BOTHEILHO	BOTELHO
BRAZELLS	BRASIL
BRIER	SILVA
BROOK(S)	RIBEIRO
BROWN	ABR(A)AO
BROWN	BRIGIDA
BROWN	BRUM
CAMBRA	CAMARA
CARDOZA	CARDOSO
CATON	CAETANO
CHAMBER(S)	CAMARA
CHARLES	CARLOS
CHARLIE	CARLOS
CITYHALL	CAMARA
COONEY	CUNHA
COREY	CORRE(I)A
CORRY	CORRE(I)A
CRABTREE	CARANGUEJO
CROSS	CRUZ
CURRY	CORRE(I)A
DAVIS	DE AVILA
DAY(S)	DIAS
DEARS	DIAS
DOMINGS	DOMINGUES
ELIZABETH	ISABEL
EMERY	AMARAL
EMMA	AMELIA
ENOS	I(G)NACIO
FELLOW	FIALHO
FERRY	FERREIRA

FIELDS	CAMPOS
FOSTER	FAUSTINO
FOX	RAPOSO
FRANCIS	FRANCISCO
FRANK	FRANCISCO
FRANKS	FRANCISCO
FRATES	FREITAS
FRAZER	FREITAS
FRAZIER	FREITAS
FREATES	FREITAS
FURNANS (?)	FERNANDES
FURTADO	STEELE
GEORGE	JORGE
GEREVAS	GERVASIO
GILL	GIL
GRACE	GARCIA
GRACIA	GARCIA
GREGORY	GREGORIO
HENAS	I(G)NACIO
IKE	AIRES
JACK	JOAO
JASON	JACINT(H)O
JEROME	JERONIMO
JOE	JOSE
JOE (KING)	JOAQUIM
JOHN	JOAO
JOHNY	JOAO
JORDAN	JORDAO
JOSEPH	JOSE
KARDOZA	CARDOSO
KENT	QUENTAL
KING	REIS
LAWRENCE	LOURENCO
LAZARUS	LAZARO
LEWIS	LUIS
LIZZIE	ISABEL
LORING	LOURO
LOUIS	LUIS
LIGHT	LUZ
MACADOO	MACHADO
MAGGIE	MARGARIDA
MARGARET	MARGARIDA
MARKS	MARQUES
MARSHALL	MACHADO
MARTIN	MARTINS
MARTIN	MATHIAS
MARY	MARIA
MEADS	MEDEIROS

MEDERO(S)	MEDEIROS
MEDROWS	MEDEIROS
MELLOW	MEL(L)O
MENDONZA	MENDONCA
MERRILL	AMARAL
MILLER	MEL(L)O
MITCHELL	MACHADO
MORGAN	MORGADO
MORRIS	MAURICIO
MORRIS	MORAES
OAK	CARVALHO
OLIVER	OLIVEIRA
PAIGE	PAIS
PEACOCK	PAVAO
PEARY	PEREIRA
PERRERA	PEREIRA
PERRY	PEREIRA
PETER	PEDRO
PETERS	PEREIRA
PHILIP	FILIPE
PINE	PINHEIRO
PRADA	PEREIRA
RALPH	RAFAEL
RIVER(S)	RIBEIRO
RIVERS	REVEZ
ROACH	ROCHA
ROCA	ROCHA
ROD(E)RICK	RODRIGUES(Z)
RODERIGUES	RODRIGUES
RODERIQUE	RODRIGUES
RO(D)GERS	RODRIGUES
RODRICK	RODRIGUES
ROGERS	ROSA
ROSE	ROSA
SAUNDERS	SANTOS
SCHWARTZ	SOARES
SEAMAS	SIMAS
SEARS	SOARES
SEVETT	SOARES
SILVAY	SILVEIRA
SILVER	SILVA
SILVER	SILVEIRA
SILVIA	SILVA
SIMMONS	SIMOES
SMITH	FERREIRA
SMITH	NASCIMENTO
SOLOMON(S)	SALOMAO

SOLOMONE	SALOMAO
SYLVAI	SILVEIRA
SILVAY	SILVEIRA
SILVIA	SILVA
SYLVIA	SILVA
TACHERA	TEIXEIRA
TASH	TEIXEIRA
TASHA	TEIXEIRA
TERRY	TERRA
TONY	ANTONIO
VASS	VASCONCELOS
VERA	VIEIRA
VIATOR	VIEIRA
VIERA	VIEIRA
VIERRA	VIEIRA
VIERY	VIEIRA
WAGER	CUNHA
WEDGE	CUNHA
WHITE	ALVES
WILLIAM	GUILHERME
WOOD	CARVALHO
WOOD	MADEIRA
WOODS	MAT(T)OS

SOURCE: Pap,1949:133-137.
        Soares, 1939:60-61.
        Lang, 1892: 17.
        Shiplists, 1860,1890,1891,1890.

FIGURE 5 - IMMIGRATION TO U.S.

1820 - 1930

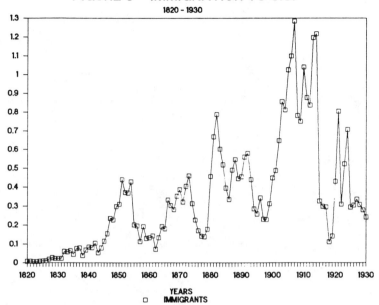

IMMIGRANTS
(Millions)

YEARS
□ IMMIGRANTS

PORTUGUESE EMIGRATION TO U.S.

1820 - 1930

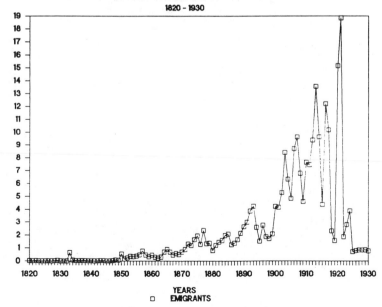

EMIGRANTS
(Thousands)

YEARS
□ EMIGRANTS

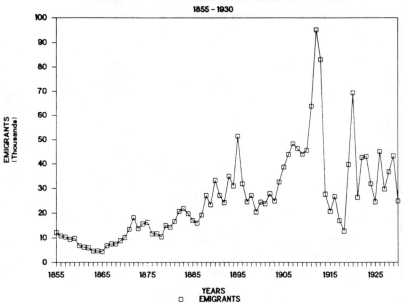

FIGURE 6 – PORTUGUESE EMIGRATION
1855 – 1930

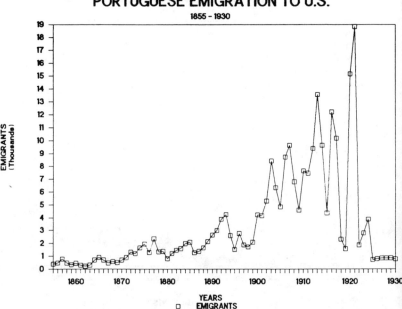

PORTUGUESE EMIGRATION TO U.S.
1855 – 1930

DRAWING OF AN EMIGRANT SHIP OF THE 1890'S

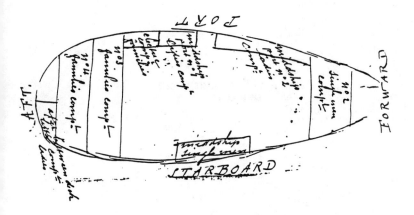

LA NORMANDIE
APPENDED TO MANIFEST # 1332, AUGUST 31, 1891
BALCH INSTITUTE

TABLE B:8 - PORTUGUESE EMIGRATION TO THE UNITED STATES 1820 - 1930
ACCORDING TO DIFFERENT SOURCES

YEAR	(1)	(2)	(3)	TOTAL EMIG. U.S	NOTES FOR SOURCE (1)
1820	35		35	8385	A) YEAR ENDED SEP.30
1821	19		18	9127	
1822	34		28	6911	
1823	25		24	6354	
1824	13		13	7912	
1825	16		13	10199	
1826	17		16	10837	
1827	12		7	18875	
1828	26		14	27382	
1829	56		9	22520	
1830	11		3	23322	
1831	2		0	22633	
1832	10		5	60482	B) OCT.1, 1831,TO DEC.31, 1832
1833	638		633	58540	C) YEAR ENDED DEC. 31
1834	73		44	65365	
1835	46		29	45374	
1836	34		29	76242	
1837	39		34	79340	
1838	32		24	38914	
1839	26		19	68069	
1840	25		12	84066	
1841	10		7	80289	
1842	19		15	104565	
1843	40		32	52496	D) JAN.1 TO SEP.30, 1843
1844	40		16	78615	E) YEAR ENDED SEP.30
1845	21		14	114371	
1846	17		2	154416	
1847	29		5	234968	
1848	87	87	67	226527	
1849	74	74	26	297024	
1850	539	546	366	310004	
1851	153	161	50	439442	F) OCT.1, 1850 TO DEC.31, 1851
1852	238	246	68	371603	OCT.1 TO DEC.31 1850 = 59976
1853	272	359	95	368645	
1854	324	340	72	427833	
1855	342	381	205	200877	
1856	480	488	128	195857	
1857	768	771	92	112123	G) JAN.1 TO JUNE 30, 1857
1858	475	480	177	191942	H) YEAR ENDED JUNE 30
1859	343	453	46	129571	
1860	447	445	122	133143	
1861	304	310	47	142877	
1862	229	229	72	72183	
1863	313	313	86	132925	
1864	694	700	240	191114	
1865	897	897	365	180339	

1866	692	695	344	332577
1867	585	511	126	303104
1868	580	555	174	282189
1869	704	714	507	352768
1870	771	852	697	387203
1871		887	887	321350
1872		1311	1306	404806
1873		1194	1185	459803
1874		1659	1611	313339
1875		1958	1939	227498
1876		1333	1277	169986
1877		2364	2363	141857
1878		1332	1332	138469
1879		1375	1374	177826
1880		810	808	457257
1881		1223	1215	669431
1882		1464	1436	788992
1883		1586	1573	603322
1884		1973	1927	518592
1885		2092	2024	395346
1886		1260	1194	334203
1887		1374	1360	490109
1888		1648	1625	546889
1889		2130	2024	444427
1890		2650	2600	455302
1891		3002	2999	560319
1892		3884	3400	579663
1893		4258	4816	439730
1894		2600	2196	285631
1895		1529	1452	258536
1896		2766	2766	343367
1897		1874	1874	230832
1898		1717	1717	229299
1899		2096	2054	311715
1900		4241	4234	448572
1901		4176	4165	487918
1902		5309	5307	648743
1903		8433	9317	857046
1904		6338	6715	812870
1905		4855	5028	1026499
1906		8729	8517	1100735
1907		9648	9608	1285349
1908		6809	7307	782870
1909		4606	4956	751786
1910		7657	8229	1041570

1911	7469	878587
1912	9403	838172
1913	13566	1197892
1914	9647	1218480
1915	4376	326700
1916	12208	298826
1917	10194	295403
1918	2319	110618
1919	1574	141132
1920	15174	430001
1921	18856	805228
1922	1867	309556
1923	2802	522919
1924	3892	706896
1925	720	294314
1926	793	304488
1927	843	335175
1928	844	307255
1929	853	279678
1930	780	241700
1931	626	97139
1932	265	35576

SOURCES: (1) YOUNG, 1871: XII-XIX.
(2) IMMIGRATION REPORTS PRESENTED TO THE HOUSE OF REPRESENTATIVES
FROM 1848 TO 1895 AND IMMIGRATION COMMISSIONER'S REPORT FOR
1897 ... 1910, AND 1920 ...1932.
(3) IMMIGRATION COMMISSION, 1910. 1911, V.I: 66-81.
P.66-- "COMPILED FROM OFFICIAL SOURCES. FOR 1820 TO 1867 THE FIGURES
ARE FOR PASSENGERS ARRIVING; FOR 1868 THEY ARE FOR IMMIGRANTS ARRIVING.
THE YEARS FOR 1820 TO 1831 AND FROM 1844 TO 1849 ARE THOSE ENDING
SEPTEMBER 30; 1833 TO 1842 AND 1851 TO 1867 THOSE ENDING DECEMBER 31.
P.70-- 1832 FIFTEEN MONTHS ENDING DECEMBER 31.
P.73-- 1843 NINE MONTHS ENDING SEP.30. P.76-- 1850 FIFTEEN MONTHS ENDING
DEC.31. P.81-- 1868 SIX MONTHS ENDING JUNE 30.
FOR THE TOTAL IMMIGRATION: REPORT OF THE COM.G.I. 1932: 186.

TABLE B:9 - PORTUGUESE EMIGRATION TO THE UNITED STATES
BY SEX, 1820 - 1930

YEAR‡	MALES	FEMALES	TOTAL	FEMALE PERCENTAGE
1820	33	5	38	13.16%
1821	19	0	19	0.00%
1822	34	0	34	0.00%
1823	24	0	24	0.00%
1824	12	1	13	7.69%
1825	15	1	16	6.25%
1826	15	2	17	11.76%
1827	11	1	12	8.33%
1828	24	2	26	7.69%
1829	51	5	56	8.93%
1830	8	3	11	27.27%
1831	2	0	2	0.00%
1832	9	1	10	10.00%
1833	636	2	638	0.31%
1834	67	6	73	8.22%
1835	40	6	46	13.04%
1836	27	7	34	20.59%
1837	30	9	39	23.08%
1838	23	9	32	28.13%
1839	20	6	26	23.08%
1840	20	5	25	20.00%
1841	10	0	10	0.00%
1842	17	2	19	10.53%
1843	35	5	40	12.50%
1844	32	8	40	20.00%
1845	17	4	21	19.05%
1846	14	3	17	17.65%
1847	22	7	29	24.14%
1848	60	27	87	31.03%
1849	53	21	74	28.38%
1850	350	196	546	35.90%
1851	119	42	161	26.09%
1852	191	55	246	22.36%
1853	242	117	359	32.59%
1854	287	53	340	15.59%
1855	307	74	381	19.42%
1856	425	55	480	11.46%
1857	608	160	768	20.83%
1858	306	169	475	35.58%
1859	235	108	343	31.49%
1860	299	148	447	33.11%
1861	211	93	304	30.59%
1862	181	48	229	20.96%
1863	199	114	313	36.42%
1864	477	216	693	31.17%
1865	554	343	897	38.24%
1866	375	317	692	45.81%
1867‡	282	184	466	39.48%
1868	305	275	580	47.41%
1869	302	205	507	40.43%

1870	450	247	697	35.44%
1871	510	377	887	42.50%
1872	960	351	1311	26.77%
1873	814	380	1194	31.83%
1874	1162	497	1659	29.96%
1875	1261	678	1939	34.97%
1876	745	532	1277	41.66%
1877	1725	638	2363	27.00%
1878	885	447	1332	33.56%
1879	916	458	1374	33.33%
1880	495	313	808	38.74%
1881	803	412	1215	33.91%
1882	931	533	1464	36.41%
1883	1053	533	1586	33.61%
1884	1260	713	1973	36.14%
1885	1372	720	2092	34.42%
1886	856	404	1260	32.06%
1887	880	494	1374	35.95%
1888	1150	498	1648	30.22%
1889	1374	756	2130	35.49%
1890	1705	945	2650	35.66%
1891	1846	1156	3002	38.51%
1892	2517	1367	3884	35.20%
1893	2706	1552	4258	36.45%
1894	1386	1214	2600	46.69%
1895	737	792	1529	51.80%
1896	1410	1356	2766	49.02%
1897	962	912	1874	48.67%
1898	857	860	1717	50.09%
1899	1101	995	2096	47.47%
1900	2386	1855	4241	43.74%
1901	2240	1936	4176	46.36%
1902	3117	2192	5309	41.29%
1903	4999	3434	8433	40.72%
1904	3867	2471	6338	38.99%
1905	2992	1863	4855	38.37%
1906	5096	3633	8729	41.62%
1907	5812	3836	9648	39.76%
1908	4019	2790	6809	40.98%
1909	2886	1720	4606	37.34%
1910	4887	2770	7657	36.18%
1911	4843	2626	7469	35.16%
1912	5938	3465	9403	36.85%
1913	8696	4870	13566	35.90%
1914	6260	3387	9647	35.11%
1915	2853	1523	4376	34.80%
1916	8010	4198	12208	34.39%
1917	4878	5316	10194	52.15%
1918	1349	970	2319	41.83%
1919	1089	485	1574	30.81%
1920	11056	4118	15174	27.14%
1921	13479	5377	18856	28.52%
1922	1077	790	1867	42.31%

1923	1973	829	2802	29.59%
1924	1254	2638	3892	67.78%
1925	436	284	720	39.44%
1926	483	310	793	39.09%
1927	653	190	843	22.54%
1928	562	282	844	33.41%
1929	450	403	853	47.25%
1930	364	416	780	53.33%

NOTES : *) YEAR ENDING JUNE 30.
         A) FIGURES FOR ALIENS ARRIVED
         B) FIGURES FOR ALIENS ADMITED
         C) QUOTA LIMIT ACT OF MAY 19,1921
         D) IMMIGRATION ACT OF 1924
         1820-1855 SAME PERIODS AS TOTAL EMIGRATION
         1856-1868 CALENDAR YEARS
         1869-1932 FISCAL YEARS

SOURCE: 1820-1855 FERENCZI, 1929:401-417
        ANNUAL REPORT OF THE COMMISSIONER GENERAL
        OF IMMIGRATION FOR THE GIVEN YEARS.

TABLE B:10 - PORTUGUESE EMIGRATION TO THE UNITED STATES
BY AGE GROUPS, 1873 - 1930

YEAR:	UNDER 15 YEARS (1)	15 - 39 YEARS (2)	40 AND OVER (3)	TOTAL	PERCENTUAL DISTRIBUTION (1)	(2)	(3)	NOTES
1873	106	958	130	1194	8.9%	80.2%	10.9%	
1874	191	1311	157	1659	11.5%	79.0%	9.5%	
1875	266	1421	246	1933	13.8%	73.5%	12.7%	
1876	123	998	156	1277	9.6%	78.2%	12.2%	
1877	290	1943	188	2421	12.0%	80.3%	7.8%	
1879	167	1026	181	1374	12.2%	74.7%	13.2%	
1880	151	570	87	808	18.7%	70.5%	10.8%	
1881	188	914	113	1215	15.5%	75.2%	9.3%	
1882	212	1112	140	1464	14.5%	76.0%	9.6%	
1883	215	1210	161	1586	13.6%	76.3%	10.2%	
1884	274	1508	191	1973	13.9%	76.4%	9.7%	
1885	275	1575	242	2092	13.1%	75.3%	11.6%	
1886	129	1024	106	1259	10.2%	81.3%	8.4%	
1887	223	987	164	1374	16.2%	71.8%	11.9%	
1888	254	1259	135	1648	15.4%	76.4%	8.2%	
1889	317	1631	182	2130	14.9%	76.6%	8.5%	
1890	415	1984	251	2650	15.7%	74.9%	9.5%	
1891	475	2156	370	3001	15.8%	71.8%	12.3%	
1892	443	3127	314	3884	11.4%	80.5%	8.1%	
1893	486	3471	301	4258	11.4%	81.5%	7.1%	
1894	242	2212	146	2600	9.3%	85.1%	5.6%	
1895	265	1105	159	1529	17.3%	72.3%	10.4%	
1897	479	1141	254	1874	25.6%	60.9%	13.6%	
1898	416	1084	217	1717	24.2%	63.1%	12.6%	
1899	477	1487	132	2096	22.8%	70.9%	6.3%	B)
1900	1105	2778	358	4241	26.1%	65.5%	8.4%	
1901	1030	2774	372	4176	24.7%	66.4%	8.9%	
1902	1439	3410	460	5309	27.1%	64.2%	8.7%	
1903	2072	5665	696	8433	24.6%	67.2%	8.3%	
1904	1426	4382	530	6338	22.5%	69.1%	8.4%	
1905	1035	3381	439	4855	21.3%	69.6%	9.0%	
1906	1821	6171	737	8729	20.9%	70.7%	8.4%	
1907	2431	6581	636	9648	25.2%	68.2%	6.6%	
1908	1697	4655	457	6809	24.9%	68.4%	6.7%	
1909	908	3404	294	4606	19.7%	73.9%	6.4%	
1910	1526	5691	440	7657	19.9%	74.3%	5.7%	
1911	1238	5765	466	7469	16.6%	77.2%	6.2%	
1912	1863	6939	601	9403	19.8%	73.8%	6.4%	
1913	2301	10366	899	13566	17.0%	76.4%	6.6%	
1914	1338	7769	540	9647	13.9%	80.5%	5.6%	
1915	638	3427	311	4376	14.6%	78.3%	7.1%	
1916	1563	9725	920	12208	12.8%	79.7%	7.5%	
1917	2172	6738	1284	10194	21.3%	66.1%	12.6%	
1918	581	1518	220	2319	25.1%	65.5%	9.5%	C)
1919	234	1232	108	1574	14.9%	78.3%	6.9%	
1920	1581	12855	738	15174	10.4%	84.7%	4.9%	D)
1921	2158	15763	935	18856	11.4%	83.6%	5.0%	
1922	351	1310	206	1867	18.8%	70.2%	11.0%	
1923	334	2278	190	2802	11.9%	81.3%	6.8%	
1924	524	3099	269	3892	13.5%	79.6%	6.9%	

1925	129	535	56	720	17.9%	74.3%	7.8% E)
1926	117	600	76	793	14.8%	75.7%	9.6%
1927	77	706	60	843	9.1%	83.7%	7.1%
1928	196	598	50	844	23.2%	70.9%	5.9%
1929	190	603	60	853	22.3%	70.7%	7.0%
1930	204	503	73	780	26.2%	64.5%	9.4%

NOTES : A) YEAR ENDING JUNE 30.
    B) AGE GROUPS ARE NOW: UNDER 14; 14 TO 45; 45 AND OVER.
    C) AGE GROUPS ARE NOW: UNDER 16; 16 TO 44; 45 AND OVER.

SOURCE: ANNUAL REPORT OF THE COMMISSIONER GENERAL
    OF IMMIGRATION FOR THE GIVEN YEARS
    FOR 1911-1919: TAFT, 1967:101

TABLE B: 11 - SEX AND AGE DISTRIBUTION OF PORTUGUESE IMMIGRANTS TO THE UNITED STATES, 1873 - 1930

YEARS	MALES				FEMALES				MALE PERCENT. DISTRIBUTION				FEMALE PERCENT. DISTRIBUT.			
	0-14	15-40	40 AND OVER	TOTAL	0-14	15-40	40 AND OVER	TOTAL	0-14	15-40	40 AND OVER	TOTAL	0-14	15-40	40 AND OVER	TOTAL
1873	55	675	84	814	51	283	46	380	6.8%	82.9%	10.3%	100.0%	13.4%	74.5%	12.1%	100.0%
1874	101	959	102	1162	90	352	55	497	8.7%	82.5%	8.8%	100.0%	18.1%	70.8%	11.1%	100.0%
1875	130	981	144	1255	136	440	102	678	10.4%	78.2%	11.5%	100.0%	20.1%	64.9%	15.0%	100.0%
1876	65	585	95	745	58	413	61	532	8.7%	78.5%	12.8%	100.0%	10.9%	77.6%	11.5%	100.0%
1877	124	1462	139	1725	166	481	49	696	7.2%	84.8%	8.1%	100.0%	23.9%	69.1%	7.0%	100.0%
1879	77	723	116	916	90	303	65	458	8.4%	78.9%	12.7%	100.0%	19.7%	66.2%	14.2%	100.0%
TOTAL	552	5385	680	6617	591	2272	378	3241	8.3%	81.4%	10.3%	100.0%	18.2%	70.1%	11.7%	100.0%
AVG	92	898	113	1103	99	379	63	540								
1880	78	364	53	495	73	206	34	313	15.8%	73.5%	10.7%	100.0%	23.3%	65.8%	10.9%	100.0%
1881	88	646	69	803	100	268	44	412	11.0%	80.4%	8.6%	100.0%	24.3%	65.0%	10.7%	100.0%
1882	136	724	71	931	76	388	69	533	14.6%	77.8%	7.6%	100.0%	14.3%	72.8%	12.9%	100.0%
1883	90	847	116	1053	125	363	45	533	8.5%	80.4%	11.0%	100.0%	23.5%	68.1%	8.4%	100.0%
1884	123	1036	101	1260	151	472	90	713	9.8%	82.2%	8.0%	100.0%	21.2%	66.2%	12.6%	100.0%
1885	147	1077	148	1372	128	498	94	720	10.7%	78.5%	10.8%	100.0%	17.8%	69.2%	13.1%	100.0%
1886	58	729	69	856	71	295	37	403	6.8%	85.2%	8.1%	100.0%	17.6%	73.2%	9.2%	100.0%
1887	128	651	101	880	95	336	63	494	14.5%	74.0%	11.5%	100.0%	19.2%	68.0%	12.8%	100.0%
1888	150	921	79	1150	104	338	56	498	13.0%	80.1%	6.9%	100.0%	20.9%	67.9%	11.2%	100.0%
1889	169	1101	104	1374	148	530	78	756	12.3%	80.1%	7.6%	100.0%	19.6%	70.1%	10.3%	100.0%
TOTAL	1167	8096	911	10174	1071	3694	610	5375	11.5%	79.6%	9.0%	100.0%	19.9%	68.7%	11.3%	100.0%
AVG	117	810	91	1017	107	369	61	538								
1890	221	1330	154	1705	194	654	97	945	13.0%	78.0%	9.0%	100.0%	20.5%	69.2%	10.3%	100.0%
1891	270	1388	188	1846	205	768	182	1155	14.6%	75.2%	10.2%	100.0%	17.7%	66.5%	15.8%	100.0%
1892	223	2083	211	2517	220	1044	103	1367	8.9%	82.8%	8.4%	100.0%	16.1%	76.4%	7.5%	100.0%
1893	254	2245	207	2706	232	1226	94	1552	9.4%	83.0%	7.6%	100.0%	14.9%	79.0%	6.1%	100.0%
1894	164	1167	55	1386	78	1045	91	1214	11.8%	84.2%	4.0%	100.0%	6.4%	86.1%	7.5%	100.0%
1895	149	508	80	737	116	597	79	792	20.2%	68.9%	10.9%	100.0%	14.6%	75.4%	10.0%	100.0%
TOTAL	1281	8721	895	10897	1045	5334	646	7025	11.8%	80.0%	8.2%	100.0%	14.9%	75.9%	9.2%	100.0%

38

1910–1917

YEAR	MALES UNDER 14 YRS	14-44	45 YRS AND OVER	TOTAL	FEMALES UNDER 14 YRS	14-44	45 YRS AND OVER	TOTAL	MALES UNER 14 YRS	14-44	45 YRS AND OVER	TOTAL	FEMALES UNER 14 YRS	14-44	45 YRS AND OVER	TOTAL
1910	795	3855	237	4887	731	1836	203	2770	16.3%	78.9%	4.8%	100.0%	26.4%	66.3%	7.3%	100.0%
1911	621	3984	257	4842	617	1801	209	2627	12.8%	81.9%	5.3%	100.0%	23.5%	68.6%	8.0%	100.0%
1912	970	4644	324	5938	893	2295	277	3465	16.3%	78.2%	5.5%	100.0%	25.8%	66.2%	8.0%	100.0%
1913	1200	7032	464	8696	1101	3334	435	4870	13.8%	80.9%	5.3%	100.0%	22.6%	68.5%	8.9%	100.0%
1914	689	5274	297	6260	649	2495	243	3387	11.0%	84.2%	4.7%	100.0%	19.2%	73.7%	7.2%	100.0%
1915	300	2403	150	2853	338	1024	161	1523	10.5%	84.2%	5.3%	100.0%	22.2%	67.2%	10.6%	100.0%
1916	777	6653	580	8010	786	3072	340	4198	9.7%	83.1%	7.2%	100.0%	18.7%	73.2%	8.1%	100.0%
1917	1213	2786	879	4878	959	3952	405	5316	24.9%	57.1%	18.0%	100.0%	18.0%	74.3%	7.6%	100.0%
TOTAL	6565	36611	3188	46364	6074	19809	2273	28156	14.2%	79.0%	6.9%	100.0%	21.6%	70.4%	8.1%	100.0%
AVG	821	4576	399	5796	759	2476	284	3520								

1920–1930

YEAR	MALES UNDER 16 YRS	14-44	45 YRS AND OVER	TOTAL	FEMALES UNDER 16 YRS	14-44	45 YRS AND OVER	TOTAL	MALES UNDER 16 YRS	14-44	45 YRS AND OVER	TOTAL	FEMALES UNDER 16 YRS	14-44	45 YRS AND OVER	TOTAL
1920	792	9826	438	11056	789	3029	300	4118	7.2%	88.9%	4.0%	100.0%	19.2%	73.6%	7.3%	100.0%
1921	1044	11917	518	13479	1114	3846	417	5377	7.7%	88.4%	3.8%	100.0%	20.7%	71.5%	7.8%	100.0%
1922	189	792	96	1077	162	518	110	790	17.5%	73.5%	8.9%	100.0%	20.5%	65.6%	13.9%	100.0%
1923	182	1701	90	1973	152	577	100	829	9.2%	86.2%	4.6%	100.0%	18.3%	69.6%	12.1%	100.0%
1924	247	2241	150	2638	277	858	119	1254	9.4%	85.0%	5.7%	100.0%	22.1%	68.4%	9.5%	100.0%
1925	61	352	23	436	68	183	33	284	14.0%	80.7%	5.3%	100.0%	23.9%	64.4%	11.6%	100.0%
1926	53	391	39	483	64	209	37	310	11.0%	81.0%	8.1%	100.0%	20.6%	67.4%	11.9%	100.0%
1927	40	582	31	653	37	124	29	190	6.1%	89.1%	4.7%	100.0%	19.5%	65.3%	15.3%	100.0%
1928	104	430	28	562	92	168	22	282	18.5%	76.5%	5.0%	100.0%	32.6%	59.6%	7.8%	100.0%
1929	94	331	25	450	96	272	35	403	20.9%	73.6%	5.6%	100.0%	23.8%	67.5%	8.7%	100.0%
1930	117	225	22	364	87	278	51	416	32.1%	61.8%	6.0%	100.0%	20.9%	66.8%	12.3%	100.0%
TOTAL	2923	28788	1460	33171	2938	10062	1253	14253	8.8%	86.8%	4.4%	100.0%	20.6%	70.6%	8.8%	100.0%
AVG	266	2617	133	3016	267	915	114	1296								

SOURCE: ANNUAL REPORT OF THE COMMISSIONER GENERAL OF IMMIGRATION FOR THE GIVEN YEAR

TABLE B:12 - MARITAL STATUS OF PORTUGUESE MIGRANTS TO THE UNITED STATES 1910 - 1930

SELECTED YEARS	MALES					FEMALES					RATIO MARRIED MALES/FEMALES
	SINGLE	MAR- RIED	WIDO- WED	DIV- ORCED	TOTAL	SINGLE	MAR- RIED	WIDO- WED	DIV- ORCED	TOTAL	
1910	2107	1931	54	0	4092	956	930	153	0	2039	2.076
1911	2213	1945	63	0	4221	967	904	139	0	2010	2.151
1912	2421	2479	67	1	4968	1192	1208	171	1	2572	2.052
1913	3631	3795	69	1	7496	1878	1605	281	5	3769	2.364
1916	3722	3447	61	3	7233	1868	1301	237	3	3409	2.649
1917	1875	1728	57	5	3665	2704	1344	302	7	4357	1.285
1920	6161	4007	86	10	10264	1749	1306	270	4	3329	3.068
1921	6659	5699	74	3	12435	1796	2192	270	5	4263	2.599
1922	518	345	25	0	888	254	297	73	4	628	1.161
1923	1000	768	19	4	1791	265	343	68	1	677	2.239
1924	1320	1046	24	1	2391	293	587	95	2	977	1.781
1925	249	121	5	0	375	61	134	20	1	216	0.902
1926	240	187	2	1	430	72	155	18	1	246	1.206
1927	384	224	4	1	613	48	86	17	2	153	2.604
1928	272	181	4	1	458	46	131	12	1	190	1.381
1929	198	151	7	0	356	58	227	21	1	307	0.665
1930	182	59	5	1	247	59	246	24	0	329	0.239
TOTAL	33152	28113	626	32	61923	14266	12996	2171	38	29471	2.163
PERC.	54%	45%	1%	0%	100%	48%	44%	7%	0%	100%	
1910-17	15969	15325	371	10	31675	9565	7292	1283	16	18156	2.101
PERC.	50%	48%	1%	0%	100%	53%	40%	7%	0%	100%	
1920-30	17183	12788	255	22	30248	4701	5704	888	22	11315	2.241
PERC.	57%	42%	1%	0%	100%	42%	50%	8%	0%	100%	

SOURCE: ANNUAL REPORT OF THE COMMISSIONER
GENERAL OF IMMIGRATION FOR THE GIVEN YEAR
NOTE: BETWEEN 1910 AND 1917 THE AGE GROUP UNDER 14 YEARS OF AGE WAS DEDUCTED.
BETWEEN 1920 AND 1930 THE AGE GROUP UNDER SIXTEEN YEARS OF AGE WAS DEDUCTED.

TABLE B:13 - PORTUGUESE ILLITERATE EMIGRANTS
TO THE UNITED STATES BY AGE GROUPS, 1897 - 1930

YEAR *	EMIGRANTS	ILLITERATE 14 AND OVER (A)	RATE	
1897	1874	800	57.35%	
1898	1717	788	60.57%	
1899	2096	1062	65.60%	
1900	4241	1881	59.98%	
1901	4176	2007	63.80%	
1902	5309	2770	71.58%	
1903	8433	4657	73.21%	
1904	6338	3318	67.55%	
1905	4855	2546	66.65%	
1906	8729	4682	67.78%	
1907	9648	5528	76.60%	
1908	6809	3315	64.85%	
1909	4606	2409	65.14%	
1910	7657	4165	67.93%	
1911	7469	3736	59.96%	
1912	9403	4234	56.15%	
1913	13566	6972	61.89%	
1914	9647	4790	57.65%	
1915	4376	2036	54.47%	
1916	12208	6228	58.51%	
1917	10194	4580	57.09%	
1918	2319		EXEMPTED TO	
1919	1574		JOIN RELATIVES	
1920	15174	865	6.36%	857
1921	18856	708	4.24%	698
1922	1867	131	8.64%	131
1923	2802	173	7.01%	173
1924	3892	203	6.03%	203
1925	720	35	5.92%	35
1926	793	55	8.14%	55
1927	843	26	3.39%	26
1928	844	24	3.70%	24
1929	853	49	7.39%	49
1930	780	65	11.28%	65

NOTES : *) YEAR ENDING JUNE 30.
    B) AGE GROUPS ARE NOW: UNDER 14; 14 TO 45; 45 AND OVER.
    C) AGE GROUPS ARE NOW: UNDER 16; 16 TO 44; 45 AND OVER.
    D) AFTER 1917 EXEMPTION FROM THE LITERACY TEST WAS GIVEN
    MAINLY UNDER SECTION 3 -- TO JOIN RELATIVES.
    E) A NEW CATEGORY NONIMMIGRANTS BEGINS THIS YEAR.
SOURCE: ANNUAL REPORT OF THE COMMISSIONER GENERAL
    OF IMMIGRATION FOR THE GIVEN YEARS
    FOR 1911 - 1919: TAFT,1967: 101.

TABLE B:14 - STATED OCCUPATION OF PORTUGUESE IMMIGRANTS AT ARRIVAL,
1897 - 1930

OCCUPATIONS	1897	1898	1899	1900	1901	1902	1903	1904	1905	1906	1907	1908	1909
ACTORS	1											1	
ARCHITECTS										1	1		
CLERGY			1	2	6		4	5	5	5	6	1	8
EDITORS								2	2		1	2	1
ELECTRICIANS										1	3		3
ENGINEERS			1		2			6	4	6	5	10	3
LAWYERS								2	2		2		
LITERARY-SCIENTIFIC									1	2			1
MUSICIANS					1			1	2	2	1		
OFFICIALS (GOV.)								6	2	4	3	2	2
PHYSICIANS							1	4	1	5	1	3	2
SCULPTORS-ARTISTS								3	2	2		1	3
TEACHERS		1		1			2	2	1		3	2	1
ALL OTHERS N. SP.	1		1	1						1	5	1	
TOTAL PROFESSIONAL	2	1	3	4	9		7	31	31	29	31	23	24
PERCENT OF TOTAL	0.11%	0.06%	0.14%	0.09%	0.22%	0.00%	0.08%	0.49%	0.64%	0.33%	0.32%	0.34%	0.52%

	1	2	3	4	5	6	7	8	9	10	11	12	13
BAKERS				1			2	3	4	3	5	16	1
BARBERS-HAIRDRESSERS	3	2	2	4	5	13	19	9	12	6	5	6	5
BLACKSMITHS	1			1	7		9	5	3	4	6	6	2
BOOKBINDERS								1					
BREWERS													
BUTCHERS			3				1	3	1	1		2	1
CABINETMAKERS								1	2	2	1	5	
CARPENTERS-JOINERS	13	3	4	6	17	38	56	35	26	56	56	44	19
CLERCKS-ACCOUNTS	6	3	1	2	10	5	8	33	26	32	44	36	11
COOPERS	2	1											
DRESSMAKERS								11	4		21	14	5
ENG.STATIONARY-FIRE							12	42	15				
ENGRAVERS						2			1				1
FURRIERS-FUR WORKERS								2					
GARDENERS		1	10	1			1				2	2	
HAD-CAP MAKERS							1		1				
IRONWORKERS							1	1			3	2	1
JEWELERS				1	1	1						1	
LOCKSMITHS							1		1	1	2	2	5
MACHINISTS						1	2	1	1	1		1	2
MARINERS	208	75	30	185	253	213	104	172	52	57	51	97	
MASONS	1	4	4	2	8	7	11	21	9	13	20	15	4
MECHANICS N.SP.				1	1		6				1	2	
METAL WORKER											2	2	
MILLERS				1	1		1	1	2	1			3
MILLINERS													
MINERS							2	1	3	6	8	4	18
PAINTERS-GLAZIERS				2	1	4	6	3	3	5	8	10	1
PATTERN MAKERS													
PHOTOGRAPERS								1	1		1		
PLASTERERS								2		1			
PLUMBERS							1			1	3		
PRINTERS								2	1	1	2	4	1
SADDLERS-HARNESS							2	1	1	1	1	1	
SEAMSTRESSES-DRESSM.	36	33	6	20	25	24	40	41	12	21	5	6	
SHIPWRIGHTS										1	2		
SHOEMAKERS	3	4	6	7	7	8	10	27	13	12	15	15	10
STOKERS										4	45	41	
STONECUTTERS		1	3	1	1	3	6	6	5	5	6	4	1
TAILORS			4	1	1	1		6	3	5	7	2	4
TANNERS-CURRIERS			1		1	1						1	
TEXTILE WORKER									1		6		
TINNERS			2		3		2					2	
TOBACCO WORKER										1	2	1	
UPHOLSTERERS												1	
WATCH-CLOCK MAKERS							1		2				1
WEAVERS-SPINNERS		2	1	1	1	4	2	6	10	9	6	4	
WHEELWRIGHTS				1									2
ALL OTHERS N.SP.		3	2		3	3	9	13	8	4	3	5	1
TOTAL SKILLED	273	136	76	238	343	332	299	409	257	277	338	358	96
PERCENT OF TOTAL	15%	8%	4%	6%	8%	6%	4%	6%	5%	3%	4%	5%	2%

AGENTS' FACTORS	4	2	3	3		2		5	1	3		1	
BANKERS			1					1					1
COOKS		3											
DRAYMEN-TEAMSTERS										2	1	3	3
FARMERS	85	120	5	1	54	4	76	31	29	86	22	46	46
FISHERMEN								67	246	174	77	150	57
GROCERS	1												
HOTEL KEEPERS	2	3	1	1					2	2		1	
LABORERS-F.LABORERS	325	364	794	1651	1371	2071	3391	2428	1771	3430	3913	2464	2102
MANUFACTURERS									1				
MERCHANT DEALERS	13	3		8	6	8	23	107	44	55	31	28	25
SERVANTS	380	418	621	1488	1425	889	1825	1076	824	1744	1308	943	666
SHEPHERDS													
ALL OTHERS N.SP.	39	26	15	22	8	10	143	1	6	13	12	17	5
TOTAL MISCELLANEOUS	849	939	1440	3174	2864	2984	5458	3715	2925	5509	5424	3653	2905
PERCENT OF TOTAL	45%	55%	69%	75%	69%	56%	65%	59%	60%	63%	56%	54%	63%
TOTAL OCCUPATIONS	1124	1076	1519	3416	3216	3316	5764	4155	3213	5815	5793	4034	3078
LABORERS - SERVANTS	705	782	1415	3139	2796	2960	5216	3504	2595	5174	5221	3407	2768
PERCENT OF TOTAL	63%	73%	93%	92%	87%	89%	90%	84%	81%	89%	90%	84%	90%
NO OCCUP.(WOMEN-CH.)	750	641	577	825	960	1993	2669	2183	1642	2914	3855	2775	1528
PERCENT OF TOTAL	40%	37%	28%	19%	23%	38%	32%	34%	34%	33%	40%	41%	33%
GRAND TOTAL	1874	1717	2096	4241	4176	5309	8433	6338	4855	8729	9648	6809	4606

OCCUPATIONS	1910	1911	1912	1913	1916	1917	1897-1917
ACTORS	1	1			1		5
ARCHITECTS				1	0		3
CLERGY	3	8	7	7	1	1	70
EDITORS		1	2	1	0	1	13
ELECTRICIANS	2		2	5	2	6	25
ENGINEERS	5	4	9	6	18	19	98
LAWYERS	1	2	1	1	1	3	15
LITERARY-SCIENTIFIC	2		2	3	1	4	16
MUSICIANS	1			2	1	2	13
OFFICIALS (GOV.)		4	5	4	10	12	54
PHYSICIANS	3	1	2	4	1	2	30
SCULPTORS-ARTISTS			1	4		1	17
TEACHERS	1	5	2	5	1	4	31
ALL OTHERS N. SP.	1	5	9	8	5	4	42
TOTAL PROFESSIONAL	20	31	42	51	43	59	441
PERCENT OF TOTAL	0.26%	0.42%	0.45%	0.38%	0.35%	0.58%	0.34%

BAKERS	10	10	22	27	12	39	155
BARBERS-HAIRDRESSERS	9	4	10	9	13	5	141
BLACKSMITHS	4	7	7	5	22	8	97
BOOKBINDERS		1	1	1			4
BREWERS							0
BUTCHERS	2	1	1		1	6	23
CABINETMAKERS		2			1	1	15
CARPENTERS-JOINERS	31	46	57	67	62	71	707
CLERCKS-ACCOUNTS	21	40	39	90	105	131	643
COOPERS							3
DRESSMAKERS	5	2	7	6	4	4	83
ENG.STATIONARY-FIRE			2			3	74
ENGRAVERS							4
FURRIERS-FUR WORKERS							2
GARDENERS	2	1	4	1	3	9	37
HAD-CAP MAKERS			1		1		4
IRONWORKERS	1		1	2	1	2	15
JEWELERS							4
LOCKSMITHS		2	1	2	1		18
MACHINISTS		4	2	6	14	14	49
MARINERS	22	38	89	78	76	83	1883
MASONS	9	17	11	18	24	18	216
MECHANICS N.SP.	0		2	3	5	5	26
METAL WORKER	1		2	1	1		9
MILLERS		3		2	4		19
MILLINERS			2		1		3
MINERS	2	2	3		1	4	54
PAINTERS-GLAZIERS	4	5	10	7	13	9	91
PATTERN MAKERS							0
PHOTOGRAPERS						2	5
PLASTERERS	1				1	3	8
PLUMBERS	1				3	2	11
PRINTERS	1	1	1		3	1	18
SADDLERS-HARNESS		1					8
SEAMSTRESSES-DRESSM.	5	22		3	13	6	318
SHIPWRIGHTS				0	0	0	3
SHOEMAKERS	9	14	22	20	24	11	237
STOKERS	39	95	40	94	24	42	424
STONECUTTERS	1	11	6	1	3	4	68
TAILORS	3	8	9	16	11	18	99
TANNERS-CURRIERS				3		3	10
TEXTILE WORKER	12	4	8	14	8	8	61
TINNERS	1	1	1	1	4		17
TOBACCO WORKER				2	1	1	8
UPHOLSTERERS							1
WATCH-CLOCK MAKERS	1		1		1	1	8
WEAVERS-SPINNERS	17	7	7	7	11	9	104
WHEELWRIGHTS							3
ALL OTHERS N.SP.	5	7	2	9	10	13	100
TOTAL SKILLED	219	356	371	495	482	536	5891
PERCENT OF TOTAL	2.86%	4.77%	3.95%	3.65%	3.95%	5.26%	4.56%

AGENTS' FACTORS	1	3	4	1	10	8	51
BANKERS						1	4
COOKS							3
DRAYMEN-TEAMSTERS	1		3	4		3	20
FARMERS	39	107	110	135	73	28	1097
FISHERMEN	115	187	164	120	77	44	1478
GROCERS							1
HOTEL KEEPERS	1	2	1	2			18
LABORERS-F.LABORERS	3586	3419	4246	6564	6352	2760	53002
MANUFACTURERS	1	1					3
MERCHANT DEALERS	27	40	44	40	79	84	665
SERVANTS	1101	995	1178	1922	1902	2842	23547
SHEPHERDS							0
ALL OTHERS N.SP.	28	69	39	29	22	36	540
TOTAL MISCELLANEOUS	4900	4823	5789	8817	8515	5806	80489
PERCENT OF TOTAL	64%	65%	62%	65%	70%	57%	62%
TOTAL OCCUPATIONS	5139	5210	6202	9363	9040	6401	86874
LABORERS - SERVANTS	4687	4414	5424	8486	8254	5602	76549
PERCENT OF TOTAL	91%	85%	87%	91%	91%	88%	88%
NO OCCUP.(WOMEN-CH.)	2518	2259	3201	4203	3168	3793	42454
PERCENT OF TOTAL	33%	30%	34%	31%	26%	37%	33%
GRAND TOTAL	7657	7469	9403	13566	12208	10194	129328

OCCUPATIONS	1920	1921	1922	1923	1924	1925
ACTORS	3		2	6		1
ARCHITECTS	1	1			1	
CLERGY	9	10	3	7	6	5
EDITORS				2		
ELECTRICIANS	2	5	1	2	4	1
ENGINEERS	11	8	3	7	10	3
LAWYERS	5	6			3	
LITERARY-SCIENTIFIC	3	4	1	3	5	
MUSICIANS	1	4		1	2	1
OFFICIALS (GOV.)	17	10	25	9	9	9
PHYSICIANS	8	6	6	5	8	
SCULPTORS-ARTISTS		6			4	
TEACHERS	9	7	3	10	10	3
ALL OTHERS N. SP.	5	1	1	5	7	1
TOTAL PROFESSIONAL	74	68	45	57	69	24
PERCENT OF TOTAL	0.49%	0.36%	2.41%	2.03%	1.77%	3.33%

BAKERS	58	67	5	22	37	8
BARBERS-HAIRDRESSERS	42	31	3	11	13	
BLACKSMITHS	31	24	1	4	8	1
BOOKBINDERS						
BREWERS						
BUTCHERS	5	7	1	3	4	1
CABINETMAKERS		4			1	
CARPENTERS-JOINERS	321	212	5	43	88	16
CLERCKS-ACCOUNTS	251	272	43	101	219	44
COOPERS						
DRESSMAKERS	12	13	1	3	11	2
ENG.STATIONARY-FIRE	3	8	4	4	5	1
ENGRAVERS						
FURRIERS-FUR WORKERS						
GARDENERS	2	5	2	2	2	1
HAD-CAP MAKERS	2	2			1	
IRONWORKERS	7	12		1	9	
JEWELERS	5	1			2	
LOCKSMITHS	34	27		3	7	
MACHINISTS	36	12		2	12	3
MARINERS	371	445	52	122	127	8
MASONS	87	101	1	20	26	3
MECHANICS N.SP.	17	20	6	5	15	4
METAL WORKER		3		1	2	2
MILLERS	5	11			2	
MILLINERS				1		
MINERS	1	18		3	5	
PAINTERS-GLAZIERS	14	13		3	10	3
PATTERN MAKERS						
PHOTOGRAPERS		1				
PLASTERERS	1	2		1	1	
PLUMBERS				1		
PRINTERS	9	11		1		
SADDLERS-HARNESS						
SEAMSTRESSES-DRESSM.	12	17	2	9	24	1
SHIPWRIGHTS						5
SHOEMAKERS	115	97	6	5	19	
STOKERS	24	17	2		7	
STONECUTTERS	6			2	1	
TAILORS	92	107	1	15	37	4
TANNERS-CURRIERS	1	1				
TEXTILE WORKER	2				1	
TINNERS	2				1	
TOBACCO MANUFACT.						
UPHOLSTERERS						
WATCH-CLOCK MAKERS	4	3				
WEAVERS-SPINNERS	28	5	3	3	8	
WHEELWRIGHTS				1		
ALL OTHERS N.SP.	30	29	8	3	8	1
TOTAL SKILLED	1630	1598	146	394	714	108
PERCENT OF TOTAL	10.74%	8.47%	7.82%	14.06%	18.35%	15.00%

AGENTS' FACTORS	3	1	1	6	8	
BANKERS	1	1	1			
COOKS						
DRAYMEN-TEAMSTERS	1	1	2	4	7	
FARMERS	588	507	30	21	35	14
FISHERMEN	126	33	1	22	25	4
GROCERS						
HOTEL KEEPERS	5		3		2	1
LABORERS-F.LABORERS	7448	9783	614	1150	1316	179
MANUFACTURERS		3	1		1	
MERCHANT DEALERS	185	176	36	69	118	15
SERVANTS	1925	1753	29	85	204	39
SHEPHERDS						
ALL OTHERS N.SP.	92	215	11	55	106	22
TOTAL MISCELLANEOUS	10374	12473	729	1412	1822	274
PERCENT OF TOTAL	68%	66%	39%	50%	47%	38%
TOTAL OCCUPATIONS	12078	14139	920	1863	2605	406
LABORERS - SERVANTS	9373	11536	643	1235	1520	218
PERCENT OF TOTAL	78%	82%	70%	66%	58%	54%
NO OCCUP.(WOMEN-CH.)	3096	4717	947	939	1287	314
PERCENT OF TOTAL	20%	25%	51%	34%	33%	44%
GRAND TOTAL	15174	18856	1867	2802	3892	720

OCCUPATIONS	1926	1927	1928	1929	1930	TOTAL
ACTORS				1	1	14
ARCHITECTS						3
CLERGY	5	1	8	1	2	57
EDITORS						2
ELECTRICIANS	1	2	4			22
ENGINEERS	1	4	5	4	4	60
LAWYERS	1				1	16
LITERARY-SCIENTIFIC	2	2		2	3	25
MUSICIANS	3	1	2		1	16
OFFICIALS (GOV.)	6	10	7	6	3	111
PHYSICIANS	3	1	3		1	41
SCULPTORS-ARTISTS	1		1			12
TEACHERS	6	1	2	2		53
ALL OTHERS N. SP.	2	5	2		2	31
TOTAL PROFESSIONAL	31	27	34	16	18	463
PERCENT OF TOTAL	3.91%	3.20%	4.03%	1.88%	2.31%	0.98%

BAKERS	3	12	1	3	1	217
BARBERS-HAIRDRESSERS		1		2	4	107
BLACKSMITHS	1	2	2			74
BOOKBINDERS		1				1
BREWERS						0
BUTCHERS			2	2		25
CABINETMAKERS		1		3		9
CARPENTERS-JOINERS	10	27	22	15	14	773
CLERCKS-ACCOUNTS	38	49	38	36	31	1122
COOPERS						0
DRESSMAKERS		1	2	1	5	51
ENG.STATIONARY-FIRE	1	1	3			30
ENGRAVERS						0
FURRIERS-FUR WORKERS			1	2		3
GARDENERS	1		2			17
HAD-CAP MAKERS	1					6
IRONWORKERS		2				31
JEWELERS		2	1	2	1	14
LOCKSMITHS	1	1	3	2	1	79
MACHINISTS		1		1	1	68
MARINERS	5	19	3	5	4	1161
MASONS	1	9	6	2	1	257
MECHANICS N.SP.	1	5	9	7	5	94
METAL WORKER	1			1	1	11
MILLERS						18
MILLINERS						1
MINERS				1		28
PAINTERS-GLAZIERS	1		3	1	1	49
PATTERN MAKERS				1		1
PHOTOGRAPERS			1			2
PLASTERERS		1		1		7
PLUMBERS	1		1	1		4
PRINTERS			1			22
SADDLERS-HARNESS						0
SEAMSTRESSES-DRESSM.				1	2	68
SHIPWRIGHTS						5
SHOEMAKERS	3	4	3	3	4	259
STOKERS	4		1			55
STONECUTTERS						9
TAILORS	3	6	6	2	3	276
TANNERS-CURRIERS						2
TEXTILE WORKER					1	4
TINNERS		1			1	5
TOBACCO MANUFACT.						0
UPHOLSTERERS						0
WATCH-CLOCK MAKERS		1				8
WEAVERS-SPINNERS		1	2			50
WHEELWRIGHTS						1
ALL OTHERS N.SP.	1	2	4	1		87
TOTAL SKILLED	77	150	117	96	81	5111
PERCENT OF TOTAL	9.71%	17.79%	13.86%	11.25%	10.38%	10.78%

AGENTS' FACTORS	4	12	4	3	3	45
BANKERS		1	1			5
COOKS						0
DRAYMEN-TEAMSTERS	2				1	18
FARMERS	37	40	37	6	10	1325
FISHERMEN	2	6	2		1	222
GROCERS						0
HOTEL KEEPERS						11
LABORERS-F.LABORERS	240	319	220	192	115	21576
MANUFACTURERS		1	1		1	8
MERCHANT DEALERS	18	32	18	23	9	699
SERVANTS	42	48	67	90	60	4342
SHEPHERDS						0
ALL OTHERS N.SP.	18	14	9	7	6	555
TOTAL MISCELLANEOUS	364	473	359	321	206	28807
PERCENT OF TOTAL	46%	56%	43%	38%	26%	61%
TOTAL OCCUPATIONS	472	650	510	433	305	34381
LABORERS - SERVANTS	282	367	287	282	175	25918
PERCENT OF TOTAL	60%	56%	56%	65%	57%	75%
NO OCCUP.(WOMEN-CH.)	321	193	334	420	475	13043
PERCENT OF TOTAL	40%	23%	40%	49%	61%	28%
GRAND TOTAL	793	843	844	853	780	47424

SOURCE: ANNUAL REPORT OF THE COMMISIONER
GENERAL OF IMMIGRATION FOR THE GIVEN YEAR

TABLE B:15 - BY WHOM THE PASSAGE WAS PAID AND MONEY SHOWN
BY PORTUGUESE EMIGRANTS TO THE UNITED STATES, 1897 - 1930

YEARS	BY WHOM PASSAGE WAS PAID				MONEY SHOWN ‡‡			PERCENTAGE DISTRIBUTION				
	SELF	RELAT.	OTHER	TOTAL	$50 OR +	LESS $50	TOTAL	SELF	RELAT.	OTHER	$50 OR +	LESS $50
1897					246	750	996				24.7%	75.3%
1898					193	737	930				20.8%	79.2%
1899					159	1131	1290				12.3%	87.7%
1900					269	2052	2321				11.6%	88.4%
1901					310	2274	2584				12.0%	88.0%
1902					365	2555	2920				12.5%	87.5%
1903					695	5625	6320				11.0%	89.0%
1904					473	3827	4300				11.0%	89.0%
1905					537	2789	3326				16.1%	83.9%
1906					598	4897	5495				10.9%	89.1%
1907					721	5678	6399				11.3%	88.7%
1908	3436	2232	1141	6809	451	4350	4801	50.5%	32.8%	16.8%	9.4%	90.6%
1909	2804	1770	32	4606	395	2761	3156	60.9%	38.4%	0.7%	12.5%	87.5%
1910	4551	2228	878	7657	539	4512	5051	59.4%	29.1%	11.5%	10.7%	89.3%
1911	4508	2381	580	7469	934	4216	5150	60.4%	31.9%	7.8%	18.1%	81.9%
1912	5118	3148	1137	9403	814	5179	5993	54.4%	33.5%	12.1%	13.6%	86.4%
1913	7260	6046	260	13566	953	8549	9502	53.5%	44.6%	1.9%	10.0%	90.0%
1914	4330	5297	20	9647	771	6671	7442	44.9%	54.9%	0.2%	10.4%	89.6%
1915	2182	2178	16	4376	457	2859	3316	49.9%	49.8%	0.4%	13.8%	86.2%
1916	6881	5287	40	12208	662	8895	9557	56.4%	43.3%	0.3%	6.9%	93.1%
1917	3829	6323	42	10194	864	6479	7343	37.6%	62.0%	0.4%	11.8%	88.2%
1920	10350	4734	90	15174	2654	8211	10865	68.2%	31.2%	0.6%	24.4%	75.6%
1921	14818	3926	112	18856	2123	11321	13444	78.6%	20.8%	0.6%	15.8%	84.2%
1922	998	821	48	1867	459	808	1267	53.5%	44.0%	2.6%	36.2%	63.8%
1923	1857	900	45	2802	558	1654	2212	66.3%	32.1%	1.6%	25.2%	74.8%
1924	2658	1176	58	3892	870	2191	3061	68.3%	30.2%	1.5%	28.4%	71.6%
1925	406	298	16	720	209	328	537	56.4%	41.4%	2.2%	38.9%	61.1%
1926	474	303	16	793	252	328	580	59.8%	38.2%	2.0%	43.4%	56.6%
1927	625	199	19	843	278	445	723	74.1%	23.6%	2.3%	38.5%	61.5%
1928	494	338	12	844	301	308	609	58.5%	40.0%	1.4%	49.4%	50.6%
1929	452	386	15	853	286	352	638	53.0%	45.3%	1.8%	44.8%	55.2%
1930	266	503	11	780	237	301	538	34.1%	64.5%	1.4%	44.1%	55.9%

SOURCE: FOR 1907 - 1916: BANNICK, 1917:41 AND 43.
ALL THE OTHER YEARS: ANNUAL REPORT OF THE COMMISSIONER
OF IMMIGRATION FOR THE GIVEN YEAR.
NOTES: ‡‡ "PERSONS OVER 20 YEARS OF AGE BRINGING MONEY"
FROM 1897 TO 1903, MINIMUM 30 DOLLARS.

TABLE B:16

STATES OF INTENDED FUTURE PERMANENT RESIDENCE OF PORTUGUESE IMMIGRANTS

DESTINATION	1901	1902	1903	1904	1905	1906	1907	1908	1909	1910	1901-10 TOTAL	TOTAL %
ALABAMA				1							1	0.00%
ALASKA											0	0.00%
ARIZONA					2		4		1		7	0.01%
ARKANSAS											0	0.00%
CALIFORNIA	483	795	1057	1028	901	1018	1198	1104	870	1386	9840	14.78%
COLORADO			5		2				6		13	0.02%
CONNECTUCUT	70	260	114	109	34	62	56	40	52	62	859	1.29%
DELAWARE				1							1	0.00%
D.OF COLUMBIA				4	10	2	1	1	3	4	25	0.04%
FLORIDA			3	9				1		1	14	0.02%
GEORGIA			1		1	1	6				9	0.01%
HAWAII	85	35	12	12	3	5	1328	1115	1	864	3460	5.20%
IDAHO			2	3	5	5	6	1	8	4	34	0.05%
ILLINOIS	4	7	14	84	6	5	6	7	14	15	162	0.24%
INDIANA								1			1	0.00%
IOWA						1					1	0.00%
KANSAS											0	0.00%
KENTUCKY									2		2	0.00%
LOUISIANA		5	2	7	7	3		2	1		27	0.04%
MAINE	1	6		2	2	7	10	16	1	5	50	0.08%
MARYLAND	1			1	0		1	1	1	1	6	0.01%
MASSACHUSETTS	2968	3109	5691	3920	2909	6042	5674	3379	2897	4228	40817	61.32%

	1	2	3	4	5	6	7	8	9	10	Total	Percent
MICHIGAN				1	0	1		1			3	0.00%
MINNESOTA					0	1					1	0.00%
MISSISSIPPI				4							4	0.01%
MISSOURI	1			23	16	1				1	42	0.06%
MONTANA	2		1	1					5	2	11	0.02%
NEBRASKA											0	0.00%
NEVADA	11	19	8	38	17	30	23	25	14	59	244	0.37%
NEW HAMPSHIRE		3	1	3		18	18	6	1	8	58	0.09%
NEW JERSEY	2	4	4	3		3	10	12	2	10	50	0.08%
NEW MEXICO								2			2	0.00%
NEW YORK	108	519	475	276	412	433	513	524	381	371	4012	6.03%
NORTH CAROLINA		1		1					1		3	0.00%
NORTH DAKOTA				1							1	0.00%
OHIO	8		6	4	21	26	15	10		1	91	0.14%
OKLAHOMA	1										1	0.00%
OREGON	2	3	1	6		9	4	1		3	29	0.04%
PENNSYLVANIA	4	5	1	12	6	13	10	4	12	5	72	0.11%
PORTO RICO			1			2	2	1		2	8	0.01%
RHODE ISLAND	421	535	1029	769	467	1020	745	534	307	614	6441	9.68%
SOUTH CAROLINA											0	0.00%
SOUTH DAKOTA			2								2	0.00%
TENNESSE											0	0.00%
TEXAS						3	2	1	3	1	10	0.02%
UTAH			2								2	0.00%
VERMONT	2		3	10	1	7	9	10	10	2	54	0.08%
VIRGINIA				1	1	6	5	2	8		23	0.03%
WASHINGTON	2		1	2	6	3	1	5	4	4	28	0.04%
WEST VIRGINIA						2					2	0.00%
WISCONSIN				3							3	0.00%
WYOMING		3		2				5	1	4	15	0.02%
INDIAN TERRITORY											0	0.00%
IN TRANSIT				10	9						19	0.03%
TOTAL	4176	5309	8433	6338	4855	8729	9648	6809	4606	7657	66560	100.00%

STATES OF INTENDED FUTURE PERMANENT RESIDENCE OF PORTUGUESE IMMIGRANTS

DESTINATION	1921	1922	1923	1924	1925	1926	1927	1928	1929	1930	1921-30 TOTAL	TOT %
ALABAMA			1								1	0.0%
ALASKA				1							1	0.0%
ARIZONA			1								1	0.0%
ARKANSAS							1			1	2	0.0%
CALIFORNIA	2254	637	428	399	113	132	52	95	82	51	4243	13.2%
COLORADO	5				1	1	1			4	12	0.0%
CONNECTUCUT	942	31	103	147	25	24	29	33	42	43	1419	4.4%
DELAWARE	8		1	3			1			8	21	0.1%
D.OF COLUMBIA	9	11	3	15	2	2	11	2			55	0.2%
FLORIDA	22	6	2	1	2	6	1		1	1	42	0.1%
GEORGIA	3	2	2	6			3	1	2	2	21	0.1%
HAWAII	9	4	3	2							18	0.1%
IDAHO	2	2	1	1				1			7	0.0%
ILLINOIS	122	1	7	14	3	8	10	5	2	3	175	0.5%
INDIANA	3		3	11		4	2	1	6	11	41	0.1%
IOWA	7	3		3						2	15	0.0%
KANSAS	1	1									2	0.0%
KENTUCKY	1		9	1		2	1		2	1	17	0.1%
LOUISIANA	10	3	7	10	1	5	2	1	2	1	42	0.1%
MAINE	4	2	1								7	0.0%
MARYLAND	8	2	8	6	3	4	1	3	2	1	38	0.1%
MASSACHUSETTS	9153	749	949	1311	249	209	164	202	181	173	13340	41.4%

MICHIGAN	29	3	8	5	3	3	4	2	3	1	61	0.2%
MINNESOTA	2	1	1								4	0.0%
MISSISSIPPI			1								1	0.0%
MISSOURI	69			1						1	71	0.2%
MONTANA	2	1	2	2							7	0.0%
NEBRASKA				1							1	0.0%
NEVADA	6	1	7	2			1	1	1		19	0.1%
NEW HAMPSHIRE	46	1	7	3	1					1	59	0.2%
NEW JERSEY	1166	20	327	545	99	113	257	150	196	148	3021	9.4%
NEW MEXICO				3			3	1	3	1	11	0.0%
NEW YORK	1387	175	482	746	100	124	189	206	208	219	3836	11.9%
NORTH CAROLINA			1				1	1			3	0.0%
NORTH DAKOTA											0	0.0%
OHIO	211	5	3	11	3	1	6	6	3	5	254	0.8%
OKLAHOMA											0	0.0%
OREGON	4	1	4			2					11	0.0%
PENNSYLVANIA	637	37	109	192	42	42	33	41	29	17	1179	3.7%
PORTO RICO				2		1		1	1	1	6	0.0%
RHODE ISLAND	2569	148	297	427	65	106	61	84	84	79	3920	12.2%
SOUTH CAROLINA											0	0.0%
SOUTH DAKOTA											0	0.0%
TENNESSE	2		1								3	0.0%
TEXAS	12	1	8	2	2	1	1	2			29	0.1%
UTAH											0	0.0%
VERMONT	4	2	2	8		1			1		18	0.1%
VIRGINIA	125	13	1	6	1	1	7			2	156	0.5%
WASHINGTON	3	3	8	2	2		1	3	1		23	0.1%
WEST VIRGINIA	13		1	3	2				1	1	21	0.1%
WISCONSIN	6	1	3		1	1		2		2	16	0.0%
WYOMING											0	0.0%
INDIAN TERRITORY											0	0.0%
IN TRANSIT											0	0.0%
TOTAL	18856	1867	2802	3892	720	793	843	844	853	780	32250	100.0%

SOURCE: ANNUAL REPORT OF THE COMMISSIONER
GENERAL OF IMMIGRATION FOR THE GIVEN YEAR

TABLE B: 17 - STATE OF RESIDENCE OF PORTUGUESE DEPARTED

STATE	1908	1909	1910	1911	1912	1913	TOTAL	PERC. DISTR.
ALABAMA							0	0.0%
ALASKA							0	0.0%
ARIZONA	1				1		2	0.0%
ARKANSAS							0	0.0%
CALIFORNIA	129	100	77	135	183	158	782	10.7%
COLORADO	1	1				1	3	0.0%
CONNECTUCUT	10	16	9	26	23	15	99	1.3%
DELAWARE							0	0.0%
D.OF COLUMBIA			4			5	9	0.1%
FLORIDA			2				2	0.0%
GEORGIA					4		4	0.1%
HAWAII	1	9		3	2	15	30	0.4%
IDAHO		1					1	0.0%
ILLINOIS	1		3	3	17	2	26	0.4%
INDIANA					1		1	0.0%
IOWA							0	0.0%
KANSAS		1	5				6	0.1%
KENTUCKY				5	1		6	0.1%
LOUISIANA				4			4	0.1%
MAINE	1						1	0.0%
MARYLAND							0	0.0%
MASSACHUSETTS	558	443	540	790	1019	943	4293	58.5%

							TOTAL	%
MICHIGAN						1	1	0.0%
MINNESOTA			1				1	0.0%
MISSISSIPPI							0	0.0%
MISSOURI	1						1	0.0%
MONTANA			2				2	0.0%
NEBRASKA							0	0.0%
NEVADA		3	6	7	13	1	30	0.4%
NEW HAMPSHIRE	1	1	3		5		10	0.1%
NEW JERSEY		3	2	5	1		11	0.1%
NEW MEXICO							0	0.0%
NEW YORK	122	126	187	249	241	213	1138	15.5%
NORTH CAROLINA							0	0.0%
NORTH DAKOTA							0	0.0%
OHIO	1	1				2	4	0.1%
OKLAHOMA			1				1	0.0%
OREGON			3				3	0.0%
PENNSYLVANIA	4	2	9	4	10	8	37	0.5%
PORTO RICO	2						2	0.0%
RHODE ISLAND	61	87	49	116	216	211	740	10.1%
SOUTH CAROLINA							0	0.0%
SOUTH DAKOTA							0	0.0%
TENNESSE							0	0.0%
TEXAS	1				8	2	11	0.1%
UTAH	1						1	0.0%
VERMONT	1	18	3	4	1		27	0.4%
VIRGINIA		1				1	2	0.0%
WASHINGTON	1	1		6		1	9	0.1%
WEST VIRGINIA							0	0.0%
WISCONSIN						1	1	0.0%
WYOMING		1		1			2	0.0%
UNKNOWN		1		3	1	3	8	0.1%
TOTAL	898	816	906	1388	1747	1583	7338	100.0%

STATE	1920	1921	1922	1923	1924	1925	1926	1927	1928	1929	1930	TOTAL	PERC. DISTR.
ALABAMA				1							1	2	0.0%
ALASKA			1	1								2	0.0%
ARIZONA		2				1						3	0.0%
ARKANSAS			1					1				2	0.0%
CALIFORNIA	728	655	378	255	302	214	174	216	225	218	33	3398	9.7%
COLORADO		3		2	1		5	1	1			13	0.0%
CONNECTUCUT	119	172	69	25	71	33	44	22	25	99		679	1.9%
DELAWARE	1		3		2	2						8	0.0%
D.OF COLUMBIA	3		4	3			2	1				13	0.0%
FLORIDA	3		3	6	14	1	9	1	2			39	0.1%
GEORGIA	3				3		2	2				10	0.0%
HAWAII		3	14	2	5							24	0.1%
IDAHO	1						2	1				4	0.0%
ILLINOIS	2	8	8	4	2	3	1	2	8	2	1	41	0.1%
INDIANA			3			1	8					12	0.0%
IOWA	1											1	0.0%
KANSAS												0	0.0%
KENTUCKY												0	0.0%
LOUISIANA	4	3	7			3	1				2	20	0.1%
MAINE	6	1	21		5							33	0.1%
MARYLAND	2	1	21	1					1		1	27	0.1%
MASSACHUSETTS	2383	2681	3771	1422	1553	2268	1874	1396	289	620	103	18360	52.5%

State												Total	%
MICHIGAN	5				4	1	3	2	3	3	3	24	0.1%
MINNESOTA	1	1	1						2			5	0.0%
MISSISSIPPI	0	1	2					3		2		8	0.0%
MISSOURI	1	1	4				2				1	9	0.0%
MONTANA								1				1	0.0%
NEBRASKA	2				1							3	0.0%
NEVADA	6	4	2	3	1		2		1			19	0.1%
NEW HAMPSHIRE	10	12	9		3	3		4		2		43	0.1%
NEW JERSEY	93	73	113	107	223	464	390	325	382	392	34	2596	7.4%
NEW MEXICO				1			2		2			5	0.0%
NEW YORK	414	361	609	300	427	392	325	289	361	356	103	3937	11.3%
NORTH CAROLINA												0	0.0%
NORTH DAKOTA												0	0.0%
OHIO	5	6	6		2	6	4	5	1	2	1	38	0.1%
OKLAHOMA	1											1	0.0%
OREGON						2						2	0.0%
PENNSYLVANIA	46	101	155	22	73	210	79	27	43	28	11	795	2.3%
PORTO RICO			2		3							5	0.0%
RHODE ISLAND	1008	1050	822	555	757	45	59	56	82	229	37	4700	13.4%
SOUTH CAROLINA			4							4		8	0.0%
SOUTH DAKOTA								2				2	0.0%
TENNESSE		1		1								2	0.0%
TEXAS	1			3	4			3			3	14	0.0%
UTAH												0	0.0%
VERMONT										1		1	0.0%
VIRGINIA		3	6	2	9	2						22	0.1%
WASHINGTON	2		4	2		1						9	0.0%
WEST VIRGINIA	6	1	9	1		1			1	2	2	23	0.1%
WISCONSIN	1			2				3	1			7	0.0%
WYOMING	1									1		2	0.0%
UNKNOWN							1					1	0.0%
TOTAL	4859	5144	6052	2721	3465	3653	2989	2363	1430	1961	336	34973	100.0%

SOURCE: ANNUAL REPORT OF THE COMMISSIONER
OF IMMIGRATION FOR THE GIVEN YEAR

SOURCES:

MANUSCRIPT

LIVROS DE REGISTO DE PASSAPORTES. For 1889 - 1891, 1899 -
1901, 1910 - 1911, 1920 - 1921. District of Angra do
Heroísmo, Biblioteca Pública e Arquivo de Angra do Heroísmo.
District of Horta, Biblioteca Pública e Arquivo da Horta.
For 1899 - 1901, 1910 - 1911, 1920 - 1921. District of Ponta
Delgada, Biblioteca Pública de Ponta Delgada.

PASSENGERS' MANIFESTS. Passengers arrived at Boston from
January to December 1860; from January 1890 to December
1891; at New York from June 1890 to December 1891; at Boston
and San Francisco from January to December 1901. Balch
Institute, Philadelphia and National Archives, Washington,
D.C..

UNITED STATES CENSUS OF 1910 . (microfilm of the manuscript)
Population Studies, University of Pennsylvania,
Philadelphia.

PRINTED

Abbott, Edith
Immigration, Select Documents and Case Records. Chicago,
Il.: The University of Chicago Press, 1924.

Bairoch, P.
The Working Population and its Structure. Vol.I of
Statistiques Internationales Retrospectives. Brussels:
Institute de Sociologie, 1968.

Bureau of the Census
Decennial Censuses of the United States. 1860...1930.
Washington,D.C.: Government Printing Office, 1864...1930.

Historical Statistics of the United States. Colonial Times
to 1970 - Part I. Washington,D.C.: Government Printing
Office, 1975.

Congressional Papers
Annual Report on Immigration Presented to the House of
Representatives. Washington,D.C.: Government Printing
Office,1848 ... 1895.

Direcção Geral da Estatística e dos Próprios Nacionaes
(former Repartição de Estatística Geral)
Censo da População Portuguesa. 1864 - 1930. Lisboa: Imprensa
Nacional, 1868... 1934.

Ferenczi, I. and Willcox, W. (ed.)
International Migrations. Vol.I, Statistics. New York, NY.:
National Bureau of Economic Research, Inc., 1929.

Immigration Commissioner
Report of the Commissioner-General of Immigration for the
fiscal year ended June 30, 1897 to 1908 and 1920 to 1932.
Washington,D.C.: Government Printing Office, 1897 to 1908
and 1920 to 1932.

Immigration Service
Report of the Immigration Investigating Commission to the
Honorable the Secretary of the Tresasury. Washington,D.C.:
Government Printing Office, 1895.

Reports of the Immigration Commission
Abstracts of Reports of the Immigration Commission. 61s
Congress, 2d Session, Senate Documents (Doc.No.633),
Washington,D.C.: Government Printing Office, 1911.

Reports of the Immigration Commission
Abstracts of Reports of the Immigration Commission. 61s
Congress, 3d Session, Senate Documents (Doc.No.747), 2
vol.s, Washington,D.C.: Government Printing Office, 1911.

Ministério dos Negócios Externos
Documentos Apresentados às Cortes. Sessão Legislativa de
1874 - Emigração. Lisboa: Imprensa Nacional,1874.

Documentos Apresentados às Cortes. Sessão Legislativa de
1885 - Emigração Portugueza para as Ilhas Hawaiiannas.
Lisboa: Imprensa Nacional,1885.

Ministerio das Obras Públicas, Comércio e Industria (after
1900 Ministério das Finanças)
Annuário Estatístico de Portugal. 1884, 1892, 1917...1930.
Lisboa: Imprensa Nacional, 1886...1934.

Movimento da População. 1887...1980, and 1901...1921.
Lisboa: Imprensa Nacional, 1890...1924.

Mitchell, B.R.
European Historical Statistics, 1750-1975. 2@ ed., New York,
N.Y.: Facts on File, 1981.

REFERENCES:

O Açoriano. Horta, January of 1887 to December of 1890.

Andrade, Laurinda C.
The Open Door. New Bedford, Mass.: Reynolds-De Walt Publs.,
1968.

Armstrong, A.
Stability and Change in an English Country Town - A Social
Study of York 1801-1851. Cambridge: Cambridge University
Press, 1974.

Bacci,M.Livi
A Century of Portuguese Fertility. Princeton, N.J.:
Princeton University Press, 1971.

Baganha, Maria Ioannis Benis
"A Emigração Vista de Viana do Castelo". Revista de História Económica e Social, 3, 1979:85-100.

"Uma Contra-Imagem do Brasileiro". Revista de História Económica e Social, 7, 1981:129-137.

"Interntional Labor Movements: Portuguese Emigration to the United States 1820 - 1930". Ph.D. Dissertation, University of Pennsylvania, Philadelphia, 1988.

"Social Marginalization, Government Policies and Emigrants' Remittances Portugal 1870 - 1930". Estudos e Ensaios em Homenagem a Vitorino Magalhães Godinho. Lisboa: Livraria Sá da Costa Editores, 1988: 431-449.

Bairoch, Paul
Commerce extérieur et développement économique de l'Europe au XIXe siècle. Paris: Mouton, 1976.

"Population Urbaine at Taille des Villes en Europe de 1600 a 1970". Revue D'Histoire Economique et Sociale. 54 (3), 1976: 304-333.

"Europe's Gross National Product: 1800 - 1975". Journal of European Econnomic History, 1976, 5: 273-340.

Bannick, Christian J.
Portuguese Immigration to the United States: its Distribution and Status. (A.B. Standford University, 1916), Thesis, University of California, 1917.

Baptista d'Oliveira, João and d'Ornellas, Vicent
"Destination Sandwich Island, Nov. 8, 1887". The Hawaiian Journal of History, Vol.XIV, 1970:3-52.

Barcelos, A.Bento
"Ilha Graciosa - O fenómeno emigratório como factor de causa e efeito na mutação socio-económica". (Outubro, 1986), Boletim do Museu Etnográfico da Ilha Graciosa, 1987:81-95.

Barclay, George W.
Techniques of Population Analysis. 7th ed., New York, N.Y.: John Wiley & Sons, Inc., 1966.

Berend, I.T. and Ranki, G.
Foreign Trade and the Industrialization of the European Periphery in the XIXth Century. Journal of European Economic History. 9/3, 1980:539-584.

The European Periphery and Industrialization 1780 - 1914. Cambridge: Cambridge University Press, 1982.

Bernard, William S.
"A History of the U.S. Immigration Policy". In Richard A. Easterlin et al., Immigration. Cambridge, Mass.: The Belknap Press of Harvard University Press, 1982: 75-105.

Bertillon, J.
Cours Élémentaire de Statistique Administrative -
Élaboration des Statistiques - Organisation de Bureaux de
Statistique - Éléments de Démographie. Paris: Société
D'Éditions Scientifiques, 1895.

Bettencourt, José de Sousa
O Fenómeno da Emigração Portuguesa. Luanda: Instituto de
Investigação Científica de Angola, 1961.

Bibliotheca Popular de Legislação
Emigração Clandestina. Lisboa: Typ. da Bibliotheca Popular
de Legislação, 1904.

Bhagwati, J.N.
"Incentives and Disincentives: International Migration".
Weltwirtschaftliches Archiv, 1984, 120:678-701.

Bodnar, J.
The Transplanted. A History of Immigrants in Urban America.
Bloomington, IN: Indiana University Press, 1987.

Bohning, W.R.
Studies In International Labour Migration. London: The
Macmillan Press, 1984.

Bowen, Frank C.
A Century of Atlantic Travel, 1830-1930. Boston, Mass.:
Little, Brown & Co., 1930.

Breton, Raymond
"Institutional Completeness of Etnich Communities and
Personal Relations of Immigrants". The American Journal of
Sociology. LXX, July 1964-May 1965:193-205.

Brettell, Caroline
Já chorei muitas lágrimas. Lisboa: Universidade Nova de
Lisboa, 1978.

"Annoted Bibliography, Nineteenth and Twentieth Century
Portuguese Emigration". Portuguese Studies News Letter. 3
(Fall-Winter), 1979: 7-16.

"Late Marriage, non-marriage, and emigration in a northern
Portuguese village". Paper presented to the Social Sciences
History Association, Nashville, Oct. 22-25,1981.

Men who Migrate Women who Wait. Population and History in a
Portuguese Parish. Princeton, N.J.: Princeton University
Press, 1986.

Brettell, Caroline and Callier-Boisvert, C.
"Portuguese Immigrants in France - Familial and Social
Networks and the Structuring of a Community". Studi
Emigrazione, 46: 149-203.

Brettell, Caroline and Rosa, V.Pereira da
"Immigration and the Portuguese Family: A Comparison Between
Two Receiving Societies". In Thomas C. Bruneau et al (ed.),
Portugal in Development - Emigration, Industrialization, the
European Community. Ottawa, Canada: University of Ottawa
Press, 1984:83-110.

Briggs, Jonh W.
An Italian Passage: Immigrants to Three American Cities,
1890 - 1930. New Haven, Conn.: Yale University Press, 1978.

Brown, Walton J.
"Portuguese in California". Unpublished Thesis. University
of Southern California. 1944

Bromwell, William J.
History of Immigration to the United States, 1819 - 1855.
New York, N.Y.: Redfield, 1856.

Butler, David and Gareth Butler
British Political Facts 1900 - 1985. New York, N.Y.: St.
Martin's Press, 1986.

Cabral, M. Villaverde
O Desenvolvimento do Capitalismo em Portugal no Século XIX.
Porto: A Regra do Jogo, 1976.

Carpenter, Niles
Immigrants and Their Children. 1920. Washington, D.C.:
Census Monograph VII, Government Printing Office, 1927.

Carqueja, Bento
O Povo Portuguez. Porto: Livraria Chardon, de Lello & Irmão
Editores, 1916.

Castelo-Branco, Camilo
Euzébio Macário. (1st ed. 1878), Porto: Lello & Irmão
Editores, 1957.

Os Brilhantes do Brazileiro. 6th ed., Lisboa: Parceria
António Maria Pereira, 1922.

Caswell,L.E.
"The Portuguese in Boston". The North-End Mission Magazine.
2(3), July, 1873:57-87.

Chatelain, Abel
Les Migrants Temporaires en France de 1800 a 1914. Paris:
Publications de L'Universite de Lille III, 1976.

Cheyet, Stanley F.
Lopez of Newport: Colonial American Merchant Prince.
Detroit, MI: Wayne State University Press, 1970.

Chiaromonte, Nicola
The Paradox of History. Philadelphia, PA: University of
Pennsylvania Press, 1985.

Chickering, Jesse
Immigration into the United States. Boston, Mass.: Charles
C. Little and James Brown, 1848.

Coale, A. J., Demeny, P., and Vaughan, B.
Regional Model Life Tables and Stable Populations. 2d ed.,
New York, N.Y.: Academic Press, 1983.

Comissão de Planeamento da Região dos Açores
"Emigração - Subsídios para uma Monografia sobre os Açores".
Typed Report (1971)

Coquelin, MM. Ch. and Gillaumin (ed)
Dictionnaire de L'Économie Politique. Tome I, Paris:
Guillaumin & Ca. and L. Hachette & Ca., 1854.

Costa, Affonso
Estudos de Economia Nacional. O Problem da Emigração.
Lisboa: Imprensa Nacional, 1911.

Cumbler, John T.
Working-Class Community in Industrial America - Work,
Leisure and Struggle in Two Industrial Cities, 1880 - 1930.
Westport, Conn.: Greenwood Press, 1979.

Cunha, José Correia da
"Determinantes Geográficas do Povoamento Açoriano". Livro da
II Semana De Estudos dos Açores. Angra do Heroísmo:
Instituto Açoriano de Cultura, 1963: 117-138.

Cunha, M. Rachel et al.
The Portuguese in Rhode Island a History. Providence, Rd.:
The Rhode Island Heritage Commission and The Rhode Island
Publication Society, 1985.

Dabney, Charles
"The Azores", Report by the American Consul. House of
Representatives, 2d ss., 48th Congr., Doc. 54, Washington,
D.C.: Government Printing Office, 1884-1885:1646-1651.

Dias, Eduardo Mayone ed.
Açorianos na California. Angra do Heroísmo, Açores: Colecção
Diaspora, S.R.E.C., D.R.A.C., S.R.A.S., 1982.

Di Comite, Luigi and Glazier, Ira
"Caracteristiche Socio-Demogragiche dell'Emigrazione
Italiana Attraverso i Registri degli Emigrati Sbarcati negli
Stati Uniti d'America (1880-1914)". La Popolazione Italiana
nell'Ottocento. Continuita e Mutamenti. Bologna: Clueb,
1985: 431-446.

Easterlin, Richard
Population, Labor Force, and the Long Swings in Econimc Growth. New York, N.Y.: National Bureau of Economic Research, 1968.

"Economic and Social Characteristics of the Immigrants". R. Easterlin et al., Immigration. Cambridge, Mass.: The Belknap Press of Harvard University Press, 1982:1-34.

Erickson, Charlotte
American Industry and the European Immigrant, 1860-1885. Cambridge, Mass: Harvard University Press, 1957.

"The Uses of Passengers Lists for the Study of British and Irish Emigration". Paper presented to the 8th International Economic History Congress, Budapest, August, 1982.

Estep, Gerald
"Social Placement of the Portuguese in Hawaii as Indicated by Factors in Assimilation." Unpublished Thesis. University of Southern California, 1941.

Evangelista, João
Um Século de População Portuguesa (1864 - 1960). Lisboa: Publicações do Centro de Estudos Demográficos, I.N.E., MCMLXXI.

Fairchild, Henry P.
The Melting-Pot Mistake. Boston, Mass.: Little, Brown, and Company. 1926.

Felix, Jonh H. et al.
The Ukulele: A Portuguese Gift to Hawaii. Honolulu, Hawaii: Nunes, 1980.

Felix, John H. and Senecal, Peter F.
The Portuguese in Hawaii. Honolulu, Hawaii: Author's Publication, 1978.

Ferst, Susan T.
"The Immigration and the Setlement of the Portuguese in Providence: 1890 to 1924". Unpublished Thesis. Brown University, June, 1972

Figueiredo, A.
Le Portugal. Lisboa: Lallemant Frères, Imprimeurs, 1873.

Freitas, J.J.
Portuguese-Hawaiian Memories. Honolulu, Hawaii: The Printshop Company, 1930.

Freitas, J.J. Rodrigues de
Notice sur le Portugal. Paris: Paul Dupont, 1867.

"A Emigração Portugueza para o Brazil" (First print, 1893), Páginas Avulsas, Porto: Livraria Chardon, 1906: 167-177.

Gebara, Ademir
"O Fazendeiro de Escravos na Cidade que Cresce." Anais de História, IX,1977:127-139.

Girão, Amorim
Geografia de Portugal. Porto: Portucalense Editora, 1941.

Godinho, Vitorino Magalhães
Estruturra da Antiga Sociedade Portuguesa. 4th ed., Lisboa: Arcádia Editora, 1980.

"L'Émigration Portugaise (XVe-XXe Siècles) - Une Constante Structurale et les Responses aux Changements du Monde". (Short Version, 1974), Revista de História Económica e Social.1, Lisboa, 1978.

Gordon, Milton M.
Assimilation in American Life: The Role of Race, Religion, and National Origin. New York, N.Y.: Oxford University Press, 1964.

Gordon, Robert J.
Macroeconomics. Boston, Mass.: Little, Brown, & Company, 1978.

Gould, J.D.
"European Inter-Continental Emigration 1815-1914: Patterns and Causes". Journal of Economic European History. 1979:593-679.

Graves, Alvin R.
"Immigrants in Agriculture: the Portuguese Californians, 1850-1970's". Ph.D. Dissertation, University of California, Los Angeles, 1977.

Graves, Nancy and Graves, Theodore
"Adaptives Strategies in Urban Migration". Annual Review of Anthropology. 3, 1974:117-151.

Greenwood, Michael J.
"Human Migration: Theory, Models, and Empirical Studies". Journal of Regional Science. 25 (4), 1985:521-544.

Guerreiro, J.V.Mendes
Regresso dos Estados Unidos da América - Açores. Ponta Delgada: Biblitheca da Autonomia dos Açores, 1894.

Handlin, Oscar
The Uprooted: The Epic Story of the Great Migrations that Made the American People. Boston, Mass.: Little, Brown and Company, 1951.

Hanson, Carl A.
Dissertations on Iberian and Latin American History. Troy, N.Y.: Whitston Publishing Company, 1975.

Heisel, Donald
"Sources of Data for the Study of International Migration".
Quantitative Data and Immigration Research. Stephen R. Couch
and R.Simon Bryce-Laporte (ed.s), RIIES Research Note # 2,
Washington D.C., 1979.

Heisler,Barbara Schmitter
"Sending Countries and the Politics of Emigration and
Destination". International Migration Review. XIX (3), 1985:
469-484.

Henriques, M.B. de Freitas
A Trip to the Azores or Western Islands. Boston: Lee and
Shepard, 1867.

Higham, John
Strangers in the Land. Patterns of American Nativism 1860 -
1925. 2d ed. (1963), Reprint, New York, N.Y.: Atheneum,
1985.

Hutchinson, E.P.
"Notes on Immigration Statistics of the United States".
American Statistical Association Journal, Dec. 1958:963-
1025.

Hyde, F.E.
Cunard and the North Atlantic 1840-1973. London: The
Macmillan Press, 1975.

Kamphoefner, Walter D.
"At the Crossroads of Economic Development: Background
Factors Affecting Emigration from Nineteenth Century
Germany". Glazier, Ira A. and Rosa, Luigi De (ed.),
Migration across Time and Nations. Population Mobility in
Historical Contexts. New York: Holmes & Meier, 1986: 174-
201.

Katz, Michael
"Occupational Classification in History". Journal of
Interdisciplinary History, 3,1973:63-88.

Kuznets, Simon
"Long Swings in the Growth of Population and in Related
economic Variables". Proceedings of the American
Philosophical Society, 102, February, 1958.

Jerome, H.
Migrationa and Business Cycles. New York, N.Y.: National
Bureau of Economic Research, 1926.

Jones, M. A.
American Immigration. Chicago: University of Chicago Press,
1960.

Justino, J. David
"A Formação do Espaco Económico Nacional. Portugal 1810-
1913." (Doctoral dissertation), Lisboa, 1986.

"A Evolução do Produto Nacional Bruto em Portugal, 1850-1910
- Algumas Estimativas Provisórias." Análise Social, XXIII
(97), 1987: 451-461.

Lacerda, José de
Algumas Palavras Sobre Interesses Açoreanos. Lisboa:
Livraria Rodrigues & Ca., 1902.

Lains, Pedro
"Exportacoes portuguesas, 1850-1913: a tese da dependencia
revisitada." Análise Social, V.XXII (91), 1986:381-419.

Lang, H.P.
"The Portuguese Element in New England." Journal of
American Folk-Lore, V.5, 1892: 9-17.

Laslett, Peter
"Family and Household as Work Group and Kin Group: areas of
Traditional Europe Compared". R. Wall (ed.), Family Forms in
Historic Europe. Cambridge: Cambridge University Press,
1983: 513-562.

Lauck,Jett W.
"The Cotton-Mill Operatives of New England". The Atlantic
Monthly, CIX, 1912:706-713.

Lee, E.S.
"Migration Estimates".Simon Kuznets, ed. Population
Redistribution and Economic Growth. United States 1870 -
1950. Vol. I, Philadelphia, PA.: The American Philosophical
Society, 1957:9-109.

"A Theory of Migration". J.A. Jackson, ed. Migration.
Cambridge: Cambridge University Press, 1969: 282-297.

Leder, Hans H.
Cultural Persistence in a Portuguese-American Community.
1968, Reprint New York, N.Y.: Arno Press, 1980.

Leeds, Elizabeth Rachel
"Labor Export, Development, and the State: The Political
Econmy of Portuguese Emigration". Ph.D. dissertation,
M.I.T., Massachusetts, 1984.

Lepetit, B. and Royer,J.
"Croissance et taille des villes: contribution a l'etude de
l'urbanization de la France au debut du XIXeime siecle".
Annalles E.S.C., (5), 1980:987-1010.

Levine, Daniel B. (et al.)
Immigration Statistics. A Story of Neglect. Washington,
D.C.: National Academy Press, 1985.

Lewis, W. Arthur
The Theory of Economic Growth. London: G. Allen & Unwin, 1955.

London, Jack
The Valley of the Moon. 1913, Reprint Santa Barbara, Cal.: Peregrine Smith, Inc., 1975.

Kettenring, N. Ernest
"A Bibliography of Theses and Dissertations on Portuguese Topics Completed in the United States and Canada 1861-1983". Essay N.4, Durham, New Hampshire: International Conference Group on Modern Portugal, 1984.

Macdonald, John and Macdonald, Leatrice
"Chain Migration Ethnic Neighborhood Formation and Social Networks". The Milbank Memorial Fund Quarterly. XLII(1), 1964:82-97.

Macedo, J. Braga de
"Portuguese Currency Experience: an Historical Prespective". Boletim da Faculdade de Direito de Coimbra, Coimbra, 1979.

Madala, G.S.
Limeted-Dependent and Qualitative Variables in Econometrics. Cambridge: Cambridge University Press, 1987.

Martins, Joaquim P. de Oliveira
Fomento Rural e Emigração. (1st ed. 1891), Lisboa: Guimarães Editores, 1956.

Marvaud, Angel
Le Portugal et ses Colonies. Étude politique et Économique. Paris, Librairie Félix Alcan, 1912.

Massey, Douglas
"Understanding Mexican Migration to the United States". American Journal of Sociology, 92 (6), May, 1987: 1372-1403.

Mata, Maria Eugénia
"A Unidade Monetaria Portuguesa Face a Libra 1891 - 1931". Working Paper N. 22, Faculdade de Economia, Universidade Nova de Lisboa, 1984.

Mateus, M and Mateus,A.
"The Agrarian Revolution in Nineteenth Century Portugal - Technological Change, Trade Regimes and the Response of Agriculture." Working Paper N. 52. Faculdade de Economia, Universidade Nova de Lisboa, 1986.

Michalowski, M.
"Adjustment of Immigrants in Canada: Methodological Possibilities and its Implications". International Migration. ICM, XXV (1), 1987: 82-97.

Miller, Ann R.
"Some characteristics of the Industrial Structure of
Employment in Latin American Countries". In Spanish
published in, IUSSP, Conferencia Regional Latino Americana
de Poblacion, Mexico, 1970 Actas 2: 83-91.

"International Variations in the Industrial Distribution of
the Labor Force. A preliminary View". Discussion Paper
presented at the Population Studies Center, University of
Pennsylvania, 1971.

Miller Jr., Robert K.
"Initial Postmigration Employment among European Immigrants:
1900-1935. International Migration Review, 15 (3), 1981:
529-542.

Minga, Teófilo A. Rodrigues
La Famille dans l'Immigration. Étude de la Problematique
dans le Domaine de l'Immigration Portuguaise en Suisse.
Porto: S.E.E., 1985.

Mondschean, Thomas H.
"Estimating the Probability of Emigration from Individual-
Specific Data: The case of Italy in the Early Twentieth
Century". International Migration Review, XX(1),1986:69-80.

Monteiro, Jacinto
Memórias da Minha Ilha. 2@ ed., Santa Maria, 1982.

Monteiro, Paulo
Luso-Americanos no Connecticut: Questões de Etnicidade e de
Comunidade. Lisboa: Universidade Católica, 1985.

Monteiro, Tania Penido
Portuguese na Bahia na Segunda Metade do Séc. XIX. Porto:
S.E.E., 1985.

Morawska, Ewa
For Bred with Butter. Life-Worlds of East Central European
in Johnstown, Pennsylvania 1890-1940. Cambridge: Cambridge
University Press, 1985.

Morison, Samuel
The Maritime History of Massachusetts 1783-1860. Cambridge,
Mass.: The Riverside Press, 1961.

Namias, J.
First Generation In the Words of Twentieth-Century American
Immigrants. Boston, Mass.: Beacon Press, 1978.

Navarro, Antonio J. Antunes
Memória Sobre a Viação Municipal em Portugal. Lisboa:
Imprensa Nacional, 1887.

Neidert, Lisa and Farley, Reynolds
"Assimilation in the U.S.: An Analysis of Ethnic and Generation Differences in Status and Achivement". American Sociological Review, Vol. 50 (6), 1985: 840-850.

Norton, Herman
Persecutions at Madeira from 1843 to 1846. New York, N.Y.: The American and Foreign Christian Union, 1857.

Nunes, Ana Bela F.M.
"A Rede Urbana Portuguesa e o Moderno Crescimento Económico". Tese complementar de Doutoramento, I.S.E., Universidade Técnica de Lisboa, Lisboa, 1989.

Oliver, Lawrence
Never Backward. The Autobiography of Lawrence Oliver A Portuguese-American. San Diego, Cal.: Neyenesch Printers, Inc., 1972.

O'Neil, Brian J.
"Dying and Inheriting in Rural Trás-Os-Montes". Jaso, XIV, 1983,44-74.

Pap, Leo
Portuguese-American Speech. New York, N.Y.: King's Crown Press, 1949.

The Portuguese in the United States: A Bibliography. New York, N.K.: Center for Migration Studies, 1976.

Peck, Emelyn F.
" An Immigrant Farming Community." New England Magazine, New Series, 31, 1904: 207-210.

Pereira, J.M.Esteves
A Industria Portugueza (Séculos XII a XIX). Lisboa: Empresa do Occidente, 1900.

Pereira, Júlio M.
Recordações dos Açores. Lisboa: Imprensa Nacional, 1893.

Pereira, Manuel F.V.
"A Emigração Há Cinquenta Anos". Boletim do Núcleo Cultural da Horta. 3(3), 1964: 483 - 485.

Pereira, M. Halpern
Livre câmbio e desenvolvimento ecónomico: Portugal na 2@ metade do século XIX. Lisboa: Edições Cosmos, 1971.

"Niveaux de Consommation Niveaux de Vie au Portugal (1874-1922)". Annalles E.S.C. (March-June), 1975:610-631.

Política e Economia (Portugal nos Séculos XIX e XX). Lisboa: Livros Horizonte, 1979.

A Política Portuguesa de Emigração (1850 a 1930). Lisboa: A Regra do Jogo, 1981.

A Persuasão. Ponta Delgada, January to December, 1891.

Petersen, T.
"A Comment on Presenting Results from Logit and Probit Models". American Sociological Review, 50 (1), 1985:130-131.

Petras, Elizabeth McLean
"The Global Labor Market in the Modern World-Economy". In Mary M.Kritz, Charles B.Keely, Silvano M.Tomasi eds. Global Trends in Migration: Theory and Research on International Population Movements. Staten Island, N.Y.: Center for Migration Studies, 1983: 44-63.

Piazza, Walter
"A Grande Migração Açoriana de 1748 - 1756". Boletim do Instituto Histórico da Ilha Terceira, Vol. XL, 1982: 465-492.

Piore, M.J.
Birds of Passage: Migrant Labor and Industrial Societies. Cambridge: Cambridge University Press, 1979.

Poinsard, Léon
Portugal Ignorado. Estudo Social, Económico e Politico Seguido de um Appendice Relativo aos Ultimos Acontecimentos. Porto: Magalhaës Moniz, Lda., 1912.

Portes, Alexandro
"Migration and Underdevelopment". Politics and Society. 8 (1), 1978:1-48.

Portes, Alexandro and Benton, Lauren
"Industrial Development and Labor Absorption: A Reinterpretation". Population and Development Review. 10(4), 1984:589-611.

"Industrial Development and Labor Absorption: A Reinterpretation". Population and Development Review. 10(4), 1984:589-611.

Qualey, Carlton C.
"Immigration to the United States since 1815". Les Migration Internationales. Paris: C.N.R.S., 1980: 32-38.

Ratti, Anna Maria
"Italian Migration Movements, 1876 to 1926". International Migrations. Vol.II Interpretations, Willcox (ed.), New York, N.Y.: National Bureau of Economic Research, Inc., 1931.

Redford, Arthur
Labour Migration in England, 1800-1850. 2@ ed., New York, N.Y.: Augustus M.Kelley - Publishers, 1968.

Rees, Albert
"Labor Economics: Effects of More Knowledge - Information Networks in Labor Markets". The American Economic Review, LVI, May, 1966:559-566.

Reis, Jaime
"O atraso económico português em prespective histórica
(1860-1913)." Análise Social, V.XX (80), 1984:7-28.

"A industrialização num pais de desenvolvimento lento e
tardio: Portugal, 1870-1913." Análise Social,V.XXIII (96),
1987:207-227.

Ribeiro, Luiz
O Emigrante Açoriano. Ponta Delgada: Tipografia "Correio dos
Açores", 1940.

Ribeiro, Orlando
"Portugal". Geografia Je Espana y Portugal, by Manuel de
Teran. Tomo V, Barcelona: Montaner Y Simón, S.A., 1955:233-
258.

Roza, M.
Gente das Ilhas. Ilha do Pico: Bandeiras, n.d..

Salazar, António de Oliveira
O Agio de Ouro. Coimbra: Imprensa da Universidade de
Coimbra, 1916.

Doctrine and Action. (1933), London: Faber and Faber
Limited, 1939.

Sampaio, Alberto
Estudos Históricos e Económicos. (1890's), Vol.II, Lisboa:
Editorial Vega, n.d..

Santos, Mário A. da Silva
O Comércio Português na Bahia, 1870 - 1930. Salvador: Irmão
Paulo, 1977.

Sequeira, M.A.
Questões Açorianas - II. Ponta Delgada: Typographia Popular,
1891.

Serpa, Caetano Valadao
"A Gente Acoriana. Emigração e Religiosidade Seculos XVI-
XX". Sep. do Boletim do Instituto Histórico da Ilha
Terceira, 34, 1976.

Serrão, Joel
A Emigração Portuguesa. Lisboa: Livros Horizonte, 1974.

Serrão, Joel and Martins, G. ed.
Da Industria Portuguesa: do Antigo Regime ao Capitalismo:
Antologia. Lisboa: Livros Horizonte, imp., 1978.

Sideri, Sandro
Comercio e Poder. Colonialismo Informal nas Relacoes Anglo-
Portuguesas. Lisboa: Edições Cosmos, 1978.

Silvia, Philip T.
"The Position of "New" Immigrants in the Fall River Textile Industry". International Migration Review, 13(1), 1976:221-232.

Smith, Eugene W.
Passengers Ships of the World-Past and Present. Boston, Mass.: G.H. Dean Co., 1963.

Soares, Celestino
California and the Portuguese. Lisboa: SPN Books, 1939.

Sowell, Thomas
Ethnic America: A History. New York, N.Y.: Basic Books, 1981.

Stevens, Gillian
"Nativity, intermarriage, and Mother-Tongue Shift". American Sociological Review. Vol.50 (1), 1985: 74-83.

Straubhaar, Thomas
"The causes of International Labor Migrations - A Demand-Determined Approach". International Migration Review. XX(4), 1986:835-855.

Sweringa, Robert
"Dutch International Migration Statistics, 1820-1880: An Analysis of Linked Multinational Nominal Files". International Migration Review, 15(3), 1981:445-470.

"Dutch International Migration and Occupational Change: A Structural Analysis of Multinational Linked Files". Paper presented to the Social Science history Association Conference, Bloomington, Indiana: Novenber, 1982.

Taft, Donald
Two Portuguese Communities in New England. New York, N.Y.: AMS Press, 1967.

Tapinos, George
L'Economie des Migrations Internationales. Paris: Fondation Nationale des Sciences Politiques/ Armand Colin, 1974.

Taylor, Philip
The Distant Magnet. European Emigration to the U.S.A.. New York, N.Y.: Harper & Row, 1971.

Thernstrom, S.
Poverty and Progress; Social Mobility in a Nineteenth Century City. Cambridge, Mass.: Harvard University Press, 1964

Thomas, Brinley
Migration and Economic Growth. A Study of Great Britain and the Atlantic Economy. (1st print 1954), Cambridge: Cambridge University Press, 1973.

Tilly, Charles and Brown, C.Harold
"On Uprooting, Kinship, and the Auspices of Migration".
International Journal of Comparative Sociology. 8(2),
September 1967:139-164.

Todaro, Michael P.
Economic Development in the Third World. 3d ed., New York,
N.Y.: Longman, 1985.

Tomaske, John
"The Determinants of Intercountry Differences in European
Emigration: 1881-1900". Journal of Economic History,
1971:840-853.

Trebilcock, C.
The Industrialization of the Continental Powers, 1780-1914.
London: Longman, 1981.

Trindade, Maria J. Lagos
"Portuguese Emigration from the Azores to the United States
During the Nineteenth Century". Studies in Honor of the
Bicentenial of the American Independence. Lisboa, 1976:237-
295.

Tucker, George
"Progress of the United States in Population and Wealth".
Hunt's Merchants' Magazine, 1843.

Um Negociante Logrado
A Emigração para Nova Orleans e o Sr. Carlos Nathan. Lisboa:
Typographia de Francisco Xavier de Souza & Filho, 1872.

A União, Angra Do Heroísmo, January-December, 1907.

United Nations (Department of International Economic and
Social Affairs)
"Manual X, Indirect Techniques For the Demographic
Estimation". Population Studies, N.81, 1983.

Vecoli, Rudolph
"The Italian Americans". L. Dimmerstein and F.L. Jaher
(ed.), Uncertain Americans. New York, N.Y.: Oxford
University Press, 1977: 201-215.

Vermette, Mary T. Silvia
The Image of the Azorean: Portrayals in Nineteenth and
Early-Twentieth Century Writings. Angra do Heroísmo:
Instituto Histórico da Ilha Terceira, 1984.

Viera, D. et al.
"Portuguese in the United States. Bibliography". Essay N.6,
Durham, New Hampshire, International Conference Group on
Portugal, 1989.

Vieira J.or, João J.
Eu Falo Por Mim Mesmo. Autobiografia. Porto: Livraria
Escolar Progredior, 1963.

Vittoz, Stan
"World War I and the Political Accomodation of Transitional
Market Forces: The Case of Immigration Restriction".
Politics and Society. 1, 1978:49-78.

Walker, W. F.
The Azores or Western Islands. London: Trübner & Co., 1886.

Warner, W.L. and Strole, Leo
The Social Systems of American Ethnic Groups. New Haven,
Conn.: Yale University Press, 1945.

Weber, A.Ferrin
The Growth of Cities in the Nineteenth Century. (1st print
1899), Ithaca, N.Y.: Cornell University Press, 1969.

Wellman, Barry and Berkowitz, S.D. (ed.)
Social Structures: A Network Approach. Cambridge, Cambridge
University Press, 1988.

Williams, Jerry
And Yet They Come. Portuguese Immigration from the Azores
to the United States. New York, N.Y.: Center for Migration
Studies, 1982.

Willcox, Walter F.
"Immigration into the United States". Walter Willcox (ed.)
International Migrations. Vol.II, Interpretations. New York,
N.Y.: National Bureau of Economic Research, Inc., 1931: 85-
122.

Wolfe, Martin
"The concept of Economic Sectors". The Quarterly Journal of
Economics. (LXXIX), August, 1955:402-420.

Young, E.
"Report on Immigration". 42d Cong., 1st Sess. (Ho. of Reps.)
Vol.I, (Doc. 1) Washington, D.C.: Government Printing
Office, 1871.

Zolberg, Aristide R.
"International Migrations in Political Perspective". In
Mary M.Kritz, Charles B.Keely, Silvano M.Tomasi eds. Global
Trends in Migration: Theory and Research on International
Population Movements. Staten Island, N.Y.: Center for
Migration Studies, 1983: 3-27.